Dangerous or Endangered?

Dangerous
or Endangered?

*Race and the Politics of Youth
in Urban America*

Jennifer Tilton

NEW YORK UNIVERSITY PRESS
New York and London

NEW YORK UNIVERSITY PRESS
New York and London
www.nyupress.org

Library of Congress Cataloging-in-Publication Data
Tilton, Jennifer.
Dangerous or endangered? :
race and the politics of youth in urban America /
Jennifer Tilton.
p. cm.
Includes bibliographical references and index.
ISBN 978-0-8147-8311-5 (alk. paper) —
ISBN 978-0-8147-8312-2 (pbk. : alk. paper) —
ISBN 978-0-8147-8331-3 (e-book)
1. African American youth—California—Oakland.
2. Urban youth—California—Oakland. I. Title.
E185.93.C2T55   2010
323.1196'073—dc22   2010015387

New York University Press books are printed on acid-free paper,
and their binding materials are chosen for strength and durability.
We strive to use environmentally responsible suppliers and materials
to the greatest extent possible in publishing our books.

Manufactured in the United States of America
c 10 9 8 7 6 5 4 3 2 1
p 10 9 8 7 6 5 4 3 2 1

Contents

Acknowledgments

This book was made possible by my family and all those who have become like family to me. Together, many people have taught me what America should be and what is required from all of us if we are going to create equal opportunities for all our children. My parents, both teachers, have been wonderful models and supports. They have provided the endless day care, meals, and housing that made this research and writing possible. They also provided a foundational commitment to social justice—whether it was through my father's stories about John Brown or my mother's efforts to challenge her parents' brand of polite southern racism. My special thanks to my Chicago family, who let a young white girl cross the hard racial lines of that city into their lives and struggles to rebuild their communities. Jackie Reed and Mary Alice "Ma" Henry, now long gone, first taught me what activist mothering meant, and that it was never okay to write off our children. Thanks to my godsons A.C. and Nathaniel for adopting me in Chicago. They have taught me the kind of strength and perseverance required for boys to become men under conditions of American apartheid. I remain amazed by their successes in the face of the many hurdles they've had to overcome.

I could never have written this book without the support of my wonderful husband, Jim, and my son, Zack, who learned to be patient with my long days and weekends writing. Being a mother has helped me understand the joy and imagine the fear and anger of many parents in this book, whose children have to face barriers our son will never face. Reading and writing stories of black parents whose children are stopped by the police or followed by security guards now makes me livid in a new way as I imagine how I would feel if I had to prepare my son for that reality. Similarly, as I imagine how I would feel if Zack were afraid every day walking to school past drug corners, I become more committed to fighting to create a nation where no children have to live in fear. Being a mother makes me feel on a visceral level the progressive possibility of a politics of childhood, at the same time as I see how easy it is to narrowly defend the privileges of your own child.

This book would never have been possible if countless Oakland community activists and public officials hadn't welcomed me into their meetings and homes, tolerated my questions, and trained me out of many errors. These gracious informants will recognize their own enormous contributions to this book, even though I refer to most by pseudonyms. The names of schools, organizations, neighborhoods, and public officials have not been changed. I also usually use real names when I quote from newspaper coverage, and for a few informants who requested that I use their names, including Van Jones, Jakada Imani, and Victor Duarte. I have never stopped being surprised at and thankful for the openness and patience of the community activists I have worked with and write about. Black community activists, in particular, had little reason to trust or take their valuable time to speak to a white, upper-middle-class woman from San Francisco. They had many reasons to doubt my intentions, or at least my ability to represent their concerns and political commitments accurately. I tried in my early career not to study black neighborhoods or black politics. The trope of white anthropologists studying black neighborhoods seemed tired and old, and there are so many amazing black anthropologists who have documented the complex stories of black communities. But my interests, passions, and history continued to bring me back to the racial divides in urban America and to writing, at least in part, about the dilemmas of black community activists. It is a testament to the commitment and hope of Oakland's activists that that so many people took the time to teach me and share their stories.

Many friends, colleagues, and mentors helped me through the endless process of writing and rewriting this book. Conrad Kottak, Matthew Countryman, Terry McDonald, and Janet Finn helped me through the early research and writing process. Sharon Stephens left her indelible mark on my scholarship and this book, although I only had the chance to work with her briefly. I am especially indebted to Barrie Thomas for her invaluable feedback on my ethnographic methods as I conducted research in Oakland. At various stages, Helena Hansen, Ping-Ann Addo, Kate Ledger, Linda Gajdusek, and Chris Rhomberg provided support and read and edited chapters. Many mentors and supportive critics have helped me identify the core argument and major contributions of this book, as well as find the confidence to write it; a special thanks to Cindi Katz, Brett Williams, Joe Hawes, Susan Hyatt, Setha Low, Caitlin Cahill, and Deborah Durham. Lastly, my colleagues Kim Coles and Keith Osajima, Denise Spencer, and my editor Jennifer Hammer helped me through final stages of revisions. David Martinez provided invaluable help editing and indexing the manuscript. And thanks especially to my colleagues Diana Sinton and Mark Kumler for carving time out of their busy schedules to produce the wonderful neighborhood maps for this book.

Introduction:
Who's Responsible for Kids?

In June 1999, recently elected Mayor Jerry Brown visited a Neighborhood Crime Prevention Council (NCPC) meeting in an elementary school auditorium at the eastern edge of Oakland, California's sprawling flatlands. Speaking to approximately fifty, mostly African American, middle-class homeowners, Mayor Brown detailed his plans for revitalizing the city, "When I talk to people everywhere in Oakland, they are concerned about crime and schools." Crime rates were declining, but "not fast enough." He knew that Oakland's citizens disagreed on how to respond; some at the meeting took "an overtly hard line on crime" while others focused on economic development, improving schools, or building after-school programs. When Mayor Brown opened the meeting for questions, an African American woman in her midthirties asked if the city had a plan to reduce juvenile crime. Mayor Brown mentioned new funding to open recreation centers longer, and then added, "Facilities are full. Even to be arrested and held, youth have to pass a test. So it is hard to discipline youth." The woman explained that she was thinking more in terms of prevention, remarking, "Locking them up doesn't work." Mayor Brown agreed: "That's our paradox. We've got to do something, but building facilities doesn't work. So what do we do?"

Talk about Oakland's present and future almost invariably turned into a discussion about youth, who seemed to simultaneously embody both the city's crises and its hopes for change. After briefly responding to an unrelated question, Mayor Brown returned to this topic: "I don't believe that I've answered this woman's question," he said.

> Prevention is an environment where young people are respected as well as disciplined. It is very hard for the state and the city to take the lead on prevention. First you need the family, then relatives, and then maybe the neighborhood. If we have to go to institutions, it's not going to work

so well. First of all, those institutions are not well funded. The rich don't want to pay for funding those kinds of programs. And there is no lobby to prevent crime, only to build prisons and lock people up. Schools are important, as are after-school programs, but schools can never be entirely responsible. Basically you are on your own. . . . These things are broken down for a number of reasons. One is that we live in a whole culture that requires there to be a bottom 5 to 10 percent that fails. We are in a system that generates failure as the flip side of success. All we can do is work block by block. There is no pie in the sky, no magic bullet. If there was, I would have discovered it as governor. I don't want to propose that the city government can solve all that.

Mayor Jerry Brown and the African American community activists at this meeting struggled with a basic problem: many of the structures that supported kids coming of age were crumbling, and the future of too many of Oakland's children seemed in doubt. This meeting highlighted significant debates over how the city should respond. What had caused things to "break down"? Were young people's problems caused by broken families or by racial exclusions and a dearth of economic opportunities? Were Oakland's children endangered or had they become dangerous themselves? Could the city and state help? Or were Oakland residents left on their own, forced to solve the urgent crises facing children by working "block by block"? This book explores the politics of youth in Oakland at the turn of the twenty-first century, drawing on ethnographic fieldwork with Oakland residents who struggled to shape the city's responses to dangerous and endangered youth. It investigates how these debates over the nature and needs of young people have fundamentally reshaped politics in the contemporary United States.

Youth is a concept that is "good to think with." A liminal category betwixt and between childhood and adulthood, "youth" offers a way for adults to think about social change, about the past and the future.[1] Oakland residents narrated complex historical changes by comparing their memories of childhood to childhood today. But young people also served as powerful symbols of the city's and the nation's future. The presence of wealthy, overprotected children living mere blocks from desperately poor kids seemed to challenge both the ideal of equal opportunity and the future of America's democracy. College graduates overburdened with debt, living at home, and looking for stable work confounded assumptions about successful transitions to adulthood. Teenage boys dealing drugs or gunned down on the corner challenged ideals of childhood innocence and highlighted our failures to ensure a safe and secure future for all our children.

Youth today call to mind a troubling set of images: kids failing school or falling behind, "babies having babies," gang members, and school shooters. These images don't begin to capture the complexity of barriers facing young people in America. Instead, they "objectify and reify young people as the problem in itself."[2] Moral panics about drug use, teen pregnancy, and crime have distorted our images of youth and our public policy responses at the turn of the twenty-first century. We are afraid for "our own kids" but deeply fearful of "other people's children." This distinction between endangered and dangerous maps complex racial, class, and gender divides in contemporary U.S. cities. Understanding the politics of youth requires careful attention to these intricate connections. We must explore the stories we tell about kids, the images we use, and the impact of both on the ways we draw the boundaries of our political community.

We usually think of children and youth as outside of politics. Kids can't vote and most are excluded from the public realm of work. We often assume that children belong in the private sphere, in the domain of family, and not in the public realm where citizens struggle over power, resources, and the role of government.[3] But feminist scholars have challenged this common distinction between private and public, between the "soft messy stuff of everyday life"— like the daily struggles of parents or young people—and the "hard" stuff of economics and politics.[4] Childhood and youth have helped craft the divide between public and private spheres that we think of as a foundational characteristic of modern states. Our shifting ideas of what kids need have reshaped the form of the welfare state throughout the twentieth century. They have also transformed city and suburban spaces. Geographer Leslie Miller argues that the idea of "dangerous streets" and "safe homes" was constructed alongside the idea of fragile, innocent children who of course "belonged" in those private homes in the late nineteenth century. Our ideals of childhood and youth have repeatedly restructured the way we draw the boundaries between public and private responsibility, public and private space, and what counts as the proper realm of politics.

Considering youth and politics together changes the story we tell about urban America and the broad political and economic shifts that have swept the nation at the end of the twentieth century and into the twenty-first. Understanding these changes requires that we explore *social reproduction*: all the messy work that must be done to raise and educate the next generation of workers. Children have certainly been affected by growing economic insecurity and a retreating and increasingly punitive welfare state. But children also serve as powerful symbols (and sometimes actors) in politics. As such, they have helped to shape contemporary political and economic transformations.[5]

The question "Who is responsible for children?" is fundamentally a political question. Young people need many kinds of care: physical care to keep them safe, fed, and dressed; love and emotional support; guidance to help them make the transition to adulthood; education and training to provide them with the skills and capacities to thrive as workers and citizens. So who does this work of social reproduction? Parents (often mothers) are the easy, default answer in many contemporary political debates. But parents don't do their vital work in a vacuum. Many institutions, spaces, and policies shape children's lives and futures and enable or constrain parental investments in children.[6] Schools, parks, playgrounds, and recreation centers are important spaces for children's development. So are neighborhoods, where children walk and play, form friendships, get guidance from other adults, and develop their own social networks. Government actions (or inactions) affect all these spaces for children. State funding for schools, zero tolerance policies, and security practices have reshaped children's daily lives in Oakland's classrooms and hallways. Federal housing policies and local urban redevelopment practices have produced wealthy, mostly white neighborhoods and devastatingly poor black and Latino neighborhoods. State and federal governments also establish taxation policies, the minimum wage, parental leave policies, discrimination laws, and social safety nets that shape the resources, even the time, families and children have together. The state literally acts as the parent for children in foster care and the juvenile justice system, deciding where children will live, with whom, and how they will be punished. In these diverse ways, the state plays a significant role in shaping children's lives, their paths to adulthood, and the very categories of child and youth.[7]

America has become a nation of radically unequal childhoods.[8] We tolerate the highest child poverty rates of any industrialized country, though we are the wealthiest nation in the world. Economic inequalities have grown in the last three decades, concentrating wealth at the top, eroding the middle class, and condemning many families to the growing ranks of the working poor. Kids born poor are likely to become poor adults—a fact that makes a mockery of our national commitment to the ideal of equal opportunity.[9] Schools more often reflect existing racial and class inequalities than provide a secure path to the middle class. We now incarcerate so many poor children that the Children's Defense Fund has begun to fight against what it calls the "cradle-to-prison pipeline." These policies have racial effects, and to some degree racial causes, despite widespread claims that race no longer matters. Black and Latino children are more likely to grow up poor and more likely to be incarcerated than white and most Asian kids.[10] These inequalities have raised fundamental questions about the meaning of race and class in the post–civil rights era, an era that has seen expanding opportunities, lingering inequalities, and new barriers for black kids coming of age.[11]

This book chronicles race and the politics of youth in Oakland and the debates among parents, community activists, politicians, policy makers, and youth activists about how to respond to these deep racial and class divides in young people's lives. The pervasive image of black youth crime placed black boys in the spotlight of Oakland politics. This book does likewise, concentrating on fears of and fears for black boys and tracing the urgent dilemmas of black parents and activists as they worked to secure safe passage to adulthood for black children. But it also explores the more complex intersections of race, class, and gender that characterized politics in Oakland. The stories and struggles of activists in this one city help us address two broad questions that face the nation: Why does the United States tolerate such inequalities in children's lives? And what kind of politics would be required to create equal-opportunity childhoods?

Children in a War on Dependence

Mayor Jerry Brown's speech embodied many principles of what scholars call neoliberal governance. He encouraged individuals and communities to govern themselves and defined government as almost powerless to solve the deep crises facing Oakland's children. His speech echoed the commonsense claim that "government can't raise children," as he characterized the state in narrow terms as a set of badly funded "institutions." Ultimately he asserted that families and neighborhoods had to reconstruct spaces and networks of care for children "on their own"—although he momentarily embraced the state's responsibility for protecting citizens from "dangerous youth." Jerry Brown's limited vision of government responsibility stemmed from his own struggles to govern Oakland in the context of massive economic inequalities and significant changes in our ideas about government and in the structure of the state.

Many scholars have explored how the state and state power have been reconfigured in a rapidly globalizing world.[12] "The state" includes the representative political bodies and bureaucracies of local, state, and national governments that make and implement laws and policies. But the state is not "a disembodied or reified object" or just a set of policy-making institutions that "somehow sits above the fray of everyday life." Rather, the state is "a set of relationships" that are "enacted through the practices of social agents" (teachers, police officers, social workers, politicians, community activists) at work, at home, and in neighborhoods.[13] The state is also a powerful and contested *idea*: What is the role of government?[14]

Since the late 1970s, conservative attacks on "big government" and the "nanny state" have radically challenged and transformed the welfare state that was built up during the New Deal in the 1930s and Great Society in the sixties.[15] Democratic and Republican administrations alike embraced free market ideologies and borrowed market models to reconfigure state institutions. State and federal governments cut taxes, reduced regulations, and curtailed spending for many health and welfare services. They transformed many federal entitlement programs (like Aid to Families with Dependent Children) into block grants administered by the states, creating a devolved and decentralized state in which private for-profit and non-profit agencies provide most social services. Historian Michael Katz argues that a "war on dependence" helped drive these neoliberal changes in state policy and practice. "Reliance for support on someone" has been redefined as "failure." Neoliberal policies encourage individual citizens and communities to act like entrepreneurs, reliant on themselves and not "dependent" on government.[16] Welfare reform embodies this critique most clearly: single mothers are no longer supposed to depend on the state but instead are expected to embrace the "independence" the job market offers.[17] This war on dependence has extended deep into the social fabric, encouraging individuals to invest in their own retirements instead of depending on employee pensions and calling for citizen volunteers to provide services once provided by government.

Neoliberal governance has not reduced state power, despite calls for small government. The rise of law-and-order politics has expanded the state's "power to punish."[18] As anthropologist Roger Lancaster has argued, punitiveness is the "real cultural logic" of neoliberalism.[19] The U.S. prison population has skyrocketed in the last twenty years, tripling between 1987 and 2007, when one out of every one hundred Americans was behind bars.[20] Children have not been immune to the rise of penal governance. A fearful public has increasingly defined youth—especially poor black and Latino young men— as dangerous thugs and gang members. All states now allow children under eighteen to be tried as adults, and the United States is the only industrialized nation that sentences children to life without the possibility of parole. California now spends roughly as much on the prison system as on higher education. These punitive public policies have decimated families and many children's life chances.[21] But the punitive logic of criminal justice has also extended deeply into neighborhoods and schools, where they have reshaped our ideas of both childhood and the state.[22] Sociologist Loic Wacquant argues that an emerging "penal common sense" is redefining the central right of citizenship as the right to sufficient police protection.[23]

These neoliberal policies have created new crises of care for children and deep inequalities in childhood.[24] Children are not autonomous agents acting in the marketplace, but by definition children are dependents reliant on adults for care. So what happens to children during a "war on dependence"? The human costs of neoliberal governance were particularly evident in Oakland's schools and neighborhoods, where poor families struggled to maintain stable housing, many middle-class families only clung precariously to their economic status, children attended schools without textbooks, and the drug war destroyed families and locked up a shocking number of the city's young black men. As Michael Katz has argued, cities in the 1980s and 1990s "could not displace misery onto other levels of government; the devolution of responsibility ended in their streets."[25]

Many innovations of neoliberal governance were forged in the crucible of cities like Oakland, which struggled to respond to the escalating needs of children and families with a limited tax base and declining state and federal funds. Jerry Brown's call for neighbors to work block by block highlights one of the central characteristics of neoliberal urban governance: an increased reliance on volunteers and community partnerships to provide basic government services.[26] Oakland's community policing initiative called for the city's residents to become partners with the police in order to create safe and orderly neighborhoods. The city's schools relied on parent volunteers as a source of funding and a vital part of daily operations. Nonprofits, funded by an unstable combination of government and foundation grants, provided a growing portion of city services for children and youth.

Each of these partnerships opened up opportunities for Oakland's activists to shape the policies and practices of local government.[27] Community policing activists gained some power to shape police priorities and some leverage to transform the historically tense relationship between black communities and the police department. Parents worked with children's advocacy groups and an expanded nonprofit sector to increase public funding for youth development and after-school programs. And, contrary to Jerry Brown's claims, they created a "lobby to prevent crime." But these different new partnerships also reshaped the way neighborhood activists framed their political identities and interests.[28] Public-private partnerships sometimes redefined ideas about what youth needed and created urgent dilemmas for community activists. How could the police make neighborhoods safe for black kids who themselves were usually the target of police sweeps? How could activists expand public investments in children at a moment when free-market ideologies had decimated progressive taxation policies that might fund equal-opportunity childhoods? How could they win support for state investments in children from a fearful public that defined youth not only as endangered innocents but also as dangerous and unworthy?

Race and the Politics of Youth

Children and youth serve as important symbols in conflicts over how to reconstruct the state in the current global economic order. Yet their role in both forging and contesting neoliberal governance has been underappreciated. This book responds to recent calls to look at neoliberalism not as unified ideology imposed from the top down but as a process shaped significantly at the local level. We need to explore the complex social and political processes, the multiple agents and interests, that drive changing regimes of urban governance.[29] *Fears of youth* and *fears for youth* motivated many activists in Oakland. The ways they framed the needs and problems of young people shaped the visions of the state they promoted and the kinds of state action they tried to secure.

"Youth" has long been a "slippery concept" invested with adult hopes but also seen as potentially and unpredictably dangerous.[30] It is a flexible identity that can only be defined in relation to the opposing categories "child" and "adult." The meaning and referents of youth change in different historical, cultural, and political contexts.[31] Child, boy, girl, teen, youth, young man, adolescent, woman, and adult are not natural categories. They are laden with dense cultural meanings that have varied globally and throughout U.S. history. From the midnineteenth century to the midtwentieth, children went from being defined as useful workers to becoming the "useless" but "sentimentally priceless" focus of middle-class family life. Most modern industrialized societies began to emphasize not only children's innate innocence, vulnerability, and capacity for change but also their incompetence and lack of cultural knowledge or moral responsibility.[32] "Adolescent" in the early twentieth century and "teenager" in the 1950s evoked other complex meanings:

idealism, exuberance, and rebellion, but also irrationality, delinquency, raging hormones, and susceptibility to peer pressure.[33] When and how a child becomes an adolescent or an adult has shifted over time, as has what we think children need in order to thrive. Do kids need free play or 24-hour education? Do they need full-time care from stay-at-home mothers or preschool and after-school programs outside of the home? Do they need meaningful work or to be removed entirely from the workforce? Do they need physical discipline or affection, care or control? Can they play in the street or should they play in more structured and supervised spaces? Do they need to be kept in "troubled homes" or removed from the influence of problematic parents? Americans don't all give the same answers today, and our public policies suggested different responses over the course of the twentieth century.

These mobile categories compel us to pay close attention to the ways community activists and policy makers talk about youth. As anthropologist Mica Pollock explains, talk is "an everyday action that shapes the world as it describes it."[34] Debates over the nature and needs of young people carry cultural weight and political consequences; they are "acts and interventions" in a political field.[35] If we describe young people in the juvenile justice system as "children," we frame them as not fully responsible and inherently reformable. However, if we describe them as "thugs," their future is already determined and the possibilities and protections of childhood are foreclosed. We may as well treat, and punish, them as adults.

Youth have often served as fertile ground for the proliferation of neoliberal ideologies of self-help and privatized family values in Oakland and across the United States. The idea that children belong in the private realm of the family could easily reify a narrow idea of family responsibility and the notion that the government cannot (and should not) help. Images of dangerous youth often justified efforts to control, contain, and exclude young people from Oakland's schools and streets. They reified the idea that youth needed discipline, not care or education, and promoted an idea of the state as a disciplinary father with expansive powers to police and regulate young people's behavior in urban spaces.

But children and youth also remained particularly powerful symbols for political projects that aimed to reconstruct a social safety net. Children's advocates and youth activists in Oakland used commonsense understandings of children as vulnerable and in need of adult protection to fight against the privatization of social responsibility for children and to secure new sources of funding for youth development. Youth activists similarly used the state's role as parent to challenge the incarceration of children.

On a national level, the Children's Defense Fund, as well as Hillary Clinton's book *It Takes a Village to Raise a Child*, tried to reclaim the progressive potential of the politics of childhood. In each of these cases, advocates used the dependence and innocence of children and youth to argue for state investments in social reproduction. Because neoliberal ideologies of choice, accountability, and self-governance falter when applied to kids, childhood may offer the most viable space for citizens to call for large-scale social programs and to bring questions of care and the social back into our political vocabulary.[36] Indeed, children and youth may be the only legitimate dependents left as neoliberalism has defined dependency as the ultimate failure of citizenship.

Race intersects with the politics of youth in important ways in twenty-first-century America. Not all children today have equal access to the symbolic power of childhood innocence and dependency. Youth of color, particularly black boys and girls, have long been linked with other symbolic associations—criminality or sexuality—that have undermined their ability to make claims on the state. As historian Jennifer Ritterhouse documents, white southerners in the Jim Crow era "rarely saw any but the very youngest black children as innocents or extended the ideal of the sheltered childhood to blacks."[37] Black parents had to train their children to survive in a racially structured world in which the "wrong" look or comment could lead to a white mob lynching, as it did with fourteen-year-old Emmett Till. On a national level, while Franklin Roosevelt declared an "end to child labor" in 1938, the Fair Labor Standards Act pointedly excluded agriculture and domestic service from the new regulations.[38] The largely black and Latino children who worked in those industries were not considered children worthy of protection.

The post–civil rights era certainly led to improvements in the lives and life chances of many black children. But an increasingly punitive state and the racialization of youth crime created new barriers and urgent problems. Since the late 1960s, black youth crime has worked as what legal theorist Patricia Hill Collins calls "a controlling image" both in Oakland and in American politics more broadly.[39] It focused black political action on the predicaments of black boys, often marginalizing attention to black girls.[40] But it has had much broader political effects as well. Racially coded images of ghetto youth have produced support for punitive public policies that treat boys as adult-like criminals in the nation's schools, streets, and justice system. They have built support for shrinking state spending for social supports while making spending on police and prisons seem absolutely necessary.[41]

The End of Democratized Adolescence

Community activists in Oakland expressed two apparently contradictory concerns about young people coming of age: children were growing up too soon, but some adult "children" never grew up. Childhood seemed to be shrinking, even disappearing, for some kids at the same time it was lengthening for others. These anxieties highlight deep disruptions in childhood and adulthood as stable, taken-for-granted, "natural" categories at the start of the twenty-first century.[42]

Neoliberal economic shifts and state policies changed the idealized path from *dependent* childhood to *independent* adulthood that emerged in the post–World War II era when an expanding economy helped produce a relatively "orderly" transition to adulthood for most young people in the United States.[43] Back then, youth would finish their education (often just high school), get a full-time job, move out of their parents' home, marry, maybe buy a home, and then start their own family. Not all young people followed that linear path, but it remained the norm against which most deviations were measured. Today the path to adulthood has many more detours and roundabouts. Economic insecurity and extended education mean that many young people leave home at later ages and remain semidependent on their parents far into their twenties, if not beyond.[44] News features and self-help books on "the mid-mid-life crisis," "boomerang kids," and "boys who never grow up" document our struggle to understand these delayed transitions to adulthood.[45] Scholars have called this new reality "emerging adulthood," and some developmental psychologists now argue that adolescence extends to the midtwenties.[46]

Changing state policies over the last thirty years have also redrawn the boundaries between childhood and adulthood in contradictory ways. On the one hand, the United States has created an ever-expanding culture of child protection. Raising the drinking and smoking age and cracking down on statutory rape, the state has extended childhood as a protected status into and beyond the teenage years. On the other hand, get tough on crime policies have led to a radical shrinking of childhood as jurisdictions around the country prosecute younger and younger children as adults.[47] Yet young people have not experienced these shifts equally. The material basis for what geographer Susan Ruddick calls "democratized adolescence" had become profoundly frayed. The category of youth itself seemed to split along racial and class lines in Oakland: poor kids, often kids of color, grew up too soon, while the protected children of the middle class never grew up.

Law and order politics has helped to codify new racial exclusions from childhood. Since the 1970s, white and middle-class youth have been removed from the juvenile justice system, their problems increasingly medicalized and treated in an expanding private system of mental health facilities.[48] At the same time, and not coincidentally, punishments have significantly increased for the largely black and Latino poor kids left in the public system.[49] California Proposition 21, the Gang Violence and Juvenile Crime Prevention Act, epitomized this get tough on youth trend. Scared by mass media reports of gang violence, voters passed Proposition 21 in 2000 even though youth crime was at a twenty-year low.[50] The ballot initiative increased penalties for a wide range of juvenile offenses, enhanced penalties for alleged gang members, and, most controversially, gave prosecutors the authority to try kids over fourteen as adults for any felony crime, including nonviolent ones.[51] Between 1985 and 1997, the number of youth incarcerated in adult prisons more than doubled in the United States.[52] Black and Latino boys are disproportionately charged and incarcerated as adults, excluding them from the category of childhood and the protections of the juvenile justice system.[53] Historian Barry Feld argues that these changes have served as "criminological triage," separating "our kids," who are seen as salvageable, from "other people's kids," who are framed as irredeemable.[54] These racial inequalities in the criminal justice system have created the popular equation between black boys and criminality that threatens to redefine black boys across class lines as potentially dangerous.[55]

These changes in the path to adulthood have increased fears across racial and class lines, while they have caused an even deeper crisis of social reproduction in black communities. As formal legal barriers to equal opportunities have been torn down, some black middle-class families have prospered as never before. But economic restructuring and criminal justice policies have created shock waves that have destroyed the foundations of many others. New gender fissures have emerged in black communities as more black women prospered while black men's economic progress stalled. Even black middle-class families have a much harder time ensuring that their children retain a secure foothold in the middle class than do white families.[56] Marita Golden, author of the popular book *Saving Our Sons*, captures the intensified risk that black boys in particular face as they come of age. For her son Michael, she explained, "the line of demarcation between childhood and adulthood was not a border, but a precipice."[57]

Oakland's Divided Landscapes of Childhood

Oakland's unequal childhoods were written into the city's physical geography, which runs from the formerly industrial flat plains along the bay up to the tall hills filled with parklands that lie between Oakland and the inland suburbs. The "flatlands" and "the hills" shaped Oakland's historical development and provided an important lens through which residents interpreted and contested deepening divides in youth. Freeways and boulevards marked both significant symbolic boundaries and real racial and class divides in this terrain. In 2000, in many areas of the East Oakland flatlands, between 27 and 52 percent of households lived below the poverty line, while in the hills above the 580 freeway there were virtually no poor households (See Figure 1).

This geographic divide provided a way to talk about the city's class exclusions that were racial, but could not be reduced in any simple way to race. Both the hills and the flatlands had become more racially diverse in the post–civil rights era, with an expanding black middle class and rapid Latino and Asian migration. But white residents still predominated in many parts of the hills, while the flatlands remained mostly black, Latino, or Asian (See Figure 2). In Oakland politics at the turn of the twenty-first century, the hills still often served as a symbol for the city's white elite and the flatlands, for the black masses. This geographic metaphor also provided a flexible way for Oakland residents to debate more complex racial and class inequalities and the contours of political power in the contemporary city.

Fears of youth crime and violence in Oakland conformed to the city's geography of inequality, with the hills generally coded as safe and the flatlands, especially in East or West Oakland, as dangerous. This general equation of space and danger reified fears of black youth, who were vastly overrepresented in Alameda County's juvenile justice system.[58] In 2000, while countywide black youth were 20% of the juvenile population, they represented 51% of juvenile arrests, 61% of adjudications, and 65% of institutional placements.[59] This conforms to a nationwide pattern: even when charged with the same offense, black youth were six times and Latino kids three times more likely to be incarcerated than white kids.[60] The disproportionate treatment is cumulative and increases at every stage in the juvenile justice process.[61]

These divided landscapes shaped the politics of youth in Oakland, creating very different coming of age dilemmas and political mobilizations that were structured in complicated ways by race, class, and place. As geographers Sarah Holloway and Gill Valentine contend, "geography matters to

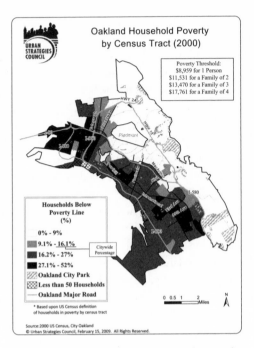

Figure 1. Oakland's landscape of poverty. (Copyright Urban Strategies Council, All Rights Reserved)

the social construction of childhood and in the everyday lives of children."[62] Oakland's neighborhoods played a significant role in creating and containing young people's dreams and opportunities,[63] but they also shaped the fears and actions of adults as they tried to understand and respond to youth in the city. Oaklanders regularly debated what the divide between the hills and the flatlands meant for children growing up in the city: Was there a ladder of opportunity to the hills for poor kids in the flatlands? Or was the path to the middle class impossibly steep? When people talked about "flatland kids" were they really talking about black kids? What was the significance of race now that the divide between the hills and the flatlands could no longer be seen in simple black-white terms?

These debates about race, place, and youth shed light on the connections between global processes and local places.[64] As anthropologists Jean and John Comaroff argue, many of the global crises and anxieties created by neoliberal capitalism "congeal in the contemporary predicaments of youth."[65] Global economic changes reverberated through Oakland's homes and neighborhoods. Decisions made at the city, state, or federal levels created patterns of investment and disinvestment that shaped children's lives. But children and adults in Oakland's neighborhoods experienced, interpreted, and reworked these global and national processes. These struggles at the local level have generated new techniques of governance, ideas of citizenship, and even concepts of the self that enable new political and economic orders to emerge.

Oakland's Complex Racial Politics

Oakland offers a microcosm of divides in youth, politics, and generation that characterize many American cities. The concerns and findings in this book echo stories that can be heard in many other cities where fears of youth have infected the populace and transformed urban policy making. Think of alleged "wildings" in New York, gangs in Los Angeles, or Chicago's curfew and loitering laws, which express broad public ambivalence about a younger generation that we have abandoned and now try to contain.[66] Or consider

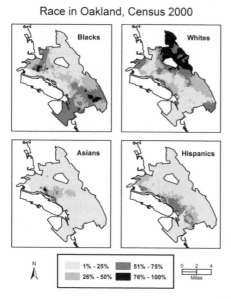

Figure 2. Oakland's complex geography of race. These maps highlight the ways white populations are concentrated in the hills, while blacks, Latinos, and Asians predominate in the flatlands. But they also show the strong black middle-class presence in the East Oakland hills and lower hills. (Mark Kumler and Diana Sinton, University of Redlands)

the more mundane frustrations adults express in towns and cities all over America when confronted with young people littering or loitering, often wearing clothes or speaking a language adults neither like nor understand. In many ways, Oakland embodies the core contradictions of urban America: racial segregation alongside rising black political power, racial liberalism and deep racial divides, disinvestment alongside gentrification.

At the same time, Oakland has several distinctive features that permit an especially rich exploration of race, class, and youth politics. Oakland is a midsized, historically working-class city that became a primary destination for black migrants during and after World War II. Consequently, Oakland's racial history and politics, in contrast to those of many other western cities, developed primarily along a black-white binary. Perhaps best known as the birthplace of the Black Panthers, Oakland has long been home to vibrant and diverse strains of black organizing and politics. Entrenched black poverty exists in Oakland, but there is also a substantial, politically powerful black middle class, which complicates the often simplistic equation of race with class or blackness with poverty. The city is home to wealthy black entrepreneurs, doctors, and lawyers who live in the hills, as well as middle-class black homeowners throughout the flatlands, who work as bus drivers, postal workers, or security guards and take enormous pride in their carefully cultivated homes and gardens as symbols of their life's work. Oakland's civil rights movement enabled black Oaklanders to amass significant local political power in the 1980s and '90s as Oakland became a majority black city. Even though many saw Mayor Jerry Brown's election as the end of Oakland's black urban regime, black politicians, civil servants, and community activists retained significant power within city government. In 2001, the city had a black city manager, chief of police, and chief of probation, and black heads of most city departments.

Oakland is also now one of the nation's most racially diverse cities—so it enables an investigation of how our concepts of race do (and do not) shift as they become less black and white. Latino, Asian, black, and white families—and many that fall neatly into none of those categories—share streets, schools, parks, and bus lines in Oakland. Childhood poverty in Oakland disproportionately affects black, Latino, *and* Asian children: 34.7% of black children, 33.5% of Asian children, and 26.5% of Hispanic children grew up in poor in 2000, compared to 17.5% of white children.[67] This diversity complicated understandings of race, class, and youth in Oakland at the turn of the twenty-first century even though a black-white binary continued to structure the way many residents thought about race and urban politics.

Oakland is a self-consciously liberal city, which enables us to explore the limits of liberalism, its failures to confront persistent structural racial inequalities, and the dangers of the color-blind ideology that has come to pervade American politics. Oakland is also home to vibrant and competing traditions of community organizing and politics. This means that Oakland politics during Jerry Brown's tenure as mayor included plentiful voices that challenged emerging forms of neoliberal governance and resisted calls for color blindness, many of which worked to revive Oakland's long history of protest politics in the face of calls for communities to partner with government to solve the city's complex problems. But it also means that neoliberal calls for community governance could draw on calls for community control that had been most prominently made by the Black Panthers. Robert Jones, a black parent and neighborhood activist in the Laurel district, explained why "city hall works with its neighborhoods."

> Look at the history of Oakland, when they were not in touch with the neighborhoods, the Black Panthers happened. So I think they found it in their interest to really be listening to their neighborhoods. As opposed to Marxist theory, Lenin's theory, it happened here. People got guns and revolted. They got guns and went to Sacramento and took the lawmakers hostage. Memories just don't go away. They are reaching out because they don't want that to ever happen again.

Studying race and the politics of youth sheds new light on the complexity of contemporary black politics. This book builds on a growing literature in political science and anthropology that explores vibrant traditions of black politics and neighborhood participation.[68] Scholars like Steven Gregory, Adolph Reed, Mary Pattillo, and Michelle Boyd have traced important changes in black politics in the post–civil rights era, exploring how complex transformations in urban political economies have deepened class divides in the ways black activists construct political identities and interests. Black activism in Oakland was reconfigured by the diverse forms of community "partnerships" that have become common in neoliberal cities. These engagements had profound generational as well as class contours. Black elders and middle-class homeowners were integrated into urban governance, working with Oakland's community policing initiative, volunteering in schools, running local nonprofits, and controlling many of the city's major city departments. At the same time, black (and Latino) youth and poor families were subjected to an increasingly punitive state apparatus. These very different kinds of relationships with state institutions helped produce deep generational and class divides in Oakland's politics. Linking the study of youth and politics sheds new light on the causes and consequences of the profound chasm between the civil rights generation and the hip hop generation.[69]

Oakland politics complicated the common assumption that fears of youth were solely white middle-class fears of poor black kids. In Oakland, fears of youth were neither confined to the white middle class nor focused solely on black youth. And *fears of* youth were closely linked to *fears for* youth who were negotiating an increasingly difficult path to adulthood. Exploring the politics of youth across Oakland's complex racial and class geography enables us to reconsider a core question in the literature on black politics: Does the fate of the black middle class remain linked to that of the black poor, and if so, does linked-fate politics remain viable?[70] It also lets us ask whether contemporary racial and class geographies are creating new linkages that may reconfigure the ways activists construct racial, class, and generational political identities. The politics of youth in Oakland at the turn of the twenty-first century suggests some significant changes in the way we think about race in the post–civil rights era. Race and class remain linked, as do race and space, but far less categorically than before the civil rights movement. Youth has become a racialized category in Oakland that marks the flexible but enduring structures of exclusion in contemporary America.

Oakland's black communities were not simply victims of urban decline and America's law and order politics. As Oakland historian Robert Self argues, black community activists have been among "the most thoughtful agents imagining and fighting for remedies to urban crises."[71] Indeed, black activists have been at the forefront of the struggle to forge a new politics of childhood that refuses to abandon some children as irredeemable. These efforts have emerged out of black political organizing and have reshaped long-standing traditions of American maternal politics. These activists may help us to imagine solutions to the fundamental crises facing many young people coming of age in early twenty-first-century America. If we are looking for a road map to create more just policies for the nation's youth, we need to learn from the urgent dilemmas and substantial roadblocks Oakland's activists have confronted and the often contradictory public policies they have promoted. As legal scholars Lanier Guinier and Gerald Torres have argued, black communities, in this case black children, may be like canaries in the coal mine.[72] They provide a critical warning and a call to national action to address the broad crises facing children and youth in America.

Are You a Reporter? Urban Political Fieldwork

This book draws on ethnographic fieldwork and historical research among Oakland's "attentive publics" or "community wardens," the active citizens, young and old, and the politicians and policy makers who shaped the city's responses to the problems of dangerous and endangered youth.[73] My fieldwork loosely corresponded with Jerry Brown's two-term tenure as Oakland's mayor. I spent 1998-2001 conducting research full-time in Oakland, and returned for periodic visits and interviews between 2003 and 2009. As with many ethnographic projects, my research methodology evolved over the course of my fieldwork, following the path of relationships I built with informants, institutional doors that opened or remained shut, and events and controversies, like Proposition 21, that created new spaces for political mobilizations.

I conducted ethnographic fieldwork in three neighborhoods across Oakland's divided geography: a largely black and Latino working-class neighborhood in the East Oakland flatlands where unemployment and high crime rates created urgent crises for young people coming of age; a mixed-income and multiracial lower hills neighborhood where many families struggled to ensure that their children would make it up a steeper and longer path to the middle class; and a wealthy, historically white neighborhood in the high hills where a local public high school brought Oakland's racial and class divides, past and present, into sharp relief. In each neighborhood, I observed the complex terrain of local politics: the youth groups, PTAs, homeowner's associations, and community policing councils that tried to shape the city's responses to the needs and problems of youth. In each neighborhood I conducted fifteen-twenty interviews with activists that explored local history, political networks, and community activism. I followed these activists to city council and school board debates about curfews, cruising, police practices, and juvenile justice policies. To understand the politics of childhood and youth also required that my methodology not reify a distinction between public political realms and the private realms of family, childhood, and parenting, so I explored activists' memories of childhood and their anxieties about the transition from childhood to adulthood as they raised children. I documented the landscapes of childhood across Oakland's geography and some of the daily conflicts over where young people belonged—conflicts that took place on street corners, in schools and parks, and in living rooms.

Many of the neighborhood activists were tightly networked into city hall and exerted a significant amount of influence over local policy making. For historical reasons, black and white activists dominated established political networks in the neighborhoods I studied.[74] Middle-class homeowners were generally the most engaged in neighborhood politics.[75] As Logan and Molotoch and many others have found, homeowners often exert more power with government and private sector groups.[76] But in Oakland the label "middle class" hides an enormous diversity in how local activists constructed class and racial identities through their political practice.[77] A central question of this study became how Oakland activists constructed racial, class, and generational identities within different political networks. I worked most closely with black political activists and parents in each neighborhood, but I also developed relationships with white, Latino, and Asian activists and parents who participated in interconnected political networks.

I explored several city and county coalitions that brought together government agencies and nonprofits to design strategies to respond to the problem of youth violence in Oakland. Moving through endless planning meetings, I met the nonprofit agency leaders as well as police, probation officers, and other government employees who led youth reform efforts in Oakland. I conducted over fifty interviews with city officials, police, and service providers. I also traced the history of Oakland's youth reform efforts through archival research in the Oakland library's history room. Since I needed to support myself financially during much of my fieldwork, I worked on a number of foundation-funded initiatives, which helped me map existing youth programs and Oakland's political networks. The world of youth service providers was a familiar one since after college I ran youth programs for a neighborhood-based nonprofit in Chicago. Instead of sitting as a silent observer, I participated freely and became "a free brain," according to one informant in a citywide collaborative. Frustrated by the fragmentation of Oakland's political networks, I often served as a bridge to bring together organizations or activists working on similar issues. Occasionally I worried that my active participation threatened a preexisting ideal of detached research or a narrow understanding of research ethics, but when I shared that worry with an informant, she reminded me of the inherently dialogic nature of knowledge: "It's not like we're some isolated tribe. You don't have to worry about contaminating our culture."

There are significant benefits and some drawbacks of studying politics by participating in multiple political networks and associations. These diverse locations helped me to develop a more subtle understanding of how Oakland's race and class divisions shaped the politics of youth. Moving through different political networks simultaneously, I became aware of multiple cleavages within Oakland's political culture, divisions between neighborhoods, between city and county service providers, and between youth activist networks and homeowner activists.[78] I could identify which networks were well connected to particular city or county departments and which were largely left out of the corridors of power. But the political networks themselves also limited my research in significant ways. As I traveled from meeting to meeting, I formed the closest relationships with the people who were already deeply embedded in the terrain of local politics and met fewer immigrants, poor parents, and young people except those already engaged in political action. I often got to know the police officers and city officials on the community meeting circuit even better than I knew activists in any one neighborhood. One particularly busy week, a police captain joked that he saw me more than he saw his wife. Following a busy schedule of meetings, I spent less time in the homes of informants and on the streets of Oakland than I would have liked. But my daily routine and my personal networks in many ways matched those of the community activists I studied who spent most afternoons and evenings in community meetings and formed close relationships with other activists in similar political networks.

My own interests as an activist and youth worker also shaped my fieldwork. When I first moved back to the Bay Area, I participated in the Critical Resistance conference in 1998 and learned about growing networks of youth activism in the Bay Area. I also began to conduct writing workshops in juvenile hall for *The Beat Within*, a Bay Area weekly magazine produced by and for incarcerated youth, which kept me in contact with the perspective of youth in the system. Although these activities were not formally part of my fieldwork, when Proposition 21 was added to the March 2000 ballot, I began to participate in planning meetings, street outreach, and rallies, both as a participant and as an observer. Youth were frequently marginalized in local politics, but they were not silent observers. To understand Oakland's vibrant youth activist networks, I interviewed youth leaders and conducted four focus groups with youth activists from the neighborhoods I studied. I observed young people on city streets and playgrounds, attended school assemblies about discipline, and watched interactions between youth and adult activists in community meetings to see the formal and informal ways young people challenged dominant discourses about what youth need and where they belong.

As I conducted this research from within very different political mobilizations, I occupied multiply marked identities that influenced people's responses to me in complex ways: a young, highly educated, upper-middle-class white woman without children, a researcher, and also a resident of San Francisco. Observing my own comfort and discomfort moving through these political networks helped to highlight the racial, class, and generational structures of Oakland's politics and geography. I felt most at home in the multiracial networks of progressive political activists in the lower hills, where I met friends to go out to bars and restaurants and used the local café as my office. When I was at largely African American community meetings in the flatlands, I "fit in" in a very different way. People often mistook me for a reporter, or a nonprofit or government employee, which was exactly where my race, class, and age located me in Oakland's political and social geography. Like other politically engaged twenty-something nonprofit workers I knew, I traveled from my childhood home in San Francisco through Oakland's poorer neighborhoods every day and night as part of my "work." I was one of the "adult children" living at home with my parents that some of my informants talked and worried about. I was significantly younger than most adult activists I interviewed and conscious of the respect that required. I simply never would have called Mrs. Jackson, an African American grandmother, by her first name, though I would do so with Victor, a sixteen-year-old youth activist, or Robert, a younger parent close to my own age. Although most names in this book are pseudonyms, I refer to Oakland activists according to the codes of respect I used in my everyday interactions.

Reflecting on my years in the field, I realize that I actively, though not always consciously, managed my identity in different ways throughout my fieldwork. With older African American activists, I often explicitly talked about how I thought racism had shaped Oakland's history, in order to overcome a kind of racial politeness that accompanied many early interviews. In professional planning meetings, I dressed up and spoke like a nonprofit worker informed about the best practices of youth reform, and I cultivated a very different style at youth-led rallies. But as I did fieldwork with youth activists fighting against police brutality as well as community policing activists, I decided that the most ethical approach was to share my emerging interpretations with my informants, along with my own political commitments and critiques.

This book leads readers on a journey through the politics of youth, race, and space in Oakland at the turn of the twenty-first century—through the memories, local histories, geographies, and fragmented state institutions that influenced debates over how to respond to the crises young people faced coming of age. These debates about children and youth occur in particular places, not only, or even primarily, in the disembodied contexts of the mass media. The first three chapters of this book are organized to highlight the importance of place, showing how Oakland's geographies of race and class shaped children's lives and the politics of youth. These chapters lead the reader from the flatlands up through the lower hills and finally into the hills. This path through the city mirrors the ways images and young people themselves move through Oakland's geography. Fears of youth in Oakland were often forged through media coverage of crime and images of the youth in the flatlands. But these representations of "inner-city kids" moved up into the hills to shape the perceptions of adults and activists in the hills. Young people themselves moved up the hill as they searched for better schools and safer places. Arriving in schools or parks in the hills, they often encountered fears of flatland kids.

Each chapter begins with a portrait of a community activist that highlights his or her memories of childhood and childrearing, analyses of what young people need, and political struggles. The chapters follow these activists into their political practice and daily lives, exploring how memory and local history shape the politics of youth. Each chapter highlights a different way community partnerships have affected political practice by influencing the way activists defined the needs of young people, the boundaries between public and private responsibility, and the idea of the state. Chapter 1 explores community policing activism in Elmhurst, examining the dilemmas of black homeowner activists whose nostalgia for disciplined youth encouraged them to construct a vision of a disciplinary state with expanded police powers. Chapter 2 examines a racially and socioeconomically diverse group of parent activists in the lower hills who volunteered their private time to try to expand public investments that would extend middle-class structured and supervised time to all kids in the neighborhood. Chapter 3 explores conflicts around Skyline High School between black middle-class parents and white homeowners who fought over whether kids at the school were dangerous criminals or innocent kids. White homeowners living in Oakland's private estates often framed youth problems as "cultural" or familial in ways that naturalized Oakland's man-made geography of inequality and helped justify California's disinvestments in the public infrastructure for children. Black parents vociferously defended their children against the image of black youth criminality that threatened to redefine them as dangerous outsiders in their own schools and streets.

Chapter 4 steps back to examine Oakland's urban redevelopment from a citywide perspective, exploring the links between the politics of youth and the city's urban redevelopment policies and practices. It begins with a portrait of MacArthur Boulevard, a main thoroughfare that embodies Oakland's fitful and incomplete transformation from a landscape of production to a landscape of consumption and the contradictory role young people have played in this process. It shows how new landscapes of childhood and community activists' efforts to save children have helped to create the privatized urban space characteristic of many neoliberal cities. Chapter 5 concludes the book with the voices of youth activists, who offer a critique of neighborhood activism in Oakland and an alternate vision of the politics of childhood and the place of youth in the city.

Oakland's activists offer important insights into the underlying question of this book: Is a more progressive politics of childhood possible? People's fears about kids are urgently real and deeply felt. We can't just wish them away. There are no simple answers to the dilemmas Oakland's activists faced, but that does not mean, as we saw Jerry Brown suggest at the beginning of this introduction, that there is nothing government can do. The inequalities in children's lives in Oakland and the exclusions of black boys from childhood are incompatible with the true meaning of democracy and the promise of the American Dream. With high levels of public support for children's health insurance and growing support for after-school funding, some public policy observers wonder whether a new wave of "kids-first politics" could reinvigorate public support for an expanded welfare state.[79] To evaluate that question we need to ask: What would it require for the United States to make good on its promise to provide equal opportunities to all of America's children and youth? What kinds of public policies and state practices would encourage democratized childhood and youth? Just as importantly, what kind of politics and activism would get the nation to make those investments? And what ideas about childhood and the state stand in the way?

1

Back in the Day

Linda Jackson had never wanted to be involved in politics. As "a preacher's kid," she was in church seven days a week doing community work. When she left home she swore, "I was never going to participate in anything else. That's the end of it." But she got "thrown back into" community work as white flight and economic decline hit Elmhurst hard in the 1970s and '80s, and she watched her neighborhood struggle with crime and blight that erased the precarious distinctions between middle-class and poor in East Oakland. Over twenty years later, when I first visited her home, Linda Jackson was frustrated by the city's failed promises, fed up with ongoing problems of drug dealing and violence, and angry at "this generation of kids that's out here shooting up people."

Linda Jackson spoke with the rhythmic cadences and broad vowels of Arkansas. "I'm just a simple little country girl," she'd say in community meetings, before her voice took on a steely tone, her impatience with city officials shining through an otherwise polite southern demeanor. An African American woman in her mid-sixties, she had attended a state college in Arkansas soon after it was integrated, retired from administrative work at a local hospital, and now ran a small family construction company with her husband out of their home.

Mrs. and Mr. Jackson raised two children, and they now watched anxiously as their two grandchildren negotiated the transition through their teenage years in East Oakland. Their ample 1940s bungalow nestled into a low hill in Toler Heights, a predominantly black middle-class community where many neighbors worked in professional or government jobs, but others lived below the poverty line. Only one block away lay the run-down 1970s apartment buildings, liquor stores, and mostly empty store fronts that cluster along MacArthur Boulevard in the sprawling and much poorer flatlands of Elmhurst.

Mrs. Jackson first joined her homeowners' association in the 1970s after a series of robberies in her neighborhood. They created a neighborhood patrol

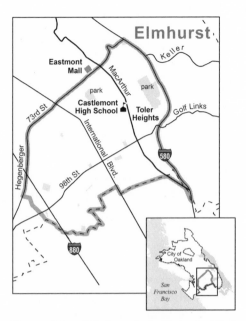

Figure 3. Map of Elmhurst: In the Flatlands. (Mark Kumler and Diana Sinton, University of Redlands)

and built a close relationship with the police department. One meeting and committee seemed to lead to another, until soon she was spending evenings and most vacations working with the association, the Neighborhood Crime Prevention Council, and neighborhood redevelopment efforts. As her grandkids began to go to the neighborhood public schools, she was drawn towards working with the schools as well.

By the time we sat down in her home to talk, Mrs. Jackson had long been a leader in neighborhood politics. She regularly spoke in front of the city council, gave interviews to newspapers, and organized with a strong network of neighbors to crack down on cruising, drug dealing, and violence throughout East Oakland. "All of us that are participating own our homes. We have chosen to stay here. We could have left but we decided not to. We decided we're no longer going to be ignored." She described East Oakland as the city's "forgotten stepchild." "People will come out and give us a lot of lip service, canned speeches. You know how many plans they've had out here?" She was fed up with watching those plans pile up, unfunded and never implemented.

"What people seem to forget is that we all have a stake in this. I heard the most ridiculous crazy man on the radio. He said he wasn't interested in education because he had no kids. This man better be interested." She knew the effects of public disinvestment. "These kids that you're leaving behind without education will be your worst nightmare in the future. The have-nots are going to be coming up robbing you." She looked back at the massive budget cuts to cities "during Reagan's time" and saw the results all around her neighborhood. "All of us have paid a price for it."

Mrs. Jackson had grown up in a strict southern household and worried that parents today weren't instilling the proper discipline in children. Her parents had raised five "strong-willed" children back in Arkansas and taught them that "you had to earn what you get." Growing up poor, she remembered picking cotton to pay for her own school clothes. "Not a one of us went to jail. All of us have been self-sufficient. We left home seventeen, eighteen. None of us ever returned home to depend on our parents to take care of us."

"My mom used to tell me, 'I wasn't brought here to be your friend. I was brought here to train you the way you need to be trained.' They kept me so afraid to do certain things until I got old enough to know better." She laughed. "I just figured if I did certain things, my parents would kill me." Nowadays, "these kids don't think anything would happen to them. In fact, the parents will be the first one running out there to jump on you if you say anything to them."

Mrs. Jackson's own kids had passed through adolescence safely. Raising kids amidst the deepening poverty, anger, and desperation of East Oakland was not easy, and drugs and violence were too close to ignore. "Everyday I thank my lucky stars that my son is not one of those kids out there on the corner, shooting and selling dope, that my daughter did not fall into that bag, getting pregnant, getting on welfare and never getting off. To me that was a certain amount of success." Her nephew, "a perfectly intelligent young man, got off into drugs," and after years in and out of treatment, was "back on the streets again." Her voice echoed the whole family's disappointment as she talked about waiting to hear about his imminent death. "I would have thought if anyone could get off of drugs it would be him."

Maternal vigilance and the iron hand of her husband had kept her own kids on the right path. "When my son was growing up, he was always devilish." She laughed. "I made sure I knew where they were." She often drove her son to school or picked her grandson up, so that they wouldn't be tempted by the streets. "If I had to get in the car and follow them, I did. I would come down and get them off that corner. . . . It took them awhile to know how I knew so much." Mrs. Jackson "talked her children to death" explaining the long-term consequences of the choices they made. But she also made sure they knew that child abuse laws didn't mean she couldn't discipline them. One day, she invited a police officer to come tell her children, "If your mama wants to whop you, I'm going to hold you down." "That took care of that problem," she explained.

But Mrs. Jackson still worried as she thought about her kids' futures. They had avoided the most obvious pitfalls. "They both work, and they are pretty well self-sufficient." But they still struggled. Her son had dropped out of college only a few units shy of graduation to take a job at UPS, and he had recently "hit a brick wall" trying to get promotions in the company. While other guys were given permission to return to college while retaining their job, he wasn't. He quit in frustration and started working for the family business. He now understood what his mother had always been telling him: "You've got to get yours before you get there." "I don't think parents teach kids this enough. If you're black you better make darned certain you are three times better qualified. Expect to be knocked down three to four times when you go out there. . . . We have to prepare ourselves."

Mrs. Jackson and her husband had helped the kids through rough patches—through divorce, a lost job—and they would do so again. "I would like them to be able to buy their own house by now, to own their home, but they do have their own apartments. I do understand in this day and age it is really hard for kids to do that. At some point in time, I may have to help them with a down payment." Mrs. Jackson's daughter struggled to afford the escalating cost of renting an apartment in Oakland despite income from two part-time jobs. A divorced single mother of two whose husband didn't pay child support, she had recently complained about her mom's community work: "Mom, you're running me out of town." Mrs. Jackson acknowledged, "It's true": economic redevelopment might displace "some of the good people."

Mrs. Jackson measured her children's success against the extraordinary risks that face black children coming of age in contemporary American cities. In Elmhurst, the children of many black homeowners had made it securely into the expanding black middle class. Some had moved to the suburbs and urged their parents to follow. But many others had struggled to finish college and maintain jobs, and some remained living at home far into adulthood. On almost every block, one could hear about some neighbor's child who had grown up too soon, about children raising children, or some young relative who fell into drug dealing, drug abuse, or jail.

Mrs. Jackson worried even more as she watched her grandkids, still in an awkward stage between childhood and adulthood. She and her husband were paying for their granddaughter's apartment for one year while she enrolled in an LPN nursing program, while still maintaining hope that she would achieve her dream of becoming a doctor. But if she didn't apply herself, they would end their support. "With kids these days, people are too lenient. You have chances. You can make good choices." Her grandson, then seventeen, loved to make comic books, but had not been applying himself in school. She had warned him recently, "You are making choices that will affect you in your life. We'll be disappointed. But you will pay the price." He had finally decided he wanted to graduate, but she knew he wasn't safe yet. "He's still at an age where he could get drawn into some of this craziness out here. I'm hoping that he doesn't."

Mrs. Jackson insisted that the neighborhood needed a long-term economic development plan. She wanted the city to build a youth center so that young people would have some alternative to "the temptation and trouble" they could get into hanging out on the street. But she worried that the neighborhood would never be able to attract any investment "if you have people shooting things up at night and there's no control. . . . We need the policemen right now to keep things under control. We realize that the policeman is not the answer to our problems, but they're the Band-Aid until we can get some things accomplished."

She didn't worry much about racial profiling because "the people perpetrating these crimes are our young black men in our neighborhood." But she acknowledged that black men in her homeowners' association were often "very leery of giving the police too much power." Even her husband had recently objected to her support for random police sweeps down MacArthur Boulevard. "Well, I haven't done anything," he insisted. But she explained, "Well, this is the situation: either we continue the way we are, or we allow the policemen to make things safer for us." She told him to avoid driving on MacArthur and if he was stopped, to do exactly what the officer said. "It's amazing, he came to realize—those were the choices."

Disciplining Youth and
Families in the Flatlands

Back in the days, our parents used to take care of us
Look at 'em now, they even fuckin' scared of us
Callin' the city for help because they can't maintain
Damn, shit done changed.

—Notorious B.I.G.

In February 2001, one of the Elmhurst Neighborhood Crime Prevention Councils (NCPC) met in a classroom at a local middle school. Bill Clay, the dapper African American NCPC president, invited two uniformed community policing officers, a tall, broad-shouldered white officer and a heavyset Asian officer, to sit up at the front of the room with him, "on the hot seat." The officers explained that they had been doing a lot of violence suppression in response to the recent rise in homicides, "flooding" particular areas with as many as twenty-five officers and "stopping everyone we can." They were targeting parolees and conducting undercover buy-bust operations at drug hot spots. Mr. Clay then told the officers to take out their pens and asked for community concerns: "Who's got the first problem?"

Mrs. Gilbert, Mr. Lawlor, Mr. and Mrs. Riles, Mrs. Taylor, and her granddaughter sat around tables with fifteen other people facing the front of the room where pictures for Black History Month surrounded the blackboard. Older African American homeowners formed a clear majority of members in the NCPC, but they were joined by a couple of white senior citizens, younger African American homeowners, one older Latino homeowner, an Arab business owner, and the school vice-principal and a code compliance officer, both African American. This NCPC was typical of most in Elmhurst. A small number of people came monthly, but more would turn out for meetings with the police chief or city manager. This NCPC could reach as many as two hundred residents through its homeowners' associations, block captains, informal phone trees, and relationships among neighbors.

Residents began to describe problems with drug dealing at specific addresses, sometimes using drug dealers' nicknames and offering details about where drugs were hidden and when drugs were sold. Mrs. Gilbert complained that she had to move her granddaughter's bedroom to the other side of the house so she wouldn't hear drug dealers' conversations from next door. "All the dealers in East Oakland are at that address." Mrs. Taylor disagreed; she still had a lot of dealers on her block. James Richards, a black man in his midforties, was discussing persistent drug dealing at a local liquor store when Deputy Chief Bryant walked into the room. "They're like cockroaches, the mess, the noise level is outrageous," he said. Turning to the deputy chief, he added, "I'm talking about across from your mother's home."

A broad-shouldered African American man with gentle eyes, Deputy Chief Bryant responded that he knew the problem well. He had grown up in this neighborhood before moving to the Oakland hills. He still attended church, visited his mother, and mentored young people in the neighborhood. Bryant described his vision for how to address Oakland's persistent problems with crime and violence. "We can't resolve the problem by locking people up, and we have locked up a lot of folks in Oakland. OPD [Oakland Police Department] is good at that. In California we have tripled the prison population and darn near bankrupted this state by trying to lock people up." He asked for volunteers to go door to door to promote a pledge of nonviolence, to hand out literature on anger management resources, and to recruit new members for community policing. The deputy chief hoped this new program would recreate the Elmhurst neighborhood of his childhood.

> People will begin to talk to each other once again. . . . In 1968 when I was at Elmhurst Middle School, if I did something wrong, my father knew when I got home. We knew each other. We have gotten away from that. Tell me what my kid's doing. This is about reaching out and building community from the ground up. The strength of the community comes from you folks. What we need is you.

Mrs. Riles, a black woman in her late seventies, spoke up. "The problem is that parents are afraid to chastise their children and teach them properly" because the kids might call the police on them. Deputy Chief Bryant insisted that the police only arrested parents in cases of serious abuse. "That's just an excuse that I can't handle. We have to get back to having children because we want to have them, and we want to raise them to be respectable parts of the community. Those values have to come from. . . ." He paused to wait for a response from the room. Mrs. Riles responded "home," while another older African American man said "the village." The deputy chief nodded, adding, "I am the most liberal deputy chief and definitely the only Democrat, but when it comes to raising children, Democrats have not done well. 'Let the government deal with it. Let child welfare deal with it.' We have to deal with it right here." He called for neighbors to become mentors and for the neighborhood to become "its own policing system."

This NCPC meeting highlighted a pervasive nostalgia in urban black communities. In almost every interview, I heard stories of a more orderly past when adults disciplined children, youth showed respect, and a more cohesive black community took responsibility for raising children as a village. African American activists in Elmhurst's NCPCs did not represent a single generation, as they ranged in age from late thirties to eighties, yet in community meetings and conversations, they constructed a body of shared memories. Repeated stories captured their sense that something was wrong with young people today. "Young people today have no respect" or "no discipline." "Youth have too much power." "These children are taking over."

Children served as vital sites of memory and nostalgic longing in Elmhurst. Anthropologist William Bissell argues that nostalgia is not "poor history" but a social practice shaped by specific spaces and politics in the present.[1] We look to the past at moments when faith in the future or in progress is eclipsed. Nostalgia in Elmhurst highlighted deep ambivalence about whether the post–civil rights era represented true progress in the black community—especially when activists looked at the hurdles young people faced coming of age in the neighborhood.

Debates about children and childrearing encapsulated fundamental debates over the role of the state and the causes of black community struggles. Were the Democrats' welfare programs responsible for undermining the foundations of black communities? Or had state intrusions into the family via child abuse laws undermined parental authority? Could the police solve the neighborhood crime problem? Or did the community have to take responsibility for discipline? Was childrearing the responsibility of parents in the home, as Mrs. Riles suggested, or of a broader "village"? These debates highlighted the complexity of black politics in the East Oakland flatlands and the ways activists combined different political ideologies. Nevertheless, nostalgia for disciplined youth shaped the politics of childhood in this neighborhood. Defining crime as a youth problem focused activists' attention on "the home" and "the family" and bolstered conservative ideologies of self-help that political scientist Melissa Harris-Lacewell argues have "deep roots in African American history."[2] Specific ideas about what children needed also helped to construct a particular vision of the state. Since many activists thought children needed patriarchal "discipline," they turned to the police as a kind of disciplinary father and supported expanded state powers to monitor and punish young people.[3] Black city officials participated actively in these memory practices in ways that encouraged Elmhurst activists to turn to the police to restore village discipline.

This NCPC meeting illustrated an interesting tension within Oakland's community policing initiative. While black homeowners campaigned for intensified police action, police officers, like Deputy Chief Bryant, often argued that the community (not the police) had to solve the neighborhood's crime problem. These calls for community self-governance were a key element of neoliberal urban governance in Oakland. Community policing became a forum through which neighbors, politicians, and the police struggled over the form of the state and through which neighborhood activists both reproduced and sometimes resisted neoliberal efforts to shift responsibility for maintaining order from government to communities and families.

Community policing reshaped the ways black homeowner activists defined their community and framed their rights as citizens in Oakland. Urban anthropologists, like Steven Gregory, Jeff Maskovsky, and Emmanuela Guano, have begun to explore the ways specific structures and practices of community participation "produce and reproduce different forms of urban citizenship and community belonging."[4] Citizenship is not just a legal category but draws on complex ideas of culture and morality to define some people or groups as full members of the nation, while excluding others. We need to explore the ways activists forged racial and class political identities within different political networks in Oakland. Community policing reinforced the power of black middle-class homeowners in Elmhurst, but often excluded poor families, renters, immigrants, and youth from the moral community constructed in these meetings.

Community policing is part of a strikingly illiberal trend in neoliberalism that legal scholar Jonathan Simon defines as "governing through crime." A narrow logic of crime prevention and security has reshaped our daily lives and politics, shaping where we live, how we raise our kids, and what we expect from our government. Governing through crime has helped to reconfigure the "purposes and tasks of the state" and the relationship between citizens and the state in two important ways. First, the criminal justice system offers "a perfect object lesson" in "individual responsibility and accountability," core principles of neoliberal modes of governance.[5] Second, governing through crime has constrained the legitimate terrain of state action and reified a vision of the state as policeman, or as Simon says, "as enforcer and protector."[6] In Oakland, nostalgia for disciplined youth helped to produce an emerging "penal common sense" that redefined the central right of citizenship as the right to sufficient police protection.[7] But community policing radically reshaped definitions of community, discipline, and care among black activists; it redefined village discipline as policing and accountability as arrests. Neighborhood activists in Elmhurst turned to the police to recreate communal discipline because they felt they had so few choices, faced with limited state resources and a massive crisis of social reproduction. As we saw in Linda Jackson's portrait, they called for more police because it was one of the few ways they could demand state accountability in a neoliberal political order.

Elmhurst: The City's "Forgotten Step-Child"

Elmhurst extends across the East Oakland flatlands from the 580 freeway to the bay, between 73rd Avenue and the San Leandro border.[8] Popular media portrays this neighborhood as a largely poor, crime-ridden black neighborhood that was labeled "the killing fields" in the early 1990s as murder rates in Oakland peaked. But Elmhurst also has many black and Latino homeowners and a long history of black community activism dating back to the early 1960s. Long-standing struggles against drug dealing and economic decline left many activists frustrated with the failures of urban renewal efforts.[9] Homeowner activists found themselves in a double bind, deeply concerned about the future of the neighborhood's children and desperate for state investment at a moment of state retrenchment. For many, community policing seemed to promise a visible state commitment to the neighborhood.

Older African American homeowners comprised the vast majority of the membership and leadership of the Neighborhood Crime Prevention Councils and homeowners' associations in this neighborhood. Most of these older residents bought homes in Elmhurst in the sixties and seventies in what was then a racially mixed and upwardly mobile working-class neighborhood, one of Oakland's "industrial gardens" where single family homes with small yards clustered near industrial centers.[10] They remembered vibrant commercial districts, neighbors who took care of their property, and children who were respectful of adult authority. But deindustrialization and the crack epidemic hit Elmhurst hard. Local activists have fought an uphill battle for years against drug dealing, violent crime, and blighted housing in their neighborhood.

Neighborhood activists resented the image of Elmhurst as an undifferentiated ghetto. In community meetings, residents regularly described themselves as "hard-working" and "tax-paying" citizens, explicitly countering media images of this neighborhood as dominated by drug dealers and families on welfare. Mrs. Jackson, whom we met in the opening portrait, complained that the city and developers "think our communities have no money to spend in our pocket," but she insisted, "some people in the neighborhood probably have more money than in the hills." A complex geography of class distinctions characterizes the neighborhood. The lower hills just below 580 include slightly wealthier middle-class households than are found below MacArthur, and this class gradation continues as one moves towards the bay.[11] But class diversity characterized the entire Elmhurst neighborhood with its mix of large Victorians, small 1940s bungalows, and scattered apartment buildings, some of which were built as subsidized housing in the 1970s. In the heart of Elmhurst between MacArthur and International Boulevard, 46% of adults have no high school diploma, but 29% have some college and 1% hold graduate degrees. Household incomes are lower than the city average but vary widely, with 18% of households making under $10,000, but 16% earning between $60,000 and $100,000 and another 3.2%, over $100,000.[12] The community is also almost evenly divided between owner-occupied (57%) and renter-occupied homes (43%).

African American activists in the NCPCs were largely homeowners, but came from a broad range of the black working and middle classes. Many retired African American men in Elmhurst started their careers in the navy shipyards or in the military, and some moved into government jobs as civil rights activism opened new opportunities. Rev. Henry Chester left the shipyard for a job in the post office before he became a community organizer with Oakland Community Organization (OCO). Mrs. and Mr. Riles bought and ran a corner store. Mrs. White retired after over thirty years as a meat wrapper at a supermarket. Mr. Lawlor, a rare younger man in his forties, worked installing cable. Ms. Knight retired early from a successful career as a lawyer and moved to the neighborhood in her midthirties. Mr. Clay, unlike most neighborhood leaders, lived in the hills but became active in the Elmhurst NCPC because he owned rental property near a drug hot spot. He retired from a managerial position in government, and at the time of my research volunteered full-time in community policing and in efforts to improve youth and senior services in Elmhurst. Some residents had bought or inherited rental properties in the neighborhood and had disposable income, while others struggled to make ends meet on fixed retirement benefits or salaries that barely met their families' needs.

Neighborhood activists had seen massive transformations since the 1960s and '70s. As the East Oakland flatlands rapidly integrated during the '50s and '60s, black and white kids increasingly shared parks and schools, and sometimes fought over these spaces of childhood.[13] Although Oakland was more integrated than many U.S. cities, rapid white flight made Elmhurst a majority African American neighborhood by 1970.[14] Deputy Chief Bryant's family experienced these racial transitions first-hand. When he was born in 1955, real estate agents still would not sell to blacks above East 14th Street. A white friend helped his parents get around these informal racial restrictions to buy their house. Like most black pioneers, his family was upwardly mobile and better off financially than many white families in the neighborhood.[15] In his kindergarten class, there were only three blacks, one of whom was the daughter of a teacher. By junior high, his school was 70% black, and when he graduated from Castlemont High in 1973, he estimated that there were only about twelve whites out of a class of eleven hundred.[16]

Most people described Oakland's white flight as a peaceful and polite "exodus," but it was nonetheless destructive. White families slowly disappeared as they took advantage of cheap, federally subsidized mortgages to move to racially restricted suburbs or to expanding neighborhoods in the hills. Mrs. Taylor maintained a good relationship with one white family on her block for years. The kids grew up and played together. The son even called her mom, but eventually he moved his parents out of the neighborhood, explaining that "there were too many blacks." Because most whites refused to buy in majority-black neighborhoods, housing values declined, and absentee landlords often abandoned properties or maintained them badly.

White flight, economic restructuring, and deindustrialization destroyed the neighborhood's economic infrastructure. As historian Robert Self documents, Oakland's white Republican city government invested in regional planning policies that systematically promoted development in nearby suburbs and underdeveloped Oakland's flatlands.[17] Businesses along the commercial corridors struggled with white flight, redlining in business loans, and the growth of regional malls. The neighborhood was rich in manufacturing jobs in the midtwentieth century, but black unemployment rates began to skyrocket in the post–World War II era; in parts of the East Oakland flatlands, unemployment ran as high as 25-30% in 1960. Younger black workers bore the brunt of job losses as industrial jobs began to relocate to nearby suburbs, but economic decline was exacerbated by black exclusions from service sector jobs.[18] Plant closures escalated throughout the '70s and '80s.[19] By 1990, unemployment stood at 9.5% in Oakland, but in Elmhurst the rate was

14.23%.[20] Even during the economic boom in 2000, 44.7% of Elmhurst children were growing up below the poverty line, and 52.4% of kids at Castlemont High remained on the state welfare program CalWORKS despite drastic declines in the welfare rolls in the state.[21]

Many neighbors traced the further destabilization of their neighborhood and the source of most of their current problems to the rise of street-level drug dealing and the introduction of crack cocaine in the 1980s. Drugs and prostitution filled the neighborhood's economic void.[22] Cheaper than powder cocaine and easy to process, crack generated an entrepreneurial drug market that radically expanded the number of drug sales locations and the violence associated with sales.[23] Neighborhood residents, who increasingly added bars to their windows and installed reinforced steel doors, described the streets as dangerous spaces where children could no longer play and where many adults, especially senior citizens, no longer felt safe. Although crime declined rapidly in the late 1990s, persistent drug dealing made most neighbors feel as though crime either had not really decreased or would soon increase again.

Black political networks dominated local politics in Elmhurst, despite the increasing racial diversity of the neighborhood as Latino and some Asian families bought houses from black families moving to the suburbs. As one marker of racial change, by 2002, Castlemont High School, once almost 90% African American, was 52.9% black, 37% Latino, 5.8% Asian and Pacific Islander, and .6% white.[24] Language was one barrier to newer immigrant participation, since few neighborhood meetings had translation services. But another barrier was that Elmhurst was broadly defined as a black space. Even though Elmhurst may have been half Latino by 2005, I would still meet African American young adults throughout Oakland who would say without qualifications that Elmhurst was a black neighborhood. Latino residents sometimes reproduced this racial definition of space when they traveled to Fruitvale, the historic heart of Oakland's Mexican American community, to meet with city council member Ignacio De La Fuente instead of Elmhurst's Larry Reid. The fact that Elmhurst organized and fought as a black community throughout the 1970s and '80s solidified Elmhurst's identity as a black space. These struggles generated deeply felt claims to neighborhood spaces— schools, parks, and streets that activists had worked to revitalize—and to political power for which black activists had fought hard.[25]

Black activists in Elmhurst took divergent paths into local politics. Some had been involved for decades, while others only became active after they retired. A few NCPC members participated actively in Oakland's vibrant civil rights and black power organizations in the 1960s. Most first became involved in community work through church, through black clubs like the Eastern Star or Knights and Ladies of Pythias, or through volunteering in their children's schools. Mrs. Gilbert was always involved in her children's and grandchildren's school and did volunteer work with her church, and then one of her neighbors told her about the NCPC meetings. She stayed involved because the NCPC gave her some way to deal with the "guys standing on the corner." Miles Johnson, one of the first black policemen in Oakland, had been a member of Men of Tomorrow, a prominent black service club that played a role in early civil rights activism in Oakland, and later became an active member of his homeowners' association. Others were motivated by personal tragedies. Mr. Lawlor felt comfortable negotiating Elmhurst's sometimes rough streets: he was young, had been a security guard, and belonged to one of Oakland's many black motorcycle clubs. But his daughter had been shot and seriously injured as she walked to the corner store. He joined the NCPC to demand more police presence so his daughter could be safe walking in her own neighborhood.

Many neighborhood residents currently active in the Neighborhood Crime Prevention Councils got their start in homeowner mobilizations in the late 1960s and '70s fighting against the growing numbers of abandoned homes, apartment buildings, and negligent absentee landlords. Mrs. Love first got involved when the Oakland Housing Authority began building scattered site housing in East Oakland to deal with the aftermath of urban renewal, which had displaced almost one-third of residents of West Oakland, the historic heart of Oakland's black community. This new housing was all located in already predominantly black neighborhoods, instead of spread throughout the city.[26] Mrs. Love's home kept getting broken into by "youth living in this public housing" next door. Since the housing authority never responded to complaints, she started organizing her neighbors and "kept going downtown."[27] Mrs. Love moved from her work in neighborhood quality-of-life politics to organizing for district elections in the late 1970s, which enabled black politicians to overturn the city's white Republican political machine.

The vibrant story of Elmhurst's community activists casts doubt on sociologist Robert Putnam's argument that Americans are less involved in civic activity today—that we are *Bowling Alone*. Black churches feed and clothe the homeless, run mentoring programs and AIDS ministries, and visit the elderly throughout the East Oakland flatlands. Many homeowners' associations, NCPC members, and members of Oakland Community Organizations have volunteered for decades, desperately trying to "hold their communities together."[28] But the challenges created by economic restructuring and public policies that shifted capital and jobs away from black urban communities were more than these volunteers could be reasonably expected to solve.[29] Many residents were frustrated by the lack of progress after decades of fighting crime, blight, and economic decline. Neighbors continued to fight the same drug corners and landlords year after year. Many residents still were unemployed, underemployed, or dependent on increasingly insecure federal aid. The commercial corridors remained dilapidated, with the most vibrant businesses—barbershops, clothing stores, beauty shops, and small convenience stores—standing out among many empty storefronts, liquor stores, and check cashing stores. Many residents expressed disappointment in the city's black leadership and its efforts to solve problems in Elmhurst. Even during the height of the black urban regime during the 1980s and early '90s, the city concentrated most public investment on revitalizing downtown Oakland.[30] Linda Jackson's description of Elmhurst as "Oakland's forgotten step-child" emphasizes both the persistent neglect of the neighborhood and her demand that the city nurture its far-flung neighborhoods.

Post–Civil Rights Nostalgia

> When I was growing up, if I did wrong, I got hit by Mrs. Green,
> Mrs. Howard, and my mother.
> —Mr. Lawlor

I first realized the prevalence of nostalgia for disciplined children as I sat one day in a meeting of nonprofit service providers talking about the crime problem in the East Oakland flatlands. A 24-year-old African American man began to explain that the problem was that young people today had no discipline: "When I was a kid, everyone laid into me. It was you against all these different people. Now a kid doesn't have to respond to anyone." This was a very familiar refrain, though quite surprising to hear from a 24-year-old who grew up at the height of Oakland's crack epidemic. Closing my eyes, I could imagine these phrases spoken by parents in the 1940s or '50s. We have a long history in the United States of blaming young people for societal decline and of seeing the past through rose-colored glasses.[31] As historian Stephanie Coontz argues in her book *The Way We Never Were*, people have been tracking the "decline" of the "American family" since at least the late nineteenth century. *Black Metropolis*, a famous ethnography of Chicago's Southside black communities in the 1940s, contains very similar complaints about how chaotic poor families fail to properly discipline their children.[32]

Political scientist Adolph Reed suggests that nostalgia for the Jim Crow South or pre–civil rights North as idyllic, unified, and safe has "attained a nearly universal status in black public discourse." He analyzes this nostalgia as "a historically specific class yearning," a patriarchal vision that secures the unchallenged role of the black middle class—the talented tenth—as role models and race leaders. Jim Crow nostalgia creates a coherent black communal identity—grounded in middle-class values—at the exact moment when deepening class, gender, and generational divides have raised questions about the idea of black unity.[33]

Reed's analysis offers important insights into the ways nostalgia operated in Elmhurst. But Elmhurst activists were not only engaged in a middle-class project of racial uplift. Black community activists were struggling with real changes in childhood and families that challenged the idea of progress in the post–civil rights era. They were engaged in an urgent project to save children in this neighborhood, including their own. We need to look carefully at the complex longings encoded in these memories to understand how they worked in the daily practice of politics.

Mrs. Gilbert and her husband grew up in Louisiana and moved into a large Victorian house in Elmhurst where they raised their children in the early 1960s. As we sat in her elegant, cluttered living room, her granddaughter did homework on the dining room table, her husband sat at a nearby computer, and her daughter came in from work. At sixty years old, Mrs. Gilbert still worked as a school crossing guard, where she looked out for everyone's children. She described her upbringing in Louisiana as

> so different. When we were growing up, we made fun. We didn't have all that stuff they had now. If we had ten cents to go to the movies or the ballgame, we were like, "Oh night out." We never had fights. In our neighborhood, everybody knew each other. . . . If you was doing something, they could chastise you. We was afraid to do anything because someone was going to tell your mother or your grandmother and you was going to get in big trouble. . . . That's a big difference today, you're just afraid to say anything to people's kids. Now kids will tell you, "Well tell her." They don't care. In my day, you wouldn't dare say, "Call her."

She laughed as she imagined herself a child once again: "Oh please don't call her. I will not do this again."

Mrs. Taylor grew up in Oakland in the post–World War II era when, she explained, "There were no drug boys." She characterized her teenage years in Oakland as full of activities for young people centered around a beautiful park in the historically black neighborhood of West Oakland that featured a swimming pool, tennis courts, and dancing lessons. She also remembered close communal and police monitoring that kept kids in school and out of trouble. The police would patrol the local theater and "shine their light to see if any children was in the theater that should be in school. Your parents had to write a note if you were going to the store and you were out sick." When she moved with her husband and children to Elmhurst in 1964, they were the third black family in their immediate neighborhood. In the late 1960s when her daughter Jean was growing up, she described kids in the neighborhood as "good kids." "They gave you the respect . . . never raised their voice, never spoke back. If you caught them outside doing something, and you'd say something to them, they'd say, 'Sorry ma'am.' Now, if you say something to one. . . ." She laughed ruefully. "You don't know what could happen." Jean Taylor, her daughter, who grew up in East Oakland in the late sixties, also emphasized how informal communal sanctions had kept kids in line: "I had the fear of God that somebody was going to see you, if you don't go to school. My mom's friend was going to pass by. . . ." They both explained that then "other parents were able to chastise your child," but now instead of kids getting their butt whopped if they skip school, "kids call the police on their mom." Mrs. Taylor added, "Adults can't enjoy life anymore because of the teenagers. They're trouble. When we were kids, there was no such thing a boy would have a weapon on him. Now everybody carries a weapon."

Mrs. Taylor and Jean Taylor even described the drug dealers in earlier generations as operating with more respect for the neighborhood. Although they were doing wrong, they were still embedded in the community, and they knew that neighbors would call the police on them. Jean explained that one young man who dealt in the old days came by recently to say hello to her mom and bring them a six-pack of beer. He had always called her mom "Mom" and her dad "Uncle." That generation of drug dealers was in prison, dead, or out of the game. Now the drug boys do not even live on their block. They just "take it as their ground." As Jean compared new and old drug dealers, she explained, "These youngsters that are coming up, they'd blow your house up. You have to be really, really careful."

Many adults in Elmhurst, like Mrs. Taylor, were simply too afraid to discipline young people on the streets today. One younger community activist thought crack had "traumatized" the neighborhood and disrupted the "child-centered" tradition of the black community. At one NCPC meeting, a middle-aged African American woman complained about cruising and cars doing donuts that had destroyed her fence, but when the police officer asked if she had seen any drug dealing, she refused to answer. "I'm not a fool. I have lived to fifty years old for a reason." Bill Clay echoed this sense of constraint: "In this day and time, you cannot walk up to a young person just because you're older. You'd get popped."

Elmhurst activists expressed a deep sense of loss and frustration that many elders no longer felt able to discipline neighborhood youth. They bemoaned the loss of a broader network of neighborhood discipline and even of neighborhood gossip—the watchful eyes of aunts, grandmothers, and neighbors who kept kids in line even when parents had to work long hours. Mabel Washington explained, "I was raised in a village setting until I came here. Now people are so transient, and there's no more shame. When I was growing up I was taught shame. If you did something wrong you should be ashamed of yourself and not let that happen again." Mrs. Gilbert highlighted the importance of a tightly knit community in establishing that sense of shame. She grew up in a big family and spoke proudly about how none of her grandmother's children had ever been arrested. "It would have been the disgrace of the neighborhood."

This nostalgia linked deeply personal concerns about their own kids and grandkids with activists' public engagements in Elmhurst politics. As sociologist Nancy Naples has documented, "activist mothering" traditions play a substantial role in the way black community activists think of their political work. Many black women in Elmhurst, as in Naples's study, described politics as a "central component" of their "mother-work and community caretaking." They emphasized "the need to politicize" their own "mothering practices" in order to prepare their children to overcome racial barriers. But they also highlighted the vital role of "community other mothers" and men in the community, whom sociologist Elijah Anderson calls "old heads." These informal caregivers and disciplinarians have been integral to broadening concepts of family in black communities.[34]

Many African American elders like Mrs. Riles blamed state child abuse laws for the decline of neighborhood discipline. Stories of children who had called the police on their parents circulated widely. According to Mrs. Taylor, her neighbors had been told that they couldn't hit their son, who was on probation. Mrs. Foster, a member of the Castlemont PTA and her homeowners' association, had a friend who lost her job and custody of her children when her daughter called the police for disciplining her after the girl had started a fire at her house. She explained that now the girl is fifteen, out of control, and on probation. Pastor John, the dynamic pastor of a very large congregation in East Oakland, pointed out the irony in such stories: "Police are still able to carry batons and beat you upside the head, but your parents are not able to correct you! If your parents could correct you at home, then the police wouldn't have to use their batons to correct you on the street." While parental disciplinary power was undermined by the state, the state still had the ultimate power to punish, whether with physical force or criminal sanction.

Pastor John's concern about discipline, like that of many other activists, was deeply personal. Many of their kids and grandkids had successfully transitioned to adulthood, completed high school or college, bought homes, and moved to the suburbs to raise their own kids, but they had seen others fall as they came of age. Pastor John was struggling to keep his own teenage son on track, fighting an uphill battle against peer pressure and what "rap culture" had defined as cool. "I'll tear my son's tail up before I let him go to jail. . . . I love my son. I'm not chastising him out of abuse . . . I'm saving this kid's life, and I'm going to whip his tail before you will. I'm gonna make sure he goes to school, gets good grades. Then he's going to college and he's going to be all he can be."

Derailed Development

Nostalgic stories of disciplined youth encoded deep fears that young people were coming of age in a time of crisis that had confused the very categories of child and adult. While Elmhurst activists told stories about kids who acted like adults, had children themselves, and grew up too soon, they also described "adult children" who never seemed to grow up. Youth in Elmhurst lived in what geographer Cindi Katz has called "derailed zones," spaces where both the promise of economic development and children's futures have been derailed.[35] The path from childhood to adulthood seemed like a highway full of blocked exit ramps and detours that challenged the future of the black community. These detours took particularly gendered forms—encapsulated in the iconic figures of a boy in jail and a teenage mother on welfare.

Many black kids in Elmhurst experienced an accelerated life course that moved directly from childhood to adulthood. As anthropologist Linda Burton argues, generations are often separated by as little as thirteen to seventeen years in inner-city black neighborhoods, so age hierarchies are unclear. Many teens are expected to fulfill adult responsibilities by helping with housework and caring for other children. They sometimes contribute to household income, and even compete with their parents for the same scarce service sector jobs. These adult responsibilities lead many teens to think of themselves as developmentally the same as adults.[36] In its most extreme form, this accelerated life course finds expression in the oft-cited feeling of some kids that they won't live past twenty-five.

The category "youth" became a catch-all category for the troublesome people caught in the neverland between an idealized protected, innocent childhood and an idealized adulthood of responsible workers. Neighborhood activists described drug dealers and other criminals as "kids," "youngsters," or "drug boys." Twenty-five-year-olds working or hustling in the street economy did not fit into the category of responsible, employed adulthood and so were categorized as "youngsters" along with the fourteen-year-olds who were growing up too soon on the streets.

Mr. Lawlor, a father of three girls, described in some detail how girls grew up too soon by playing adult sexual roles. He would see girls who still had "baby features" wear

> low cut or very revealing tops, bare midriffs or a skirt too short. . . . I know the potential for the destruction in that. . . . Some men are not strong enough to say, "That's a child. I won't cross that line." They will take advantage of her. In my neighborhood, that's exactly what happens. A couple of years down the line, that child is pushing a baby carriage.

Mrs. Jackson insisted that "children having children" didn't know how to raise kids. "I've been out in public places where you have these mothers, teenagers, they're kids really. They have these kids with them, and they're calling them every name under the sun, smacking them on the head. What can that poor kid learn? It's sad." She thought "this generation of kids that's shooting up people" was "a product of some of those teenagers not having raised them."

Reverend Chester described how boys grew up too soon; they dropped out of school and got lured into the drug game. He explained that some parents indulge kids who deal drugs "because the child might be paying the light bill, might be paying rent or PG&E and everything. . . They don't care because as long as he is bringing in a dollar they can sit back and relax." Mrs. Taylor had watched one of the biggest drug lords in East Oakland grow up. He helped pay his grandmother's bills, and she helped keep him informed about community policing efforts by attending meetings and reporting everything that went on. His economic support was so crucial that she ended up losing her house after he got arrested. Mrs. Taylor and Reverend Chester described an upside-down world where teenage boys took on the role of family provider, and some parents became dependents with neither the power nor the desire to push kids in the right direction.

Jermaine Ashley, a sixteen-year-old youth activist, described the pressure to grow up fast in his East Oakland flatland neighborhood:

> Here's a place where right is wrong and wrong is right. Dope runs the streets and those who are supposed to serve and protect are common enemies. . . . You have to grow up fast just to keep up with our peers. Stepping out of your house is like stepping into another world. No love, not knowing who you can trust. . . . But you can't be scared to walk out of your house, can you? *No!* Why? Because I'm a hard young *man*. Why? Because I have to be. It's either be the beast or be eaten by the beast. Elders look at me and think I'm a menace to society, but they do not know I'm doing the best I know how. I tried to get a job. I put in an application. I even got an interview, but no one taught me how to present myself, so that job is down the drain.[37]

Young men had to become "hard" in order to survive on streets where neither adults nor the state seemed able to exercise control or offer real opportunities. Jermaine's comments echo the findings of anthropologist John Devine, who found that in the toughest schools in New York, young people ultimately were responsible for their own security.[38]

Mr. Bennet, another Elmhurst NCPC member, thought drug dealing had fundamentally shifted power from adults to kids. He had retired from the post office, owned his own house, and had worked hard, but he was on a fixed income. He had an older model car and rarely had more than an extra fifteen or twenty dollars in his pocket. He explained that "the kids" dealing drugs in his neighborhood couldn't relate to the older people in the neighborhood because "on a given day they might have two or three thousand dollars in their pocket. So it's hard to tell somebody when they see that I'm broke down and on a cane." Reverend Chester agreed: "You can't tell a kid there is a better way than selling drugs when he's looking at that guy out there driving big cars with all this money, and you're working for nine dollars an hour."

Black youth and young adults in Elmhurst occupied very insecure positions in the labor market. Youth unemployment rates are routinely twice as high as adult rates, but black youth unemployment rates remain far higher. In the summer of 2003, California's youth unemployment rate was 22%, while for African American youth it was 56.3%.[39] Black youth unemployment quadrupled from the 1960s to the mid-1980s, while white youth unemployment remained relatively stable.[40] One study of Elmhurst in the late 1980s estimated that youth unemployment rates were as high as 75%.[41] In this same period, most government funding for youth employment and summer job programs dried up. Young black men have experienced particularly substantial drops in income and employment rates, even as black women have made some significant gains in employment, income, and education in the post–civil rights era. Women's gains have not translated systematically into higher family incomes and lower child poverty rates, however, because they are often either single parents or in families with men whose economic status has stagnated.[42]

High unemployment levels in Elmhurst made it hard for many young people to achieve the markers of adult independence—a full-time job and an apartment.[43] African Americans often leave home at later ages than whites and have a much harder time escaping poverty than white youth.[44] Reverend Chester explained that too many men and women remained dependents living at home without real jobs even as they entered their thirties and forties: "When our generation came up, we were glad to get eighteen years old and get ourselves a job. We got some parents now who have kids thirty-two, thirty-eight, forty years old and have never worked, and they are still their babies." He blamed overprotective parents who let kids get away with anything, but also acknowledged that the economy had changed. "When I came along we could get a job, even if it was just digging holes." Now everything was automated: "they've got back hoes."

Economic restructuring and mass incarceration have reshaped coming of age in black neighborhoods like Elmhurst. Sociologist Loic Wacquant argues that a new deadly symbiosis has emerged between the prison and the ghetto at the turn of the twenty-first century. Jail and prisons have become the main way we manage economic and social marginality.[45] Between 1987 and 2007, the prison population nearly tripled, so that one out of every one hundred Americans was behind bars. But for African American men aged twenty to thirty-four, the rate was one in nine.[46] Sociologist Devah Pager reports that "over the course of a lifetime, nearly one in three young black men—and well over half young black high school dropouts—will spend some time in prison."[47]

Mass incarceration has destroyed black families and deepened black men's economic marginality.[48] Pervasive arrests, and felony convictions, make it much harder for black men to get or keep the stable jobs required as cultural and economic markers of adulthood. In her book *Marked: Race, Crime, and Finding Work in the Era of Mass Incarceration*, Pager argues that the prison expansion has legitimated and reinforced "deeply embedded racial stereotypes" of black young men as criminals. These stereotypes have reduced economic opportunities for all black men. In experimental tests, Pager found that black men with no criminal record had the same chance of getting jobs as white men with criminal records.[49] Black young men themselves have been redefined as criminal.[50]

The criminal justice system has fed the adultification of black boys. The drug war, with its harsh mandatory sentencing laws, encouraged drug dealers to recruit younger and younger boys for the most risky street-level dealing.[51] By 2000, the most common juvenile felony arrest in Oakland was for possession of narcotics.[52] This created a vicious cycle in which boys "grew up too soon" and a fearful public supported trying children as adults, thus excluding them from the protections of childhood. Sociologist Christopher Jenks argues that by excluding violent children from childhood, representing them as "demonic man-children," adults have been able to secure the sanctity and purity of our ideals of childhood.[53]

Drug markets and the drug war spread guns and violence in urban America so that coming of age sometimes became a matter of life and death. Miles Johnson experienced the intimate costs of violence. One of Oakland's first black police officers, from a prominent old black middle-class California family, Mr. Johnson and his wife raised two sons in Oakland. One became a police officer who was almost killed in the line of duty. The other was in prison for killing a police officer. He was big as a teenager and frequently experienced police harassment in Oakland. Later in college when some police officers harassed him and his fraternity brothers, he struck out violently. He told his father, "I just couldn't live in that bullshit world." When Marie Spencer received an invitation to her ten-year high school reunion in the late eighties, she saw many successful Castlemont graduates, but realized that almost 50% of the men in her class were dead.

There was a deep crisis of social reproduction in Oakland's flatlands. The path to adulthood was no longer a clear progression from dependence to independence. Parents were sometimes dependent on children who provided for the family. Children became parents before they had achieved any kind of independence, responsibility, or adult maturity. Many adults remained unemployed or underemployed for decades, unable to attain full independence from their parents. Some hard-working middle-aged adults or senior citizens had less disposable income than young street-level drug dealers. And too many kids, especially boys, simply died before they grew up. These urgent crises were not private concerns, but motivated a wide range of black public engagements in Oakland.

Faulty Families and the Disciplinary State

I sat one day talking with Reverend Chester and Mr. Robertson in the small storefront on International Boulevard that served as a community outreach office for the police department. Reverend Chester and Mr. Robertson had worked closely together in neighborhood politics for over twenty years. They both worked with Oakland's community policing initiative, the Elmhurst Blight Committee, and Oakland Community Organization to address problems of crime, blight, and economic development in their community. Both men gave very complex and divergent explanations for changes in the neighborhood.[54] They described how economic shifts and political decisions had abandoned a generation of black children. They worried that there was "no common labor" anymore so it was hard for young people to make a living without an education. New high-tech businesses were bringing in immigrant workers from "India or Korea" to fill new professional jobs instead of making sure unemployed black men were trained for them. Even as they demanded that the police arrest drug dealers in their neighborhood, they also worried that sometimes "it seems like they want to get every black kid on probation." But Rev. Chester and Mr. Robertson returned repeatedly to identify families as the problem. Rev. Chester worried that kids were raising themselves because women were at work and families had been broken up by welfare. Mr. Robertson returned to the mantra, "The home is where it starts and the homes are broken down. Until we get back to that family life, we've got a problem." Talk of structural forces quickly receded as the conversation turned towards complaints about broken families and nostalgia for parental authority.

At a city council hearing, city council member Larry Reid drew on these nostalgic narratives as he called on the black community to support cracking down on crime.

> I am an African American man. Last year there were 113 homicides. Eleven were *not* African American. If you look at my district, the people dealing drugs look like me. People that look like me are making [the neighborhood] unsafe. I don't want to keep locking up people that look like me and making them part of the criminal justice system. But I don't know when we begin to hold people accountable for their actions, and when we begin to hold *parents* responsible.

To applause from the audience, he repeated for emphasis, "When we begin to hold parents responsible, parents who've disengaged themselves from their children's lives."

Explicitly addressing youth activists who earlier in the meeting had defined drug dealing as "a crime of poverty," he continued:

> Let me tell you about Valerie Reid. Valerie Reid is my mother. In the city of Cincinnati, she had ten children in the projects. . . . I know what it's like to eat Spam and how many ways to make corn bread. Don't let anyone say it's a crime of poverty. People can pull themselves up by their bootstraps. Stop making excuses for people standing out there selling drugs on the corner. . . . Be proud that we didn't give up our neighborhoods to those who choose not to be productive citizens. We fought for our children to get a good education and live in a neighborhood where they can play outside in front of their homes. And these seniors who have worked hard deserve to be able to walk to the corner store.

Many black homeowner activists, like Larry Reid, resisted claims that young people today were trapped in poverty. Their political culture and analyses were shaped by a set of common experiences with the more explicit racial exclusions of the Jim Crow era.[55] Bill Clay told me about a conversation he recently had with his granddaughter, who married a man in jail. She had told Bill that he just didn't understand how it was for young black men. "They had to make a living. There was no other way." Bill thought young black men needed a lesson in how it was before, when he couldn't even get a union job. "Now there are opportunities, and you just have to take advantage of them." Bill Clay recognized the continuing significance of race, but his own success proved to him that overcoming racism or rising out of poverty was a matter of personal strength. "I tell kids that if you work hard, you can make it no matter what color you are."

Larry Reid never explicitly identified "youth" as responsible for crime, but his repeated popular call to hold parents accountable reproduced the widespread equation between youth and crime. The story of his virtuous mother reinforced a pervasive nostalgia for family discipline that blamed faulty families for neighborhood crime. These comments drew on a long-standing "politics of respectability" in black communities based on a "class- and gender-inflected moral valuation of motherhood and proper childrearing."[56] Anthropologist Brett Williams argues that black urban politicians embrace these nostalgic images because "they have no money, and little political power, to address the inability of the poor to find decent jobs, affordable housing and stimulating schools." Nostalgia and calls for self-help "deliver them from this quagmire." In this way, black politicians become complicit in disavowing federal and state responsibility for addressing the massive costs of contemporary urban inequalities.[57]

Locating children in the private sphere can easily erase the ways in which public actions fundamentally shape family life and children's worlds. Our normative definition of childhood locates children in the family, safe and secure in private homes, and off the street. Even the common criticism of state child abuse laws drew narrow boundaries of responsibility for children and blamed the state for interfering in the sacred space of the family. We see clearly here how focusing on the bad choices of children and parents can reify a false distinction between public and private that forecloses several important questions. How did changes in the class structure that Mr. Robertson identified affect the ability of young people in Elmhurst to work their way out of poverty? How did state crackdowns on drug dealing and crime along with increasingly punitive justice policies themselves serve as barriers to social mobility? How did economic transformations that decreased the availability and security of well-paid "common labor jobs" impact the ability of families to raise, supervise, and discipline their children? How had rising housing costs affected the stability of many low-income families? How had state cuts in education and social services affected the security of the path from childhood to productive adulthood?

Defining crime as a private disciplinary problem had far-reaching effects on political action in Elmhurst. It certainly did not encourage demands for the state to invest in education, create a living wage, expand drug rehabilitation programs, or create paths to work for former prisoners. Instead, as Gregory argues, these narratives framed "black youth as subjects in need of discipline and policing instead of community services."[58] These stories left the state little role except protecting citizens from the results of failed socialization. When Larry Reid called on Elmhurst activists to defend their community, many answered his call. They supported Mayor Brown's efforts to hire an additional three hundred police officers and to expand police powers to seize vehicles involved in drug busts or cruising, and they campaigned for intensive police actions targeting drug dealing, prostitution, and other street crime.

Neighborhood activists built these partnerships with the police in part because they desperately wanted to save youth from lives of crime. Reverend Chester explained,

> We will call the police if we see a drug dealer or young prostitute because we feel like we don't want them in our neighborhood. We don't want them standing out there selling drugs because the first thing happens with that

young man is that he gets busted for drugs. They give him a criminal record. Then if a good job comes around and he wants to work, he can't get a job any place.

By not clearing the corners of drug dealers, Mr. Lawlor agreed that the police "endanger that generation that's coming up to see that 'Man, that's easy money. Why should I go out and get a job when I can make four thousand dollars or five thousand dollars a week selling drugs?'"

Partnerships with the police provided a way for elders to recreate village discipline and to restore the authority of community other-mothers and fathers in the neighborhood.[59] Mrs. Taylor complained that she could no longer discipline drug boys and other neighborhood youth: "I don't say anything to them. I don't bother them because it's dangerous." She explained that she used to sit on her porch with her daughter and watch the drug boys ride their bikes up the street. "They would stare at us on our property, and one would ask, 'Why you looking at me?' He would make this a habit everyday. I called George (her community policing officer) and they found him and they disciplined him. George said if they bothered us again, he'd jack them up." She chuckled as she explained that the drug dealers believed him and didn't bother them anymore.

Community policing activists, like Mrs. Taylor, constructed a broad model of state power that had the police acting "in loco parentis" as disciplinarians. Elmhurst activists mobilized to support truancy ordinances, antiloitering laws, curfews, and anticruising ordinances. They did not want the police just to arrest kids but also to set limits, to hold kids accountable, and to keep them off the street and away from a life of crime.

At one Elmhurst NCPC meeting, city manager Robert Bobb called for daytime and nighttime curfews to reduce crime and to keep kids in school. To a chorus of "That's right" from many black homeowners in the room, he insisted that it might even take putting a parent in jail to make parents realize that they "have to be accountable for their child." Bobb suggested that the state could discipline the family itself, by reestablishing proper parenting and divisions between public and private.

This idea of the state as disciplinarian built on the nostalgia for both patriarchal and physical discipline prevalent in Elmhurst. Many older African American activists used the phrase "to discipline," "to chastise," or "to correct" specifically to refer to physical discipline. "Discipline" needed to be grounded in a clear hierarchy between children and adults and a model of adult authority based on fear as well as love and respect. African American

Figure 4. A disciplinary state: Oakland police stop and question a young black teenager in Elmhurst. (Photo by author)

men (and some women) often emphasized the importance of a father's role as strict disciplinarian. Mr. Lawlor described the discipline he received from his father as the foundation for the village discipline that existed when he was growing up. "Without that father figure, without that basic respect, which is based on fear of repercussion, these children are not going to respond. . . . They feel no responsibility to you or I. You have to basically frighten those kids, like I do." Since kids did not fear parental or village discipline, Elmhurst activists could use the threat of the state's power to use force. The police could become the ultimate male authority figure and instill fear and discipline in youth.

This nostalgia did not on its own lead community activists to create a vision of a disciplinary state. Pastor John drew on similar memories of communal discipline when he brought his congregation into Castlemont High School to reduce violence and improve education. Oakland Community Organization drew on activist mothering traditions in its campaigns to demand state investments in after-school programs and small schools that would nurture youth in the flatlands. Individual residents also reached out to young people and their families. Bill Clay volunteered to mentor two children at the local middle school and worked with other NCPC members to donate computers, buy walkie-talkies for the school, and raise prize money for a student essay competition. Mrs. Taylor hosted block parties and bought toys and equipment for home daycare providers on her block. Mrs. Gilbert watched a young girl she met as a crossing guard after school so her mother could keep going to classes at City College. In these cases, visions and memories of communal solidarity laid the groundwork for a politics of inclusion that involved older African American citizens working to reconstruct communal bonds, often reaching across generations and sometimes even across the divide between "law-abiding" and "criminal" citizens.

Defining crime as a youth problem often led to questions about whether the police were the right answer. Black homeowner activists always talked about investing in education and social services for youth. Many NCPC and homeowner activists supported expanded policing while simultaneously asserting that the police could not solve the problem. Mrs. Gilbert, an active member of the NCPC, insisted, "I don't think locking up people works. Education is key." Reverend Chester worried that police enforcement only bred resentment and hostility among young people instead of respect and discipline. We need to look more closely at the structures of the local state and community activism to understand why homeowner activists in Elmhurst used so much social capital and political power to demand more policing and to expand the disciplinary state.

Partners in Policing

City manager Robert Bobb spoke at a large public meeting in East Oakland to announce a new program to better track and supervise parolees in order to reduce violence. In a community room in the Elmhurst mall filled with NCPC members, homeowners, and black church members from throughout East Oakland, Robert Bobb urged the audience to raise "an uproar" to combat high murder rates. "The community has to be angry enough." A fifty-year-old African American woman, a member of a prominent black Baptist church, quietly said to the man sitting next to me, "We are. We want jobs." Robert Bobb continued, "The cost to the community is so high. . . . When guys in white hoods came in to our communities, we'd beat them. When we're killing each other, the enemy is in our neighborhood. We have to go after it with as much aggressiveness." Robert Bobb, much like Larry Reid, called for the black community to defend itself against criminals, as the enemies within.[60] His public reference to memories of black historic struggles against the Ku Klux Klan reframed policing as a core aspect of black communal self-defense. Clearly, not all audience members agreed that the policies he proposed would solve Elmhurst's problems. But in important ways community policing did work to reshape relationships between the black community and the police. Oakland's community policing initiative was successful, not so much in reducing crime as in rearticulating the relationship between black citizens and the state. The Neighborhood Crime Prevention Councils redrew the boundaries of "the community" and, somewhat surprisingly, brought the police into a "black self-help" initiative in Elmhurst.

Criminologist Wesley Skogan has described community policing as the most significant innovation in policing, but it means many different things to different people. Community policing tries to create relations between "beat cops" and citizens, who can then serve as "the eyes and ears of the police force." Sometimes it tries to get police officers out of cars and onto regular foot patrols. It often includes a broader focus on improving neighborhood "quality of life," instead of just responding to 911 calls for service. Some describe community policing as a specific formula that assigns beat cops to meet with neighborhood groups, but others describe it as "a philosophy" that must pervade and reshape the whole police department. Community policing is often described as the opposite of enforcement (police sweeps, drug busts, and arrests), but in practice, many police departments combine these two strategies. In Oakland, community policing officers both met with community groups and took part in massive drug and violence suppression operations with names like Operation Bullseye. Scholars continue to debate whether community policing is simply "rhetoric" or represents real change.[61]

Community policing became the official strategy of Oakland's police department in 1994. The city created a unique system of fifty-seven Neighborhood Crime Prevention Councils, each staffed by a civilian police employee, the Neighborhood Services Coordinator (NSC), and a community policing officer.[62] These NCPCs served as the centerpiece of Oakland's efforts to increase community involvement in local governance. Oakland police chief Richard Word, an African American officer who rose through the ranks and became chief in 1999, described his hope that community policing could lead to a true partnership in which police would not "work against or separate from community but . . . be a part of community."[63] City and police leadership regularly called on "the community" to take more responsibility for solving crime problems. The police could not do it alone. These calls for "partnership" and "self-help" drew both on new technologies of urban governance and also on black self-help traditions. And Elmhurst activists eagerly embraced this call for partnership, organizing some of Oakland's first and most active Neighborhood Crime Prevention Councils.

Oakland's community policing initiative drew on earlier local efforts to change the historically hostile relationship between black communities and the police. Oakland experienced periodic protests against police brutality as early as the 1930s, but these tensions escalated in the post–World War II period.[64] The Oakland Police Department launched its first effort to organize district councils in the 1950s, created a community affairs office in the early 1960s, and formed the nation's first home alert groups in 1967. While the department described these efforts as generically about improving "community-police relations," they had their origins in the escalating racial tensions between the police and black communities at the height of black political protest in the city.[65] In 1966, the Black Panthers took up arms to defend their community against police brutality, describing OPD as "an occupying army" and the white Republican city council as a colonial government.[66] People still tell stories in Oakland about how the police department imported white southern recruits in what seemed like a racial war between the police and Oakland's black communities. In the 1960s, Oakland's home alert groups, district councils, and, later, the African American Advisory Committee on Crime reached out to bring black community leaders into new kinds of partnership with the police department.[67]

Oakland's community policing initiative also drew on new models of community policing developed and funded by federal think tanks and the Department of Justice in the 1990s.[68] In the aftermath of the Los Angeles riots, attention focused once again on community-police relations, which had deteriorated nationally with the expansion of gang sweeps and the drug war. A federal 1994 omnibus crime bill created Community Oriented Policing Services (COPS), a multi-billion-dollar grant program, which provided funding to police departments if they embraced community policing. COPS provided the fiscally strapped Oakland Police Department with fifty new grant-funded officers for several years, money for equipment upgrades, and funds for ongoing training in new models of community policing.[69] OPD brought in consultants and model programs from particularly "successful" cities that had achieved large crime reductions with elements of community-policing strategies.[70] Even as federal funding to cities declined in most areas, sociologist Eric Klinenberg argues that COPS "created new fiscal incentives for cities to expand their policing capacities" and to place law enforcement agencies at the core of a restructured local government.[71]

Community policing helped resolve some of the tensions created by Oakland's ambitious efforts to reduce crime in Jerry Brown's first term as mayor. It enhanced support for the police department within a politically powerful segment of Elmhurst's black community as the city increased police sweeps and cracked down on quality of life crimes like cruising, loitering, and drinking in public.[72] Chief Word often explained that Oakland wanted to "keep citizen complaints low" even as it tried to emulate New York City's success in reducing crime. A police department training session led officers and community leaders through several scenarios that showed how better communication could build trust and insulate the police department from protest when claims of police brutality or harassment emerged.

Oakland's black urban regime helped reshape the oppositional relationship between the city's black communities and the police department. As political scientist Adolph Reed has argued, black professional workers have "increasingly assumed administrative control of the institutions of urban governance."[73] This has institutionalized the black middle-class role in managing deep racial and class marginality in urban America. Oakland's police chief, probation officer, and city manager gave a very public face to the black regime. Most neighborhood service coordinators (in charge of the NCPCs) were African American women. Black entrepreneurs ran many of Oakland's group homes for youth, and many county probation officers as well as private security officers were African American. Even the Oakland Police Department had diversified, with 54.5% minority and 25.9% African American employees in 2000.[74] Many black city employees, including some police officers, remained networked into historically African American flatland neighborhoods through extended families, churches, and service organizations. As Oakland's city manager, police chief, other black police officers, and city officials circulated through community meetings, these relationships and the solidarities they engendered were often evident. Activists remained frustrated that increased black political power and their relationships with city officials had not led to substantial improvements in neighborhoods like Elmhurst. And these close relationships did not always prevent protest, but they did break down a clear opposition between the state—and specifically the police—and the black community that historically undergirded many black political mobilizations in Oakland.[75]

Black activists in Elmhurst embraced community policing because it built on long-standing demands for police accountability and community control that were most explicitly articulated by the Black Panthers.[76] Participating in NCPCs gave activists symbolic power, and some real power, over an important arm of the state, one that had a particularly racially charged history in Oakland. They could call police brass and city leaders on their private numbers and generally count on a prompt (if not always satisfying) response to their call. They could focus police drug investigations on specific blocks or corners and sometimes shape department priorities, for instance, by insisting that the city assign a specific community policing officer to each beat or reinstate drug and violence suppression units. Captain Bobbie Daniels, an OPD officer who grew up and worked in East Oakland's flatlands, explained that the history of police disrespect in black communities made community activists hold on tightly to the limited power that community policing offered.

Black community activists often framed their demands for city services and for better policing as claims for racial equality and justice.[77] They criticized a broad government abandonment of Oakland's black flatlands and argued that the police department never would tolerate the drug dealing and disorder if Elmhurst had been a white neighborhood or a neighborhood in the hills. They criticized absentee landlords in the suburbs and hills who profited off the neighborhood but failed to maintain their properties or screen their tenants. They condemned suburbanites who used Elmhurst as a regional drug market, confining the chaos and social costs of the drug war to black, not white, neighborhoods. And they criticized Oakland's history of building low-income housing only in the flatlands. In these ways, Elmhurst activists highlighted the ways in which burdens and resources were racially structured across Oakland's geography.[78]

Demanding police action was one way Elmhurst activists struggled for a visible state commitment to the neighborhood. They often used community policing meetings to demand expanded state action, much to the frustration of city politicians like Chief Word, who criticized the NCPCs for their shotgun approach and for "unloading" too many issues on the police. Linda Jackson insisted, in a letter to the city manager, that the city wasn't holding up its end of the community policing partnership: "If we do our part of the partnership, you need to do yours." Community policing did not produce ideal neoliberal self-governing citizens in Elmhurst,[79] but it did have significant effects on local politics, reshaping the kinds of demands activists made and the ways they constructed their rights as citizens.

Community policing made significant strides in overcoming an oppositional relationship between "the black community" and the police. African American residents built close, trusting relations with individual police officers and with police department leadership. At Elmhurst NCPCs, popular officers were regularly given rounds of applause when they gave their reports and were occasionally presented with community awards. Bill Clay explained that the police got to know the "good people" in the community, and "a lot of people who didn't like the police officers before, they stop seeing the gun. That's when I know they've been converted." These relationships of trust changed community policing activists' responses to claims of police brutality and harassment. When four Oakland police officers were arrested for planting evidence and beating suspects in what became "the Riders" case, most NCPC activists defined those officers as individual bad apples instead of as evidence of a broader culture of disrespect or abuse within the police department. At a city council hearing for an antiloitering law in 2003, Ms. Eva Blanton, an African American activist in her midsixties from Elmhurst, described how community policing allowed her to build real partnerships and trust with the police department so that she no longer believed racial profiling was a significant threat in her neighborhood. While there was "a time when laws like the antiloitering law would have a negative impact on African American communities, at this time we are confident that the antiloitering ordinance would help all law-abiding citizens."

People rarely raised concerns about police harassment or brutality in community policing meetings, but this did not mean that there was no resistance to partnerships with the police, just that it was largely silent. Younger black men in their forties remained more reluctant to support expanded police powers. Richard Stevens was a member of the NCPC and his homeowners' association who worked closely with Linda Jackson, but he was profoundly disturbed by the law and order focus of East Oakland's political leadership. He worried that African American neighborhood activists saw every young person as a potential problem and were helping to criminalize black children, but he said that people who shared his concerns often stayed quiet. "They still have to live here. It's a very tight community where everyone knows everyone."

Redefining Moral Community, Root Causes, and the Rights of Citizenship

Oakland's community policing initiative reached out into neighborhoods throughout the city in ways that restructured black politics. Elmhurst had a broader network of thirty-seven homeowners' associations that dated back to the 1970s, an active community district board responsible for distributing federal economic development funds, powerful churches, youth organizations, and periodic community organizing efforts by Associated Communities Organizing for Reform Now (ACORN) and by Oakland Community Organization (OCO), which mobilized residents through church-based organizing committees. These community organizing groups worked to build community power, engage low-income residents, create tension, and make demands on the state. The NCPCs operated separately from this activist infrastructure, although individuals sometimes crossed political networks. The "community" in community policing was neither representative nor a transparent reflection of a preexisting unified community voice. Oakland's community policing initiative privileged the concerns of older black homeowners and deepened class divides in the ways activists constructed political community.[80] The specific structures of the NCPCs reshaped the ways black activists defined the root causes of crime, drew the boundaries of their community, and described their rights as citizens.

The Oakland Police Department often described community policing as a vital part of its effort to move beyond crime suppression to address the "root causes of crime." City leaders and police were frustrated by their inability to achieve long-lasting reductions in drug dealing and violent crime simply by arresting people in many of Oakland's flatland neighborhoods like Elmhurst. Community policing officers often served simply as "a tactical squad" focused on drug- or violence-suppression activities, and some officers didn't see problem solving as "real police work."[81] Nonetheless, the police department continually tried to restructure and retrain all officers to work with citizens on "long-term problem solving" instead of traditional enforcement activities.

The emphasis on problem solving in Oakland's community policing initiative provided a flexible frame within which neighborhood activists could define the "root causes" of the neighborhood's crime problem.[82] Bill Clay frequently spoke about the importance of providing training and rehabilitation for criminals while they were in prison or insisted that the city had to improve schools and provide after-school programs and jobs that could keep kids from turning to crime. City manager Robert Bobb provided a very broad interpretation of what problem solving in the NCPCs could entail. "On 96th Ave., if it's a socioeconomic issue, we'll deal with it. . . . I saw in the paper that they are increasing the number of high-tech visas to 240,000. We could do problem-solving around that and how we can get some of those jobs. Maybe we need jobs, recreation." While activists and politicians sometimes defined neighborhood problems broadly, the structure of the community policing initiative made it hard for community activists to mobilize for political action around these broad visions and instead encouraged demands to expand police enforcement.

Community policing, in practice, most often redefined the root causes of crime in terms of *problem places* or *problem people* instead of economic or racial inequalities. At an NCPC meeting in East Oakland, Chief Word described the department's new focus on proactive problem solving instead of simply responding to 911 calls: "Instead of just arresting the drug dealers, they had to look at the source of the problem. It might be a crack house down the block. Maybe it's an absentee landlord. Maybe it's an old landlord, and they didn't know how to evict someone." An African American police captain explained his understanding of problem solving: "I am a true believer in the broken windows thesis. Most crime issues are attached to grime issues, trash, loitering, problem businesses. . . . If it looks bad, people act bad."

Oakland's community policing initiative had embraced "the broken windows thesis," which defined disorderly behavior as the cause of crime and the primary threat to urban neighborhoods. As Steven Gregory argues, this thesis creates a revisionist history of crime that locates the root causes of crime in blighted housing, fear, and declining public decency instead of economic insecurity, educational disinvestments, or racial exclusions.[83] Oakland city officials often redefined the root causes of crime in these terms and tried to decrease crime rates by decreasing "grime." City officials routinely went even further, defining crime and grime as the *causes*, not consequences, of Oakland's economic woes. As city council member Henry Chang explained, "Under leadership of Robert Bobb, Oakland will not tolerate crime and grime . . . economic development will follow."

With this definition of "root causes" of crime, the police and NCPC leaders did move beyond trying to arrest their way out of East Oakland's crime problem. Oakland embraced a range of zero tolerance policies, using the full spectrum of the city's powers to maintain social order. The police and community policing leaders worked closely with code compliance and other city agencies to regulate liquor stores, shut down problem motels, crack down on illegal dumping and public drinking, and target landlords of problem properties. This expanded vision of the state's role in maintaining order probably encouraged community policing activists to turn to the state to control the behavior of undisciplined young people in the neighborhood.

The structure of community policing, which divided neighborhood participation into fifty-seven NCPCs tied to police beats, made it hard for neighborhood activists to address broader structural causes of crime and encouraged participants to frame their analyses of neighborhood needs in very localized terms. By decentralizing citizen participation to the level of specific police beats, neighborhood activists focused less on broad policy changes that might impact crime, and began to view the problem of crime as located on particular corners and at particular addresses that could be cleaned up by the police. At an ACORN meeting on neighborhood safety, when a neighborhood activist raised a call for more jobs to solve crime problems, a police captain explained that the only thing he could do about jobs was to point young people to already existing job-training programs. At the same meeting, the chief seemed frustrated by his inability to respond to broad demands for jobs, respect, and community development. He suggested that the people provide the captain with some more "specifics, some problems, some corners so that we can have that list to work from." The chief only took notes at this meeting when neighbors identified problems with drug dealing or abandoned cars at particular addresses in the neighborhood and implicitly defined the role of the police as solving problems only through enforcement at particular corners or specific streets.

Since the police and code compliance officers were usually the only agents of the state at NCPC meetings, if neighbors wanted action, they learned to formulate their demands within the language of policing or neighborhood cleanup, calling for action on particular corners or at particular addresses, instead of more general calls for jobs programs or youth centers. While some NCPCs continued to work on issues of economic development or youth development programs, community policing made the police the most accessible government agency. Whatever frustrations community policing activists had with the failure of the police to control crime, at least police officers were available monthly at the NCPC meetings, and often on cell phones between meetings, to respond to neighborhood demands. Since through the NCPC structure, the state most easily responded to community problems with law-enforcement practices, activists were encouraged "to represent and indeed experience their concerns through the tactical logic of controlling community space."[84]

Elmhurst activists redrew the moral boundaries of their community as they participated in the NCPCs. Community policing activists, like Eva Blanton and Linda Jackson, often constructed a clear opposition between decent, hard-working, and tax-paying citizens and other people in the neighborhood who were drug users, criminals or generally "lowlifes." These were not preexisting stable categories of "street" and "decent" orientations, as sociologist Elijah Anderson has argued, but were distinctions produced through particular public policies and structures of community participation.[85] As community activists came to monthly meetings and talked about neighborhood crime problems with the police, they constructed a kind of moral community of respectable taxpayers struggling with the police as their partners against people, trash, noise, and crime that they framed as undermining the sanctity of their homes and the security of their lifetime's investment.[86] Mrs. Jackson described people "drinking and selling drugs" as her "nightmare." "Get them out. I want my nightmare to go." Her frustration with crime made her question abstract rights of citizenship and think "we shouldn't have to treat the bad guy equal."

Community policing activists learned to see the streets through the eyes of the police, to understand, and sometimes resent, legal constraints on the police. Community policing activists often used police language, speaking of "hot spots," "buy-bust" operations, and "hitting corners." They often began to define "proactive policing" in terms of sweeps and arrests. Police routinely explained how hard it was to get a good case on a drug dealer because of constraints on their rights to search. Officers portrayed the juvenile justice system as lenient and complained that juvenile hall generally would not hold juveniles at all unless they already had long records. Through these conversations, neighborhood activists and police constructed a shared sense that "drug boys" and criminals had more rights than citizens.

Activists often used community policing to try to recreate the community of their memories, Elmhurst's midcentury industrial garden suburb where homeowners strived to maintain codes of middle-class respectability. They fought against street vendors, taco trucks, and men who repaired cars on the streets, defining these working-class and poor economic survival strategies as violations of the neighborhood's moral order. They campaigned against any expansion of low-income housing and against overcrowding and illegal conversions of garages. These actions implicitly excluded many poor families, renters, and sometimes immigrants from full community belonging.

The ways community policing activists constructed their political identity also posed problems for the ways activists responded to the needs and problems of neighborhood youth. Many community policing activists desperately wanted younger people to participate in community policing. But the NCPCs were not spaces where people came together across generational lines. Only one teenager came regularly to the NCPC meetings I attended, and she was Mrs. Taylor's granddaughter. Other teenagers and young adults I spoke with were hesitant to come to a meeting run by the police. As one man in his early twenties who was handed a flier for an NCPC said, "If the police are there, it ain't for us."

Young people were often implicitly excluded from the moral community constructed at these meetings. The absence of youth in NCPC meetings encouraged older activists to blame youth for crime and to frame youth as subjects in need of discipline instead of as political actors who could improve the neighborhood. As community policing activists worked closely with the police to control neighborhood spaces, they increasingly defined all youth on the streets as problems. I noticed this in my own responses to young people. The more I attended NCPC meetings, the more I started to identify all kids on the street as drug dealers. When I mentioned this to Mrs. Taylor and her daughter Jean, they both quickly replied, "They probably are."

Community policing activists were less likely to be affected by enhanced police suppression than younger residents. A black police officer told me that he had heard Elmhurst activists tell the police to "go on and profile," but he added, "to be honest, they are not the ones who are likely to get beat up in a backyard. They are not going to be the target of profiling." Many older male and female activists acknowledged that they were less likely to be stopped by the police than younger men walking or driving in the neighborhood. Reverend Chester suggested that "driving while black" might be better described as "driving while young and black." "John and I can get in a Lincoln Continental stretch and drive all the way downtown on East Fourteenth and never get stopped. But you put a young man in that. . . ."

Most NCPC leaders could avoid heavy police enforcement since they had the basic accoutrements of a middle-class lifestyle, particularly a car. Since police enforcement in Elmhurst often focused on "clearing corners," travel by car could insulate them from some of the effects of state disciplinary practices. When Linda Jackson's son and husband worried that they would be the focus of police suppression demanded by the NCPC, she warned them to avoid MacArthur Boulevard and drive straight to the freeway. They were able to structure their lives in ways that avoided the most heavily policed commercial corridors, which lower-income and underage residents had to use as they shopped and waited for buses. This provides an interesting counterexample to a common assumption of the broken windows thesis that law-abiding citizens will return to public space with a more proactive police presence. Enhanced enforcement may actually encourage black middle-class adults to avoid public spaces so that they avoid being targeted by the police.

Many community policing activists fundamentally felt they had little choice but to ally themselves closely with the police department. Linda Jackson bemoaned state and federal cuts in aid to schools and youth programs under Reagan for creating "this generation that's out here shooting up everything." But Linda Jackson's own choices as a community activist had been significantly shaped by state disinvestments, economic transformations, and the structure of Oakland's community policing initiative and its fight on crime and grime. These partnerships transformed the way activists framed their rights as citizens. As Simon argues, governing through crime helped redefine the legitimate terrain of state action and reify a vision of the state as policeman. As we saw in her portrait, Linda Jackson was willing to give up some of her own rights as long as doing so would help police crack down on crime in her neighborhood. As she explained, "people back in the old days had no rights. . . . Now the crooks have all the rights. Somebody needs to start looking at the people have some rights instead of the killers." Though she described the police only as a Band-Aid, Linda Jackson accepted that economic redevelopment would not come to her neighborhood until crime was under control. As activists worked within community policing, they embraced a reconstructed and limited notion of their rights as citizens, and demanded their right to sufficient policing.

Community policing drew on and reconfigured black nostalgia for disciplined youth in troubling ways. Community activists described nuanced systems of care and accountability for children. Stories that described the importance of physical discipline and "fear" could support a role for the police as disciplinarians. But just as often, activists defined shame, respect, close communal relationships, and love as the keys to creating disciplined youth. These core activist-mothering values motivated a broad commitment to trying to save youth in Elmhurst. Working within the community policing initiative, however, encouraged activists to adopt criminal justice models of accountability and choice that left jail and exclusion from the community as the way to hold people accountable.

Conclusion

At an NCPC meeting in January 2000, Bill Clay and other residents engaged in a lively debate about how the community could best discipline youth and hold them accountable. Proposition 21 would come up for a vote in two months, prompting discussion throughout Oakland about whether kids as young as fourteen should be tried as adults. Bill Clay hoped that Proposition 21 would motivate a new generation of young people to get involved in their community. "The only people doing anything out here are over forty. We need to encourage our grandchildren so we can sit back, and they can make changes. . . . We need to be asking kids what's wrong and how to fix it. You will hear a lot about after school programs. If we don't give them something else, we can't lock them up."

Neighborhood activists afraid of kids on the street formed an obvious constituency for get tough on youth crime proposals like Proposition 21. Bill Clay reminded me that since I didn't live in the neighborhood, I couldn't understand the appeal of Proposition 21: "When you live in the neighborhood, and you see how youth disrespect you, it's going to be a hard sell. They are going to say you should try twelve-year-olds as adults because they see those twelve-year-olds out there on the streets. Older guys recruit younger guys to do their work for them." With twelve-year-olds dealing drugs, the divide between childhood and adulthood became so blurred that many activists did support trying juveniles as adults and turned to the police as disciplinarians.[87]

But Bill Clay and other activists at this meeting still insisted that the village could reach out and incorporate troubled kids. James Richards told a story of catching a kid drawing graffiti on his fence. "I told him, 'You are quite an artist. Why don't you go over to [the youth center] and take classes.' You see a lot of kids are not that bad. I came to his level, and I got to know him. I think we can deal with children, but we have to deal with their parents too." Bill Clay returned to the juvenile crime bill: "If we can't come up with something better, people who are afraid to come out of their houses will vote for it."

Black homeowner activists in East Oakland had struggled for decades for a visible state commitment to their neighborhood, but they faced unacceptable choices in their political practice. In the context of retreating state commitments to social welfare and new forms of community-based governance, black neighborhood activists often embraced a vision of the state as disciplinary father. Elmhurst homeowner activists wanted to recreate village discipline, and they forged partnerships with the police in order to keep young people in line. But here is the surprising twist: community policing inserted the police into this imagined black community as the disciplinary father necessary to save black children. Nostalgia for disciplined youth helped reframe tensions between the police and the black community in familial terms as generational tensions between rowdy youth and adult authority.[88]

Community policing encouraged the formation of an organized law and order constituency that had a disproportionate impact on setting city priorities. NCPC members became the most recognized leadership in Elmhurst. An aide to council member Larry Reid described them as "hard-wired into city hall." These were the community representatives that the city manager, police chief, and mayor called whenever they sought support for new city initiatives to reduce crime or violence. These community-police partnerships were fragile, and activists were often frustrated by changes in police strategy and the rapid turnover of community policing officers, but community policing did relentlessly refocus Elmhurst activism on demands for more (and more effective) policing in ways that ironically intensified the danger that jail would become part of coming of age for young men in the neighborhood.

Community policing illustrates some of the problems neoliberalism poses for political action. The decentralized NCPC structures made it hard for activists to make broad demands on the state. Community policing also promoted "partnership," "collaboration," and "consensus" in ways that delegitimized protest politics. Police and NCPC leaders often described the more confrontational "demands" of Alinsky-style community organizing groups like OCO or ACORN as inappropriate holdovers from the 1960s. Police encouraged those groups to participate in the NCPCs, where they would form partnerships and take community responsibility instead of just demand state action and community control. These calls for communal self-help often hid the unequal resources and burdens available for individuals and communities. Neighborhoods and blocks with established networks of politically connected homeowners were able to "help themselves" far easier than renters were. These partnerships risked reifying Oakland's class divides and shrinking the space of politics and the rights of citizenship.

2

Trying to Get up the Hill

"What I see in Oakland is everyone doing this shift up the hill." Liz Walker explained that parents in the Laurel district often drove their kids up to Montclair Recreation Center in a wealthy enclave in the hills and tried to get their children into schools farther up the hill. Families from the flatlands did the same thing, coming into the lower hills to find safe spaces and schools for their kids. "Everybody's trying to get up, up, and up. . . . I don't want to drive my kid up the hill for everything. Why don't we have anything going on right here?"

Liz and Robert Walker first moved to the Laurel district in 1991, happy and surprised to find a house they could afford in this "vibrant neighborhood" in the lower hills. When they first drove through the neighborhood of small bungalow houses and storefronts, Robert thought, "Oh my God, look at this." There was everything they might need along MacArthur Boulevard: a bank, a veterinarian, a drugstore, a karate studio, a hardware store, and a couple of restaurants. Soon the World Ground Café opened and quickly became a new center of community life.

Robert, a tall and lanky African American man in his late thirties, with dreadlocks grown just to his ears, was raised in a mostly white neighborhood in San Francisco and marveled at finding "a true black community" with a thriving black middle class in Oakland. An interracial couple raising a young son, Robert and Liz particularly appreciated that the Laurel district seemed like a racially mixed, but stable neighborhood "where people were settling down and staying." As Liz, a white woman in her late thirties, explained, "We seem to have a pretty diverse working-class population that isn't necessarily going to be displaced. It's not all black and turning white. It's mixed."

Liz and Robert bought a house right next to Laurel Elementary School, where they saw on a daily basis the effects of Oakland's decaying public infrastructure on children and youth. The Laurel school had only one old kindergarten play structure for its five hundred students and no organized after-school recreation program. The school yard was often "packed with kids after school, but there was no instructor, no balls, no bats, nothing to do." Robert bought three basketballs and told the kids where to find them next to his house. They could borrow them as long as they kept bringing them back. "I have become a Rec director just by having balls and bats. That's what gave me entree to the kids. If they are cutting up, smoking or drinking, I am going to come out, and I am going to have a lot to say. But they also know that I'm not going to call the cops on them unless they are doing something highly illegal."

Robert became frustrated with the complaints of many neighborhood merchants about "all the kids, walking up and down the street." He imitated an older business owner, his voice dripping with indignation: "They walk into my business, spending money. . . ." In his own voice, Robert explained, "Well, at least they are spending some money. People don't want kids around, that's what I see. Especially when they're not their kids, and they tend to be black and brown. There is just 'a problem.'" He asked merchants, "If you don't want them around, where do you want them? What do you want them to do?" "The answer was deafening silence, which meant to me that a lot of people come out to attack these kids, but when it came down to tangible solutions, no one was talking tangible solutions. Let's look at our neighborhood. There is nothing for these kids to do."

"We've lost a couple of generations in Oakland." Unless they went to school in the hills, Robert explained, children in Oakland had been "robbed of education" and now risked being tossed aside by the wave of gentrification sweeping across the city. Liz added, "They just haven't had a thing in schools. It's just stripped down to nothing. It's pitiful. It's just disgusting. It makes me so angry. And of course, the people that suffer the most are people of color."

Liz and Robert both became deeply engaged in the local public schools and in trying to rebuild safe and nurturing spaces for young people in the neighborhood through their own volunteer labor and activism. Between Liz and Robert, they knew just about everyone involved in local politics in the Laurel district. Liz attended the Laurel Community Action Project (LCAP) to work on commercial revitalization and joined the new Neighborhood Crime Prevention Council (NCPC) that met in Laurel Elementary School. Robert had been more hesitant than Liz to join the NCPC, "or to deal with the police in any way shape or form," but slowly he was pulled into the whirlwind of neighborhood meetings and became an officer in the NCPC.

Over the next few years Liz and Robert helped forge close relationships with the NCPC, the PTA, and neighborhood schools. They were particularly adept at working across the subtle racial and class lines that crisscrossed community politics in the neighborhood, forging relationships with business

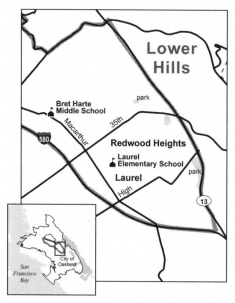

Figure 5. Map of Laurel: Nestled in the Lower Hills.
(Mark Kumler and Diana Sinton, University of Redlands)

owners, African American church women, white and black middle-class homeowners, retired white women or stay-at-home moms who wanted to do something for youth, and working-class women or women on welfare across racial lines, whose kids attended the local school.

Liz and Robert struggled occasionally with how to prepare their son for the realities of being a black man in America. Liz was often more protective and didn't want her son, Jayden, walking anywhere alone, but she also believed in giving him a lot of freedom to express himself. Robert, "raised by a conservative black woman," believed in the stricter family rules of his childhood. Kids should be "seen and not heard, which might not necessarily be good for their inner child, but it is going to keep them alive in this society. And this society is harder on black males. We are not so many years down the road from when you could see a black person being hung every weekend. That's why I say kids have too many damn rights."

Robert trained Jayden how to deal with the police from a very young age. "If the police tell you to, stop. You don't have a right to do shit. You have a right to sit yourself down and stop. Don't be acting like your little white friends because you ain't them. Period." He paused, reflecting, "Maybe I'm a bit rough on Jayden, but I'm no rougher on him than this country is going to be. That's my bottom line. Some people think I'm absolutely brutal until I ask them, 'How will this country treat him when he grows to be eighteen, six foot four, two hundred pounds? What are you going to do? You're going to run from him.'" Robert insisted that Jayden "better come out better educated than me and his mother combined." "I tell him, 'You've got to be better because you're not getting a break. All these people, who are very nice to you when you're little, will not employ you.'"

Liz joined the PTA a whole year before her son was old enough to attend kindergarten. She worked with other parents and kids to paint murals, clean up the school yard, and hold fundraisers. Eventually she became part of a public-private collaborative to bring new after-school programs to the elementary and middle schools in the neighborhood. Even though Liz had volunteered many hours to bring additional resources to the school, she still "really struggled" with the decision to put her son in Laurel Elementary School. She worried that he wouldn't get a well-rounded, quality education and that her son might be "exposed to a lot of bad language, violence." It only takes a few kids "not getting their basic needs met to disrupt things for everyone. . . . He's our only child and we don't want to make any sacrifices. We just want him to have the best." But "we also want him to be like us, to be able to deal with different people. . . . Luckily our son is extremely bright. If he had any special needs, we'd have to go to private school."

Even before their son entered kindergarten, Robert began to teach him the discipline that would protect him from racial stereotypes and fears as he grew up. "He's going to be really structured. . . . He's five years old, and he needs to control himself. I'm very dogmatic about that. I don't want him doing certain things. I don't want him sitting certain ways." When he goes to school next year, "Guess what? The schoolteachers are going to tell him to be quiet, and they want him to be quiet. Or all of a sudden he will have ADD. In Oakland . . . if a talented black male is a little verbal, he is diagnosed as ADD." Then in seventh grade, they will look at his test scores and say, "Look he's gifted." "You are a fuckup. Oh no, you are gifted." Based on his own experiences in Bay Area schools, Robert said, "I don't trust teachers. I don't trust schools, and I am going to be a very hard parent to please."

Robert explained that the twenty-first-century realities of limited budgets and limited funding for social programs meant there was often a large gap between "what we should do" and "what we can do." Robert and Liz, along with many other volunteers, tried to fill that gap in the Laurel district. They spent free time volunteering in classrooms, raising money to build new play structures for the school, writing grants to secure state-funded after-school programs, and lobbying for the city to invest in recreation facilities for youth. But they worried that their volunteer efforts weren't enough to make up for overburdened parents, underfunded schools, and a frayed social safety net. Liz knew that as "movers and shakers" in the school, she and Robert could closely monitor their son's progress, even choose his teachers. "Of course we're going to be really involved." But Liz added, "If we see it having detrimental effects on him, we'll pull him out of the environment. I really want to make changes at Laurel, but I'm not sacrificing my child to do it." As a new fiscal crisis washed across Oakland in 2003, Liz worried that if the money wasn't there, all the efforts of parents and volunteers would be insufficient to secure the kind of education she wanted for her son. Robert reflected on the increasing needs and the decreasing budgets: "The thing is, as the economy gets worse, the more we need those services. And the less we're going to get them. But the more we're going to get police. It's really funny. The governor can't fund a lot of education, but he came up with two hundred million dollars for the prisons."

Dangerous Times

Reconstructing Childhood in a Volunteer State

In May 2000, the Laurel Redwood Heights NCPC gathered in the Laurel Elementary School auditorium for a town hall meeting with Mayor Jerry Brown. The mayor sat alongside the local city council member and assorted other city, county, and school district officials at a long table on the stage at the front of the room. Neighborhood activists had advertised the meeting well, and at its height well over a hundred people filled the room. Participants reflected this neighborhood's political networks: slightly more white than black, with a few Asian and Latino residents, ranging in age from the late twenties to the seventies, mostly homeowners and business owners but also a good number of renters from the apartment buildings around 39th Avenue.

Mayor Brown described Laurel as "one of the most dynamic neighborhoods" in the city. "Oakland is on the move, in the right direction, but we are not there yet." The police captain reported major improvements in the city's crime statistics. "We are on the way to a safe city, but next we have to make a reputation for the city being safe." He called on neighbors to stay involved: "You folks are the folks that can really get things done."

Discussion ranged across a wide variety of local concerns: storm drains and traffic, truancy and schools, commercial development and beautification plans. But residents and NCPC organizers continued to return to issues that concerned neighborhood youth—in particular the desperate need for parks, playgrounds, and organized recreation programs. The new Parks and Recreation director for the area, a slightly built African American man, spoke about the importance of expanding after-school programs for kids. "Education is not an eight-hour job. Twenty-four-hour activity is needed for our children to be competitive. . . . We have to make sure that during school hours children are safe and learning and that they are also safe and learning after school." He announced plans to hire Robert Walker to coordinate after-school activities at the Laurel school. Soon, he added, "your kid and mine will be here" taking advantage of new learning opportunities.

Robert Walker, in his role as parliamentarian of the NCPC, discussed recent NCPC successes: securing better lighting along 39th Avenue and a greater police presence at bus stops at MacArthur and 35th Avenue where "waves of children" gathered after school. He commended the great work of Friends of Laurel School, "an offshoot of the NCPC," which had launched the Laurel Jazz Festival to raise thirty thousand dollars to build new play structures at the school. "Have you seen how eager kids are to play? But they have nothing to play on." Several neighbors echoed Robert Walker's call for more parks, green space, and playgrounds in the neighborhood. A white parent, his long, curly hair pulled back into a ponytail, talked about his work with the Laurel PTA and NCPC trying to improve the school yard: "If you look out here at the yard, it's still just concrete." He turned to speak directly to the mayor: "We gave you this city on a platter. We have high expectations. We've worked hard to make little things happen. It is time for the city to step up. This is now the opportunity to get money for the city parks." Another white woman in her forties with curly brown hair echoed his call for the city to invest in spaces and programs for kids: "I don't have kids, but I've really liked the kids in this neighborhood." She described them as "sweet" and complained, "Some of these adorable kids are left with nothing to play on except garbage cans. It is a shame on all of us. They should be our social priority. They're good kids. They don't want to get in trouble. Teenagers too."

This community meeting highlighted the potential for a politics of childhood that repoliticized children's needs and expanded public responsibility for their care. Residents in the Laurel district drew on long-standing ideas of children as "sweet," innocent, and vulnerable to call on neighbors and the city to invest in schools and to create new safe places for kids to play. The Laurel district's geography and political networks broke down barriers between "our kids" and "other people's kids."[1] It brought together black, white, and a few Asian parents, and included professionals, families barely holding onto the middle class, and poor families living in run-down apartments, all of whom shared concerns that Oakland's schools and recreation programs were no longer adequately providing the care, supervision, and education kids needed to compete in the twenty-first century. By bridging racial and class lines, neighborhood activists built broad support for public investments that could secure a safe passage to adulthood for all kids.

Parents and neighbors in the Laurel district united behind a growing local and national effort to expand public investments in after-school programs.

They worried that "free time" was dangerous, repeating the refrain, "Kids don't have enough to do after school so they get into trouble." These concerns highlight a broad crisis of care that left working parents (both poor and middle class) struggling to provide care and supervision for children after school. But the Parks and Recreation director's call for 24-hour education hinted at new anxieties about the path to adulthood, a sense that kids need more education and preparation than ever to "be competitive." After-school programs were so appealing because new middle-class parenting practices have changed what is considered "normal" and necessary for healthy youth development. Middle-class children increasingly spend their time out of school in structured, supervised, and "productive" educational activities, as their parents try to secure their kids' progress up a steeper path to the middle class. These middle-class parenting practices have deepened class divides in children's lives and exacerbated worries about the dangers of free time. So activists in the Laurel district mobilized to build a public infrastructure that would enable all Oakland's youth to have middle-class structured time. They fought an uphill battle to secure the material basis for a democratized childhood and adolescence.

Laurel activists' efforts to rebuild public landscapes of childhood offer important insights into the dilemmas of activism in the context of what I call "the volunteer state."[2] Children's welfare, education, and recreational needs have always been met by a complex, shifting mix of public and private initiatives in the United States, but broad attacks on "big government" in the 1980s helped popularize the notion that private markets, volunteers, nonprofits, and faith-based organizations could best meet the needs of children and families.[3] Sociologist Robert Putnam's book, *Bowling Alone*, served as an influential rallying cry to rebuild civic networks and to reengage the "volunteer spirit" of Americans in order to repair our fraying safety net and revitalize American democracy.[4] These calls had bipartisan appeal. President George H. W. Bush called for citizens to become one of the "thousand points of light" that would replace government programs, while President Bill Clinton helped launch America's Promise to recruit volunteers and build public-private partnerships to support children and youth. Historian Michael Katz describes America's Promise as "the apotheosis of volunteerism," the severely limited "response of a downsized, reinvented government to the crises of youth in inner cities, which it had done so little to alleviate."[5]

We need to do more than simply celebrate these volunteer efforts or bemoan their absence. Calls for civil society and voluntary nongovernmental organizations (NGOs) to play a more central role in governance have gone global, from India and South Africa to Chile. As with community policing, we need to explore how these new partnerships between state and civil society are reshaping our ideas of the state, our concepts of citizenship, and the everyday practices of state institutions.[6] Activism in the lower hills showed complex and shifting boundaries between public and private efforts to care for children as neoliberalism became the reigning ideology at the turn of the twenty-first century. Middle-class parents often retreated to private schools and an expanding market of private services that promised to provide the care and 24-hour education children need to compete in the global economy. But many parents and neighbors in the Laurel district created new landscapes of childhood that were neither purely public nor private. These volunteers devoted their *private* time and money to rebuild the crumbling *public* infrastructure. They *had* to be active volunteers in order to negotiate a decaying school system and to create and maintain services for children— like after-school programs and parks—that were once provided by local government. Local and statewide activist efforts successfully expanded state funding for after-school programs, and thus extended public responsibility for children's care, supervision, and education beyond the traditional school day. But these new publicly funded programs were run by private nonprofits that had to compete for grants in a growing and increasingly entrepreneurial "third sector."[7] These nonprofit agencies addressed urgent needs of Oakland's children, but they also often reproduced very narrow visions of what youth need and what the state could provide. They could not bridge the vast gaps left by increasingly insecure state investments in children and their families. Indeed, the volunteer state sometimes reinforced deep racial and class inequities in children's environments.

In the Slants

Robert Walker described the Laurel district as "a lot like the country. It is very diverse, a lot of people with good educations, a lot of single parents, a lot of gay people. We are right in the middle. We do not have quite as much money as the people up on the hills. We aren't quite as lower income as the people below 580. . . .We are the prototypical middle class. That's what I see." The Laurel district lay between two freeways that mark the clearest borders between the hills, above Route 13, and the flatlands, below 580. The same economic transformations that had decimated Elmhurst had significantly transformed the Laurel district. Once an aging, white, working-class community, the Laurel district now embodied many of the contradictions of a political and economic order that generated massive increases in wealth and poverty, a fragile middle class, and significant divides in children's lives. Robert captured the neighborhood's precarious location in Oakland's geography with the term "the slants," evoking the ease with which the neighborhood could still slide down the hills towards the flatlands.

The Laurel district was "an up-and-coming" neighborhood. Its small commercial corridor, charming mix of 1920s bungalows and older Victorians, and burgeoning café culture had begun to attract young professionals looking for relatively affordable houses. With the high-tech boom, home prices in the Laurel district skyrocketed in the late 1990s. Richard Jones, a white professional active in local politics, described the Laurel district and Redwood Heights (just up the hill) as "yuppie-ized," but "because it was Oakland," "yuppie" didn't simply equal "white." The neighborhood was racially diverse, with "African Americans, Asians, and whites," and a lot of people who were "just making it in the [social services] agency world," which made the neighborhood "very progressive in orientation."

But Laurel was far from a uniformly gentrified neighborhood. Many working-class or poor families crowded into tiny houses, apartment buildings, or dilapidated motels right next to newly remodeled homes.[8] In what many neighbors described as a "zoning nightmare," hundreds of apartment buildings were built along the MacArthur corridor in the 1960s, many of them clustered along 39th Avenue. The neighborhood resisted many of these apartment complexes, in what one long-time resident described as a "battle between the little bungalow dwellers and the developers." These fights had both racial and class overtones. The Laurel district was on the edge of an area called the "Bible Belt," where white homeowners "carved out a homogeneous racial space" in the flatlands and lower hills that lasted through the 1970s.[9]

The Laurel neighborhood had become increasingly racially mixed since the seventies, with a substantial black and rapidly growing Asian population. The Laurel Community Action Project estimated that the neighborhood had an equal percentage of black and white residents, who together formed 60% of the neighborhood, while the remaining 40% was split among Asians, Pacific Islanders, and Latinos. Several Chinese Americans and African Americans ran businesses on the MacArthur commercial strip, and Cornerstone Baptist, an African American church, had bought a substantial amount of property when it was cheap and commerce was declining along MacArthur in the 1980s. The stores themselves, all built into beautiful but often deteriorating Art Deco store fronts, highlighted the neighborhood's race and class contradictions: new upscale clothing boutiques and cafés with wireless access were scattered among 99-cent stores and laundromats, black barbershops and nail salons, cheap doughnut shops, no-frills takeout Chinese restaurants, and working-class bars.

The neighborhood's diversity obscured a more complex racial geography. Some blocks were 40-50% Asian, predominantly first-generation Chinese immigrants. Just across the street, however, might be a block that was 50% black. Jenny Chin, a second-generation Chinese American woman in her late twenties, who grew up and still lived in the Laurel district, described it as "a Black and Asian neighborhood." The apartment building she grew up in was all Chinese but was just across the street from another apartment building that was African American. She had formed close relationships with some of her black neighbors, but her immigrant parents had labeled the neighboring apartment building a "crack house."

The neighborhood became both wealthier and whiter as one moved up the hill towards the Redwood Heights neighborhood, which had an excellent public elementary school, a beautiful park, and a new recreation center. Redwood Heights was one of Oakland's few majority-white neighborhoods (roughly 69% white, only 10% Asian, and 8% black), the historical legacy of informal efforts to resist racial change by a home improvement association formed in 1944 by white Republican homeowners.[10] Sam and Judy Turner, a white couple who lived near MacArthur and were active PTA and NCPC members, explained that the "higher up in the hills you go, the more money you have. Three blocks up, they think they are better than us." A real estate agent had told them, "Every foot above MacArthur counts."

The Turners described their racially diverse block on the edge of the Laurel district:

> The neighbor across the street is Japanese who was interned during the war, next to him a Chinese family, next a little old [white] lady who doesn't talk to anyone and is kinda paranoid. Next to them are two houses owned by these large families from El Salvador that are childcare centers, Tongan and Samoan, African American, white, Portuguese that distinguish themselves from Anglo-Saxon white.

A "yuppie African American couple" had just moved to the neighborhood, but there were "very few African Americans on this block. You could be any ethnic group but black and it's unremarkable, but [most of] the African Americans live in the apartment buildings." According to the Turners, several owners wouldn't rent their houses to blacks and some of the older neighbors, like their Japanese neighbor, described blacks as the cause of neighborhood decline.

There was not a simple equation of race and class, or blackness and poverty, in this neighborhood. Many poor black families lived in the apartments on 39th Avenue, but they lived alongside a substantial number of poor white and Asian families. In one census block, 46% of white kids lived in poverty alongside 14% of black kids and 24% of Asian kids.[11] There were upper-middle-class black, Asian, and white families, but there remained significant racial disparities when one looked closely at the distribution of family income levels. In the heart of the Laurel district, only 23% of black families made more than sixty thousand dollars, while 46% of Asian families and 59% of white families did. At the lower end of the class ladder, 28% of black families earned less than thirty thousand dollars, compared to only 10% of white families and 16% of Asian families. A good number of families across racial lines were concentrated in the precarious middle-class range of thirty to sixty thousand dollars: 49% of black families, 37% of Asian families, and 31% of white families.

Laurel's location "in the slants" helped create a distinctive kind of politics of childhood. Black, white, and Asian middle-class professionals, prospering in the high-tech boom, lived in close proximity to Asian immigrant, black, and white working-class families, some of whom were struggling in an increasingly polarized economic order. The local NCPC was different from many in the city in that it not only included older homeowners but also had actively reached out to incorporate two groups not frequently engaged in neighborhood politics: renters and public school parents.

The NCPC often defined the apartment buildings on 39th Avenue as problems where, as Robert Smith explained, "there's lots of low-income people packed in on top of each other." Families were "crammed into small apartments," and their kids "were on the streets." This focus on 39th Avenue, while stigmatizing renters and their kids, also had the surprising effect of encouraging some renters to join the NCPC. The NCPC created a separate committee to focus on 39th Avenue, in order to increase street lighting, crack down on drug dealing, and push "slumlords" to beautify their buildings, hire private security, and evict problem tenants. Tanesha Johnson, a black single mother raising her three sons on disability payments and part-time work, first came to a community meeting to defend tenants and her landlord from what she perceived as unfair attacks. She worried that all the pressures on her landlord to paint and landscape his buildings would just lead to higher rents and her eviction. But she stayed involved because she hoped the NCPC could do something for neighborhood children. She had moved to the Laurel district to get her sons away from the violence that plagued the East Oakland flatlands where she grew up. She found a cheap apartment, where most tenants were "really really low income." The landlord charged only $675 a month and was "really forgiving of late rent." One block in any direction was "paradise," but her apartment complex was not. Young black men often hung out in front of the building, and she didn't know whether they were still dealing drugs. She wondered if the city should "just tear them down," but she knew that "if it weren't for these apartments, I would probably be in a worse place."

Liz Walker helped forge relationships with the local elementary school, which brought middle-class and working-class parents into the NCPC. She encouraged Jean Schmidt and Bobbie Taylor, both working-class white parents who lived on 39th Avenue, to join the NCPC and PTA. She also invited Sandra Collins, an African American homeowner and businesswoman with an MBA, who was a single mother active in the PTA. Sandra joined the NCPC hoping to beautify the school so it would "look less like a prison and more like an elementary school." She wanted to create a friendly, caring neighborhood that would watch over her son as he grew up. Since she got to know so many neighbors through her activism, she felt more comfortable with her son walking around the neighborhood. "At least he could have *some* freedom."

Parent participation enabled the Laurel NCPC to break out of the institutional boundaries of community policing and to forge a broader mandate that extended beyond disciplining kids to caring for kids. Some middle-class neighborhood activists, like Robert, Liz, and Sandra, sent their kids to public schools alongside working-class and poor kids. So they shared interests and investments in the public schools and playgrounds. But these connections extended to neighbors without kids and parents whose kids went to private school. Mary and Peter Thomas were relatively prosperous white homeowners and active members of the NCPC and LCAP, where they worked to attract new upscale businesses to the Laurel district. Mary was a stay-at-home mom, and they sent their daughter to a private bilingual French school. As they worked alongside parents in the NCPC, they became concerned about kids in the public schools, so they helped found Friends of Laurel Elementary School and led fundraising efforts and beautification projects around the school.

Sharing the same streets, and sometimes the same schools, parents and neighbors became painfully aware of the inequalities in Oakland childhoods. As one white middle-class parent volunteer said, "It has been heartbreaking to absorb the magnitude of social neglect in Oakland. We are witnessing a massive loss of human potential. Most people are oblivious or insensitive to the deep suffering of these children."[12] Sam and Judi Turner's son was best friends with a kid named Peter who was growing up in the "rental cottages next door," whose parents were alcoholics and who went to a county-run alternative school. They sometimes worried that Peter would "drag our son down with him," but they cared for him since they "had semi-raised him." This kind of intimacy broke down clear boundaries between "our kids" and "other people's kids" and led some parents towards deeper engagements in public schools and towards activism that would reshape the ways children used time and space in the neighborhood.

Divided Landscapes of Childhood

Parents and neighbors who grew up in Oakland in the 1960s remembered well-maintained parks, good schools, and school yards where Parks and Recreation staff ran supervised after-school recreation programs. When Bobbie Taylor grew up Oakland, "they let the kids play ball till five o'clock," but by the time her daughter attended Laurel Elementary School in the 1990s, that program was gone. Now as a white single mother struggling to making ends meet in an apartment on 39th Avenue, she worried, "It's not as safe." She didn't feel comfortable letting her daughter play Kick the Can unsupervised on the street as she had as a child. "There is a lot less for kids to do . . . and everything now costs money too. A lot of people don't have the money." From where Bobbie sat, the public affordable infrastructure for Oakland's kids looked very different in the late 1990s than it had in the 1960s. Her memories capture two important changes in children's environments in Oakland. From the early 1970s through the mid-1990s, public investments in children's environments, especially schools and recreation facilities, declined precipitously, deepening class divides in the landscapes of childhood in Oakland. But the pervasive sense of decline was also shaped by drastic changes in the kinds of structures and education that we think kids need to successfully make the transition to adulthood.

Oakland's basic infrastructure of schools, parks, and recreation facilities had developed in the early twentieth century alongside our modern ideals of childhood and youth as "age-graded phases in the life cycle."[13] By the 1920s, child labor laws and mandatory schooling had restructured childhood in the United States, excluding kids from the workforce and consolidating a definition of childhood as a time for school and play. But this new concept of childhood also produced new problems, in particular new worries about what children would do with their "leisure time" and how they would transition from a protected childhood to adulthood. Many of the institutions we associate most immediately with childhood and youth—playgrounds, the Boy Scouts, YMCA, Boys and Girls Clubs, summer camps, and organized sports activities—developed during this period as efforts to fill young people's newly idle time. Oakland's first public playgrounds were built by the Oakland Club, one of many women's clubs that formed part of a broad "child saving" movement in the late nineteenth and early twentieth centuries.[14] By the 1920s, the city of Oakland had created the Recreation Department to take on the responsibility of establishing and maintaining a network of supervised playgrounds throughout the city.

Oakland mobilized again to combat the "tragic misuse of leisure" during the Great Depression in 1933. The Coordinating Council of the Community Chest, a collaboration of private social welfare organizations, churches, and citizens groups that was a precursor to the United Way, published a booklet calling on Oakland residents to donate funds to make sure "your son or daughter" spent his or her "precious" leisure hours in "character-building activities." The accompanying headlines suggest that without this protection, boys in particular might end up "setting fires," hurting each other, or even going "to jail." But the images of the smiling faces of white boys and girls in scouting-style uniforms captured the fundamental belief that with the proper support they would become "all-American" children (See Figure 6).[15]

Calls to fill kids' free time cropped up again urgently during World War II. Oakland created youth canteens to supervise youth while mothers worked and fathers were away. Even after the war, youth reformers worried about "broken families and truancy," but also about unsupervised youth socializing in "commercial amusement establishments," dance halls, and movie theaters that were cropping up in commercial strips throughout the city. The Oakland Police Department created a new juvenile bureau and a special juvenile patrol division to monitor places where juveniles might "congregate" during school hours.[16] These child-saving efforts always combined attempts to control working-class kids and their families with efforts to expand care for children, but middle-class reformers never were entirely successful at transforming the ways kids used time and space.[17] Working-class youth in cities like Oakland created and maintained vibrant street cultures through the twentieth century, and middle-class kids through most of the twentieth century still had plenty of unstructured free time.[18]

We could look at this history as the heyday of "civil society," when people organized themselves (without the government) to meet the needs of children and youth, but this would misinterpret how Oakland's park and recreation

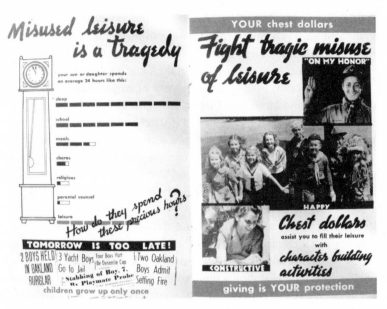

Figure 6. Tragic misuse of leisure, a recurring twentieth-century fear. This 1938 brochure was published by the Oakland Community Chest. (Oakland History Room, vertical files)

infrastructure was built.[19] While some of Oakland's recreation infrastructure (like the playgrounds, YMCA, and Boys Clubs) were initiated by private social welfare organizations, these organizations always worked closely with city agencies and often helped advocate for expanded public infrastructure for children and youth. By the 1920s, Oakland city government had taken the responsibility for providing supervised children's playgrounds throughout the city and even ran a public summer camp at Feather River. The federally funded Works Progress Administration (WPA) helped significantly expand the number of Oakland parks and build new recreation facilities. WPA funds even helped launch the first nonprofit "Boys Club" (now Boys and Girls Club) in Oakland.[20] By the 1950s, Oakland had developed a substantial and nationally renowned Department of Parks and Recreation that ran after-school programs at most public schools and coordinated juvenile delinquency prevention efforts for the city.[21] Adults in Oakland remember not just playing in these facilities but also finding their first summer jobs in them.

Oakland, and California as a whole, had invested in a basic infrastructure for children and youth in the midtwentieth century that included decently funded public schools, recreational facilities, and a rapidly expanding public university system. These public investments promoted an almost democratic or egalitarian childhood and youth, where kids across class (and to a lesser degree racial) lines at least participated in the same public institutions. Oakland also had a vibrant private infrastructure of neighborhood movie theaters, roller rinks, and businesses that provided inexpensive places for young people to play and socialize. The Laurel district had a small public library, two movie theaters, a neighborhood music store, and daily organized recreation activities in the school yard. As geographer Susan Ruddick argues, our midtwentieth-century ideals of childhood and youth depended on exactly this kind of "impressive array of public institutions that were part and parcel of the Keynesian welfare state."[22]

Nevertheless, Oakland in the fifties and sixties was far from an egalitarian paradise for black children, and forces were already in motion that would destabilize the public and private infrastructure for Oakland's kids. Freeways promoted white flight and capital flight to the suburbs, starting a precipitous decline in commercial districts and in the city's tax base. Black children in West Oakland and in the East Oakland flatlands were confined to the most crowded industrial areas of the city, while white families fled to the hills with its vast parklands and new schools. The white Republican city council remained committed to a low-tax and limited-government philosophy, even as they shifted public funding and services away from the black flatlands and to the hills. As black kids grew into their teenage years, they faced a hostile police force that often trampled on their rights to public spaces.[23]

White flight reshaped California state politics, empowering a white suburban constituency that began campaigning to limit public spending in cities. Proposition 13, the signature victory of California's white suburban tax revolt, passed in 1976 and decimated the public infrastructure for kids in Oakland just as black activists were finally securing local political power.[24] Reagan- and Bush-era federal funding cuts further shifted responsibility for children's welfare onto cities already struggling with declining tax bases and increasing inequalities.[25] By 1983 Oakland's Parks and Recreation staff was reduced to half of its pre–Prop 13 levels.[26] School funding dropped continuously and precipitously through the early 1990s. By the early eighties, the small storefront branch library in the Laurel district had closed and Parks and Recreation no longer provided after-school recreation activities at the local school. California lost over $17 billion in federal funding between 1997 and 2002 alone.[27] Oakland politicians and citizens tried to hold together the city's disintegrating landscapes of childhood by cultivating public-private partnerships like Friends of the Library and Friends of Oakland Parks and Recreation, and by saving money through contracts with nonprofit service providers.[28] Oakland school board member and youth advocate Gregory Hodge maintained that declining schools and recreation programs were symbols of the state's failure to invest in kids: "We've pretty much sent the message to kids that we don't care."

Oakland city government struggled in the late 1990s to rebuild some of the public infrastructure necessary to sustain all the city's children. Peg Gordon, an activist in the Laurel district for the last twenty-five years, thought that by the late 1990s in Oakland, there was "a great deal more consciousness to do something for youth. People are willing to vote for school bonds. We know that the next generation needs to be nurtured and cared for, and that it will create more problems by not nurturing them. It is a standard concern, but now we know that it must be a social concern." Starting in the late 1980s, Oakland voters passed a series of bond measures and special parcel taxes, trying to make up for decades of state and federal disinvestment in spaces for children and youth in the city. These local bond measures injected vital resources into Oakland's parks, recreation centers, and schools and began to make a dent in problems caused by two decades of deferred maintenance in Oakland's aging infrastructure for children.[29] The booming economy in the late 1990s enabled the city and the schools to slowly rebuild funding for children's environments and staffing for programs.[30] But California's structural deficit and the boom-bust economy of the turn of the twenty-first century made these local investments very fragile.[31] Every few years Oakland would face a new fiscal crisis that once again threatened to decimate schools and children's services. During the California budget crisis of 2002-2003, children's programs sustained more than 75% of the $9.4 billion in reduced spending.[32] And the state raided city and county budgets, as it did in every budget crisis. Supervisor Keith Carson estimated that Alameda County lost about $1.6 billion to the state between 1993 and 2003.[33]

Landscapes of childhood were deeply divided in the Laurel neighborhood at the turn of the twenty-first century. Many middle-class families in Oakland had dealt with the crises in public schools and recreation by retreating to private markets to meet their children's needs. Robert Smith complained that many middle-class residents in the Laurel district had fled to private schools or tried to move "up the hill" where they bought expensive homes within the boundaries of a "good" elementary school. "A certain demographic," the white middle class, had "abandoned" the public schools. Margaret Duncan, a lawyer and white homeowner, sent her son to Bret Harte Middle School, but she was rare among her friends. Her friends sometimes sent their children to public school in the hills for elementary school, but most moved "through the tunnel" to Orinda or sent their kids to private school after elementary school as schools began to draw from broader geographic areas. Christine Rollinson, a real estate agent and a good friend of Margaret Duncan's, agreed that a lot of upper-middle-class people in Oakland hear about teenagers having sex, smoking pot, and cutting school and simply retreat from public schools and city life.

Sociologist Barrie Thorne calls these deeply "privatized childhoods." Nannies and private day cares, with low-wage immigrant women as the care providers, provided much of the daily love and care for children while parents worked. Private schools and tutoring services took the place of well-funded public schools, and private play facilities replaced vibrant parks and public spaces.[34] As more middle-class families moved to the Laurel district, it began to attract these kinds of private investments, such as a new kids' dance studio (See Figure 7).

A nearby public recreation center advertised "Mommy and Me" classes at a Laurel café, but at thirty dollars a class they were out of the reach of Laurel's working-class parents. Middle-class parents could drive up the hill to the SCORE! Learning Center, a for-profit tutoring company, whose website promised to propel its clients up an increasingly steep educational "path to success" so they could join the "Academic all-stars."[35] As geographer Cindi Katz has argued, these privatized strategies may protect and propel some kids up a steeper path to the middle class. But they also fuel the public abandonment of many children whose parents cannot afford to pay for services in the private market.[36]

The Laurel district included families living these very different public and private childhoods. As Robert Smith explained, some Laurel residents "could afford to take their kids up the hill," but others couldn't, so they "just let their kids run wild outside the door." Many Laurel parents were only precariously holding onto their middle-class status, or striving to make it out of poverty. That's why, according to Robert, the lower hills communities had to "fight a lot harder" for services for youth. Parents in the Laurel district could not necessarily afford to pay for all the accoutrements of a middle-class lifestyle for their children. They paid "very high taxes" but were often "underserved in terms of city services." The flatlands had obvious needs and got a lot of city resources, while in the hills, parents didn't need city resources because they could "pay for ballet lessons, music."

Figure 7. Private landscapes of childhood in the Laurel District. (Photo by author)

Controlling the Dangers of Free Time

Parents varied significantly in how, and how much, they tried to structure their own kids' free time. Some drove their kids to and from school, kept them in structured after-school programs, and supervised them very carefully. Others let their kids have more freedom to bike around the neighborhood or to take the bus as they got older. Nevertheless, every parent and neighbor I interviewed in the lower hills described "free time" after school as a problem, often a dangerous one. Chris Quan worried that kids "coming from broken homes" or with "parents working late at night" weren't getting "the guidance they need." She wanted schools to stay open late so they would not be "just left to do whatever." Surveys in the Laurel district confirmed these broad concerns about children's free time. The community's three highest priorities were "after-school activities for youth," "recreation facilities," and "child care." Parents also wanted academic mentors, tutoring, and extended music and arts classes that would provide more education and structure for kids during their free time.[37] Free time posed different kinds of dangers for children across race, gender, class and age categories, but the fear itself crossed racial and class lines and drove efforts to structure children's free time in the Laurel district.[38]

Most parents described unsupervised elementary school kids as "endangered" by cars and adult predators on the streets. News coverage and police dramas about kidnapping and child sexual abuse, as well as teenage sex and drugs, have left many parents terrified to let children have any unsupervised free time in public places.[39] Anthropologist Roger Lancaster argues that these panics have created "a dark picture of childhood encircled by sinister forces, menaced by innumerable threats." They have also promoted an "ever more expansive culture of child protection."[40] At one NCPC meeting, an African American mother asked for more police patrols because "kids say that cars are coming and stopping to try to talk to them." Tanesha chimed in, saying, "it would be so sad if some little child got taken."

Even older girls were generally described as "endangered" by free time. Neighborhood activists frequently talked about high school boys and older men "coming and preying on the young girls" at the bus stops or as they walked home. Jackie Patterson, the Neighborhood Services Coordinator, told me a story about one middle school African American girl who rode in a stolen vehicle with a man she didn't know without thinking that she could become another headline about kidnapped children. She thought that girl would quickly end up pregnant because she was "looking for love in all the wrong places. . . . They don't realize the dangers they get themselves into."

Neighborhood activists defined older boys as both endangered and made potentially dangerous by free time. Many concerns focused on boys, especially the poor African American boys who "hung out" in the apartment buildings on 39th Avenue. Liz described what she had seen happen when poor black boys grew up without adequate support, structure, and supervision. A kid named Isaiah at Laurel Elementary School

> was just a natural born leader. He was always willing to help sell tickets [for fundraisers], helping organize the whole thing, but he had little parental influence. His dad wasn't around and his mother was whatever. . . . You could just see it happen to him. Now he's out on the street. You know that these kids are bright. You can't just, by the time they're in ninth grade, say "here's a karate class." They need to have support starting in elementary school.

Many neighborhood activists blamed poor kids with too much "free time" for the Laurel district's crime problems. That's why the NCPC first started to build after-school programs, as Jackie Patterson explained. "There was a lot of crime on the MacArthur corridor—theft, robbery, commercial burglary, drug activity—that's not captured by the data." They surveyed students, who said, "There's no space in the Laurel. Ain't nothin' to do." They were mostly having trouble with preteens so they developed after-school programs "to keep them away from getting in a lot of trouble." Activists in the Laurel neighborhood reproduced a long-standing duality in child protection efforts: children must be protected from the dangerous public sphere, but the public also must be protected from dangerous children.[41]

Tanesha Johnson, on 39th Avenue, never let her sons play outside. She worried about everything: traffic, sexual predators, random violence, and especially the lure of "easy quick money" that seemed to pull so many young black men into drug dealing. She drove her sons to and from school because "kids get beat up going to school." When one of her sons got suspended from school, she spent several months sitting in on his classes. "There is no lax time when my children are unattended, and if there is no lags in time, then maybe they'll be safe." She hesitated, "maybe . . . at least that's my assumption." Tanesha thought that she might be "a bit paranoid," but her comments highlight the ways race, class, and gender structured fears about free time. Free time posed particular kinds of dangers to poor black boys: that they would become or be seen as drug dealers, the ultimate "bad boys." Tanesha often had little money, and poor health sapped her energy, so her kids mostly stayed inside and played video games. Tanesha worried that keeping her kids confined in the house wasn't good for them. "Normal kids do play outside on their block." She wished they had a creek, a park, or a yard to play in. But she looked at the young men hanging out in front of her apartment and thought that their parents had not kept them "in the house" as she did with her sons.[42]

Bobbie Taylor worked part-time as an after-school monitor at Laurel Elementary so she could supervise her daughter after school. She occasionally let her go to the playground after school, but worried that she might get into drugs or "the wrong crowd." There was little for her daughter to do with her free time since she rarely had the money for bus fare, entrance fees, or movie tickets. We see here clear limits on parental choices. Like Tanesha, Bobbie could arrange her schedule so she could volunteer at her children's schools. She could keep her children in the house, but she did not have the money "to choose" to live in a house with a back yard in a safe neighborhood or to take advantage of the emerging private landscapes of childhood in Oakland.

Middle-class professional parents had more choices, but they too worried about free time. Sandra Collins described providing care for her son before and after school as a "big concern." Her professional position gave her the flexibility to arrange her work schedule so that she could be with him after school without sacrificing income. He got himself to school after she left for work, but they got home at the same time so they could unwind together, get homework and chores done, and play together. She bought him a cell phone to keep in touch during the day and she tried to get to know his friends and their parents. As her son was getting older, she was "trying to be more structured with him" because "now it's more serious. It's going to be high school time." He participated in a baseball league and a program at the YMCA and had a tutor. She also found a special after-school class in robotics for him to take. But she realized that most parents didn't have those luxuries. She thought "kids needed more care" after school before parents came home from work. "Nine out of ten don't want to get in trouble, but they're bored so they do."

These concerns about "free time" after school point to a deepening "crisis of care" that affected families across class lines.[43] High rates of maternal employment and single-parent households have decreased the number of parents who stay home to provide childcare. In Oakland, at least 64% of students in the city lived in families with two parents working or a single parent working.[44] Many parents worked longer hours or two jobs to make ends meet and struggled to find childcare for children and supervised activities after school for older kids. While some parents could rely on relatives to care for their kids after school, others could not. There were fewer grandparents and "other parents" on the street to informally monitor kids after school.[45] Jenny thought kids should be off the street, but "maybe they don't want to be home. That's another problem." Not all homes were safe and caring spaces for kids.

National reports and surveys echoed these broad-based concerns that "free time" led to trouble and argued that after-school programs could turn a "risk" into an "opportunity." As the influential Carnegie Foundation report, *A Matter of Time: Risk and Opportunity in the Nonschool Hours*, explained, "unstructured, unsupervised, and unproductive" time often led young people to drug and alcohol abuse, crime, and violence.[46] The Carnegie Foundation described adolescence as "a crucially formative phase that can shape an individual's entire life course and thus the future of society." Coming of age was a complex process that had to be actively managed: "In the critical transition from childhood toward a still-distant adulthood, adolescents have a lot to learn . . . families help. Schools help. But increasingly they are not enough."[47] This report argued that we needed to turn to the "third side" of the "developmental triangle," to community organizations and youth programs. After-school programs could provide "an array of engaging and meaningful experiences" that would help America's youth develop into "responsible" and "productive" members of society.[48] They could keep youth on the right track and ensure they would not "veer into another course of development."[49]

In the mid-1990s, youth advocates in Oakland and across the nation launched efforts to shift the terms of the debate from fixing youth problems to promoting "healthy youth development."[50] Oakland's *Call to Action: A Blueprint for Youth Development* described how community agencies could ensure that all young people had secure spaces and relationships with caring adults to safely make it to adulthood. Young people inevitably "will find somewhere to turn for their sense of belonging and care. The question is whether they find it with family, resort to an informal peer group, find their way into a gang, or turn to a community alternative which provides consistent bonds with caring adults." The *Blueprint* highlighted Omega Boys Club as a model youth development organization, and quoted founder Joe Marshall explaining, "We don't do programs. . . . We're an extended family. . . . You just take care of kids who aren't your own. You do them the way you would your own children."[51] These advocates attempted to challenge the focus of many youth institutions (like schools and the juvenile justice system) on controlling, containing, or punishing kids. Instead, they tried to revalue care and to extend responsibility for children beyond the boundaries of the family.

After-school programs became the consensus solution to a multitude of problems facing youth by the late 1990s. Sociologist Anita Garey found that diverse advocacy groups pushed the California state legislature to expand funding for after-school programs in 1998. School officials looked to after-school programs to help them meet the higher expectations for academic progress especially after the passage of No Child Left Behind. Working parents looked to after-school programs to help provide care and supervision. And law-enforcement and crime-prevention groups promised that after-school programs could prevent crime in the crucial hours between 3:00 and 6:00 P.M.[52] Nonprofits also developed sophisticated lobbying efforts to expand government funding.[53] These combined efforts produced a massive expansion in federal, state, and local funding for after-school programs at the turn of the twenty-first century.[54] Many cities have developed comprehensive citywide after-school systems, like Los Angeles's BEST and New York City's After-school Corporation.[55] By 2006-2007, 17.89 million public dollars were being spent in Oakland to provide comprehensive, free, after-school programs that served approximately 25% of public school students.[56]

After-school programs were increasingly framed as a necessary public investment for middle-class kids as well as poor kids who were struggling to make their way up a steeper path to adulthood. An After-School Alliance poll found that 84% of U.S. voters thought there should be a "national commitment to ensuring that every child has a space in an afterschool program."[57] Advocates for after-school programs drew on long-standing ideas that children needed to be supervised and protected to argue for expanded public responsibility for children's after-school time. But they also drew on new ideals of and anxieties about childhood that had emerged in response to fundamental economic restructuring that had created deeper divides in the paths young people took to adulthood.

Falling Off a Steeper Path to Adulthood

Young people at the turn of the twenty-first century are taking a bumpier road to adulthood and making the transition at later ages than in the mid-twentieth century.[58] Pervasive economic insecurity has escalated adult fears about youth coming of age; one Carnegie Foundation report described half of all U.S. adolescents as "at-risk" of "not achieving productive adulthood."[59] In the late 1990s, 60% of American adults and 77% of black adults thought that children were worse off than when they were kids.[60] We saw in Elmhurst how economic restructuring and the ongoing significance of race decimated black working-class neighborhoods and many children's lives. Adults worried both that kids were "growing up too soon" and also that without good schools and secure work, they might never fully grow up. But the road to adulthood has become longer, steeper, and more risky for middle-class children as well. Middle-class parents have responded to these risks by creating a new culture of intensive parenting that has transformed children's daily lives and reworked our ideas of what children need. Activists in the Laurel district developed after-school programs that would enact and democratize these new ideals, by extending middle-class structured time to all kids in Oakland.

Broad economic changes created intense "fears of falling" in this neighborhood.[61] Globalization and the shift to a service economy have generated massive inequalities not just between rich and poor but also *within* the middle class. Most new jobs created in California are at the extremes of the wage spectrum, with far fewer jobs created in the middle-income levels.[62] While some upper-middle-class families have seen enormous gains in income, most middle-class families experienced stagnant wages or downward mobility. Between 1976 and 2006, the income of the top 20% of California earners increased 18.4%, while the middle percentile increased a meager 1.3%.[63] This emerging class structure has increased competition for the few well-paid jobs at the top and exacerbated parental fears that their children might easily fall down the class ladder.

Families also had to contend with what political scientist Jacob Hacker has called the *Great Risk Shift*, as jobs, health care, retirement, and family income have all become much more insecure.[64] First blue-collar and then many white-collar educated professionals saw their jobs downsized or outsourced and their incomes stagnate or fluctuate wildly. In California, many middle-class families were able to maintain their income levels over the last three decades only because of the increased number of working mothers, a coping mechanism that, given a mostly unchanged gendered division of household labor, has only deepened the crisis of care in working families. As anthropologist Brett Williams has argued, and the 2008 housing crash made only too visible, many families have only held onto their precarious middle-class status—and tried to pass it on to their kids—by racking up unsustainable levels of debt.[65]

College and graduate school have become increasingly required for access to well-paid jobs in this insecure and polarized economy. But this extended education has left many young people struggling to attain culturally expected markers of adulthood. As author Anya Kamenetz chronicles in her book *Generation Debt*, many young people leave college massively burdened with debt that exacerbates their economic insecurities in an already-risky job market. Others find they need to earn graduate degrees or to take unpaid internships to advance in their chosen professions. With the soaring cost of home ownership, another marker of adult success slipped out of reach for many in the Bay Area. Even college no longer seemed to guarantee a safe transition to adulthood. As the cost of college skyrocketed, Margaret Duncan said that many kids in the lower hills worried, "Am I going to be able to afford to go to college at all? Is it really going to make a difference? Can I afford to stay in?"

Anthropologist Janet Finn argues that our understanding of youth has changed as "our standard cultural scripts about middle class upward mobility no longer seem to work." In the midtwentieth century, experts described adolescence as "a volatile stage en route to adulthood," in which experimentation, risk taking, and rebellion were expected and seen as normal, if not necessarily desirable. Finn argues that today few youth "have the luxury" to experiment and "'try on' adult roles" but instead are "in training for a race" for the few "openings" available in the professional middle class. In this context, adolescent risk and experimentation are increasingly seen as pathological and far more dangerous.[66]

Many middle-class parents in Oakland worried that the normal mistakes and distractions of adolescence might fundamentally endanger their children's future. Margaret Duncan, who had raised two sons in the Laurel district, described the escalating pressures on parents and kids. "The freedom to be a kid and make mistakes and experiment [is] more constricted." Everything's become "so scripted." Parents have become so worried about "safety issues, having your kids out at night, having your kids out with a helmet practically every time they walk out of the door. It gets overwhelming." She found herself constantly evaluating whether her youngest son, who was "extremely bright," was "really concentrating well" enough in school: "If your kid isn't a total sit-in-your-seat kid, well, do you medicate him or not?" Sixteen years before, with her first son, "You just didn't worry so much." Margaret complained about the "hype" and "competition" to get into universities and the emphasis on testing. Margaret tried to resist those pressures, but she often felt herself drawn into the almost inescapable logic of escalating competition. She wanted her kids "to be economically viable. I don't have the kind of personality that could deal with some kid coming home and staying with me till they were twenty-five or thirty. I don't think it's right for them."

Many middle-class kids now experience a radically extended adolescence as they climb this steep path to adulthood.[67] Margaret Turner, reflecting on her stepsons, thought it could extend into the late thirties. "I think kids remain kids for a hell of a lot longer. My stepsons, none of them are married. It drives me nuts. . . . Something is wrong with this picture. . . . There is something about not quite growing up. . . . It's not just the single part, but still relying on your parents. If you screw up, you end up back at home." She added, "The economic opportunity is really a problem. If I were young, I never would stay in the Bay Area. It's not feasible to stay here. Where are they going to go to start their families? And how are they going make it unless they're super-educated?"

This precipitous path to adulthood has sharply increased the amount of care, time, and education we think children need in order to "keep up" and "get ahead."[68] Middle-class parents now orchestrate 24-hour learning environments for their children, reshaping the way kids use their free time so that they can become "super-educated." Sociologist Annette Lareau calls this new culture of parenting the "logic of concerted cultivation."[69] An ever-growing number of products and services promise to offer our children competitive advantage "in an era of economic anxiety."[70] Parents spend "floor time" playing with infants and buy educational toys that promise to turn "play time" into an endless opportunity for learning and skill building. New videos and video games promise to teach preschoolers how to read (and to give frazzled parents a few minutes of adult time almost guilt-free). Parents drive older children to ballet lessons, soccer practices, after-school tutoring, art classes, and science camps. Parents are even encouraged to extend learning opportunities into the womb by playing Mozart to their developing fetuses.[71]

The new culture of middle-class parenting has fundamentally reshaped the ways kids spend their "free time" out of school and has deepened class divides in the experience of childhood.[72] Middle-class kids (across racial lines) now spend more and more of their "free time" in structured, supervised, and often expensive after-school activities. In contrast, working-class and poor kids still spend their "free time" in less structured activities, playing independently with friends, visiting with relatives, or watching TV.[73] One report found that while 83% of eighth graders in the highest socioeconomic category participated in organized out-of-school activities, 40% of low-income youth participated in none.[74] This 24-hour learning culture has redefined our sense of what is normal and required for children to compete in a global economy. It has also deepened the chasm between poor kids and middle-class kids, who are learning to multitask and blur lines between "work" and "play," skills that are increasingly required for professional work in contemporary capitalism.[75]

Parents in the Laurel district experienced fears of falling and felt the pressures to prepare their children to compete in the global economy in a particularly acute way. They didn't have to look far, up or down the hill (or even next door), to see the massive inequalities in children's lives and trajectories generated by the current economic order. Deep class divides in the temporal rhythms of childhood exacerbated fears about free time in the Laurel district. Parents and neighborhood activists fought for after-school programs to offer middle-class structured time to all public school kids. These programs would help both poor and middle-class kids meet escalating requirements as they climbed the increasingly rocky path to adulthood.

Race also shaped the politics of childhood in significant ways in the Laurel district. Black middle-class parents shared with their white and Chinese American neighbors deep fears of falling, but race, class, and gender intersected to create additional barriers for their children on the path to adulthood. Black families in the United States have a harder time securing the future class status of their children than white families.[76] Instead of being upwardly mobile, recent studies have found that a majority of black children born to middle-income parents grow up to have less income than their parents: only 31% of black middle-income children exceed the income of their parents compared to 68% of white children.[77] Black children in the Laurel district faced a steeper path to the middle class for several reasons. Black middle-class families tended to cluster in the lower-income fractions of the middle class, while many white families clustered in the higher-income brackets. Black families also tended to have significantly less wealth than white families, even when they made the same income. This wealth gap, built up by generations of discriminatory hiring and housing policies, meant that black families had less money to invest in their children's education or to survive temporary economic disruptions like job losses.[78] Many black middle-class families lived in close geographic proximity to poor black families and attended the same schools. As sociologist Mary Pattillo McCoy has shown, this geographic proximity means that black middle-class children often attend inferior schools and get drawn into peer groups that pull them off the path to higher education and income security.

Black boys faced additional barriers on the path to adulthood. As Sandra Collins's son entered middle school, she began to worry more about his future. Middle school is "a different world," she explained, "with a lot of tough kids and more peer pressure." "My biggest worry right now is him not succeeding in school, really failing and not being able to get a good job and falling into the wrong crowd." Her son was getting picked on for hanging out with white and Asian kids, and he was text messaging her all the time from school, a sign he was struggling. He fell behind and had to repeat a grade, but to her dismay, his teachers didn't seem particularly concerned. "He's in danger! You'd think maybe the teachers would be watching." But even though she was active in the PTA, she "didn't get a progress report or anything." Her son's failure was unremarkable to teachers at his school, who had come to expect (and thus help produce) black boys' educational disadvantage. At the same time, her son also faced intense peer pressure to self-identify with the powerful image of black boys as "tough."[79] Eventually Sandra decided to send him to a small private school, which prepared its mostly African American students for elite high schools and where her son would get the kind of individual attention he needed to get back on track.

Sandra Collins kept reiterating that her son was "a good kid with a really good heart," but she worried that people would assume "he's a bad kid" who was "going to do something bad." Although Sandra was confident that he would "steer himself in the right direction" and "not fall into that trap," he nevertheless had to contend with people's assumptions that he was up to no good. When her son was in sixth grade, the police were investigating some robberies near the school and they pulled over her son, who was walking with a group of kids. The boys were "scared, searched, and really treated badly." She talked with her son, warning him "not to let your anger get away with you because if you act mad, they're just going to be more aggressive toward you." As a young woman growing up, she had never experienced this, but she knew that as her son grew older "and started to drive, that will happen more" and they'd have to "talk about it more."

Black parents struggled to secure their children's future in the context of declining investments in children's environments and increasing surveillance and policing of black youth. The difficulties black middle-class families faced in ensuring their children's safe and successful passage to adulthood worked to produce a sense of "linked-fate" politics in this neighborhood. The specter of black youth criminality was not confined to the flatlands and did not only affect poor kids. Black parents across class and geography had to contend with the ways this image threatened to redefine all black boys as potentially dangerous, especially as they crossed the fuzzy boundary between cute kid and teenager. Black middle-class parents had to walk a fine line, giving their children the sense of middle-class entitlement that would propel them up the class ladder, while at the same time preparing them for rituals of submission that might be required to protect their lives. Many parents, like Robert, taught their sons how to carry themselves so they would not be labeled as bad boys in school. They trained their kids how to deal with policemen when they were stopped on the street. These dilemmas of black middle-class parenting extended beyond the home to shape politics in Oakland. In the Laurel district, these concerns encouraged black middle-class parents to work alongside poor parents to make schools and the neighborhood safe and secure for all kids.

Taking Back the Schools

Robert Smith described an almost moral commitment to the public schools: "You have to take the schools back and to follow through on all the liberal rhetoric to take care of children. I ask very pointed questions to people who espouse these liberal policies to find out where's your bacon? Where's your beef?" We both laughed, and when I asked if he meant "Where are your kids?" he said, "Exactly, that's pretty much what I ask. Where do your kids go to school?" The struggles of activists in the Laurel district to "take back the schools" and to expand after-school programs for youth offer important insights into the dilemmas of activism in the context of the neoliberal volunteer state. Parents and neighborhood activists in the Laurel district worked to revitalize the public infrastructure for children with their own volunteer labor. They invested their time and skills to improve the public schools and to expand the publicly funded infrastructure for after-school programs.

Neighbors and parents in the Laurel area worked hard to fill the gaps left by increasingly insecure public investments in children's environments. Some parents volunteered daily and many others weekly at their children's schools. Robert became volunteer recreation director at the Laurel Elementary School playground simply by buying equipment. Neighbors led by Marie and Sam Thomas started Friends of Laurel School to raise money for playground equipment. Marie also combined her love of gardening and community work to organize planting trees around the cement school yard. When Pat Jackson retired from her work as a preschool teacher, she became the de facto youth coordinator for the NCPC, helping to plan new after-school programs at the public schools. Several parents in the lower hills, like Liz Stewart, joined the PTA the year *before* their child began school. They not only got to know teachers and principals but also became integrated into the daily management of the school. PTA and NCPC members spent weekends cleaning and painting school portable classrooms, created school websites, led fundraisers, and helped write grants and plan after-school enrichment programs. A "hills parent" on a local education blog explained that Oakland schools "do best when parents treat them as a co-op. . . . The demands on parents are not just for funds, but for time; time in classrooms, time for meetings, time to fight on unjust or poorly managed issues."[80] Jenny Chin explained why she volunteered her time: "This is a public school. It's free. There isn't tuition where they can spend money. That's why it's up to volunteers." Parents were optimistic that their volunteer work in the lower hills schools would produce positive results more easily than they might in flatland schools. At Laurel Elementary, Liz explained, "We don't have a horrendous battle, it's very possible. Our test scores are 50%." Unlike elementary schools further down in the flatlands, "It's not eleven hundred kids on an overcrowded campus."

Women did most (though not all) of this volunteer labor, given the long-lasting gendered division of labor that holds mothers ultimately responsible for their children's care. For this reason sociologist Sharon Hays defines the new culture of middle-class parenting as the ideology of intensive mothering.[81] Some middle-class mothers stayed home, while others took more flexible jobs, so that they could be available to help their children solve any problems that emerged in school or so they could pick up their children after school. Some working-class mothers—like Bobbie Taylor and Jean Schmidt—also took jobs in the schools or as after-school monitors so they could forge close contacts with their kids' schools. But women often found their public mothering roles constrained by their paid work, unlike women in the progressive era, who carved out a space for their participation in the public realm through their role as mothers.[82]

Parent activists insisted that you *had* to have *free time* to volunteer if you wanted to ensure your child received a good education in the Oakland public schools. Chris Quan, a parent volunteer at Skyline High School, echoed the importance of parent volunteers. "If the kid wants an education, they can get it in public school. But you have to follow up on it. You have to go to the school. You can't count on somebody else to do for it you. If you don't have the time, that's what private school's for." Margaret Duncan took her older son out of Bret Harte Middle School in the mid-1980s when she was starting a new job as a lawyer. There were problems every day at schools with students stealing, taking money, even once bringing a loaded gun to school. "I was not going to have the time to go downtown and go to school and protect my son." Later, when she changed jobs and had more time to be involved, Margaret moved her younger son from private school back to public elementary school. "I'm probably the only person in the universe to go back to public schools."

These kinds of volunteer efforts in Oakland public schools are shifting the boundaries between public and private responsibility in complex ways. They are not exactly privatizing childhood, since parents are using their private time to try to revitalize public schools and to reinvest in publicly funded after-school programs, but they are helping to blur the boundaries between public and private. When parents volunteer on a daily basis in the public schools or take jobs in the schools to be able to better monitor their kids, they reinforce the notion that public agencies are "co-ops" that legitimately depend on volunteer labor to function. As anthropologist Susan Hyatt has argued, this emphasis on volunteers facilitates a shift toward neoliberal ideas of citizenship, in which empowered citizens, not the state, take responsibility for maintaining the public sphere.[83] Volunteering may also reinforce the tendency among middle-class parents to construct a private security bubble around their own children instead of addressing the fundamental gaps in public funding and support that create the needs for volunteers in the first place.[84]

Parent volunteers were also integral to efforts to build publicly funded after-school programs in the lower hills. Liz Smith had been talking about the "need to go after grant money" to bring more resources to Laurel Elementary because the PTA had limited capacity to raise funds, but she didn't really have the time or knowledge to secure grants. A neighbor put her in touch with the Bret Harte Collaborative, which had begun planning for a Healthy Start grant with the support of a parent who worked for the school district in this program and thus had the knowledge and contacts to launch the complex process of applying for a federal grant.

The Bret Harte Collaborative is in many ways a true success story. They secured a planning grant and hired a coordinator, who built a partnership among schools, parents, and nonprofit providers in order to take advantage of the growing pool of public funding for after-school programs and school-based social services. Middle-class parents and neighbors, working alongside poor and working-class parents, used their flexible time and cultural and social capital to expand publicly funded after-school programs for children in the neighborhood. By 2001, Bret Harte Middle School had received well over five hundred thousand dollars in grants from the federal, state, and local governments, while Laurel Elementary received additional government funding. Roughly three hundred kids spent three hours every day at Bret Harte doing homework, playing sports, taking art or dance classes, and participating in nature and science programs. They sometimes even led weekend trips to ski or participate in rope courses. Nonprofits and independent contractors ran most classes and also provided family counseling. These supervised activities reduced working parents' anxieties about the dangers of "free time" and offered kids fun and challenging after-school activities.

Limitations of the Volunteer State

Efforts to rebuild public landscapes for children in Oakland also highlighted substantial limitations of the volunteer state that hampered efforts to expand public responsibility for social reproduction. Many people told me that "the Laurel was good at making noise" or "raising hell." Liz argued that to be successful in their efforts to attract public investment in children, the Laurel district had to establish clear priorities and "be vocal about it." Neoliberal models of urban governance encourage neighborhoods, individual schools, even youth programs to "organize, lobby and apply political pressure to achieve [their] goals." As anthropologist Delmos Jones argued, this model "holds out the promise of results (if a group is patient, waits its turn and plays by the rules), but fundamentally masks the conditions and constraints that ultimately determine success."[85]

Volunteer efforts were a risky strategy for ensuring equity in children's environments. Middle-class parents in Oakland's hills had more resources—time and money, as well as social and cultural capital—to invest in their children's schools than most working-class and poor parents in the flatlands. Parent volunteers and PTA members were disproportionately middle-class professionals with flexible work schedules, and mothers who worked part-time. Middle-class parents also felt more entitled to participate in the schools, to nudge their kids towards the best teachers, and to intervene to shape their children's environments.[86] Bob Yuen and his wife both had professional jobs that gave them the luxury of flexible schedules. They spent a lot of time volunteering in their kids' schools and usually could drive their kids to after-school activities. But he knew that most of his children's friends' parents, who were first-generation Chinese immigrants, did not volunteer in the same way. Working-class and many immigrant parents had less flexible work schedules, less autonomy on the job, less free time, and also felt less entitled to intervene in their children's education. Liz Walker said that people always complained that "parents didn't participate in flatland schools." But she insisted that schools rarely did extensive outreach and parents had not "necessarily been welcomed." "In the hills people know it's their right to be in the school, but a lot of people don't come from that perspective. Some just think, 'Thank God I got into [this] school.'"

Parent fundraising abilities most clearly highlighted the ways volunteer efforts could reproduce stark racial and class inequalities in children's schools. PTAs in the hills, even the lower hills, were able raise substantially more money than the schools in the flatlands. Since the schools in the hills were also smaller, that money went much farther. In 2003, Horace Mann Elementary School in the East Oakland flatlands, where 63% of students are poor, held one school fundraiser that raised $900, the equivalent of $1.77 per student. In contrast, Redwood Heights' PTA organized six to nine major fundraisers a year and raised $106,000 the same year, $380 per student, money that funded a librarian, field trips, a lunch supervisor, office equipment, and classroom grants for teachers. Stepping up even further into the hills, at Hillcrest Elementary parents raised $150,000, a total of $549 per child.[87] These parent contributions directly follow Oakland's class-segregated geography. Sociologist Allison Pugh describes these parent-raised funds as a form of "self-taxation" that "expose a weakness in concepts like 'privatization.'" Neither fully private nor fully public, these parent fundraising efforts occupy a "middle ground," similar to gated communities, where "the collectivity is so limited that the public is in effect privatized."[88] Volunteer time, likewise, concentrated resources in middle-class schools, thus reinforcing racial and class inequalities in children's educational environments.

Playgrounds developed through volunteer efforts like the one in the Laurel district similarly show how volunteer efforts can exacerbate inequalities in public investments in children's play environments. The Laurel school could rely on a vibrant commercial district, some middle-class parents, and wealthier neighbors who had committed to help the school. Friends of Laurel Elementary School raised the first eight thousand dollars for a new play structure. This private fundraising effort attracted political attention and public funding. Jean Quan, then a school board member running for city council, committed herself to raising the rest of the money needed to build two new play structures at the school. This new playground, along with murals and trees planted by volunteers, helped transform the concrete school yard. At the same time, in the Elmhurst flatlands, most children's playgrounds remained concrete yards with old play structures and faded paint marking four-square and dodge ball courts.

The story of the Bret Harte After-School Collaborative also underscores several problems with using volunteer labor to "take back the schools." Expanded state and federal funding for after-school programs, along with grants for mental health care and violence prevention, provides a false sense that there are plentiful resources available to invest in children and youth. But the competitive process of applying for grants hides several fundamental constraints. New state and federal grant programs are rarely adequate to meet the needs of all children, or even all lower-income children. They are not entitlements, but block grants or discretionary grant programs.[89] So each city, school, or nonprofit group has to apply and compete in an increasingly entrepreneurial environment for grants to provide after-school programs and children's services. Specific grants and programs also come and go, so it is difficult for cities, schools, and nonprofit youth providers to sustain investments in children's environments over time.[90] When federal Healthy Start funding ended, Bret Harte struggled to maintain the same counseling services, nonprofit partners (whom it could no longer pay), and high-quality programs that corresponded to kids' interests.[91]

The competitive grant-making process may disadvantage the poorest schools and make inequalities in children's environments worse. The social and cultural capital of Bret Harte's engaged middle-class parents helped it build one of the first and most substantial after-school programs in the city. But not all schools could draw on the flexible work schedules and grant-writing skills of professional parents. Principals in overcrowded larger schools in Oakland's flatlands, which are full of poor kids whose families struggle with a multitude of crises, spent most of their time "putting out fires," as one

Elmhurst Middle School principal told me. They had less time to apply for grants. Likewise, working-class and poor parents rarely have the time, skills, or contacts that would enable them to volunteer to write the grants themselves. These hidden constraints may explain noteworthy inequalities in the distribution of state funds. California schools with the lowest test scores got 30% less state bond money for improving school facilities than they should have because the state allocated money on a first-come, first-served basis instead of on the basis of need.[92] A 2006 study found that the East Oakland flatland schools were underserved by public after-school programs, with only 29% of funding for 40% of the Oakland public school students.[93]

The devolved and decentralized structure of the state services has shifted the boundary between public and private in other significant ways. State and local governments increasingly provide social services through block grants and nonprofit social service agencies, which have expanded rapidly since the 1970s. An Oakland directory of youth programs in 1994 listed 160 organizations and ninety additional organization sites.[94] And one study found that community-based nonprofits had launched fifty-four new youth-serving programs just in West Oakland between 2000 and 2005.[95] This growing entrepreneurial nonprofit sector provided an increasing proportion of social services in Oakland. As historian Michael Katz argues, in this increasingly devolved and decentralized state, any clear "distinction between public and private in provision of social services finally collapsed" in reality, if not in political rhetoric.[96]

Activists with INCITE! Women of Color against Violence have been more critical, labeling these partnerships the Non-Profit Industrial Complex and stressing several ways nonprofits may constrain grass-roots activism.[97] Nonprofit organizations are by law "forbidden to advocate for systemic change."[98] Facing pressures to professionalize, they often create governance structures that value the knowledge and experience of middle-class professionals more than those of poor families or kids. Public-private partnerships and the constant quest for grants also often force nonprofits to embrace narrow definitions of community problems and "program-specific categories and remedies."[99] These critiques call for a more careful look at the ways nonprofit partnerships reshape ideas of the state, concepts of citizenship, and the everyday practices of state institutions.

In Oakland, these partnerships helped redefine "good government" along market models. They consolidated a model of the state and citizens as "consumers" who shop around and "choose" the best available public-private services.[100] An evaluation of the Oakland Fund for Children and Youth (OFCY), the city's major funding source for kids, quoted extensively from city manager Robert Bobb's favorite book, *Reinventing Government: How the Entrepreneurial Spirit Is Transforming the Public Sector*. Government had to become "a skillful buyer," shopping around for the most effective and efficient service providers in order to "squeeze more bang out of every buck" and to preserve "maximum flexibility to respond to changing circumstances."[101] These flexible partnerships helped local government adapt to the reality of budget cycles that oscillated between fiscal crises and budget surpluses. They also shifted responsibility for the quality of services onto private nonprofit organizations. OFCY insisted that "trying hard is not good enough. We need to be able to show results to taxpayers and voters."[102] Even though city and state agencies rarely provided sufficient funds to cover the general operating expenses of nonprofit organizations or individual youth programs, they held nonprofits accountable for demonstrating substantial results. The Oakland city council often responded to demands for more resources for youth with arguments about the amount of grant money they already spent. They blamed nonprofits for failing to reach young people that needed services.

Nonprofit youth programs were forced to embrace a narrow and depoliticized definition of what children needed as they tried to prove their "success." The Oakland Fund for Children and Youth developed an elaborate evaluation to measure increased skills and assets of each child and to track improvements in educational levels and reductions in juvenile crime. They measured "customer satisfaction" and calculated the "cost per unit hour of services" in order to maximize results from their grants.[103] But the ways OCFY defined "success" embraced a deeply individualized model of youth development.[104] A visual representation of youth risks and resiliencies in one report portrays two young people navigating a maze of risk factors, including truancy, drugs, gangs, guns, violence, and peers (See Figure 8).

The young person with low "protective assets" gets lost in the maze and ends up at a "brick wall" representing antisocial behavior while the young person with full assets makes it quickly through the maze to the "whole world of opportunity." With enough assets provided by family, school, and community, "a youth learns to walk through the 'risk factor mine field' without stepping on the 'mines.'"[105]

Oakland parents, neighborhood activists, and nonprofits argued for state investments in building up youth assets, but in significant ways, this popular risk and resiliency model shifts accountability to individual kids. This model effectively tries to explain how one poor child growing up in a single-parent

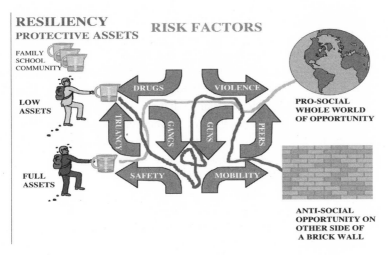

RESILIENCY
PROTECTIVE ASSETS   RISK FACTORS

FAMILY
SCHOOL
COMMUNITY

LOW
ASSETS

DRUGS   VIOLENCE

TRUANCY   GANGS   GUNS   PEERS

SAFETY   MOBILITY

FULL
ASSETS

PRO-SOCIAL
WHOLE WORLD
OF OPPORTUNITY

ANTI-SOCIAL
OPPORTUNITY ON
OTHER SIDE OF
A BRICK WALL

Figure 8. Resiliency in a maze of risks for contemporary youth.
(Image produced for Oakland Fund for Children and Youth by Peter Ellis)

household can successfully graduate high school while another drops out and turns to a life of crime. Protective factors, like relationships with caring adults or high expectations set by families, schools, and communities, can certainly help children escape poverty, violence, and crime, but focusing on how some kids "succeed against long odds" doesn't encourage children's advocates and nonprofits to try to change the odds themselves. This model completely ignores systemic structural barriers kids face and suggests that if we create enough social services to fill kids' "cups" with assets, these deep structural exclusions won't matter. Poverty, increasing economic inequality, and Oakland's racialized geographies of exclusion are not even listed as risks. Instead, they are turned into parental deficiencies, individual educational failures, peer influences, and "crime in neighborhood." This focus on youth assets reaffirms the "unbridled valorization of individual agency" characteristic of neoliberalism.[106] Ultimately youth must negotiate the maze of risks alone.

After-school providers had to tailor their goals and programs to meet constantly shifting funding priorities, as they chased grants for education, crime or violence prevention, and obesity or pregnancy prevention. When the Department of Education began to supervise expanded funding under California Proposition 49, nonprofit providers faced new pressures to help schools meet strictly educational goals.[107] The Bret Harte program had to focus more on "academic interventions," but the coordinator explained that doing so left them struggling to hold onto the "higher-risk kids," who generally felt alienated from school and thought, "I'm not having a good time in the first place. Why should I come back here and do more?" Indeed, Garey argues that advocates in California often focused on education and crime in ways that marginalized, even undercut, claims that children had a right to care.[108] Framing after-school programs as "crime prevention programs," while politically strategic in the context of broad fears of crime, also reified the already powerful idea that youth were dangerous. These fears of youth repeatedly got in the way of efforts to shift state spending patterns away from policing and incarceration, priorities that helped to produce the consistent crisis in funding for children's education and care in California in the first place.

More problematic, advocates for after-school programs failed to confront California's overall structural deficit, which was created by politicians and voters who often voted for expanded public services but resisted *any* tax increases that might pay for them. This structural deficit meant that expanding after-school programs often came at the expense of education or other core funding for children and families. While California funding for after-school programs increased from $200 to $750 million between 1996 and 2003, welfare spending for families declined by more than one-third, and funding for childcare programs increased modestly or stayed flat.[109] Neoliberal welfare policies often shift funding in this way from income or housing supports to professionally provided services. These policies rely on moralizing distinctions between the virtuous and the undeserving poor. They reframe poor kids and families as clients, not citizens, and have the bizarre consequence of exacerbating the crises of low-income families and then funding youth development and social service agencies to pick up the pieces. The structural deficit also created an endless cycle of feast and famine for California's children as funding for public schools, children's health care, and social services for families would increase slightly in an economic boom, only to be slashed again when the bust came.

Oakland kids, especially poor kids, needed more than after-school programs. They needed stable housing, parents with jobs that paid a living wage, health care, schools that challenged and encouraged all children, and neighborhoods that were caring, not frightening places. After-school programs are great, but not if policy makers have to choose between them and giving children health care, paying teachers, or creating tax and welfare policies (like expanded low-income tax credits) that would reduce the number of families and kids in poverty.

Conclusion

Geographer Cindi Katz has argued that in the current global economy, state commitments to children (in the form of adequate education, housing, health care, and income supports) have become voluntary, neither the entitlements of citizenship nor the responsibilities of the nation.[110] The way parents and activists respond to these deep changes in the political economy of youth has the potential to reshape politics at the local and national levels. If parents rely on private strategies, like buying homes in the right school district, keeping kids inside, retreating to private schools and recreation centers, it will be very hard to build a unified movement to reinvest in all of our children. Activism in the Laurel district offered hints of an alternate and more progressive politics of childhood. Black, white, and Asian parent activists did not work only to ensure their own children's safe passage through school system, into college, and into the professional middle class. They also used their volunteer labor to campaign for expanded public responsibility for social reproduction. Given the pervasive racial and class segregation in children's environments, volunteering in our own kids' schools and neighborhoods is not enough. But if middle-class parents join with working-class and poor parents, as they did in the Laurel district, there is at least some hope that we can to reconstruct the public supports that can sustain a democratized childhood and adolescence.

After-school programs provided a focus for local activist demands that Oakland reinvest in children. But new after-school policy networks, nonprofit providers, and funding streams also helped to shape their understanding about the kinds of care and support children need. They consolidated the emerging idea that what kids needed most was more structure, supervision, and education in the after-school hours. Professional parents and neighborhood activists used their own flexible work schedules to reshape the ways kids used time so that their kids and other people's kids would be prepared to compete in a new economy. They brought middle-class structured time to poor kids, which would help some of these kids build the skills and capacities to pull their way up the class ladder. These new networks helped to extend state responsibility for children into the after-school hours but also simultaneously limited local activists' visions of (and demands on) the state.

Efforts to expand public responsibility for children and youth were constrained in significant ways by the devolved and decentralized structure of local government. The investments Laurel activists fought for in schools and after-school programs remained vulnerable, dependent on securing competitive grants and the substantial investment of volunteer time by parents. As long as state funding relies on the entrepreneurial efforts of neighborhoods and nonprofits, the infrastructure for America's youth will not develop equally. Fundamentally these local endeavors, like too many children, are left to succeed or fail on their own. In 2003, as another budget crisis washed across Oakland, I talked to Pat Jackson in World Ground café. She was worried that the budget for the Bret Harte Collaborative would be cut, and she said that they would just have to rely on volunteers to make up the difference. Already the YMCA, one of their core partners, had to cut a quarter of its staff and issued an open call in the *Oakland Tribune* for volunteers to become mentors, tutors, and coaches in their after-school programs.[111] Volunteers could temporarily mask, but not solve, the fundamental crises of care and the structural deficits that destabilized efforts to reconstruct children's environments in Oakland. Volunteer time would not be enough to reconstruct public schools for Oakland's children.

This new fiscal crisis and the state takeover of Oakland public schools threatened to undo much of the work Liz and Robert and other parent volunteers had put into the elementary school. Oakland public schools had tried to increase teacher pay and invest in school infrastructure, but declining enrollments and budget cuts during the recession of 2002-2004 had plunged the school district into a $50 million shortfall. In March 2003, the Oakland Unified School District sent layoff notices to seven hundred staff, including over four hundred teachers and counselors.[112] The schools again faced cuts in art and music programs, teacher layoffs, expansion of class sizes, and cuts in after-school programs that threatened much of progress parent activists had made in the Laurel district. Just as disturbing for Liz and Darryl, two new dynamic young African American male teachers at Laurel Elementary had received layoff notices. They had looked forward to their son having a black male teacher as a role model and thought their close relationship with the school administration would have secured him a place in one of their classes. With the imminent departure of these teachers and the chaos created by another round of budget cuts, Robert and Liz decided to pull their son out of the public schools, only two years after he had begun. The next year, he would attend the same small private school where Sandra Collins sent her son. Although Robert and Liz believed this was the right decision for their son, Liz felt guilty to be leaving behind their friends at Laurel Elementary School. She knew that Tanesha, Bobbie, and Jean could not afford to flee the public schools even if they could get the partial scholarships available at some private schools. The fragile coalition of parents, renters, and homeowners that they had built in order to bring new resources to the public schools and build after-school programs would not last. Soon Tanesha would grow frustrated with the NCPC's focus on cosmetic changes and its failure to really change things for kids in the neighborhood. She stopped attending the meetings, and few middle-class parents followed in Liz and Robert's efforts to use the NCPC as part of a broader effort to transform the schools.

Protecting Children in the Hills

In January 2001, a white man in a Rolls Royce was driving up the tree-lined street to his home in the Oakland hills when he saw some young people spray-painting a sign for Skyline High School. They were students painting a new sign as part of a school project, but that is not what he saw. Primed with mass-mediated images of "youth criminality," he saw a group of young people wearing hoodies and baggy pants, holding spray paint, and he immediately assumed they were vandals. He stopped his car and threatened them with a gun before driving off.

A few weeks later I sat with Dr. James Smith and his wife, Loraine, talking about the joys and struggles of raising three black boys and one girl in the Oakland hills, including one son who was then a junior at Skyline High School. Though the incident at Skyline was very unusual, for the Smiths it highlighted a much more common problem. "As minorities in the hills," Loraine explained, they often heard the question, "Where do you live?" at PTA meetings or community meetings. If they had to deal with that as parents, Loraine wondered, "imagine what our children are facing, when our children walk to school. That was our concern about the gentleman with the gun."

The Smiths lived in a beautiful home perched on the side of the steep hills below Skyline High School with wood decks and an indoor pool with windows that offered stunning views of the bay. Because of all the negative stories they had read in the newspapers, they initially "did not want to live in Oakland" when Dr. Smith joined a surgery practice in the East Bay. But as their realtor drove them down Highway 13 through the Oakland hills, they saw that Oakland was "a beautiful, incredible, wonderful city."

The Smiths led very active political lives fighting to improve Oakland public schools. Dr. Smith, a tall, scholarly-looking man with small, round glasses, worked in a surgery practice in a nearby suburb. He had grown up in Detroit during the tumultuous 1960s, "right down the street from where the riots started." His mother was a teacher and his father was a dentist. They had not been particularly engaged in civil rights struggles, but he began to read radi-

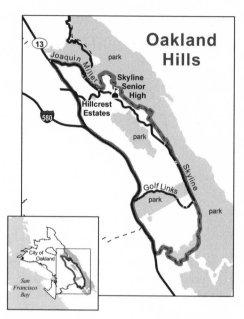

Figure 9. Map of Oakland Hills: The bucolic ideal around Skyline High School. (Mark Kumler and Diana Sinton, University of Redlands)

cal papers, and that activist consciousness "just kind of stuck." For Loraine Smith, parent activism was basically a full-time job. She grew up in rural Mississippi, where her mother was a teacher and her father a principal active in civil rights struggles, so she had "always been involved" in her children's education. She participated in the PTA, volunteered regularly at Skyline High School, and worked with an African American women's club to encourage black students to pursue higher education in the health professions.

The more involved Mrs. Smith became with the public schools, the more she saw the struggles of black students, who were rarely in AP or gifted classes but were disproportionately suspended or expelled. Too often Oakland public schools were "dream killers." Teachers had low expectations, and most kids would "live right down to those expectations." She helped found the African American Education Task Force and became president of Concerned Parents of African American Students at Skyline High School.

Dr. Smith worried that Oakland Public Schools only made the divisions between the haves and the have-nots worse in an information economy where education was so important. Kids coming through overcrowded elementary schools in the flatlands have "fewer resources, more uncredentialed teachers, poorer physical plants." Yet when kids from these flatland schools arrived up at Skyline, people compared them to kids educated in the hills and wondered, "Why they aren't prepared?" "People are becoming now more of a permanent underclass. The walls are growing even larger."

Dr. and Mrs. Smith instilled high expectations in their children. Their eldest son was already away at college, and the others would soon follow. "If they don't get their education, they won't be able to go anywhere." They fought against rampant materialism, refusing to buy their kids brand-name clothes so they would remember not to get focused on possessions. And they shared with their sons the importance of a broader engagement in Oakland's black community and a responsibility "to try to bring along others to also succeed."

During our conversations they repeatedly returned to their efforts to prepare and to protect their sons from the stereotype of black youth criminality that endangered black boys across class lines in Oakland. Mrs. Smith discouraged her kids from wearing baggy pants. "Pull them up. It's a little more respectful." When she took her eldest son shopping, she instructed him, "'Have your money in your hands. Put what you're going to buy in your hands. Don't wear any long coat.' By the time I finished, he said, 'I don't want to go.' We have to train our boys . . . that somebody is going to think they're potential criminals. That's very difficult. Most of the time we just tell them to stay home."

The Smiths had built a pool and installed a pool table to create a safe and comfortable place for their kids to hang out with friends. When their eldest son was a teenager in the mid-1990s, they thought conditions were even worse than today, "the way that they were going after black males at that time. . . . We just wanted him home. I just wanted him where I could see him. He always tells us, 'Guys, you never let me go to anything.' That's true. We wouldn't."

But the incident at Skyline High School was a painful reminder that some neighbors in the Oakland hills interpreted the presence of black youth on the street in the hills as a problem and a sign of criminal intent. Dr. Smith's son was standing out "right in front of his own house" one day with a couple of his friends, when some police offers asked to see his ID. He reached in his pocket for his wallet, saying, "Wait, Wait." Afterwards, Mrs. Smith told him, "You could be shot. Never make any sudden moves. I don't care how much money you have, how much money your parents have and how you look, you are going to be pulled over. You have to watch yourself." She explained, "Every parent we know says the same thing."

The Smiths were incensed when they attended their first Skyline Task Force meeting and heard a neighbor propose "to build a wall, a concrete wall" around the school. Mrs. Smith thought their "primary issue" was how they could make the school "more prison-like." When she visited the Laurel Neighborhood Crime Prevention Council, she was surprised to see how different it seemed from neighborhood activism around Skyline. "They were talking about the grants they had gotten for the school."

The Smiths insisted they were never afraid of kids. The problems at the high school were "normal teenage stuff." "I would walk up to any kid at Skyline," Loraine Smith explained. "First I always look them in the eye and say, 'how are you doing? By my watch you were supposed to be in class.'" Then she'd take them by the arm and lead them to class. "They are so used to people not looking at them and being invisible." Dr. Smith was once installing computer equipment in a classroom full of kids with disciplinary problems at Skyline. "These kids who were such troublemakers were also respectful and wanted to learn about these computers. If you gave them the impression that you cared about their well-being, they were fine. Keep remembering that these are still children. They aren't even eighteen yet. You can't just throw them away." Mrs. Smith explained that because many kids feel as though everyone sees them as trouble, they start to withdraw from adults. "We have to own the kids."

Youth in a "Private Estate" in the Oakland Hills

In January 2001, five high school students came to the monthly Skyline Task Force meeting to present their idea for creating a Youth Center at Skyline High School. Youth Together, a multiracial youth leadership and organizing group, had been organizing high school students to prevent youth violence, especially interracial violence in the public schools. Luis, a junior and long-time youth organizer, explained that the Youth Center would increase the number of students in AP classes, offer tutoring, and provide health services and counseling. He carefully argued that the center would benefit the neighborhood as well as the school. By providing supervised activities for students, the Youth Center would raise student self-esteem, improve behavior, and build a "sense of responsibility to the community." When the students finished their brief presentation, neighbors peppered them with questions. "What hours would it operate?" "How many days would it be open?" "How late?" "Where would it be located?"

Neighbors worried that the Youth Center would draw more youth to the Skyline campus, keep them in the area longer, and increase security problems. As one neighbor insisted, "This may just give them more time to be up here and make a mess. At least now they leave at four o' clock." At Task Force meetings, neighbors regularly complained about students littering at the bus stops, fighting in the streets, and "invading" the neighborhood by walking down private streets or coming onto private property. They blamed Skyline High School students for any theft or vandalism in the neighborhood. Students invited Task Force members to participate in a meeting to develop a plan for the Youth Center, but one neighbor said, "If you want my input now, it needs to be put in a location to have minimal impact, as far as possible away from neighbors."

Nate Miley, then a city council member and later a county supervisor, convened the Skyline Task Force in 1997 to bring city and county agencies together to solve the wide range of problems that neighbors identified as coming from Skyline High School. Over the next three years, the Task Force worked to improve security around the school, to discourage students and parents from using the neighborhood's private streets, and to improve bus service and food at the school. But many students and parents remained skeptical of neighbors' interest in meeting student needs. One Youth Together member thought neighbors were only interested in keeping youth on campus and off their private roads, remarking, "They don't like us."

The Task Force met monthly in the school library, with Nate Miley's staff facilitating, and often included Oakland school police officers, security guards, school representatives, Alameda County Transit officials, or sheriffs (responsible for bus security). Task Force meetings were usually small gatherings of eight to ten adults, though sometimes a conflict would swell the numbers to twenty or thirty. I was first invited to the meetings by a white couple whose son was a junior and who described the meetings as "better than a movie." The Task Force meetings were animated, often rippling with tension between people who introduced themselves as "neighbors" and those who introduced themselves as "parents" or "parent advocates" as well as "neighbors." Those who identified themselves as "neighbors" were all middle-aged or older and white, while "parents" included white, Asian, and black parents, including the Smiths. "Parents" and "neighbors" sat at different small tables scattered around the library, though Theresa Thomas, one of the "neighbors," told me that at the next meeting she might "sit on the parents' side. . . . I think it will really shake them up. It will make some uncomfortable if they have one of the homeowners just plop myself down at their table."

Youth Together and the Task Force continued to meet, to plan, and to fight over the next five months about where the Youth Center would be built, what hours it would have, and what programs it would offer. People sent a flurry of emails and arranged meetings with the superintendent of schools, school board members, and Supervisor Nate Miley. Youth Together staff reported that one neighbor had called the major foundation funding the Youth Center to complain and put their grant at risk. Supervisor Nate Miley reassured worried neighbors that the center would focus on making kids into "better students and members of society as opposed to providing a place to hang out, have dances, play sports and billiards." But his emphasis on reforming kids reinforced some neighbors' fears that it would be a place for "problem kids." One white neighbor said that when she first heard about the Youth Center at her homeowners' association, "It sounded like they were going to have a mental ward up there."

At a May 2001 Task Force meeting, some of the percolating tensions came to a boil. After ongoing complaints about the proposed Youth Center location, Dr. Smith responded in frustration,

> We've been dealing with this for three years. Some things have to be said. They're talking about ways to hide them. They are our kids, not outside kids. This isn't the juvenile authority. This isn't Santa Rita [the county jail]. These are *our* kids. Youth Together has bent over backwards to accommodate you people. The consultants said this was the most cost-effective place to put it.

A few moments later, Joan Nelson, a white "neighbor," objected to Dr. Smith's characterization: "It was wrong and provocative to say that we think students at Skyline should not be seen. I state that for the record. It is upsetting to have statements like that made." Mrs. Smith responded, "Certain behavior generates certain perceptions," and added that she was "from the city where the KKK burned the most crosses on people's lawns" so she knew what she was talking about.

The Skyline Task Force meetings were often tense and explicitly racially charged. Parents who attended Task Force meetings complained that "neighbors" described Skyline students as criminals, not as children, while white "neighbors" complained that they couldn't talk about their concerns without being labeled racists. These conflicts enacted fundamental debates about the meaning of race, class, and generation in post–civil rights America. On a daily basis, neighbors, parents, and youth confronted the glaring inequalities in Oakland's schools and neighborhoods, divides that were racialized yet not reducible to race. But they offered competing explanations for Oakland's unequal childhoods and constructed divergent politics of youth.

The history of Skyline High School shaped the politics of childhood in this neighborhood and made conflicts in the Task Force particularly racially charged. Today Skyline High School is a predominantly black and Asian school located in one of the city's wealthiest neighborhoods, but in the 1960s and '70s, Skyline was a white school in an all-white neighborhood, a symbol of the "de facto" segregation that characterized many northern and western cities.[1] The contested history of Skyline's integration and white flight from the public schools produced deep divides between this school and its neighbors.

Conflicts around Skyline High School show how white, middle-class retreat from public institutions often stands in the way of creating a progressive politics of childhood. Neighbors around Skyline High School lived on private streets, rarely sent their children to public schools, and expected to be able to retreat from the city and "its problems" to their peaceful private neighborhood. Retreating to their private estates, neighbors drew very different boundaries of political community than we saw in Elmhurst or the Laurel district. They rarely defined the kids at Skyline as "their kids." Instead, they framed Skyline students as outsiders in the hills, as kids from Oakland's flatlands who threatened to bring the problems of the flatlands with them into the hills. These defensive definitions of community posed real dangers to Skyline students. Drawing on stereotypes of flatland youth as criminal, "neighbors" demanded more policing and surveillance of young people and embraced the use of zero tolerance policies to exclude the "bad kids" from the school and neighborhood.

Politics in this neighborhood offers a clear case of what sociologist Eduardo Bonilla-Silva has called *Racism without Racists*.[2] Most of the hills' white neighbors embraced a strict color-blind liberalism. They actively resisted any talk about race, speaking instead in terms of generation, class, or culture. They saw their own success and the rise of many black families into the middle class as proof that there was equal opportunity in the post–civil rights era and as disqualifying claims that race still mattered. They framed the existing inequalities between the hills and flatlands as natural, as "just the way it is." And they insisted that cultural differences explained ongoing racial disparities between the hills and the flatlands.[3] But this color-blind ideology left many white neighbors blind to the ways racial inequalities had been built into Oakland's class structure, schools, and neighborhoods and the ways state institutions like schools served to reproduce those inequalities.

White neighbors' color-blind commitments led some of them to rewrite the history of Oakland's public schools and the history of the city itself. They blamed black activists and politicians for making race matter and argued that flatland youth and their faulty families were responsible for the poor state of the city's public schools. Similar narratives have had wide-reaching effects on public policy in California. They have helped produce and justify a broad public abandonment of schools in California and have made existing racial inequalities seem like the natural products of individual effort and family choices. Politics in this neighborhood shows how the stories we tell about children can shrink public responsibility for social reproduction.

Parent advocates, like the Smiths, created an alternate politics of childhood that built on a long tradition of black parent activism. They challenged the color-blind ideology of white neighbors because the image of "bad kids" remained a racial image that posed a threat to their children both in school and on the streets of the hills. Parent advocates at Skyline High School demanded that we claim all of Oakland's public school kids as "our kids" and fought against the exclusion of black boys from the protections of childhood. This was a necessary precursor for their fight to make equal access to educational opportunities a reality.

A Bastion of Bigotry

Perched on the top of Skyline Boulevard, overlooking a canyon towards the east, Skyline High School looks more like a typical suburban California campus than like most Oakland high schools—typically three-story blocks surrounded by concrete yards and worn grass fields. The school sprawls over forty acres of land with long, one-story buildings connected by outdoor walkways and small courtyards. Wooded paths covered in pine needles lead down to football fields and worn tennis courts.

A chain-link fence separates the sprawling school complex from the neighborhood, but many neighbors thought that this fence was not high enough or strong enough to protect them from the high school. Lax security allowed students and outside visitors to come on and off campus at will. Neighbors were shocked by boisterous and sometimes disruptive student behavior, which the school and police could not seem to control. Their complaints were not so different from those in other neighborhoods. But the history of Skyline High School made the politics of childhood in this neighborhood very different from elsewhere in Oakland.

Skyline High School was built as a white-flight school. It was developed in 1961 to relieve overcrowding as baby boomers moved into their teenage years, and white hills residents successfully lobbied to locate it in the rapidly developing hills instead of the Central East Oakland flatlands.[4] In a radical shift from precedent, Skyline's attendance boundaries were drawn so that they included *only* hills communities, unlike all existing high schools, whose boundaries cut across the city to include the flatlands and hills. Skyline's boundaries stretched one mile wide for ten miles along the top of the hills and effectively created a white, wealthy school in Oakland just as upwardly mobile black homeowners moved east and integrated neighborhoods like Elmhurst (See Figure 10).

In the 1960s, Oakland public schools found themselves at the center of white resistance to integration and of Oakland's black civil rights movement.[5] Married couples with children formed the vast majority of white residents fleeing the flatlands. Historian Robert Self suggests that their "experience of

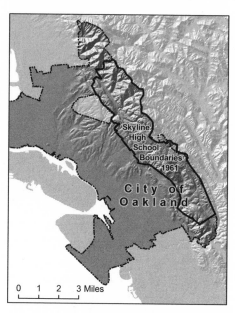

Figure 10. Building a school for the hills: Skyline High school boundaries, 1961. (Mark Kumler and Diana Sinton, University of Redlands)

desegregation was mediated by children and the social spaces of childhood: schools and recreation centers." One East Oakland resident told a University of California interviewer, "I wouldn't think of sending my kids to Castlemont H.S. There are too many colored."[6] Into the mid-1970s, Skyline High School served as a retreat for white families fleeing racial change in the flatlands.

Skyline High School became an important symbol for the movement to desegregate Oakland public schools in the early 1960s. The NAACP and Donald McCullum called Skyline the "bastion of bigotry" and led the charge against this "private prep school paid for by public funds."[7] In May of 1964, Skyline finally admitted two hundred students from other areas of the city through open enrollment, but the stated impetus was overcrowded schools and allowing "parents more free choice," not achieving racial integration.[8] Some charged that this limited open enrollment actually exacerbated problems of segregation as white parents in the flatlands transferred their students to Skyline and quickly fled schools like Castlemont High.[9] Further efforts to change the boundaries of Skyline to promote integration were actively resisted by some Skyline parents.[10] In January 1965, under significant public pressure by state education officials, the NAACP, and Oakland Federation of Teachers, the school board implemented a plan to allow unlimited open enrollment for Skyline High School specifically for students from three predominantly African American middle schools in West and East Oakland. However, the school board did not actively recruit students from these middle schools and the same year cut subsidies for Skyline transportation.[11]

Tensions remained high between Skyline students and students from flatland schools in the late sixties and early seventies, often erupting in racial fights at sports games. Several current white participants of the Task Force remembered their children getting beaten up when Skyline High School teams went to play at other schools in Oakland. One article about a fight between Skyline and Castlemont students at a basketball game in 1969 quoted a student from the flatlands saying that after seeing the facility at Skyline, "I'll be frank about this. I was bitter. Skyline gets better books, and it really looks more like Orinda [a wealthy suburb]." Robert Pritchard, a teacher who sat with Castlemont students at the game, said that he began to feel excluded himself from "that beautiful school sitting up there on a hill." He saw in the faces of Castlemont students "expressions of intense hatred and envy that transcended the circumstances of losing only a football game." He recommended that Skyline drop out of the Oakland public school league and play with private schools until "we solve the problem of racial and class hatred in this city and country."[12]

Skyline became more integrated as white parents began to flee the public school system, as more students took advantage of open enrollment, and as a growing black middle class moved into the East Oakland hills. In 1970 Skyline was 20% minority, but only three years later had increased to 35% minority. This process of integration was not without tension. There were racial fights or "riots" in 1976, when black students tried to stop white students who had organized a walk-out to protest an optional assembly for Black Appreciation Day.[13]

The story of Skyline High School's integration highlights a small piece of the long history of black parent activism to expand educational access and equality for black children. In the 1950s and early '60s, black parents focused on integrating public schools, as many bought homes in formerly white neighborhoods, joined PTAs, and advocated for their children's equal education in small-scale battles in individual schools. By the mid-sixties, black educational activists no longer focused on desegregation, which rapid white flight had made irrelevant in most Oakland neighborhoods. Many began to criticize the underlying logic of desegregation efforts, which often reproduced assumptions of black inferiority and white supremacy.[14] Instead, activists focused on quality education, community control, and equity among Oakland schools. Skyline remained an important symbol in this campaign for equity as well, as black community activists continued to complain that "all the money for quality education is being spent in the hills."[15]

Political mobilizations in the 1960s and '70s helped make the hills and flatlands a potent and lasting metaphor for Oakland's racial and class divides. The hills remained the bastion of Oakland's white Republican political regime, which retained power through the late seventies. Black political activists targeted the hills as symbols of Oakland's white power structure as they demanded increased investments in Oakland's flatlands. The black political regime that came to power in the seventies and eighties helped redefine the flatlands as the center of a new political community, as the heartland of the city.[16] Decades later this history continued to shape the ways community activists in the hills and flatlands framed their political identities and interests.

In 2000, the hills remained a central metaphor for the white upper class of the city, despite the emergence of a significant upper-middle-class black and Asian population. One city staff person explained the divide between the perception of the hills and its new reality. "They are rich and you don't have to be white to be rich these days." He described the Campus Drive area below Skyline High School as one of "the most ethnically diverse in the entire city." But he added, "It's been a common Oakland theme that there are white rich people up in the hills. That's the perception. . . . The other perception of the hills is they are racists or they are very culturally insensitive."

The neighborhood around Skyline High School remained significantly whiter and richer than Oakland but was far from a white enclave. Census tracts around Skyline High School varied between 50 and 70% white, 12 and 45% black, and 5 and 15% Asian, with very small Latino populations. Most of the private roads directly off Skyline Boulevard in the Hillcrest Estates had larger white populations, while areas farther off Skyline Boulevard and farther east had significantly higher African American populations.[17] Persistent racial gaps in wealth influenced these subtle racial patterns in housing, even within the hills. Since white, upper-income families have on average three times the wealth of black families in the United States, white families were more likely to be able to afford the larger properties in Hillcrest estates.[18]

This hills-flatlands divide continued to structure Oakland politics at the turn of the twenty-first century. In the 1998 election, in District 6, which includes Skyline High School and cuts straight across the hills and flatlands in Central East Oakland, incumbent city council member Nate Miley won every precinct below the 580 freeway and lost every precinct above it.[19] A political staff person told me that one white woman in the hills explained, "We just thought Nate was another one of those Lionel Wilson, had been in power for thirty years, African-Americans from the flats who doesn't care about us up here. We had Elihu Harris and before that we had Lionel Wilson and they ignored us up in the hills." The staff person first thought this comment was racist, and then realized it might have been true. Residents in the hills often complained that their issues were ignored as politicians focused on the more visible problems of the flatlands, and a frequent refrain of flatland activists was that the city would have addressed their problems much more quickly if they lived in the hills. Nate Miley's careful attention to the concerns of hills residents, in venues like the Skyline Task Force, helped him to overcome his earlier lackluster performance in the hills to win election as county supervisor in 2000.

By the end of the twentieth century, Skyline High School was a majority black, Asian, and Latino school in a wealthy, though no longer entirely white, neighborhood. White flight from the public schools accelerated so that 44% of white families in Oakland sent their kids to private schools compared to 11% of black families and 9% of Asian families.[20] Skyline High School's student population in 2000 was 47% African American, 25% Asian, 15% Latino, 1% Pacific Islander, and only 12% white.[21] But gaining access to Skyline High School was no panacea for black children. Skyline remained deeply internally divided by race, and black student achievement lagged far behind that of white and Asian students. In 1994 only 15% of blacks were tracked into AP and honors classes compared to 85% of whites and Asians.[22] And there were still racial tensions among students, but not always along black-white lines. Fights between Asian and black students in 1999 helped propel Youth Together to expand antiviolence efforts at the school.

The history of this school and neighborhood made the politics of youth in this neighborhood particularly racially charged. Whenever white neighbors complained about the school and its students, black parents and school officials interpreted their fears as part of the longer history of white opposition to Skyline's integration. School officials often resisted simple requests from white "neighbors" and denied their claims that students posed any danger to the surrounding community. Sometimes the school's resistance was standard-issue bureaucratic inertia, common throughout the city, but school officials, especially black school officials, also harbored deep suspicions that white neighbors were racially motivated and responded with passionate defenses of the innocence of Skyline students. White neighbors often interpreted this bureaucratic resistance through a racial lens as well, as evidence that Oakland's black urban regime was once again ignoring the needs of their hills community. This divide between the school and "neighbors" in the Skyline Task Force was exacerbated by the narrow ways white neighbors in the Skyline Task Force drew the boundaries of their political community.

Defending Hillcrest Estate's Bucolic Ideal

Early every weekday morning, Alameda County (AC) Transit buses stream from all over Oakland toward the Central East Oakland hills to bring students to class at Skyline High School. As buses drive up the hill on 35th Avenue past the Laurel district, modest one-story bungalow homes almost imperceptibly sprout second floors and yards grow to fill larger lots. The names of Oakland's main boulevards change as one goes up the hill. Thirty-fifth Avenue becomes Redwood Road, and these name changes create another marker of the fluid yet real boundaries between the hills and the flatlands. Across Highway 13, up a long, steep hill, rows of houses, yards, and sidewalks no longer line the major road but instead newer, suburban-style developments of large, single-family homes or condominiums cluster along private roads or circular courts, sometimes hidden behind gates or nestled into the hillside. As buses turn onto Skyline Boulevard, they drive through an almost rural landscape where tall pine trees grow in a wide center divide. The road is lit at night only by small lights built into the pavement. The lights of the entire Bay Area spread like a blanket below the hills.

Theresa Thomas lived quite close to the high school, in a rambling house with extensive gardens that extended over an acre lot. As we sat at her kitchen table, she explained why she loved her neighborhood and didn't want to sell her home despite the problems she had with students on her property. She described the neighborhood as "the last stronghold of the estates," a realm of privacy, with homes painted so that they faded into the trees, surrounded by horse stables, deer, foxes, squirrels, hawks, and hummingbirds. "People love the area because of the trees. I'm not particularly a tree hugger, but . . . because of the trees, we have a lot of good air. That benefits the whole community." Gesturing down to the flatlands, she added in playful tone, "We have plants cleaning the air for you folks."

The housing development immediately around Skyline High School is quite distinctive. Opened to development in 1948, Hillcrest Estates includes a series of private roads along a ridge of the Central East Oakland hills.[23] An active homeowners' association protected this distinctive identity in the

1990s by creating a new building code designation that prohibited any house in the neighborhood being sold on less than one acre. With this new regulation, few streetlights, and no sidewalks, neighbors fought to keep the private "estate" atmosphere that Theresa described and that another neighbor defined as "affluent country living." Most neighbors drive on and off the hill except when walking their dogs along the dirt path along Skyline Boulevard or in the many nearby parks. Many streets are private and prohibit nonresidents from walking or parking in the neighborhood.

Oakland hills' private rural estate atmosphere was created by a series of public investments throughout the twentieth century. Skyline Boulevard and Hillcrest Estates lie just adjacent to thousands of acres of wilderness parklands that run along the entire ridge of the Oakland hills, with miles of hiking and horseback trails, lakes, and golf courses, most of which are owned and maintained by the East Bay Regional Park district. The first parks were developed by the Works Progress Administration in the 1930s, and over the years ballot initiatives have helped the city of Oakland and the East Bay Regional Park district develop additional wilderness areas and parks. Much of this investment went into more park space in the hills instead of the flatlands, both because the hills had undeveloped space and because Oakland's white Republican political elite prioritized the needs of Oakland's white hills homeowners who were fleeing the rapidly integrating East Oakland flatlands. The city built two new golf courses in the hills in the sixties and seventies, even as kids in Oakland's flatlands struggled to find enough parks to play in.[24] Near Skyline High School, residents can walk in a small redwood forest, explore thirty-eight miles of trails, fish in a lake, and swim in a public heated swimming pool.[25]

Theresa loved her house and the woodsy atmosphere of the neighborhood, but she frequently complained about how Skyline students at the bus stop near her house threatened her home's bucolic ideal. She told me stories of catching kids going into her garage, trying to steal things, setting fires on her property, and smoking pot in her yard. Frequently in our interviews she teased me for being naïve and not recognizing the dangers coming from students. She told me about a young man who had once threatened her with a gun when she asked him to leave her driveway, where she thought he was dealing drugs. He pulled back his jacket and showed her that he had a gun and said, "You are telling me you want me to move?" She asked him again to "please get off my property and walked off to the house, a nervous wreck. I could have been dead right there." I asked if she filed charges, but she said, "Girl, get a grip. I would have to identify him and his little gang. We are unprotected most of the time from any kind of retribution." Theresa had tried to hire a security agency, but insisted that they had quit out of fear of the students. She thought the police were "scared shitless."

Theresa Thomas recently built an eight-foot-tall cyclone fence around her property so that she wouldn't feel scared on her own property, but students had already damaged the fence several times. She wished she could have built a fence with "steel bars close together, fifteen to twenty feet high, covered with barbed wire." In community meetings talk about disrespectful youth, vandalism, and crime multiplied and intensified fears of Skyline students and extended these fears to many hills homeowners who rarely interacted with students.[26] Neighbors described littering and loitering as crimes or even, in a post–9-11 moment, as "terrorism," blurring these mundane concerns with fears of student fights and much rarer threatening encounters.

Hillcrest Estates and Theresa Thomas's cyclone fence represent an extreme example of a much broader middle-class retreat from public institutions and spaces in many cities. As documented by anthropologists Theresa Caldeira in Brazil and Setha Low in the United States, fears of crime and deepening economic inequalities have led many upper-middle-class homeowners to build symbolic walls and real gates around increasingly privatized communities.[27] Hillcrest Estates homeowners expected to be able to retreat to the peace and quiet of their wealthy neighborhood, far above the crime-ridden and disorderly flatlands, and they defended this bucolic ideal against any threat, whether from real estate developers or from high school students roaming through their private streets.

Skyline Task Force meetings often began with introductions that ritually enacted a clear divide between "neighbors" and "parents" and highlighted the narrow political boundaries many "neighbors" drew around their private estate in the hills. At one Skyline meeting during the months of debate about the Youth Center, Shirley Casey, a Skyline Task Force regular, introduced herself as a "parent" and a "neighbor." Joan Nelson asked Shirley, "Where do you live?" in a challenging tone, with a veneer of aimless curiosity. When Shirley responded, "In the area," Joan asked again, "Where in the area?" Shirley responded, using the city's community policing beat boundaries, "In the area, in Beat 25 Y." This interaction was formally cordial and polite, with both women wearing forced smiles and speaking in tense, honeyed voices, but Joan's persistent questioning suggested that Joan didn't consider Shirley a "real" neighbor and reinforced a clear distinction between neighbors and parents.

Theresa, Joan, and Bob Peterson all regularly attended meetings and described themselves as "neighbors." They served as conduits of information (and sometimes mobilization) to a broader network of hills residents organized through the Hillcrest Estates homeowners' association and NCPC. Their participation in the Hillcrest Estates homeowners' association encouraged some Task Force members to define their "neighborhood" primarily by its boundaries and "estates" identity—narrow boundaries that excluded many other hills residents, like Shirley and the Smiths, who lived in other nearby developments. At one meeting Joan made clear the narrow boundaries she drew around her community, saying, "by 'community' I mean neighbors, not the school community."

Like the Smiths, Shirley had two children at Skyline, spent an enormous amount of time at the school, and spoke as a forceful advocate for students, particularly black students. Shirley had curly blond hair and clearly confused "the neighbors." One older white neighbor guessed she was "a guilty white liberal." Shirley grew up in the Oakland flatlands, sometimes spoke with slight inflections of Oakland's working-class streets, and had married her childhood sweetheart, an African American man. Shirley explained that sometimes people couldn't place her race and so asked her, "What are you?" She would answer, "Today Hispanic. Ask me tomorrow, it will be my Asian day." Shirley's playful comments point to the fluidity of racial identification in Oakland, where families and individuals often crossed racial lines and thwarted simple equations of politics and identity. Some white or Asian women fought for black children as their own, not because of abstract "liberal" ideals but because they "mothered" black children and had learned intimately the human costs of racial stereotypes and hierarchies.

"Neighbors" would never accept appointing "parents" as official representatives of the Skyline Task Force. Even "parents" who lived in the hills were excluded from representing the "neighborhood" and its interests. One Asian parent, who sometimes attended the Task Force meetings but mostly observed the conflicts, said, "It always seems to be us against them. It doesn't help if you're a neighbor, but also a parent. You are one of them. If you're not a neighbor, you're definitely one of them. If you're a student, you are one of them. It didn't seem that there were very many students who they would respect."

This binary distinction between "neighbors" and "parents" simply presumed that hills residents did not send their kids to Skyline High School. The school's changing racial demographics fed this sense among many white neighbors that the school was no longer a *neighborhood* school. Middle-class flight from public schools accelerated in the eighties and nineties, so that by 2000, 25% of all Oakland's school-aged students attended private schools, 10% higher than the state average.[28] Even though "neighbors" recognized the existence of black middle-class homeowners, they assumed these wealthy neighbors wouldn't send their kids to Oakland's "bad" public schools. One white parent and hills resident said that when she attended the Task Force, neighbors "were shocked" to find out that her kids went to Skyline. "They didn't know that nice kids went to Skyline. . . . They assumed I had nice kids because of the way I looked and talked."

Neither "parents" nor "neighbors" in the Skyline Task Force accurately represented the diversity of the school or neighborhood. "Parents" who attended the Task Force meetings were almost all middle-class homeowners who lived in the hills and lower hills, and the most vocal participants were the parents of black children. Most participating "neighbors" were white and lived very close to the school or the few private streets students used to get off the hill. Their concerns did not represent some general "hills public opinion" about Skyline High School, as was made evident by a youth-led survey of 366 households along Skyline corridor that found that 85.7% of residents said that Skyline High School affected their day-to-day life either not at all or only to a limited degree.[29]

These neighbors drew fundamentally different boundaries between the public and the private than I found in other neighborhoods in Oakland. We have seen how parents in the lower hills worked alongside neighbors to develop school-based programs to get children and preteens back into safe spaces of school and home and off the streets. Accepting that public schools worked best as a co-op, they blurred boundaries between public and private responsibility. These parents (like many parents at Skyline) used their volunteer labor to expand public investments in schools and spaces for children. They defined students as their own kids and framed public schools as an integral part of the neighborhood.

In the hills, by contrast, neighborhood activists literally and figuratively extended the boundaries of their property into the privatized streets. They considered public use of the streets in front of their homes as unacceptable and boisterous youth behavior or fights in the streets as a direct affront to their rights as property owners. Many neighbors defined their entire neighborhood as a private space that had the *right* to remain separate from the city and its problems, which lay below the hills. Mrs. Tyler, a Hillcrest Estate homeowner and occasional Skyline Task Force participant, explained,

The people that are living up here are not used to that sort of thing. They have not been living down in the slums of Oakland. Maybe some of them did originally, I came pretty close. But they managed to work their way up to this and they feel they do not have to be put into that kind of problems. If you don't like our neighborhood, get the hell out.

Neighbors insisted that the state protect their expansive notion of private property. They demanded greater police presence after school and more security at school events. Mrs. Tyler grounded this right to state action in her identity as a tax-paying homeowner who paid a lot of money but did not use public services. "People up here pay enough taxes. . . . Most don't have kids in school. But we pay a tremendous amount of money. That should be given consideration."

The way white neighbors drew the boundaries of political community had significant material effects. They excluded public schools from this private community, defining them as dangerous and inadequately controlled public spaces that called into question the safety and innocence of the youth within them. They defined all Skyline students as outsiders in the hills, erasing the presence of Asian, black, and white students who both lived in the hills and attended the public schools. They defined the neighborhood not only as rich and resistant to the public school but also implicitly as white, reproducing a clear equation of race, space, and identity that no longer held true at the turn of the twenty-first century.[30] This narrow definition of community posed a real problem for black parents and children. Some white hills residents defined black teenagers on the street as a problem and a sign of criminal intent. A Latino police officer told me he had received a message from a white hills resident complaining, "There are black kids walking through my neighborhood. What can I do to get them removed?" He asked, "What exactly am I supposed to do in response to that?" But other police officers reproduced these exclusions. Black parents like the Smiths regularly told stories about how their boys were stopped by the police in the hills, asked for identification, or asked what they were doing there.

Framing youth in the streets as dangerous outsiders had equally frightening effects when neighbors themselves tried to enforce their rights to an exclusionary private community. Two white men had approached Shirley's son as he walked in the neighborhood, called him "boy," and spoke to him in a threatening manner that reminded her of the South. When the man in the Rolls Royce threatened students with a gun as they painted the Skyline High School sign, the Youth Together coordinator told the Task Force "right now students think there is someone up here who wants to kill them."

Colorful Language and Color-Blind Liberalism

Racial animosity pervaded Task Force meetings, frequently erupting in debates over whether or not youth at the school were dangerous or criminal. At one meeting, "neighbors" and "parents" engaged in an extended argument over whether or not there had been "riots" after a basketball game at Skyline. Bob complained that the neighborhood had been terrorized the previous three weeks by "roving gangs" and one attempted "car-jacking" around the school. He asked for a schedule of after-school events so that the neighbors would "at least have a chance." The principal, an African American woman, objected that she had never seen "a riot" at the school. And Shirley insisted, "What you call a riot at the schools may have been a loud discussion. . . . It's all subjective. If you look up the incident, it's clear there was a disturbance, but it doesn't say there was a riot, R-I-O-T." Joan responded, "That's just semantics."

White neighbors developed a complex racial etiquette for talk about problem youth.[31] Joan complained that she couldn't even "speak English" anymore because certain words were regarded as racist. Nevertheless, she learned to edit her speech because complaints about youth had racial undertones that remained perilously close to the surface. Fears of "riots" and of "gangs" have profound racial histories in American cities. They are central metaphors from the sixties and nineties, respectively, for fears that the collective rage or alienation of youth of color would break violently out of control. As anthropologist Steven Gregory has argued, "youth crime" and complaints about dangerous youth are "over-determined by an ideology of black crime."[32]

Neighbors' careful racial etiquette should not be interpreted as simply cynical, nor "as proof" that whites were "repressing or occulting racist motivation."[33] But we do need to consider how the "central frames" of neighbors' color-blind ideology redefined race and racism in a post–civil rights era.[34] White neighbors, like many Americans today, defined racism as a problem of hearts and minds, of hidden ideas and "intentions" embedded in the minds of white folks. One of the legacies of civil rights–era legal victories has been to define racism as morally bad, and to imply the inverse, that good people can't really be racist.[35] We talk about racism in a language of sin, guilt, and innocence. This moralistic understanding of racism left white neighbors with few ways to talk about race, racial inequalities, or racism in the past or present.

Calls for color-blindness have become quite common in politics and public policy debates, from Proposition 209, which prohibited affirmative action in public school admissions, to the California Civil Rights Initiative, which voters rejected but which would have stopped the state from tracking race for any purpose at all. Anthropologist Mica Pollock calls these efforts "color-muteness" because "such actions seek to erase race words from public discourse in an exceedingly race-conscious way."[36] The color-blind ideology of white neighbors in the Skyline Task Force both denied and reproduced deep racial inequalities in Oakland and fed a neoliberal turn in American politics that privatized responsibility for creating equal opportunities for children.

When I asked Joan whether she thought there was any way to talk about race without divisiveness, she paused a long time before answering and hesitated frequently as she spoke.

> I am trying to remember when I was a kid how my family talked about race. I don't think there was anything divisive about it, you know. And I'm not trying to say that that proves me to be a wonderful person. The people who lived next door to us were a black judge and his wife. Their kids were mostly grown, and really I didn't think anything about them being a different race. They were one of very, very, very few black families in the town where I grew up, and they had a granddaughter who was around my age. I used to like to read a lot and my mom was always trying to get me to go outside. [Laughs.] One day. . . . I was commanded to go outside and play with their granddaughter. I went outside and I looked at her, and she was quite brown, and I said, "Well, at least your mother isn't always telling you . . . to go outside and play."

She laughed a bit uncomfortably and added, "I believe that . . . teaching kids respect for other people is the way to talk about race. . . . Just basic rules about what it means to be human and to have regard for other human beings." Joan's parable of childhood color-blindness, or, more importantly, seeing the color brown but not caring, serves to argue that if we just ignore race, it won't matter.

Neighbors never talked about the race of students causing problems, except to deny that they were talking only about black boys. Joan insisted, "The kids are not all African American. There are Caucasians, young ladies. I'm not trying to pick out African American students." Joan was angry that Mr. and Mrs. Smith described white neighbors as racist.

> Presumably they think that if it were white kids doing this—of course, oftentimes it is—that it would be okay with us. That's just not true. A lot of the littering, I happen to notice in the parking lot across from here is

one area where a bunch of Asian kids hang out in. Littering amongst the students and at least some of their parents does not know any boundaries of race. I have all the empirical evidence. It is so frustrating because it has nothing to do with race.

White homeowners used their own successful paths to the hills—and that of their black neighbors—to argue that kids today faced no clear structural barriers to equal opportunity. As Mrs. Tyler insisted, "I grew up in the flatlands and obviously I am not acting like that. My dad left when I was twelve years old, but I had grandparents and a place to be and a place to go. So if I can do it, they can bloody well do it too. I'm not so special at all."[37] She dismissed claims about the ongoing significance of race as "bullshit." "Do you realize how many black families now live in this particular neighborhood? They've moved up in the world and gotten jobs and they're doctors and lawyers, realtors, whatever, and they are just the same as everyone else."

Neighbors sometimes couched their local fears of youth in the context of the broader national conversation about school shootings, particularly in the aftermath of Columbine. In one Task Force meeting, Theresa talked for several minutes about her fears that neither the police nor private security guards could protect her from students invading her property. After commenting that she was "glad her kids no longer went to Skyline," she paused as if recognizing that she had just painted a very grim portrait of students, and added, "I say that only in light of the recent campus shootings." Joan also referred explicitly to school shootings several times in an interview. She complained about "the irrational reaction" by many parents and youth to a recent proposal to bring officers from Oakland's police department into the public schools, saying, "You can't say that you are not going to have proper security in the schools. Why court disaster? I find it kind of ironic that when it comes to why they don't want to have police in the schools, Cincinnati is invoked [where a police officer had recently shot and killed an unarmed nineteen-year-old black man], but Columbine is never invoked by those people." These references to Columbine and school shootings raised a particular image of violent white suburban youth that reframed fears of youth as racially neutral and justified neighbors' calls for increased security and surveillance in and around schools.

Neighbors often insisted that they didn't think all Skyline students were bad kids or were criminals and that only a certain number of "bad apples" caused the problems. These "bad apple" estimates ranged from one hundred kids to 2%, 5%, or 10%, but all consistently erased race and class from the calculations. As Mrs. and Mr. Tyler, explained, "The majority of kids, they are nice kids. They always are. It's the bummers that are causing the problems." Mr. Tyler insisted that the "bummers" or "the ten percenters" crossed all walks of life. "It is true of doctors or janitors or teachers or anyone. There is always 10% of this group, whatever group it is, that are going to be losers, and it is the same thing with students in school. This is the problem we have at Skyline High School." They reframed fundamental social divides in the United States as between "losers" and "good guys," not between categories of race, class, or age. This analysis defended neighbors from the criticism that they were afraid of poor kids, black kids, or, in the geographical metaphor of Oakland, flatland kids. They identified "bad kids" as simply part of the natural order, a natural "category of 'undesirable' people, people who are truly and objectively the 'scum' of any race" or class.[38]

White neighbors insisted that race only mattered because "people," implicitly black activists, like the Smiths, "made it matter." Joan asserted,

It becomes a self-fulfilling prophecy, self-verifying proposition. It makes it hard for me to understand. . . . The people who are trying to put everything in those terms, what is it that they really want? . . . What is driving them? It's nothing good. . . . What is it that they would really like to see happen? Maybe they would like to see every house in this area burn down? I don't know. Sometimes I get that sort of feeling.

For Joan, talk about race is divisive, even dangerous, raising the bizarre specter of a riot in the hills.

White neighbors sometimes expanded this color-blind ideology to rewrite Oakland's recent history in a very race-conscious way. Mrs. Tyler thought that

the black community in Oakland, I am afraid, has used race ever since the sixties as a way of trying to shut up the white community. Everything you say, it becomes you're prejudiced. Everybody shuts up. They took over the city of Oakland and damn near ruined it. [Politicians and administrators] had to be black. . . . The fact that they knew what they were doing or not did not matter. . . . It took Jerry Brown to come in and try to get things sorted out. It still has a long way to go, but at least we are more on the right track than we were before. We were going down the tubes.

Sensing the ways that this comment might sound racist, Mr. Tyler quickly interjected that Robert Bobb, Oakland's black city manager, was a "great guy" and that this was not about race. "You can be green, purple, or puce." Mr. Tyler's use of color here makes race an insignificant (even fanciful) trait disconnected from any meaningful social categories. The black community not only inappropriately brought race into city politics, but in so doing put the city itself at risk. This version of Oakland's history suggests that black politics led to the city's decline. If Oakland could not "get beyond" race, these white hills residents insisted, the city would remain in the dysfunctional racial past, unable to become the revitalized city that it could be.

This story erased all the ways in which white people made race matter in twentieth-century Oakland and built racial inequalities deep into the East Bay's economy, schools, and neighborhoods. Public decisions (past and present) shaped the contours of race, space, and wealth in Oakland, as in all other U.S. cities and suburbs. Federal housing policies in the post–World War II era and the more informal actions of real estate agents and white homeowners built racial inequalities into Oakland's class geography. These policies subsidized loans for white families to buy homes (and build capital) in the hills and suburbs, while excluding blacks from similar opportunities. This recent history created the contours of current inequalities in education, income, unemployment, and poverty.[39] Terrible public schools in Oakland's flatland neighborhoods continued to reproduce unequal educational outcomes by race and trapped working-class blacks and Latinos in the most insecure areas of the labor force. Oakland's geography itself helped reproduce racial inequalities in the post–civil rights era. But homeowners often interpreted Oakland's geography in moral terms that justified existing inequalities.

Busing, Borrowed Communities, and the Decline of Skyline High School

Neighbors often identified "kids on the buses" as the source of most problems. Theresa Thomas explained that kids in the "cars they got for Christmas" worried her less, as did the kids whose parents picked them up. A Skyline school police officer agreed, insisting that some kids at Skyline "should not be here. They bring problems with them." Reproducing a common equation of space and danger, they assumed kids on the buses were "flatland kids" who brought the disorder of the flatlands into the hills.

Stereotypical images of Skyline students as poor, probably dangerous kids from Oakland's flatlands fed white neighbors' fears of Skyline students. Mrs. Tyler drew on these stereotypes as she argued that the youth center should be in Eastmont Mall, near Elmhurst, "down where the kids live." Now "at least you get rid of them by about four o'clock. They are on their way somewhere, to the latest drug den, or home, or what have you." She worried that if they didn't stop the trouble now, "we could fear for our lives up here just like they do down in the flats." Her casual equation of drug dens and student homes in the flatlands highlighted the role of mass media in forging popular ideas of poor families and neighborhoods: "All you have to do is turn on Jerry Springer and you'll see what people are really like out there in the flatlands."

Oakland never had a formal busing program to achieve racial integration, but public buses allowed students to cut across Oakland's racial and class geography in a quest for better education. It is hard to estimate exactly how many of Skyline's students came from "the flatlands" compared to "the hills" since these are not stable sociological categories that Oakland public schools could track. Skyline's catchment area now extends down into the flatlands, and many students from Castlemont High School in Elmhurst transferred to Skyline, either for specific programs like drama or simply because they saw their neighborhood school as academically limited or too dangerous. Still, Skyline High School had few very poor students compared to other schools in Oakland. In general, only the most stable working-class and middle-class families from the flatlands had the social capital and commitment to negotiate the bureaucratic process of applying for intradistrict transfers. In 2000 only 2.5% of Skyline student families received welfare compared to 57.9% at Castlemont High School.[40]

"Kids on buses" and "kids from the flatlands" all served as subtle ways to mark class and race without explicitly acknowledging the significance of either race or class as structures of exclusion. Oakland's geography naturalized structures of inequality so that the "flatlands" became a moral category, like the underclass, that enabled white neighbors to talk about race and class as "culture." This geography allowed neighbors to avoid talking about race, even while they relied on and reproduced racial stereotypes of the ghetto poor. Flatland youth and their faulty families became powerful forces that explained not only ongoing racial inequalities but also historic changes in Oakland's public schools.

Many older white residents blamed open enrollment and "busing" for Skyline's troubles and for the school's apparent decline. Their fond memories of Skyline as a "great," "clean" school were juxtaposed with stories of the disorderly and dirty campus today. These stories often dramatically condensed the school's long and contested racial transition, as did one woman from the lower hills: "The year they integrated Skyline High School, it had a brand-new plant, but it was totally trashed in a couple years. That is just reality."

Meredith Clark, a white homeowner and former public school teacher who lived in Redwood Heights, provided the most detailed description of the way Skyline's integration led to its decline. "I think one of the *main* things that really changed it was when they allowed the beginning of open enrollment in schools. . . ." She described Skyline High School's boundaries as "one of the biggest divisive things in the whole city." "Immediately this group that was not in that district, they just thought, 'Well. Why do they get a new school?' They did anything. They lied like fire to get into Skyline." Mrs. Clark explained,

> It wasn't an organized group, but just parents who thought their kids should have this nice new school. McClymonds High School at that time had one of the best schools. They had excellent teachers and more material things to work with than any other school in the town. . . . Parents immediately, they thought some magic thing would happen if their child got to Skyline. It was a lovely school. But we were up there a couple of years ago. We went to a basketball game. I have never been so disgusted in my life to see how they had let kids come in and ruin something. . . . It was absolutely filthy. . . . There was total lack of authority.

Neighbors often fumbled with their words, in what Bonilla-Silva describes as "rhetorical incoherence" when they tried to talk about race.[41] Mrs. Clark completely avoided talking about race in this story. She hesitated to ever say explicitly who was "lying" to get into Skyline High School. But McClymonds High School lay in the heart of historically black West Oakland, so this was a deeply racial story of how open enrollment led to Skyline's decline. When I pressed for further details, she added,

> They had kids that came from all over town. They came out of their neighborhoods. They took a bus at MacArthur and 35th . . . up to Skyline. . . . Kids who were from this neighborhood were like, "Heck, we're being pushed out of our neighborhood or anything decent." . . . It's just . . . I don't know. I don't really blame any particular race of people in any state or form because there are wonderful people. We have close friends of all ethnic backgrounds, really close, and two daughters. I call them daughters, and they call me mother. They are just as close to me as my own kids. So it doesn't mean, uh, it just means, uh, I guess [pause]. But that was the ruination of the schools. It made the parents lie. They'd say they live at such and such an address.

She later explained, "It's not a thing of race in my opinion. It's a thing of class and education and . . . the . . . desire . . . to have family that you're proud of."

Meredith Clark was a Christian woman, critical of white flight, who talked about two black women as daughters (though she was so averse to talking about race that she hesitated to say they were black). She refused to acknowledge that struggles for open enrollment at Skyline were demands for racial integration or equality. She denied that this story was about race. But without the racial explanation, she almost couldn't explain what this story meant. Ultimately, she recoded race as class, education, and a commitment to a decent family life.

This story highlighted several important ways in which white neighbors used the geography of the hills and flatlands to naturalize existing inequalities Oakland. Suggesting that "people" should stay in "their own neighborhoods" made Oakland's neighborhood boundaries seem like natural and transparent expressions of identity and community. But Oakland's neighborhoods (and schools) had been made racially segregated by white investments in maintaining white neighborhoods through the 1960s. Indeed, in 1964, 70% of Oakland hills residents voted for Proposition 14, a California ballot initiative that overturned the state's "open housing" law and prohibited the state from denying a person the right to rent or sell property to "any person he chooses."[42]

Resources were vastly unequal across Oakland's racial geography. Meredith's insistence that McClymonds was one of Oakland's best public schools, with "more materials to work with" than other Oakland public schools, is simply false. Even after decades of parental activism for equity, in the 1980s, McClymonds High School had no science labs, no AP classes, and such a shortage of books that students couldn't take them home to read or study.[43] Black activists called for open enrollment at Skyline not out of selfishness, but rather to demand equal opportunities for their children.

Neighbors constructed a moral geography that turned racial and class divides into cultural and moral conflicts. Theresa acknowledged the material divides between the hills and flatlands: "Below MacArthur are Afro-Americans because housing is cheaper. . . . Most of the people who are in low-cost housing are not Caucasians [but] primarily Latino, Asian, and Afro-Americans. There is the racial barrier alone in economics." But later she explained this divide in terms of culture and community:

> I think there is a very different concept of community among different sections of Oakland. . . . I think that some of it is probably the haves and the have-nots. . . . If you do not inherently get the pride of keeping your

neighborhood together and being responsible for helping your neighborhood stay clean, crime free, watch out for your neighbors' kids, then you don't have any respect when you come up to a borrowed community to go to school. . . . Where are the kids going to learn a sense of community? The school tries to do what they can.

Theresa reframed the divide between the haves and have-nots in terms of a "sense of community," defined as an inherent set of values and a bounded "culture" tied to space.

Neighbors drew on popular theories about the urban underclass as they blamed parents in Oakland's flatlands for failing to teach students the proper sense of community and respect.[44] Most popular and academic writing about the underclass implicitly argues that "aberrant" families have failed to properly raise young people in American ghettos, and this is why they are poor. As sociologist and black feminist theorist Patricia Collins argues, these analyses implicitly "use race to explain class disadvantage and gender deviancy to account for racial difference." Through this commonsense "causal" chain, theories of the underclass "rationalize black poverty."[45] They rely on a faulty understanding of culture as static, inherited, and unaffected by changing material and economic realities. The cultural category youth helped forge these commonsense links among race, class, and culture. The family is the crucial site for reproduction of culture, instilling the correct mores, attitudes, and behaviors necessary for "civilized" society.[46] But since the family remains the commonsense site for biological reproduction as well as cultural reproduction, talk about faulty families maintains an ambiguous tie to older biological notions of race. Sociologist Paul Gilroy argues that these two commonsense ideas of family help to turn "social processes into natural, instinctive ones."[47]

This cultural analysis of Skyline High School encouraged neighbors to focus on fixing what they considered a cultural deficit among Skyline students. As Mrs. Tyler explained, "These kids up here are a bunch of savages. They have never learned any manners or any caring or anything at home, which is not their fault, but on the other hand the school is going to have to teach common civility and concern for others. There are certain things you do and don't do in society." Neighbors wanted to set up a "citizenship training" that would teach kids "manners" and "respect for private property." This focus on culture opened up the possibility that kids could be fixed. But defining flatland kids as threatening outsiders, as savages who belonged "in their own neighborhood," turned culture into something almost natural, something one inherently got or didn't get from one's neighborhood or family. This more "biologized" notion of culture encouraged zero-tolerance policies to suspend, expel, or arrest students if they could not be "civilized."[48]

This narrative defined youth problems as essentially private, cultural deficits and thus ignored many urgent predicaments youth faced at Skyline. Racial disparities in suspension and graduation rates or in honors classes became not racial barriers but simple problems of morality or behavior. Concentrated poverty and violence in the flatlands became not a political crisis, a legacy of racism, or an effect of economic restructuring, but a problem of culture. The solution became to fix these poor children, or to keep them out of the neighborhood, but not to address problems of poverty, racial inequality, or California's failure to invest in equal opportunities for all young people.

White neighbors' privatized analysis of youth problems bore a striking resemblance to the nostalgia of Elmhurst activists for disciplined youth. But it had a different underlying logic. In the hills, this analysis was disconnected from ideas of activist mothering—that these were "our kids" we were trying to save—that served as important counterweights to privatizing discourses in the flatlands. White hills activists' color-blind commitments prohibited any broad critique of the ways in which the neoliberal order reproduced existing racial inequalities.

The color-blind stories white neighbors propagated had broader political effects. They relied on, and reproduced, deeply racially coded images of "ghetto youth" that have been central to efforts to shrink state spending for children and their families. Political scientist Peter Schrag argues that Prop 13, California's taxpayer rebellion, was caused by the resistance of an aging white electorate unwilling to pay for public services that were increasingly shared with the state's growing population of poor, youth, immigrants, and people of color. Antitax advocates defined themselves as "homeowners" and "taxpayers," implicitly (and falsely) distinguishing themselves from recipients of public services who they often described as unworthy.[49]

As American studies scholar Ruth Gilmore has argued, stereotypes of "dangerous boys" and "teenage mothers" frame black children as essentially dangerous and thus fundamentally unworthy. Images of dangerous youth naturalize state disinvestments in children's environments, while authorizing investments in systems of surveillance and control.[50] When Howard Jarvis, one of Prop 13's authors, was asked about libraries closing as a result of the initiative, he justified state funding cuts by drawing on these stereotypes: "It doesn't bother me a damn bit . . . because most of the children they're for can't read."[51] As American studies scholar Dan HoSang argues, these racialized images produce a particular "'truth'—that prisons for brown, black, and poor bodies are a 'required' expenditure but schools for those same bodies 'throw money at the problem.'"[52]

The ways white neighbors told the history of Skyline High School ignored massive structural changes in Oakland's schools and economy that threatened American ideals of equal opportunity. Proposition 13 had both generational and racial effects. In many ways, it mortgaged the future of all children in California. It enabled older property owners to pay very low property taxes even as their homes escalated in value, at the same time as it made it harder for subsequent generations to buy property or to get a decent public education. In 1970, before the passage of Prop 13, California was ranked number one in school spending, but fell to forty-first in 1996. The state increased investments substantially in the economic boom of the late 1990s, so the state ranked twenty-seventh in 2000. But repeated budget crises in the early 2000s eroded many of those gains. California fell back to thirty-fourth in 2005, and that was prior to the massive budget cuts that would follow.[53]

Youth in Oakland public schools were left with schools that struggled for basic resources. Prop 13 cut most significantly into the resources of cities where growing numbers of children of color lived. Increasingly, white voters lived in racially and class-segregated suburbs or neighborhoods, and wealthy families could pay for private schools, extracurricular activities, even private policing. California's taxpayer rebellion created an endless cycle of budget crises that decimated Oakland's public schools. When neighbors saw a declining and dirty Skyline campus, they were seeing one small measure of these structural changes on Skyline High School's physical plant, not the simple effect of open enrollment or a failure to teach children manners. Skyline used to employ sixteen landscapers in addition to several janitors. By 2001, the entire Oakland public school district had only sixteen landscapers.[54]

Declining state investments decimated equal educational opportunities in Oakland. In the 2000 census, Oakland was ranked the eighth most educated city in the country, with 34.3% of adult residents having graduated from college. But the city has basically imported this educated workforce. The city attracted a growing number of college-educated people as part of the Bay Area high-tech economic boom.[55] But young people who grew up in Oakland faced a deeply troubled public education system with poor test scores and a massive high school dropout rate. Over a four-year period, 21.8% of students drop out of Oakland schools. Skyline students fared significantly better, with only 8.6% of students dropping out.[56] But even at Skyline High School, one of the best schools in the district, only one-third of students in 2000 graduated with the course requirements to go to a California public university.[57] Most Oakland public school students were not being prepared for professional jobs. As Cindi Katz argues, in an increasingly globalized economy, cities no longer have to reproduce their own labor force to ensure economic growth.[58]

White neighbors' color-blind commitments left them unable to see that the ladder of opportunity into the hills had many missing rungs. But young people in Oakland's public schools understood the significant barriers they had to overcome. One student, an African American girl from Oakland's flatlands, expressed longing and despair at the chasm she saw standing between herself and the glimpses of the good life she saw in the hills. "Every time I come up into this neighborhood, I see houses. It's nice up here. I wish I could live up here, but I don't know how to get there."

Reclaiming Childhood for Black Children

Parent advocates went to the Skyline Task Force meetings girded for battle, ready to challenge "neighbors" every time they even hinted that Skyline students might be dangerous. Black parents actively resisted the color-blind ideology of white neighbors and pointed out every race-coded comment because they saw the real effects of pervasive stereotypes of black boys as dangerous in their children's daily lives. Talk of riots, car-jacking, and crime around Skyline High School implicitly defined the school itself and its students as dangerous and potentially criminal. These images reproduced a broader societal tendency to represent and treat black children, especially boys, as "not child-like," as sociologist Ann Ferguson documents in her book *Bad Boys: Public Schools and the Making of Black Masculinity*. According to Ferguson, black children have been "constituted differently through economic practices, the law, social policy and visual imagery." An ensemble of images of black boys as "dangerous thugs" or as "an endangered species" means that black youth violence or educational failure, unlike that of white youth, prompts little soul searching in America. It is expected, seen as "inherent in the kids themselves," as natural (or maybe cultural) expressions of black racial difference.[59] These racial images and exclusions from childhood, combined with color-blind ideology, foster pernicious public policies and institutional practices that affected black families across class lines in Oakland.

Black parents worried that the image of black youth criminality had transformed public schools, naturalizing black educational failure and defining black students as in need of control, not education. Even upper-middle-class parents at Skyline had to confront the troubling racial contours about who was defined as gifted or a troublemaker in school.[60] When Mrs. Smith and Dr. Smith's first son arrived at Skyline High School in 1994, he came in with a 3.83 grade point average and recommendations from his middle school counselors for honors classes, but when they received his class schedule, he was in no honors classes. Mrs. Smith was furious and instantly met with the principal. Her son was quickly transferred into honors classes, but other black parents confronting the same problem were told that the honors classes were full.[61] Dr. Smith said, "We had to fight to get our kids into honors classes at Skyline High School in liberal, progressive Oakland. It was shocking."

African American parents at Skyline gathered data and learned that honors classes at Skyline were 85% white or Asian. Black students with over 3.0 averages were routinely not offered honors classes.[62] The explanation schools gave for these inequalities drew on common stereotypes about the deficiency of black families and the cultural deprivation of black students. The principal explained to a local newspaper that the numbers of minorities in honors classes were low because they are traditionally underrepresented in college-going populations.[63] This circular logic denied the ways schools reproduced inequalities in college attendance by assuming that existing patterns were expressions of student capacity and predictions of future student achievement.

Racial and class inequalities were built into Oakland's schools through its geography. As part of an organizing campaign on overcrowded schools in the flatlands, Oakland Community Organization created a map that highlights the stark educational inequalities across Oakland's landscape (See Figure 11). Elementary schools in the hills were smaller, had nicer physical plants, more experienced and credentialed teachers, and higher test scores than schools in the flatlands.[64] Teachers in hills elementary schools were paid on average ten thousand dollars more per year than teachers in the flatlands. Over the course of six years of elementary school, this means the state spent approximately sixty thousand dollars more to educate kids in a hills elementary school classroom than in a classroom in the flatlands.[65] In 2000 civil rights groups launched a landmark class action lawsuit, *Williams v. State of California*, documenting pernicious racial and class inequities in education. Despite decades of activism, money and resources in Oakland and the nation continued "to follow white children."[66] The state legislature, in a 2004 settlement, guaranteed that all students should have the basic right to books and other instructional materials, schools in good repair, and qualified teachers, and it pledged almost $1 billion towards creating more equity in children's learning environments.[67]

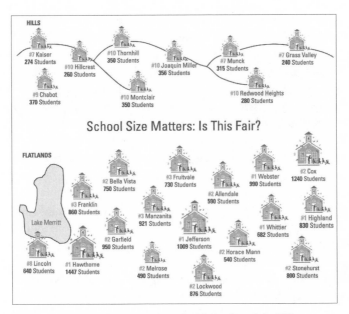

Figure 11. Unequal educations across the Flatlands and the Hills.
(Map produced by Oakland Community Organization)

School systems in California do not just mirror preexisting inequalities. They "distribute opportunities along racial lines" and produce stark racial effects.[68] In what anthropologist Michelle Fine describes as "an institutional choreography," school districts and individual schools track students by race in districts throughout America. As mostly white and Asian students from hills elementary schools were tracked into honors classes, schools made whiteness (and now maybe some Asians, as model minorities) appear naturally or normally "meritocratic" while being black or brown appeared "deficient."[69] In California, white children are much more likely to attend the state's highest-performing schools, while black students are almost three times, and Latino students seven times, more likely to attend the lowest-performing schools.[70] In 2001, only 16% of Oakland's black students and 17% of Latino students met state proficiency standards in math, compared to 60% of white students. On language arts tests, roughly 30% of black and Latino students met the standard, while 67% of white students did. The OCO map asked in bold letters, "Is it fair?"[71]

Ferguson documents the ways schools act "as sorting systems" that produce the social identities gifted, at-risk, good kid, and bad kid. Even in elementary school, teachers often give white boys "masculine dispensation" and interpret their misbehavior as "boys being boys," while black boys are quickly labeled as "willfully bad."[72] Instead of seeing children's behavior as "something to be molded and shaped over time," schools often interpreted black children's behavior as adult-like, as "evidence of their future place in the social order." Consequently, schools often punished black boys "through example and exclusion rather than through persuasion and edification," as they did with white boys.[73] Ferguson demonstrates how black boys construct their own identities "in relation to these expectations." They sometimes "threaten, misbehave, reciprocate in kind, displaying a power that reproduces the very stereotype of dangerous youth."[74]

The image of black teenagers as dangerous and potentially criminal led to massive racial disparities in suspensions in Oakland, often for ambiguous offenses like "defiance of authority." These disparities only increased during the 1990s as schools nationally embraced "zero tolerance policies" that expel students for bringing any drug or weapon to school (including sometimes Tylenol or fingernail clippers).[75] Oakland school suspensions rose 65% between 1991 and 1996. Black and Latino boys were disproportionately suspended and expelled. Boys represented 80% of suspended students. Black youth comprised 50% of public school students, but received 70% of suspensions. Latino suspension rose fivefold in the same time period, far outpacing the significant growth in Oakland's Latino population.[76] Dropout rates began to increase for black boys nationally in the 1990s as a combination of high-stakes testing and zero-tolerance policies pushed some out of school.[77]

Black parent advocates knew that "bad kids" and "flatland youth" were categories that retained deep racial connotations. So their children remained at risk as long as disproportionate numbers of black kids in Oakland public schools were tracked into lower-level classes and identified as "bad kids." Shirley Casey's biracial son experienced how easily he could slip from being a "good" to a "bad" kid. She explained that people weren't always clear about "what he was" or where he fit in Oakland's racial and class landscape. He was always very polite and used to be clean cut. But recently he had started to grow small dreads, and he suddenly found that teachers were no longer treating him as a "good boy." His teacher at Skyline had explained that she didn't call on him in class because of "the energy that surrounds him because of his rough and tumble appearance. I wouldn't be able to control my class." When Shirley asked her son, "Do you want to cut your hair now because they don't perceive you as a sweet little white boy?" he answered, "No, this is who I am, at least for now."

White parents often defended Skyline High School's reputation, but like many white neighbors, they often assumed that there was a clear distinction between "good kids" and "bad kids." Christine Rollinson, a white mother active in the PTA, explained that Skyline was a safe school for middle-class kids despite popular perception. "The bad boys and girls tend to just self-destruct or tend to take it out on friends. . . . They go away. That's what we want them to do. We want them to go away and stay away from our kids." Christine didn't challenge the ways black and Latino kids were systematically defined as bad kids, tracked into lower-level courses, and disciplined so that they disappeared from this hills school. Many middle-class white parents and school officials, like white neighbors, accepted those inequalities as normal, as transparent expressions of Oakland's racial and class inequalities or as expressions of differences in parenting and culture in Oakland's flatland communities.

Dr. and Mrs. Smith helped formed Concerned African American Parents at Skyline to fight against these kinds of institutionalized racism. Parents pressured the school to create more formal criteria for admission to honors classes and Advanced Placement courses so that schools would not simply reproduce racial stereotypes of who was "gifted." Monthly meetings of Concerned Parents of African American Students at Skyline educated black parents to be more effective advocates and counselors to help their children get to college. Another African American parent advocate at Skyline insisted that "African Americans can't just drop their kids off at school and assume they'll get the same education as Caucasian kids. Many of the teachers really have lower expectations of these kids. And if you're not there, it's perceived that you're not concerned."[78]

Mrs. Smith defined her work in the schools as part of a long tradition of black activist mothering and parent activism for racial equality in education. She saw it as part of her job as a parent to worry about all black children. She explained that once Skyline administrators and parents learned her husband was a doctor and they lived in a big house in the hills, they treated her differently, as if they were thinking, "You're one of us now." Mrs. Smith wondered, "Did I stop being black?" The principal said, "Don't worry, Dr. and Mrs. Smith. We'll take good care of your son." The implicit message was that they didn't have to worry about the other kids. But she refused to settle for her son being one of the few black kids in the AP classes. "I want the best education for my child and for the other kids."

Motivated by this broader mission of racial uplift, Concerned Parents of African American Students at Skyline High School joined with Oscar Wright, an Oakland civil engineer and long-time advocate for black children in the public schools, to push Oakland to sign a voluntary resolution with the U.S. Department of Education's Office of Civil Rights to monitor Oakland Public Schools. The voluntary resolution required the school district to provide more access to textbooks, Advanced Placement classes, trained teachers, and classes taught at grade-level standards in Oakland's majority-black schools in the flatlands.

Black parent activism in the hills illustrates interesting similarities and striking differences when compared to such activism in other neighborhoods in Oakland. Middle-class parents in the hills and lower hills volunteered actively in the public schools, trying to secure a safe passage for their children through fraying public schools. As in the Laurel district, they also worked to insulate their children from the damaging effects of institutionalized racism that too often led to lowered expectations for black students.

Many scholars have documented increasing divides between the black middle class and the black poor in the post–civil rights era. Black families in the hills benefited in many ways from Oakland's geography of inequality. Their kids automatically went to Oakland's best public elementary and middle schools, and so came to Skyline with built-in educational privileges. Upper-middle-class parents could afford to send their kids to private school or move to the suburbs, and many did. The hills themselves physically insulated their children from Oakland's most dangerous streets, as did the privileges wealthy parents could offer their children in the form of large homes, yards, cell phones, cars, and home computers wired to the internet. But these private spaces and class privileges did not fully insulate their children from the pervasive image of black youth criminality. This "controlling image" continued to partially link the fates of black parents and children across class and geographic lines in Oakland.[79] National campaigns by the NAACP Legal Defense Fund and the Children's Defense Fund against the "school to prison" or "cradle to prison" pipelines indicate the political power of these fears for black children.[80]

The polarized racial politics around Skyline High School led black parent activists to engage in different spatial politics in the hills than elsewhere in Oakland. In the flatlands and lower hills, many black parents and neighborhood activists embraced efforts to clear youth off the streets "for their own good." Black parents in the hills often kept their kids at home to protect them, but they also often defended young people's rights to public space. They did this not only to protect their own children from being identified as "outsiders from the flatlands" in front of their own homes but also to challenge the implicit equation of race, class, and space that erased the presence of black middle-class families from the hills.

Conclusion

The Skyline Task Force enacted fundamental debates about the meaning of race, class, and generation in the post–civil rights era. White neighbors' calls for color-blindness, while often well intentioned, were premature and only exacerbated pervasive inequalities in California. Fifty years after *Brown v. Board of Education*, we remain far from attaining racial equality in educational opportunities or outcomes. If we cannot talk about race, we cannot see or address the persistent ways schools reproduce racial inequalities.[81] We will return again and again to trying to fix individual young people or youth culture instead of addressing racial inequalities that have significant structural causes. As anthropologist Mica Pollock argues, kids in multiracial California do not belong to simple racial groups, but "when it comes to inequality," too often "we do."[82]

Americans engage in deep debates over why these racial inequalities remain. These disagreements often boil down to three central questions: Are racial inequities explained by culture (values) or structure (economic or spatial exclusions)? Are they the legacy of past racism or does racism still work to create inequality in the present? Do individuals control their own destiny or do outside forces impinge upon us and shape our life paths? These debates often obscure more than they elucidate, in part because they misunderstand culture, structure, *and* individual choice. Culture is not a stable set of beliefs or values, separate from the material world. Culture is always contested, changing, emergent—reshaped by our daily engagements with the world around us, even as our ideas and actions shape that world. Individual choices matter, but our choices are fundamentally shaped by the contexts (ideological and material) in which we grow up, live, and raise children.

White neighbors in the hills were face-to-face with the city's obvious failures to support and educate all of its children. These kinds of exclusions of young people exist in deep tension with idealized relationships between generations. Youth remain still on the border of childhood, with its attendant moral responsibilities for adult nurturance. We have a significant commitment to ideals of equal opportunity, particularly that children can become whatever they want through effort and education. Adults either must engage with the needs of youth or work hard to bolster ideologies of equal opportunity that justify existing inequalities.

Roger Sanjek argues that quality-of-life concerns focused on children can enable neighbors to recognize that people of all races "share a common fate at the hands of city planners, realtors [and] politicians" and want effective policing, good schools, and recreation facilities.[83] Sanjek argues that the terrain of local politics is particularly important for creating a multiracial public sphere. In Queens, he found that the definition of "our people" and the boundaries of community changed as black residents, and later Korean and Latin American immigrants, began to participate in community politics. We saw a similar phenomenon in the Laurel district, where defining public school students as "our kids" led to an inclusive civic politics.[84] But in the Oakland Hills, most upper-middle-class neighbors didn't share a "common fate" with the working class or lower middle class. While many wealthy adults bemoaned the state of public schools, they rarely personally invested in improving the schools. Hills residents often didn't even understand the limited resources available in public schools. While they demanded better city services for their neighborhood, during times of budget cuts they could always simply pay for private services. They could retreat in their private cars to their private streets and into their luxurious homes and private schools. This distance from a common fate with other citizens in the city encouraged hills residents to construct a defensive community and to argue that it was their right to remain distinctly separate from the rest of the city.

This middle-class retreat was certainly not unique to the Skyline neighborhood, nor was it evidence of an unusual racial or class hostility on the part of these white neighbors. Retreating from a disorderly and truly public sphere increasingly characterizes the way the upper middle class lives in cities.[85] What was remarkable about this neighborhood was that Skyline High School prevented what most of the urban upper middle class takes for granted, its effective isolation from problems that may affect the rest of the city. Retreating into the private sphere simply could not fully isolate these neighbors around the school from the problems youth face in Oakland. They couldn't escape the real effects of massive state disinvestments in youth and the effects of youth poverty, whether manifested as violence among youth, as claims to the private spaces of neighbors, or as a dirty campus. This proximity often fed efforts to erect defensive walls between the school and the neighborhood, but it could offer real possibilities for developing a more progressive politics of childhood.

There were some incipient moves towards a politics of inclusion within the Skyline Task Force. As "neighbors" met with students and parents planning the Youth Center, white homeowners without children in public schools began to understand some student needs and to move beyond calls for more surveillance and policing. They joined with parents and students to demand better food in the cafeteria, better bus service, and alternatives to suspension.

Neighbors learned, and expressed shock, that Skyline High School didn't have a full-time school nurse or counselors to address the students' mental health needs. One white neighbor was horrified at a Task Force meeting to hear a young woman's most basic request for toilet paper in the girl's bathroom. When Task Force members focused their frustration on the school administration, instead of on students, they could occasionally find points of agreement with parents. The Task Force neighbors finally agreed to support the Youth Center, built exactly where the students wanted it from the beginning, and the students reassured neighbors about security plans.

Shirley Jackson told a story that captured what a more inclusionary politics might look like and why it is important to treat all kids—even those acting like bad boys—as our own. One day about a dozen kids were throwing things at the bus stop and something hit and damaged her car. Shirley confronted the students, full of street language and attitude: "Who threw the mother-fuckin' stuff at my car?" She demanded that they step up and take responsibility. The kids got pissed off and called back, "What are you, a bitch?" Soon the police came and had one kid in the back of the car. When the police asked, she said, "Yes, press charges." But then a white man came by and asked, "What are they doing now? Did they break into your car?" Shirley paused and, reminded of how often white neighbors defined black young men as criminals, she turned to the man, saying, "My son and I are having a family conflict. There's no problem." Then she apologized to the young man. "Sorry I came at you like that. My name is Shirley Jackson. What's your name?" From the boy's "stone cold face," she saw "tears welling up in his eyes." They drove back up to Skyline High School with the police to call the boy's mom, who gave them permission to do anything, including spank the child. Shirley made the young man call her Auntie Shirley, show her his report card, and make dinner that night for her. Now they are close: "I love that boy. That child is my heart."

Cruising down the Boulevard

One spring day in 2003, as I took pictures along MacArthur Boulevard in the Laurel district, a fifteen-year-old African American girl asked me what I was doing. When I told her I was writing a book about youth in Oakland, she asked if I knew that they were trying to move the bus stops from the corner of 35th and MacArthur. She added in a matter-of-fact voice, "They don't want youth in this neighborhood." Every school day at 2:30 in the afternoon, a trickle of students wearing backpacks and holding bus passes turned into a flood, filling the bus stops along the MacArthur corridor. Some came down the hill from Skyline High School or from nearby Bret Harte Middle School. Others waited to transfer buses as they trekked home to North or East Oakland. Black, Tongan, Chinese, Latino, and some white students filled the sidewalks, sometimes spilled into the streets, or roamed down the boulevard in search of food and fun. Some kids listened quietly to music on headsets; others were more boisterous, play-fighting with their friends, throwing nutshells, or tossing insults and shouting across the streets to friends. On occasion, the crowd gathered in a circle to watch the excitement of a fight. Two Oakland police cars often sat near busy bus stops casually monitoring the corner for signs of trouble—accepted as a natural, normal part of the Oakland street scene.

Two years earlier, on a clear, cold day in January 2001, I walked down the boulevard with Jackie Patterson, an African American mother of a thirteen-year-old and the neighborhood services coordinator, and Pat Jackson, a spry older white woman who served as the NCPC youth coordinator. The Laurel Neighborhood Crime Prevention Council led a broad effort to clear kids off this commercial corridor starting in the late 1990s. They campaigned for more police, hired private security, tried to move the bus stops, and developed after-school programs to keep kids off the street. As we walked, they identified individual businesses that either helped or hurt the neighborhood. They pointed to World Ground café and Farmer Joe's organic marketplace as signs of neighborhood revitalization, but complained that one Chinese

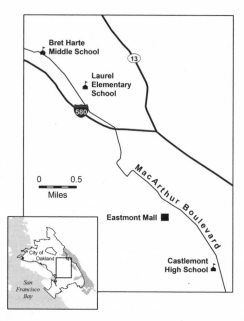

Figure 12. Map of Macarthur Boulevard. (Mark
Kumler and Diana Sinton, University of Redlands)

restaurant needed to be closed because it drew crowds after school with its
hand-written signs advertising one-dollar meals. We stopped at small grocery
stores, liquor stores, and beauty salons where Jackie explained to merchants
that students had been "warned to stay away from here after school. They
were told to go straight home, or they don't have to go home, but they have
to leave here. They can't loiter." Pat Jackson most clearly framed the problem
when she explained to the owner of a nail salon, "People don't want to come
and shop here if there are crazy kids everywhere." Youth seemed to stand in
the way of the fragile revitalization of this commercial corridor, which had
struggled for decades as waves of urban restructuring washed over the city.

The history of MacArthur Boulevard traces Oakland's fitful, and certainly
incomplete, transformation from a landscape of production to a landscape of
consumption—and the contradictory role young people have played in the
process. Moving east along MacArthur Boulevard through the Laurel district
into Elmhurst, you can see the ways Oakland's urban landscape has been
made and remade by successive redevelopment efforts. Small commercial
districts with art deco storefronts and abandoned movie theaters dot MacAr-

thur Boulevard, evidence of the village centers built up along the Key System streetcar routes in the 1920s and '30s to serve the expanding industrial garden suburbs that had sprouted up in East Oakland's lower hills and flatlands. Motels, hot dog stands, burger drive-throughs, auto-repair shops, and abandoned gas stations mark the street's development in the 1940s and early '50s as the main highway which led an increasingly mobile and car-loving population to the heart of downtown Oakland and San Francisco. Now rundown motels highlight Oakland's deepening economic inequalities. Covered with "no loitering signs" and the logos of private security companies, they serve as informal low-income housing and homeless shelters where a mix of families, prostitutes, and drug addicts live week to week when they can't afford the cost of an apartment's security deposit.

The empty storefronts that dot MacArthur Boulevard tell another important story. Civic boosters in the 1950s worked to reshape and promote Oakland as an "all-American city." Concerned about the city's image, the *Oakland Tribune*, run by the politically powerful Knowland family, had an editorial policy forbidding the use of the term "slum" or "ghetto" to describe any Oakland neighborhood.[1] City leaders invested in a regional development strategy, creating a new network of freeways and the Bay Area Rapid Transit (BART) system, which they hoped would help Oakland's city center better compete with San Francisco. These freeways and BART carved deep divides into Oakland's neighborhoods, displacing many in West Oakland's historic black community, facilitating white flight to the emerging suburbs, and redirecting traffic away from Oakland's commercial corridors. The long-time owner of a music shop in the heart of the Laurel district, explained that after the MacArthur Freeway was completed in the early 1960s, it "just killed" the commercial heart of the neighborhoods. There was "no more traffic on the street."[2]

The Eastmont Mall, located on MacArthur Boulevard at the edge of the Elmhurst neighborhood, provides an apt symbol of the city's troubled efforts to reinvent itself in the wake of deindustrialization and suburbanization.[3] From the 1920s through the '50s, a Chevrolet plant was one of many factories in the East Oakland flatlands that provided well-paying and often unionized blue-collar jobs. But by the early sixties, this plant and most others were closed. In its place, Hahn and Company built the Eastmont Mall, bringing their pioneering concept of the mall as "a cool place to hang out as well as shop" from the suburbs to the city.[4] The mall was briefly successful in the 1980s, when black teenagers and multiracial families hung out at the movie theater, ate in the food court, and shopped at a full complement of department stores and small boutiques, as well as the grocery store, drug store, and library, which met basic neighborhood needs. But after anchor tenants JC Penney's and Mervyn's left the mall in the early 1990s, the mall slowly emptied out. Walking through the mall, one feels and hears the retail abandonment of Oakland's flatlands in the echoes of footsteps and isolated voices bouncing off undecorated walls and empty stores. The bustle and consumer frenzy, the mall as entertainment, the palace of consumer goods is gone.

These changes along the boulevard left gaping holes in spaces for Oakland's youth. Movie theaters closed, as did a major bowling alley and a roller rink in East Oakland that had provided spaces for young people before deindustrialization and white flight. In the late 1980s young people began to reclaim the semi-abandoned commercial spaces of East Oakland. Black teenagers and young adults gathered on weekend nights in the Eastmont parking lot to play music, dance, and show off candy-painted Corvettes and Mustangs with gold rims. Slowly they invented an Oakland original: a hip hop–influenced car culture and form of cruising called the Sideshow. Young people blasted music from open car doors and windows as they pushed their cars through slow acrobatic dances, swinging their cars in donuts and figure eights, "dipping" by alternately hitting brakes and gas in time with the music, and sometimes "ghost-riding" as they danced on top of or around cars that drove themselves, demonstrating their driving skill and courage.[5]

Many former participants, and even some observers, describe Sideshows in those early years as relatively peaceful. Yakpasua Zazaboi fondly recalled, "It was just black folks and cars everywhere. It filled up the whole lot . . . people was walking around just talking, having fun. . . . People weren't looking at us as if we were a threat. [It] was more like a welcoming thing, like, 'Man, you see us. Now get out of the car and be with us.'"[6] Promoted by local hip hop artists, the Sideshow grew larger and began to draw black and Latino revelers from all over the Bay Area.[7] But new city regulations and police sweeps in the late 1990s pushed Sideshows out of the Eastmont Mall and other large commercial parking lots. As a result, it became a roving, rowdy party that unexpectedly cropped up throughout residential and commercial corridors in East Oakland, even downtown, as the police and drivers played an increasingly expensive and sometimes dangerous game of cat and mouse. Even Chief Word acknowledged that Oakland Police Department "made a mistake, by pushing them out of the parking lot of Eastmont Mall and into the neighborhoods."[8] Sideshows literally marked the MacArthur corridor with circular black tire skid marks that served as a constant reminder to frustrated neighbors that the city had not yet overcome its image as a disorderly and too often dangerous place.

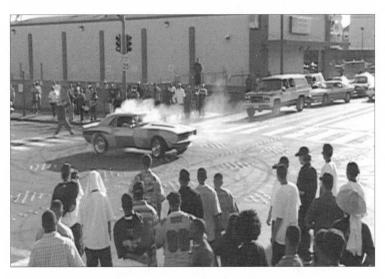

Figure 13. The Sideshow's spectacular claims to public space.
(Image courtesy of Yakpasua Zazaboi, Sydewayz)

Eastmont Mall tried to reinvent itself once again at the turn of the twenty-first century. Its "innovative solution to retail" was to replace stores with social service providers and government agencies. A large security office, a computer training center, a library, a senior citizen activity center, and public health department offices lay interspersed among the few remaining stores—Young's Wigs, beauty supply stores, a cell phone provider, Fashions for Dolores, All African Imports, a Black Muslim Bakery, and a dingy store called Value Plus with threadbare industrial gray carpet, partly burned-out fluorescent lights, and big signs advertising low interest rates. The welfare self-sufficiency center was the most stylish office in the mall. Finally, in 2000 the mall found a new anchor tenant when the police department located its new East Oakland headquarters in the empty Mervyn's store. With the secure image this new tenant provided, a new grocery store (one of few in the neighborhood) finally moved into the mall.

Linda Jackson, the black homeowner activist whom we met in chapter 1, described her hope that a redeveloped MacArthur Boulevard could make her Elmhurst neighborhood look more like the Laurel district, or even like Rockridge, one of the most solidly gentrified walking districts in the city. She wanted to be able to walk down to MacArthur to go to a Starbucks, to visit a fitness center and boutique dress shops, and to sit at a restaurant with tables and chairs outside. She hated the Sideshow. "I want to be able to walk down without hearing all these cars, loud music." She wanted to see "kids walking down the street polite, without pants hanging down to their knees and foul language, nobody hanging on the corners with a bottle in their hand and throwing it out in the street when they're done." Young people hanging out along MacArthur Boulevard—and the black marks from donuts on the corners—captured community activists' worries that the promise of urban redevelopment had not yet reached Oakland's far-flung neighborhoods. They reified an image many neighborhoods like Elmhurst were desperately trying to escape. As Mrs. Jackson complained, many investors refused to see East Oakland as a space for investment: "Unfortunately people have this idea that we're so poor that we can't afford anything."

Potential Thugs and Gangsters

Youth and the Spatial Politics of
Urban Redevelopment

On February 25, 2003, Oakland City Council held a public hearing on a new ordinance that would "prohibit loitering in public for the purpose of engaging in illegal drug activity." This law was narrowly crafted to target drug dealing, not kids hanging out on the street, but the debate at the hearing was almost entirely about how the law would or should affect Oakland's youth. Oakland's multiracial youth activist organizations had mobilized close to one hundred young people and several parents and grandparents to testify that this law would increase the racial profiling and harassment youth already faced on Oakland's streets. As one nineteen-year-old African American young man explained, "People think I'm on the block dealing because I wear a beanie and a pea coat. And I'm waiting for the bus."

Bill Clay, the black community policing activist in Elmhurst, was frustrated by these claims that the law targeted young people, but he had to educate both supporters and opponents alike that the antiloitering law wasn't about kids. The many African American adults and senior citizens who spoke in favor of the new law hoped it would positively affect the behavior of all young people in the city, particularly black kids. James Collins, wearing graying cornrows and a Raiders jacket, insisted, "We don't want to endorse the idea that it's okay to be on the corner. It's not okay." Rev. Henry Chester hoped, "This law would . . . give some of these young people that are applauding here tonight the opportunity to learn how people are supposed to live in the city."

This hearing demonstrated the pervasive idea that we have seen across Oakland's neighborhoods: that "youth" were responsible for most of the crime and disorder in the city.[9] It also highlighted conflicting views over the ways young people used urban space and profound race, class, and generational cleavages in Oakland's politics. Black, Latino, and Asian youth activists, city officials, and older African Americans at this meeting struggled over the meaning of "kids on the corner." Were they kids waiting for the bus? Or kids on the fast track to criminality?

Community meetings in Oakland often produced "a moral vocabulary of landscape."[10] Proposals for youth curfews, antiloitering laws, and anticruising ordinances popped up every few years in Oakland politics, as if replaying an endless loop.[11] Supporters argued that there were right and wrong ways for young people to use public spaces in the city. The "corner" and "the streets" served as metaphors for many dangerous turns on the path to adulthood. "Kids on the corner" became the most common shorthand for drug dealing in Oakland's working-class flatland neighborhoods. Black homeowner activists from Elmhurst worried that the streets literally turned "kids" into drug dealers. As Jean Taylor explained, "Kids don't need to be out there with those dealers. . . . It hasn't failed me yet. Young boys hanging around watching . . . begin to do. They have no business there. I just don't see kids hanging on the corner who are good kids." Because of their urgent fears about black youth coming of age in the disintegrating environments of Oakland's flatlands, these black elders often led efforts to get kids off the street.

But efforts to clear youth off the street extended far beyond Oakland's flatlands into the city's commercial corridors and even downtown. We've seen a wide range of efforts to change the way youth used space across Oakland: from police sweeps and proposed curfews to expanded after-school programs. These divergent efforts relied on and reproduced a particular spatial organization of childhood and youth—one that defined youth on the streets as "matter out of place."[12] Teaching young people the proper way to "live in the city" seemed to hold the key to Oakland's future in two interconnected senses. Youth had to be taught not to hang out on the streets so that they could make a successful transition to adulthood—but also so that Oakland's fragile commercial redevelopment effort could succeed.

Oakland city government under Mayor Jerry Brown embraced a neoliberal urban development model. They tried to create the vibrant public spaces and "distinctive places of consumption" that would make Oakland "a destination city" and "an entertainment venue for the middle classes." Many critics have argued that these "urban redevelopment efforts have often led to the virtual privatization of urban space," what Sharon Zukin calls "domestication by cappuccino."[13] Cities like Oakland faced new pressures to manage their image in order to compete for increasingly mobile capital investments. But Oakland's carefully crafted image was built on shaky ground. The city struggled to make itself "safe for gentrification" in the context of deep class divides, crime, and recurrent budget crises.[14] Responding to these pressures, Oakland city government intensified its efforts to make public space feel safe by expanding government regulation of the ways people use space.[15] These spatial regimes of governance, as anthropologist Sally Merry explains, apply the "logic of zoning": they "manage opportunities for behavior rather than the behavior" itself. Antiloitering laws, curfews, stay-away orders, and "quality-of-life" policing—based on the "broken windows thesis"—all regulate spaces and produce public order instead of trying to reform individual offenders.[16] Cities like Oakland have increasingly turned to these spatial strategies of governance because they have had to "govern more while spending less."[17] The city hoped that redesigned streetscapes, along with new laws and police sweeps to regulate the use of space, would create the appearance of orderly public spaces needed for the city to realize its redevelopment dreams.

The literature on urban redevelopment largely ignores youth. Scholars often mention young people only in passing and note that youth–especially youth of color—are increasingly defined as "undesirable occupants" of public space.[18] But they have not sufficiently explored the important role children and youth play in urban restructuring. Changes in childhood have helped to produce changes in urban spaces both in the past and in the present. In the late nineteenth century, new ideals of childhood helped produce the idea that the private space of "home" was a "haven from the heartless world" of industrial capitalism and an emerging commercial culture.[19] These ideals shaped urban planning and encouraged the creation of Oakland's industrial garden suburbs with their small houses and private backyards. They also fed repeated attempts over the last century to segregate children from a potentially polluting public sphere. Sociologists and reformers wrote extensively about the dangers of the corners in the early twentieth century, as in William Whyte's *Street Corner Society* and Clifford Shaw's *Jack Roller: A Delinquent Boy's Story*. They made the familiar argument that hanging out on corners lured kids into crime, and they created separate age-segregated spaces (like playgrounds or youth canteens) that were integral to defining the categories of "childhood" and youth.[20] But these changes in childhood also helped produce new ideas and contours of public and private space in urban America.

Changes in childhood, and efforts to save children, are again fundamentally reshaping urban space in twenty-first-century neoliberal cities. Parents, children, and neighborhood activists are producing new landscapes of childhood (and landscapes of consumption) in Oakland as they struggle to respond to deepening divides in childhood and youth. Many middle-class children are experiencing an extended adolescence, but as we have seen, some kids, particularly African American boys, face real exclusions from childhood. In response to urgent concerns about coming of age (real and imagined), neighborhood activists, parents, and children have changed the ways kids live in the city. Explicit struggles over appropriate uses of public space—like the loitering hearing—have reshaped the contours and boundaries of public space in Oakland. But so have changes in the ways parents and children use space in their daily lives.

These new landscapes have removed many young people from city streets and set in motion new meanings of "kids on the corner."[21] Neighborhood activists increasingly identified kids on the street as potential gangsters, as present or future members of Oakland's underclass, an underclass that both was marked as black and crossed racial lines. This is why young people on the streets became a potent symbol of the present and future class status of neighborhoods across the city. Oakland's young people became the living equivalents of the many "broken windows" that marred the city's commercial corridors, evidence of the deeper disorders that stood in the way of Oakland's redevelopment dreams.

Geographer Don Mitchell asks, "Who has the right to the city and its public spaces—and to what degree are we willing to shrink public space in an ongoing effort to control 'undesirables' whether they be teenagers, homeless or political activists?"[22] Most adults at the antiloitering hearing converged on the same answer: youth did *not* have a right to the city and its public places. But this attempt to erase youth from Oakland's streets was not the simple result of white, middle-class adults demonizing black kids. Black activists and politicians in Oakland were a vital part of constructing Oakland's neoliberal urban regime and reconstructing urban space. They tried to create a "geographic fix" to fundamental inequalities in childhood—combining intensified policing with after-school programs in order to secure a safe passage to adulthood for all of Oakland's kids. This geographic fix helped consolidate new landscapes of consumption that increasingly privatized and securitized urban space. But it also threatened to define young people who remained on the streets as criminals who could be excluded from the category and protections of childhood.

Chasing the Dream of Urban Redevelopment

In 1998, newly elected Mayor Jerry Brown described his vision for the city in a community meeting: "We want to make Oakland a drive to instead of a drive through." His inaugural address laid out four main goals: to decrease crime, to revitalize downtown, to improve public education by creating charter schools, and to create "centers for art and creativity" in Oakland. These goals together encapsulated Brown's dream that he could reinvent Oakland as what many have called a "theme park city" that would lure the professional managerial class to experience the excitement of urban life.[23]

Oakland worked hard to reshape its image as it tried to catch the wave of the high-tech boom that was transforming the Bay Area. Oakland fought against two primary negative images: that it was simply a bedroom community—that, as Gertrude Stein insisted, "There's no there there"—and that it was a dangerous city. Oakland launched an advertising campaign with ads posted at BART stations and bus stops in San Francisco, pointing out the advantages of Oakland's warmer weather and the fact that Oakland was closer to San Francisco than much of San Francisco. For several months, whenever I drove from San Francisco to Oakland, I passed a large billboard with a picture of Lake Merritt and Oakland's skyline and the caption "Oakland. It's Time." This ad campaign captured the hopes of the city development office and many Oakland residents. But many worried that Oakland's image as a poor black city—as a ghetto itself—stood in the way of its redevelopment dreams.

Mayor Brown crafted a neoliberal development regime that aggressively adopted market-oriented growth strategies.[24] He explained that Oakland had to compete "to be more attractive than" other cities where developers could put their money. He acknowledged that the global high-tech economy had generated substantial inequalities, but insisted that the city couldn't place any burdens on private investors, "no matter how well intentioned."[25] Brown resisted efforts to mandate low-income housing set-asides in new development projects or to pass living-wage and tenant-rights legislation, explaining that Oakland had "to create an investment- and development-oriented city government" so the "private market" could "work its magic in the City of Oakland."[26] This description of the "magic" of the private market expressed an almost blind faith that the benefits of the market would "trickle down" to lift all boats in Oakland.[27] As historian Michael Katz argues, many cities embraced these kinds of pro-growth urban development policies in the 1990s. Since little help was forthcoming from state and federal governments, cities tried to develop their way out of complex urban fiscal and social crises.[28]

Mayor Brown's urban regime embraced gentrification as its central urban redevelopment strategy.[29] He launched an ambitious plan to bring ten thousand new residents into downtown and promoted a vision of downtown as a place where residents could "live, work, and play in 'a spirit of elegant density.'"[30] He formed close relationships with Bay Area developers and fast-tracked many downtown housing and upscale retail developments. Political scientist Owen Kirkpatrick quotes one Brown advisor who said that whenever a desirable business—like software communications and biotech—expressed interest in investing in the city, Oakland would act like a "good venture capitalist" and develop an "innovative package of goodies to dangle in front of companies." The city offered tax breaks, public subsidies, and publicly maintained fiber optic cables and used its powers of eminent domain to promote private investment and residential development, especially downtown.[31] Responding to critics' concerns that low-income residents might be displaced, the mayor said, "I'm not ashamed to know capitalists. . . . We need more capital in Oakland."[32] One "pro-business" advocacy group credited his two terms in office with major successes in luring "quality jobs, retail and housing."[33]

Jerry Brown's transformation from an icon of the liberal 1970s to a pragmatic city leader received accolades in neoliberal policy circles and the press. The free-market think tank Manhattan Institute awarded Mayor Brown an "Urban Innovator Award" in 2001. The institute's magazine *City Journal* reported that both the mayor and City Manager Robert Bobb were "cleaning up a barnacle-encrusted city government," leaving behind "decades of racial politics," and "shaking off the failed orthodoxies of the Great Society." The article celebrated Brown's recognition of the city's "basic needs for order and private development" and his commitment "to beat down all opposition to achieve them."[34]

There were significant social costs and a growing opposition to this pro-development regime, which critics called "Jerrification." Tenant advocacy groups documented a massive 300% increase in no-cause evictions in the first eighteen months of Brown's first term. These evictions hit low-income neighborhoods and black tenants disproportionately. The average rent for a one bedroom apartment in Oakland soared 17% in the same time period despite a city law that capped increases at 3%.[35] A study in 2000 found that "two out of five Oakland families were already experiencing problems with housing costs," and prices continued to soar.[36] The median cost of a home rose from $290,268 in 1999 to $467,373 in 2003.[37] These rapid changes helped launch a renewed wave of affordable housing activism, union organizing, and youth activism in Oakland. People began to ask, Who was Jerry Brown redeveloping the city for? And who would be displaced in the process?[38]

Oakland's economic development strategy focused on making city spaces feel safe to businesses and middle-class residents. The city manager, as we have seen, adopted the "broken windows thesis" into his mantra for the city. In one interview Robert Bobb referred to Disneyland as a model for this strategy. "In community meetings, I ask people who's been to Disneyland and whether they put their hamburger wrappers on the street there. 'If you lit-ter,' I tell them, 'it says it's okay to commit crime.'"[39] Oakland, like New York, where the "broken windows" theory was created, embraced many zero-tolerance policing practices to reduce "quality-of-life crimes" like public drinking, gambling, drug dealing, prostitution, and cruising.[40] The city also tried to regulate the ways "risky" people used space, implementing curfews for people on parole, creating intensified supervision for serious youth offenders, and placing video cameras in high-crime areas. Neighborhood activists often complained that Oakland did not implement these strategies consistently enough, in part because it didn't have the large numbers of police officers required to maintain a New York–style crackdown on quality-of-life offenses.

Oakland's commercial revitalization strategy also relied on creating vibrant streetscapes, not just securing safe streets. This strategy rejected the wholesale retreat to privatized space that characterizes suburban gated communities or the private estates in the hills.[41] Oakland's downtown development efforts mirrored that of many other U.S. cities in the early twenty-first century: creating an uptown arts district and mixed-use waterfront redevelopment projects along the estuary harbor and around Jack London Square, where a new upscale food emporium modeled on Seattle's Pike Market was planned. These plans included small parks and open space, pedestrian walkways and bike paths, and open plazas with café and restaurant seating outside.[42] As geographer Neil Smith argues, retaking the city for the middle classes involved "more than gentrified housing." It required constructing entirely new landscapes of "recreation, consumption, production and pleasure."[43] The city abandoned its efforts to lure department stores downtown and focused instead on marketing "downtown's sense of place and character," which could "offer the leisure-time shopper an authentic alternative to the mall."[44] An Oakland's Economic Development Agency study found that Oakland was losing up to $9.5 million in retail sales tax because residents often had to leave the city to shop.[45] By revitalizing downtown, the city hoped to lure middle-class hills and lower hills residents to spend their money in the city.[46]

A Benetton Ad, Not a Poor Black City

Despite Jerry Brown's efforts and the real estate boom at the end of the twentieth century, Oakland was far from a fully gentrified or "theme park" city. Oakland's commercial districts were torn between their efforts to create inviting and lively landscapes for consumption and fears that these public spaces would attract "disorderly" participants. Young people were at the heart of these struggles, but the city's response can only fully be understood by looking at the intersections of race and class in Oakland's diverse public spaces. Geographer Loretta Lees points to "an underlying ambivalence about diversity" within neoliberal urban redevelopment efforts. City efforts to "foster a genuine public culture on the street often subvert that very goal" as their "efforts to secure urban space stifle its celebrated diversity and vitality."[47] Oakland touted the city's diverse image, proudly proclaiming on its economic development site that Oakland was one of "most diverse cities in the United States" according to the *USA Today* "diversity index."[48] But only some young people embodied this marketable ideal of diversity. Others, especially unregulated crowds of predominantly black youth, represented the prime signs of "disorder" in Oakland's commercial districts.

Young "hipsters" were sometimes described as a key force in recreating vibrant public spaces and landscapes of consumption in Oakland. A series of articles published in 2007 in *San Francisco Magazine*, called "It's Oakland's Turn," celebrated the "youthful hipness" and "diversity" of the city's burgeoning art scene, hipster bars, and restaurants. The author described these new bars as "the epitome of Oakland cool." "The young and the nicotine-addicted hang out here to swap stories about their art, their tats, their day jobs, and their hangovers past, present and future."[49] This description celebrates the "risk and hedonism" that geographer Susan Ruddick describes as typical not only of new consumer cultures but also of new entrepreneurial cultures of work, most visible in the startups of Silicon Valley and San Francisco.[50] Ruddick argues that "youth, youthful bodies, and youthful energy and creativity have become the defining ideal of contemporary Western culture." Young and older adults "are increasingly encouraged to actively construct themselves as 'youthful' in their ability to retool intellectually, to embrace uncertain career paths and—even in cultures of the body—to dress and discipline their bodies to appear younger, fitter and more energetic."[51]

The youthful energy, "hip consumerism," and diversity in Uptown's gritty art scene promised to bring vibrant street life to downtown Oakland that would help the city complete its successful transformation from a landscape of production to a landscape of consumption.[52] News coverage emphasized the diversity of the new uptown bar scene; one article described "the mix" in an uptown bar as "so perfectly multi-ethnic it seems like the set of a Benetton ad."[53] The meaning of diversity was shaped by the racial and class composition of the emerging uptown scene. The "Benetton" mix included many young white artists and professionals of all races, many of whom had the cultural capital, if not always the income, that led many to define them as an engine of redevelopment. This race and class mix marked the uptown scene as distinct from other, more segregated, working-class black and Latino youth cultures. The uptown scene did capture part of Oakland's real racial and class mix, but it also helped replace an image of dangerous black city with a more benign and marketable idea of diversity.

Predominantly black clubs downtown were not permitted to celebrate Oakland's more youthful and gritty elements. Several had to close their doors, establish strict dress codes that prohibited "street" or hip hop styles, or change their format to respond to worries about violence. Hip hop itself was often defined as a potentially dangerous and criminal black youth culture. As one news article reported, "hip hop oriented clubs" attract "younger, more violence prone crowds," crowds they explained full of "young, mostly African-American patrons."[54] Strict code enforcement and a new permitting process, which assessed higher "safety costs" for police, security, and insurance, reduced the number of facilities that held youth-oriented hip hop events in Oakland.[55] When asked where the younger hip hop crowd was going now, one club owner responded, "Maybe San Francisco."[56] Hip hop journalist Davey D criticized the city's divergent responses to different kinds of downtown nightlife, saying that Oakland wants "a vibrant attractive nightlife scene"; "they just don't want black folks to be a part of it."[57]

Oakland has a long history of ambivalent responses to unregulated gatherings of black youth, as do many other U.S. cities. In the early 1990s, Lake Merritt became a popular hangout and cruising spot, where crowds of black youth would gather outside of the popular Festival of the Lake, extending cruising from East Oakland into one of the city's most desirable public spaces, "the Jewel of the City."[58] This cruising generated profound discomfort among many neighbors as well as concerns, expressed by black and white adults at a 1996 City Council hearing, that it would "chase all the business out of Oakland."[59] The city council implemented police sweeps and passed an ordinance that prohibited passing between two designated checkpoints twice in four hours. Heavy policing at the popular Festival of the Lake escalated into an outright mêlée between the police and black young men in 1994.[60] The organizers first moved, then abandoned the popular festival in 1997, but cruising continued in East Oakland, and the city spent roughly five hundred thousand dollars a year on police overtime to control Sideshows throughout the late 1990s and early 2000s.[61]

By 2001, Sideshows had made Oakland a destination for teenagers and twenty-somethings from around the Bay Area who were looking for after-hours excitement. As a police captain said, "It's becoming the place to be." One police study estimated that 38% of Sideshow drivers came from surrounding suburbs.[62] Images of Sideshows appeared in several popular hip hop videos, and local production companies released videos with titles like *Oakland Gone Wild* and *Sydewayz* that documented the wild street parties, car tricks, and almost ritualized conflicts with the police. Jack London Square became a new site of conflict that spring. With one of the only multiplex theaters in the city and safe open spaces, Jack London Square provided a much-sought-after public space for young people to gather on weekend nights. As crowds gathered, drivers would sometimes show off, play loud music, squeal their tires, or do donuts. Sideshows began to break out as nearby clubs closed, and caravans of cars spilled into East Oakland's streets.

This was not the kind of destination city Oakland wanted to become. Jerry Brown made eliminating Sideshows a priority, first in 2001, and then again in his second term in 2005, as he prepared his campaign to become California's attorney general.[63] The police department doubled the number of officers and intensified patrols of East Oakland's streets on weekend nights. The city and state legislature passed new laws in 2002 that allowed the police to seize the car of anyone participating in the Sideshow, and then in 2005 another law that allowed police to ticket spectators.[64] The patrols issued five thousand traffic citations and towed seventeen hundred vehicles in the first seven months of 2005.[65] "Sideshow" became a label quickly applied to any large youth gathering, street disorder, or violence in the city.[66]

Heavy police actions in Jack London Square prompted complaints by the NAACP and African American downtown business owners. "They're messing with our sons," explained Dorothy King, the owner of Everett and Jones Barbecue, a prominent Jack London Square restaurant. "You have to have the police mess with your son to really understand how it hurts you inside." The police had impounded her eighteen-year-old son's car for thirty days after a police officer determined that he was playing his car stereo too loud. Another officer threatened to arrest King's daughter if she didn't drive off immediately when she stopped her car outside the family's Broadway restaurant one weekend night. Her daughter explained, "Anytime they decide there are too many black people, they come down hard." Dorothy King began to take a bullhorn outside to tell the police to stop harassing young people in front of her restaurant. At an NAACP hearing, King demanded that the police "leave the African American children alone. They just want to do like the white children."[67]

Many black neighborhood activists in Elmhurst campaigned actively against Sideshows, which had turned their residential neighborhood into an outdoor party venue. But they also recognized, like Dorothy King, that many black kids and young adults were only looking for access to some public space. At one meeting with the Elmhurst police captain in 2001, May Johnson, an African American mother in her forties who had grown up in the neighborhood, insisted that Oakland needed more bowling alleys, roller rinks, or movie theaters, as it had had when she was growing up. Bill Clay wondered if instead of spending so much money on policing Sideshows, they could actually build something for youth: "Kids just want to go where they can be seen." A 21-year-old African American woman explained the appeal the Sideshow held for young people not yet old enough to go to clubs:

> We would meet up at Jack London Square, wait till everyone was cleared by police, and get on the freeway to East Oakland. So you'd dance and get out of the car and walk around, then people would start doing "donuts" and show off other driving skills. . . . I can honestly say the sideshows are a haven for Oakland youth in a city where you are constantly being harassed by police that don't understand you and there is a mayor who does everything in his power to make your life miserable. The result is youth rebellion.[68]

City council member Desley Brooks tried in 2001, and again in 2005, to build support for a plan to create a legitimate Sideshow in Oakland Coliseum parking lot, where licensed and insured drivers could perform for paying crowds. Some police officers agreed, frustrated that their twenty-year-old suppression effort had caused as many problems as it had solved.[69] Supporters of this effort noted that San Diego and Sonoma had successfully created legitimate drag racing courses, where young people paid to show off their cars and race, sometimes against the police. But the mayor and most of the city council rejected the plan. The Coliseum declined to open its parking lot; a white business owner in Elmhurst thought that even legal Sideshows "would have a bad impact on business." These proposals, like so many other attempts to create unstructured spaces for young people, foundered on the basis of two presumptions: that Oakland's hip hop street culture was itself criminal and that young people should not be hanging out in the streets.

Black youth socializing in Oakland's commercial corridors became prime signifiers of Oakland's ghetto past that many city leaders wanted to leave behind. Their uses of public space served as a sign of Oakland's incomplete transition to a more gentrified landscape of consumption. As they prepared to vote on a new Sideshow ordinance in 2005, council member Pat Kernihan explained her support: "I'm tired of the negative press the city is getting on this." And council member Larry Reid added that the ordinance would "help us attract retailers to the MacArthur corridor."[70]

Hanging Out on the Boulevard

Neighborhood activists also wanted their neighborhoods to become destinations, to lure middle-class residents to shop in revitalized commercial districts. The city spent millions of economic development dollars to redesign the city's streetscapes to create distinctive neighborhood commercial centers. In the Laurel district, the city built two huge, green, wrought iron arches, decorated with metal laurel leaves to demarcate the heart of the commercial district. Matching dark green decorative benches, garbage cans, old-fashioned lampposts with colorful laurel leaf banners, and large, decorative terra cotta flower pots created a sense of neighborhood identity—even a brand—along the walking district. Even in Elmhurst, much redevelopment money was spent on infrastructure projects that aimed to make the neighborhood look good, such as placing electrical wires underground and funding façade improvement projects.

Community groups in the Laurel district actively promoted this effort to create a "pedestrian friendly," commercially vibrant neighborhood. Neighbors and business owners worked together in the Laurel Community Action Project (LCAP) and later the Laurel Village Association to get rid of businesses like liquor stores and bars, which many identified as problem properties, and to replace them with more upscale restaurants and shops. They hosted village music festivals to create a lively street life and a Business Improvement District to pay for extra private security and street cleaning to make the streets feel safe. The LCAP website urged merchants and homeowners to "become part of this exciting, up-and-coming district in Oakland." They lovingly described the neighborhood's historic buildings—the "simple lines and human scale" of the 1920s brick two-story buildings, accented with the "streamlined pizzazz of the 1930s art deco" and "some 1950s glitz." This marketing strategy proclaimed the neighborhood as perfectly poised to become the next Rockridge or Piedmont, gentrified neighborhoods full of small specialty boutiques, upscale restaurants, bookstores, cafés, and "top-flight retail outlets."[71]

This careful marketing effort demonstrates that neoliberal urban development has extended to the neighborhood level. Individual neighborhoods—not just cities—now compete with each other and market themselves to attract businesses and professional workers. As anthropologists Judith Goode and Jeff Maskovsky have argued, neighborhood activists, working in this competitive context, often embraced calls to make themselves "more attractive" to investment by purging "their ranks of the undeserving poor."

This often seemed to be "the only option for neighborhood improvement and development."[72] Clearing youth off the streets was one of the major ways the Laurel district tried to make itself more attractive to investment.

Neighborhood activists and business owners frequently framed young people as impediments to commercial redevelopment along MacArthur in the Laurel district. When I asked Jackie Patterson where teenagers spent time in the neighborhood, she said that they didn't anymore. "They've been told to get up out of here. If they are in the after-school program, that's fine but otherwise they have to get out of the area because the area's off-limits." She told me about a man who had opened a restaurant with pinball machines on the 4400 block of MacArthur. He was "shut down by the community . . . because kids were using [the restaurant] as a hangout spot." She mentioned that the same thing had happened at the ¼ Pound Burger and the car wash next to it. Many convenience stores posted no loitering signs and let only two or three kids in at a time. For almost a year, at the insistence of neighborhood activists, the Taco Bell on the corner of 35th and MacArthur closed for service between 3:30 and 6:00 except for its drive-through so that crowds of youth could not gather inside. Kids coming down the hill from Skyline High School had also "been told to stay out of that area . . . unless they're contributing something positive to the community." Patterson later offered that some kids went to the two karate schools, which, like the after-school programs, provided supervised and structured activities, but her basic assumption was that youth normally did not contribute to this commercial district, and the efforts of the NCPC helped to ensure that youth would not become major consumers in the Laurel district.

Youth in Oakland's commercial districts were not defined as integral parts of the economic order. Instead they were framed as the source of potential disorders that might disrupt the safety and comfort of adult landscapes of consumption.[73] This position echoes a broad ambivalence about youth as consumers throughout the United States, where some retail outlets have embraced bizarre techniques to keep youth from congregating, like playing classical music and high-pitched noises only teens can hear, marketed as "Mosquito: Stop Teen Loitering."[74] Adults and business owners often defined youth in commercial spaces and city streets as challenging "the moral code of well-ordered consumption" that increasingly defines public space.[75] Many complaints about kids in Oakland's public spaces highlighted their refusal to recognize adult middle-class ideals of social interaction and consumption. They "hung out" and "loitered" in large groups instead of shopping or moving smoothly through the streets.[76]

Positioning youth as barriers to commercial revitalization is deeply ironic given the economic power of the youth market. Preteens, teenagers, and young adults constitute one of the most desirable consumer markets and are the targets for a wide range of marketing efforts. This youth market is no longer simply defined by white, middle-class suburban kids. Urban youth, especially black kids, increasingly produce and define "the popular" in music, clothes, and culture as hip hop has become the dominant force in popular culture. Author Naomi Klein documents the strange tension between "the commoditization and criminalization" of street cultures, an argument that extends easily to youth cultures: "When the street has become the hottest commodity in advertising culture, street culture itself is under siege."[77]

Businesses and neighborhood activists were afraid that more lucrative adult consumers would avoid the Laurel commercial district if the streets were filled with teenagers. Many neighbors were intimidated by the crowds of teenagers that gathered on the sidewalks, at bus stops, or in front of Taco Bell on MacArthur. As Jenny Chin explained, "a sidewalk can only hold three," so when she found herself having to wade through a crowd of twenty kids who wouldn't move aside, she was scared. A school vice principal who lived in the Laurel district recalled arriving one day at the corner of 35th and MacArthur where a "big knot" of twenty to thirty kids were waiting at the corner in front of the Taco Bell. He found himself thinking, "This is a gang. This is a riot. There's something happening there. But I caught myself. . . . I said, if this was thirty white kids standing on the corner would you be thinking this is a riot, this is a gang? Is this a piece of my own racism coming up? It probably is." But he had seen that kind of gathering on the corner "explode" into fights before, so he was also "aware of the potential for violence there."

Neighborhood activists often hesitated to talk explicitly about race and their fears of youth on MacArthur Boulevard. But they did sometimes mention the racial fears of others—either white hills residents or the older generation of neighborhood residents who represented the more racist past of this multiracial city. One white activist, who described herself as becoming more radical in her old age, complained that many people from further up the hill "in Redwood Heights won't shop in the Laurel because they say they are afraid." When I asked why, she pointed to the "rough, boisterous youth population around the buses." Some people were "not accustomed" to "African American social patterns." Richard Thomas was committed to "neighborhood shopping" but afraid that "we'll never have it while people are afraid of MacArthur Boulevard." Racism, he explained, was "surprisingly close to the surface." As the Laurel district tried to compete with other neighborhoods in what seemed like a zero-sum game for commercial investment, neighborhood activists worried that youth of color on the streets could stand in the way of commercial revitalization.

Thuggish-Looking Kids

Jackie Haley, an African American lawyer with grown children, was a board member of her homeowners' association and did a lot of volunteer work with "at-risk kids" in Oakland's flatlands. She lived in the solidly professional Redwood Heights neighborhood. As we talked about changes in her neighborhood, Mrs. Haley said,

> There was a time when it seemed like Laurel was creeping up. . . . I looked and I saw these kids with their pants down to their butt—a lot more minority kids. And I'm black, and I thought, "Oh no." I'm just being honest. And I very much identify with the issues and recognize discrimination, but when it came down to the value of my house, I didn't want to see a lot of thugs . . . thuggish-looking kids. . . .

Jackie Haley's description of these "thuggish-looking kids" reveals a very complicated conflation of youth styles, race, class, gender, and space that was used by many neighborhood activists as they tried to describe "problem youth." We cannot necessarily interpret Jackie Haley's reference to baggy pants and "minority kids" as a coded way to talk about black youth alone. Adults couldn't always tell the difference between "kids on the corner," itself a criminal category, and black, Latino, or Southeast Asian kids who happened to be on the corner waiting for the bus. Kids on the street could be drug dealers. But they could just as well be black, Asian, or white middle-class school kids dressed in the newest hip hop styles leisurely walking home from school with their friends. Oakland's neighborhoods were simply too diverse for blackness to be equated with poverty or for blackness alone to define youth as a problem.

Talk of thuggish kids may indicate significant changes in the way we think about race and class in the post–civil rights era. Racial categories are not stable, despite their deep inscription in material hierarchies. Rather, they are always in process. Anthropologist Virginia Dominguez's work on race suggests that pragmatics in the long run determines semantics—in other words, the ways we talk about race (and use racial labels) can change the meanings of racial categories over time.[78] Race remained significant in Oakland, but its meanings shifted with the rise of the black middle class, increased immigration, and deepening poverty for far too many black kids, but also too many Asian and Latino children. Race and class remained linked, as did race and space, but more flexibly and less categorically than before the civil rights movement. These changes made race and age intersect in new ways.

At least since the late nineteenth century there have been curious crossings between the language used to describe youth and the language used to describe racial others and the lower classes. One of the first to define adolescence as a distinctive stage of life, G. Stanley Hall used race as his central metaphor for youth, describing "adolescent races" and raising children as a civilizing process.[79] Hall and other early-twentieth-century reformers borrowed racial stereotypes of native tribes to describe children and youth, while in turn "natives" and blacks were frequently described as childlike. In the late twentieth century we saw a resurgence of this traffic in images. In the 1990s criminologists described violent youth as "super-predators," compared youth to primitive tribes and to animals, and labeled gangs as "wolf packs." A panicky media often described youth as "present-oriented," without moral reasoning and impulse control, all images previously used to justify the exclusions of African Americans.[80]

Youth has become an almost racial category that marks the flexible but deep structures of exclusion in contemporary America. Race and class were often hopelessly conflated in Oakland politics, but it was relatively easy for most adults to distinguish between middle-class and poor adults. Black, Latino, and Asian homeowners "fit" perfectly well in the Laurel district or in the "estate atmosphere" of the Oakland hills near Skyline High School. Their class position was securely marked by home ownership, so white homeowners found them unremarkable and unthreatening. Young people were a different matter. Young people's future class status is always somewhat unknown and insecure. They must attain the education, postgraduate degrees, and jobs to become or stay securely middle class. So youth became the focus of many racial (and class) fears in the city.

Adults in Oakland struggled to discern whether young people were on the right or wrong developmental path. They looked to body posture and baggy pants for evidence of defiance. They looked to backpacks as an indicator of school engagement. They distinguished kids on the bus from those whose parents picked them up—at least a mark of a "good" family, if not of a family's class status. They tried to read young people's faces for more subtle signs of "hardness" or sophistication that might mark them as "thugs" instead of children. But they also looked carefully at how young people used space in

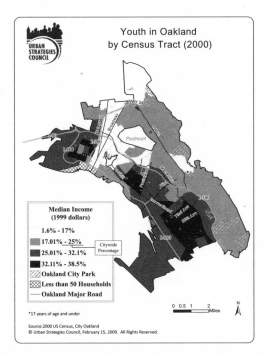

Figure 14. Oakland's geography of youth. Kids under eighteen
are concentrated in the flatlands, especially in far East Oakland.
(Copyright Urban Strategies Council, All Rights Reserved)

the city—reading signs of young people's class status and trajectories by how
they moved through the city.

Oakland's deep racial and class divides were perhaps most visible in the
unequal landscapes of childhood in the city. When Jackie described kids on
the street as "the Laurel creeping up," she pointed to the ways Oakland's geography of the hills and flatlands was also a generational geography. Children
and youth were concentrated in the lower-income minority flatlands, and
there were fewer children and teenagers in the hills. But young people moved
across Oakland's divided geography as they took buses in search of better
schools, safe parks, and recreation facilities and places to hang out with their
friends. These mobile kids blurred the porous boundaries between Oakland's
wealthy and poor neighborhoods in ways that highlighted the insecure status
of Oakland's redevelopment efforts.

Many adults used the public expression of hip hop style as a sign of trouble or a sign that a young person was on the wrong path. Performance stud-

ies scholar Nicole Fleetwood has argued that fashion has become the primary "signifier of racialized adolescence."[81] As we saw in chapter 3, when Shirley's son began to grow dreads—a hip hop style popularized by Bay Area rappers—his teacher began to define him as having a "rough and tumble appearance." In the teacher's mind, his style marked him not just as black but as the particular kind of black young man that would be disruptive. Hip hop style became a marker of a young person's affiliation with Oakland's streets—a statement of what historian Robin Kelley calls "ghettocentricity."[82]

Jenny Chin described how race, age, and hip hop style became a proxy for a troublesome kind of masculinity that invoked fear in Oakland. "When I see kids, maybe it's just the way that they're dressed now, I get really scared. I know there are Asian gangs, black gangs, Cambodian, even Mien gangs. I'm not strong." She described the style: "the head bands, the jackets that hang way down, a lot of shirts hanging out, the baggy pants." When she saw this hip hop–influenced style, especially with kids all the same race, "It feels like a gang." She knew it was "a fashion statement," one that some of her own nephews enjoyed, and thought, "I probably shouldn't be judging." But she found herself doing it, "especially if they have their boom box blasting" and souped-up cars. Chin acknowledged that black kids predominated at the bus stops in the Laurel district, so some of this was a fear of black kids, but she also pointed to the ways these fears could extend to other racialized kids who had adopted "ghettocentric" styles.

The ways young people used public space itself became a way of distinguishing between "good kids" and "thugs." Kids hanging out on the street, across racial lines, were often defined as threatening "underclass" kids because of broad changes in the landscapes of childhood in Oakland. Parents and neighborhood activists in Oakland had responded to broad anxieties about children coming of age by radically restricting children's free and independent access to public spaces. In neighborhoods like Elmhurst, where drug markets operate openly, many parents kept their kids inside to keep them safe from dangerous streets. But middle-class efforts to "cultivate" their kids through structured and supervised activities in the hills also radically reshaped the ways kids use space.

Parents and neighborhood activists had produced the new landscapes of childhood that fundamentally removed kids from the streets. Robert Walker described middle-class kids in the Oakland hills as "yard kids—maybe they have a big old yard and tree house. . . . Their parents take them everywhere. They don't play in the street. Or they go to Gymboree. I call those places urban escapes. It's those places you pay to go in to play. It automatically eliminates the low-income." Robert points to several defining characteristics of middle-class urban life: private space, private transportation, and the money to purchase private spaces of leisure and pleasure. He also highlights broad changes in the landscapes of middle-class childhood, which have increasingly become what sociologist Barrie Thorne calls "gated childhoods."[83]

These changes in childhood helped produce new urban landscapes of consumption and specific ideas about the proper use of urban public spaces. As Sandra Collins explained, she let her thirteen-year-old son have "some freedom" to enjoy walking and riding his bike in the Laurel district by himself. But she insisted that he had to be "in a specific place. He's not roaming around the streets. There has to be a specific destination." The streets were not spaces for socializing, hanging out, or loitering but instead spaces for a pleasurable stroll to a private destination, a café, a store, or a friend's house. Kids might still pass through, but not linger on, the streets as they moved to or from structured and supervised activities. Activists in the Laurel district tried to make the streets safe for youth to use in this circumscribed way, hiring "Safe Passage" monitors and private security to patrol the commercial corridor, to bring the public space of the streets under the watchful eyes of adults during the after-school hours. These "Safe Passage" monitors worked to secure young people's safe movement through the streets, but also served to symbolically secure the safety of transitions to adulthood.

Landscapes of childhood were sharply divided in Oakland between what geographer Sharon Zukin described as "landscapes of consumption and devastation."[84] Middle-class youth lived in homes with more private space and in neighborhoods with more vibrant landscapes of consumption. They could always drive and pay for access to structured and supervised leisure activities throughout the city. Working-class and poor kids were concentrated in neighborhoods with far more limited public and private spaces. Even when parents like Tanesha and Bobbie Taylor moved to the Laurel district, in a search for safer neighborhoods and schools, they rarely had the money to pay for the new commodified landscapes of childhood. They often just kept their kids inside to keep them safe. Both of these strategies removed young people from public space to create safe transitions to adulthood, but they created very different kinds of gated childhoods.

These new gated childhoods have changed the meaning of kids in the street. Now the very presence of unsupervised young people hanging out on the streets raises questions about their class status and defines them as potentially dangerous members of the underclass. By this I mean two things. People assumed youth on the streets simply came from poor families, and that their parents were not adequately supervising them. Popular discourses about the faulty families of the underclass were prevalent in Oakland, as we have seen. But they also assumed that kids who hung out on the streets, no matter what their class of origin, were likely to "grow up too soon" and become members of the underclass because they were not getting the kinds of structure, supervision, and education that were increasingly defined as requirements for access to the middle class. Youth on the streets (and also in public schools) became a suspect, racialized category because of how easy it seemed to slip down the class ladder into the underclass.

These new landscapes of childhood have redefined public spaces as "naturally" or "normally" an adult space. As geographer Gill Valentine argues, since children no longer "produce the street" as a "children's space" through their performative acts of play, the street has increasingly become a place where children and youth are defined as "out of place."[85] Youth who continued to use the streets were more and more often seen as "bad kids" who were a "menace to the moral order of neighborhoods."[86] Groups of children and youth on the street became mobile "broken windows" in Oakland politics. They represented the city's stalled progress in constructing vibrant landscapes of consumption. They served as signs of deeper disorders—as evidence of failed parental supervision or socialization that threatened economic development. And they had to be "cleaned up" off the streets or fixed so that crime and disorder would not follow them. Only then would economic development take hold.

Saving Youth with a Geographic Fix

The Laurel NCPC conducted an assembly at the local middle school in January 2001 that highlighted the connection between the efforts to save youth and the efforts to restructure space in Oakland. Jackie Patterson and Robert Walker spearheaded this effort to change what they saw as the increasingly outrageous behavior of young people on the streets near the school. Jackie had distributed fliers to all middle school students and sent fliers home to parents. The flier announced "WARNING" in big letters, explaining that school staff, Oakland police, merchants, parents, and neighbors would be "monitoring the activity of youth" and would take "appropriate action" if students committed any violations. A list followed that blurred distinctions between "defiance of authority," minor offenses, such as jaywalking or littering, and more serious criminal acts like sexual assault, concealing weapons, and drug dealing. The flier echoed the common assumption that small violations could be signs of more serious crime or violence to come. But this strange list also implicitly redefined all children's misbehavior on these corners as criminal. This flier included three clip art cartoon pictures that provide an interesting symbolic representation of the vision of law and order implicit in this campaign. In the upper right hand corner a young woman with blond hair and big eyes runs carelessly down a city street dropping pieces of paper behind her on the ground. In the left corner a judge, complete with wig and gavel, stands behind the bench and stares down sternly through wire-rim glasses. At the bottom of the page stands a police officer, fists clenched, mouth wide open, barking an order with such force that his whole body shakes. Although the flier says that all adults will be watching youth, the criminal justice system alone watches and speaks in these pictures. The order to youth implicit in these pictures is written in a highlighted box below: "The best thing to do is leave the area when school lets out!!!"

Throughout this assembly in front of three hundred eighth graders Robert and Jackie tried to draw clear lines between the spaces where students belonged—home and school—and the spaces where they didn't—the streets and corners. They explained that the police would be monitoring the corners and that any misbehavior (from throwing eggs and "spit balls" to fighting and drug dealing) could lead to arrest. Robert Walker tried to drive home their point, saying, "Seriously speaking. When you're out on that corner. . . . I'm not saying all of you are on that corner. I believe most kids here are good kids. I'm at City Hall everyday convincing people that this is not a school full of potential thugs, potential gangsters." As Robert spoke, many students laughed, several raised their hands, and one African American boy shouted out his question, "What corner?" Robert thought he asked this question to be disruptive (and he may have), but the question fundamentally rejected the definition of the corner as a space that turned children into thugs and gangsters. Students at this assembly understood the symbolic weight of "kids on corners." But for them, the corner was both a practical necessity (a bus stop) and a relatively safe place to relax in an unstructured way with friends after school. There were not many such spaces in Oakland. Indeed, fears of youth repeatedly stood in the way of efforts to create unstructured and minimally supervised spaces for youth.

Later in this assembly Jackie and Robert used Proposition 21's recent passage to define the street corner as a space that could literally and metaphorically turn children into adults. Jackie asked students if they knew about the recently passed "Proposition 20—" She hesitated, trying to recall the exact number. Several students called out "Proposition 21." Jackie had all the kids fourteen and over raise their hands. With about half the hands in the room raised, she announced, "You are now considered adults by California if you commit a crime." Here Jackie exaggerated the effects of Proposition 21. While it allowed fourteen-year-olds to be charged as adults for "serious and violent felonies," it stopped short of redefining all youth criminals as adults.

Robert went even further as he tried to get an increasingly restless room to pay attention. "Did you hear what she said? If you are fourteen years old in the state of California, you're an adult." No room full of eighth graders was going to let that comment pass. Students laughed and began debating loudly about what they should then be able to do. An African American girl raised her hand determinedly and said, "If you consider us adults, why can't we drive or drink?" The whole room burst into applause. Jackie tried to clarify her point. "If you commit a crime—three strikes—you are an adult. But . . . don't go home and say you can do whatever you want. You are not an adult in the real world—only if you commit a crime."

This interesting distinction between the status of children in "the real world" and the criminal justice system highlights Robert and Jackie's attempt to make real a world in which children are confined to the safety of home and school. If, however, youth step outside of this "real world" to misbehave on the corners, "Three strikes—you're an adult." This was not simply a metaphor. An increasingly punitive state treated at least some kids as adults. And these legal and symbolic exclusions from childhood, especially of black boys, made these efforts to keep kids off the streets more urgent. Robert and Jackie were not suggesting that African American children in the streets should be treated as adults or as criminals, but that they would be, no matter what their class status or where they lived.

At the end of the assembly, an African American boy asked if the police had "the right to beat us down?" Robert effectively answered yes. "You have to bring yourself under control. If you don't, the police have the authority to use any force because to them, you're out of control."[87] As students filed out of the assembly, several young people went to talk to Robert. One young woman asked, "Why do you want us to go to jail instead of get an education?" Robert didn't want her to go to jail, as he explained, but he did think that self-restraint was an absolute necessity for black kids—especially boys—who had to overcome both the image of black youth criminality and the accompanying harsh forms of social control. Robert justified the need for an expanded police presence in terms of his fears about police power, explaining that a few years before, the police had broken up a student fight with liberal use of pepper spray and handcuffs. "We don't want the cops to feel outnumbered because a scared cop is a dangerous cop." By threatening students with police surveillance (even violence), Robert and Jackie were trying "to scare kids straight" and thus to save them from material forms of policing and exclusion that had intensified in the post–civil rights era.

Many black parents across Oakland worried that black kids were no longer being given the tools they needed to survive in what was often a law-and-order state. Robert thought that black traditions of vigilant discipline for black young men had been disrupted. "Somehow as black parents, we feel we can just let our kids go. . . . I see it as actually a sign of progress. Thirty-five years ago in Oakland you could not let your son walk the street because the police would pick them up. Now they can walk the street, and they only worry about other black males." But he worried about the police as well so he tried to instill the discipline necessary for his son to come of age safely. "You can't say, 'You can do everything,' to a minority that gets locked up at three times the rate of white people. You do not have the same rights, and you learn that very early on. What you think is right—and what should be right—in America is not. The sooner you figure it out—the sooner you can adjust—and not be angry your whole life."

Dr. Smith and Mrs. Tucker thought that post-civil-rights–era California made the significance of race opaque for many parents. "A lot of them think that they're in wonderful liberal California, and their kids are a different color than what they are. That's sad. We had more protective environments. Our parents gave us armor to handle things." Dr. Smith added, "Plus we grew up in the middle of things—the civil rights movement, Vietnam War—so not only did our parents teach us, but we could see it right in action. It was on the evening news tonight. These kids don't know about it. If their parents don't teach them, they have no idea." The Smiths did not argue for a model of childhood innocence in which children should be protected from the harsh realities of the world. Even as they tried to keep their children safe in the house and in school, they insisted that black parents had to give their children the armor to make it in a world where race still shaped the path to adulthood.

Linda Jackson in Elmhurst, Robert Walker in the Laurel district, and Dr. and Mrs. Smith in the hills all gave their own version of the speech that "young people today have too many damn rights." Mrs. Jackson and Robert were simply baffled by youth activists' demands for their rights to the street at the loitering hearing. As Robert explained,

Kids need structure. I don't know that the street is a good place for teenagers. There's nothing there. They need to be in programs. They need to be being kids. They don't need to be locked in the house. But on the other hand, it's not their right to hang out on the corner. Being on a corner is not getting you to Cal or getting you a degree from Yale.

The streets posed two connected dangers for teenagers: they interfered with successful transitions to adulthood (getting into college), but they also stopped kids from "being kids" since "normal" childhood has been redefined as being "in programs."

Robert and Jackie's presentation redefined kids on the streets as adults in way that posed a real problem for their efforts to save kids. They drew on and reinforced a "protectionist approach" that framed children as dependent, innocent, and vulnerable.[88] But the assumption that good kids are not found on the street made it easy to define any kid on the street as up to no good. They became not innocent "angels" but folk "devils" ineligible for the protections of childhood.[89] Youth on the street became symbolically "dirt" or "matter out of place." As anthropologist Mary Douglas explains, "dirt is that which must not be included if a pattern is to be maintained."[90] Youth on the streets had to be excluded either from the streets *or* from childhood to secure the foundational links between public and private/adult and child.[91] Robert told me that "on the street, it's a different rule of law." Unlike in school, no one was "obligated to teach" young people or "get on their case," so students were "on their own in the streets." In this analysis, student misbehavior on the streets became "criminal" instead of "delinquent" and adults were no longer responsible for their care and education. This is an example of a growing tendency to exclude from childhood anyone who challenges ideals of childhood innocence.[92] By excluding youth on the streets from the protections of childhood, adults secure the sanctity and purity of childhood as an ideal.[93]

Black homeowner activists throughout the city consistently campaigned both for more money for after-school programs and for more policing and surveillance of the streets. Local geography and structures of community participation shaped these demands and the way the city responded. In the Elmhurst flatlands, homeowner activists often focused on demanding more police to keep young people off the streets, while in the Laurel community activists used their own volunteer labor to build new spaces for children that would offer poor kids the same structured and supervised educational opportunities increasingly characteristic of middle-class childhoods. Both these efforts consolidated the definition of youth on the streets as out of place. Young people who remained in public spaces, whether waiting at bus stops, hanging out with friends, or dealing drugs, were subjected to intensified police sweeps and private security surveillance.

At a community meeting in the spring of 2001, Jackie Patterson described the success of their effort to get kids off the street in the Laurel district: "By 3:30 or 4:00 kids are basically gone." As an example of progress, she said, "A kid sitting on his porch" had seen a police officer pass by and gone inside. "So there's been a big improvement." We see here a deeply privatized vision of both childhood and public space, where even a kid's use of his porch is suspect. The streets became a no man's land for children.

Oakland's neighborhood activists were essentially looking for a "geographic fix" for the massive racial and class inequalities in childhood in the city. As Don Mitchell describes, they were creating "a geographical solution for what is a social—and a political-economic—problem."[94] They fought to get youth off the streets as a way to save children and reconstruct childhood in the context of a retreating welfare state and an increasingly law-and-order response to urban problems. This geographic fix may have been particularly appealing in the context of a broader state abandonment of efforts to reform young people—that, following Michel Foucault, we might call disciplinary technologies of governance.[95] Many black activists worried that parents, schools, and the juvenile justice system no longer adequately instilled discipline in children. In place of disciplinary technologies that aim to retrain the soul, schools and even the juvenile justice system increasingly relied on "zero tolerance policies" that simply punished or excluded youth for misbehavior.[96] Black homeowner activists regularly complained that state disinvestments in young people had helped produce the disorder on Oakland's streets, and they supported youth programs that would instill self-discipline. But in the context of increasingly insecure state commitments, they hoped that getting youth off the streets could at least help young people negotiate the precipitous transition to adulthood safely while protecting youth from an increasingly punitive state.

Nowhere to Go

There was a pervasive sense among Oakland's youth that they had "nowhere to go" and "nothing to do."[97] These complaints frustrated many Oakland policy makers and adult community activists. Oakland had significantly increased its investments in programs for children and youth since the late 1990s. At a community meeting in 2001, city council member Dick Spees complained that with Kids First and other programs, "now Oakland is spending thirty-seven million dollars for children's services." He wondered "where the money is going when kids are still telling us there's nothing to do." Councilman Spees' quandary points to several shortcomings in Oakland's expanded infrastructure for youth. The fragmented structure of nonprofit youth services often left young people with insufficient knowledge about existing programs. But there was a bigger problem. These complaints mostly came from *teenagers*, who didn't necessarily want the kind of services the city was funding.

Oakland had built up its infrastructure of school-based after-school programs, which helped fill urgent gaps in care and supervision for younger kids. But many older teens didn't want to stay in structured and supervised after-school programs. Few programs targeted teens and virtually none funded activities at night and on the weekends.[98] As one 19-year-old told me, she was "too old for the Boys and Girls Clubs." Many didn't want to stay in school-based programs, especially kids who were struggling as they came of age, because school was not a positive or supportive environment. Public schools are rarely spaces where young people are recognized as full human beings and where they can freely express their needs and desires.[99] Students considered most "at risk"—those who were suspended, frequently absent, and with low test scores—were only 25% of participants in Oakland's after-school programs.[100] Tanesha Miller's three sons in the Laurel district, who got teased a lot at school and were frequently suspended, didn't participate in the after-school program at Bret Harte. She explained, "My kids don't want to stay in school any longer than they have to."

Public spaces may be particularly important for youth, who are in the process of forging independence and crafting both individual and social identities.[101] The need is urgent for poor youth, as legal scholar Regina Austin observes: "Many seek leisure outside their homes and in public places because they do not have basements, backyards, or other safe private spaces to use; the streets are their chief recreation and socializing venues."[102] Youth studies scholars Hall et al. identified a pervasive problem with local efforts to "provide a place for youth to go" like those in Oakland. Many youth centers or after-school programs "may provide much valued space for association, expression and the exploration of identity," but they "simultaneously serve to corral young people, containing and supervising their activities." This leads to a recurring cycle in which older teens leave structured settings as they search for autonomous spaces, younger kids take their place, and policy makers wonder why teens still think there's nothing to do.[103]

Youth wanted safe and cool places of belonging, not programs designed to fix their educational, social, or cultural deficits.[104] In surveys and interviews, young Oaklanders asked for informal spaces where they could socialize with peers, play sports, and explore creative arts no longer available in schools. They wanted lounges where they could watch TV and movies, or play pool and arcade games. They envisioned teen centers that would be staffed by teens, have youth-led conflict mediation, and employ aggressive, youth-designed publicity.[105] This need for space was particularly urgent for poor youth growing up in the East Oakland flatlands. Youth activists mapped public schools, parks, and recreation centers throughout Oakland—and found stark differences between the hills and flatlands. In the hills, they found "abundant, safe, and usable" facilities, while in the flatlands "facilities, where they exist at all, are dilapidated."[106]

Young people also wanted to participate in the life of the city, to see and be seen, to enjoy the pleasures of window shopping, going to the movies, and socializing with friends in public. They often did not want to be segregated in kids' spaces. Youth I spoke with often said that they had to leave Oakland "to have real fun." They went "to Berkeley, Richmond, or San Francisco to hang out with friends in arcades, in shopping malls, or public places where adults hang out too." There were too few movie theaters, fairs, and festivals in Oakland, and the shopping malls "are run-down or there's nothing to buy." Jack London Square was the only place in Oakland where they could go to popular movies. Otherwise they had to travel to suburban malls like Bayfair, Southland, or South Shore. "There's no place in Oakland that stays open late enough for teens to hang out together."[107] Teenagers wanted spaces where they could exercise autonomy but also where they could play safely at young adult behavior. In focus groups at both Skyline and Castlemont High School, students complained that they were excluded from many adult things. Most of all, they wanted a "club to go dancing" that might be open late Friday and Saturday nights. Luis, a Castlemont senior, said, "Not all youth got to go home at midnight. Some youth have a late curfew, and they want to use it up as much as possible."

The spaces young people wanted were the very spaces that adult policy makers and neighborhood activists have been the most hesitant to provide. Oakland's Youth Commission tried to develop a teen center in 2000 that would have live music, dances, and poetry slams, but they ran into perennial concerns about safety, drugs, and sex, which shut down the idea of "a teen club." Spaces that became informal youth hangouts on MacArthur Boulevard were targeted and closed by community activists. We saw how at Skyline High School Nate Miley insisted that the Youth Center would *not* be a place to "hang out" but would provide services that would make youth better citizens—services that would "fix" kids. In contrast, when Skyline Task Force

Figure 15. Dance battles at Youth UpRising. (Dancer: D-real, photo courtesy of Yoram Savion, Youth UpRising)

youth described their vision for a youth center, they often talked about wanting "just a place where you could go . . . hang out with your friends. Like if you don't wanna go home after school."

Youth UpRising, a publicly funded youth center, promised to be this kind of cool hangout when it opened in the East Oakland flatlands in 2005. Planned by young people, including members of Youth Together, Youth UpRising's architecture and programming embraced Oakland's streets and youth cultures. It has provided a valuable venue for public performances of Oakland's indigenous hip hop culture, hosting popular and usually peaceful dance battles for young people to demonstrate their skills to an audience of up to four hundred mostly black teenagers and young adults in its outdoor amphitheater.

But Youth UpRising (YU) also demonstrates significant dilemmas of building these kinds of cool places. The dance battles helped attract more street-affiliated youth, but the center sometimes found it hard to keep them in more formal classes and programs. Grounding the center in hip hop culture—which remains marked as "authentically" black despite its appeal across racial lines— also made it hard to create a multiracial youth space. In a neighborhood that was half Latino, YU attracted mostly black kids. Youth

UpRising was also publicly attacked for promoting "thug culture" because it worked with local hip hop artists. And even Youth UpRising was not staffed at levels that allowed it to stay open late into the evening and weekends.[108]

Conclusion

Changes in childhood, and these campaigns to save children, have helped reshape urban space and emerging forms of governance at the turn of the twenty-first century. Parents and children have produced new landscapes of childhood, and the daily movements of young people through these landscapes invested new meanings in Oakland's public and private spaces. They helped produce new landscapes of consumption that redefined what counted as proper use of public space in the city. Paying attention to childhood and youth does not just add details to our understanding of neoliberal restructuring. Neoliberal urban redevelopment was fought out and fundamentally remade through local struggles over youth and social reproduction.

Black homeowners and activists in Oakland have been a vital part of constructing Oakland's neoliberal urban regime. They were deeply concerned about the safety and security of children. And they supported intensified efforts to reshape the way young people used space in the city to help youth negotiate an increasingly precipitous transition to adulthood. The terrible irony is that many black activists supported expanded policing and surveillance of youth in order to protect black kids from being criminalized by an increasingly repressive state. In the process, black activists helped to construct the heavily policed and privatized spaces characteristic of neoliberal cities. These efforts risked exacerbating Oakland's geographies of exclusion.[109]

Oakland's deeply unequal childhoods cannot be solved by after-school programs, truancy programs, or loitering laws, no matter how valuable some of those programs might be. "Creating proper urban geographies" for children cannot replace progressive policies that provide living-wage jobs, affordable health care, stable housing, equal educational opportunities, and healthy food for children, youth and their families. Oakland alone cannot solve these vast inequalities—but defining youth on the streets as broken windows may get in the way of efforts to do so. As Mitchell argues, "regulating space can easily be substituted for concerted progressive policies designed to attack social problems and to expand the content of urban social justice."[110] The geographic fix may even bolster the current political and economic order that has produced such deep divides in the landscapes of childhood. Adults may stop asking why young people are hanging out on the corner, insisting instead that they do not have the right to do so. Kids on the street become potential thugs, a dangerous image that justifies efforts to control, restrain, or exclude youth instead of to care for them.

We see here a deep problem with the logic of the broken windows thesis—especially as it applied to youth in Oakland. Legal scholar Bernard Harcourt, and many other scholars, have argued that broken windows policing does not actually reduce crime. Harcourt points out that increased police surveillance also comes with "a big price tag": enormous increases in spending on police, significant increases in civilian complaints, and deepening distrust of the police in communities of color.[111] Oakland's relentless focus on reducing crime statistics and producing public order certainly increased tensions between the police and youth of color. As Oakland hip hop artist and activist Boots Riley of The Coup explained, the city's zero tolerance policies and police crackdowns targeted Oakland's young people of color "as potential criminals" and made them "feel unwelcome in their own neighborhoods."[112]

Young people were not silent in these struggles over childhood and public space in Oakland. At the loitering hearing, at the school assembly, and in the city's streets, young people repeatedly contested their exclusions from public space. Students at the assembly and the loitering hearing directly refused the definition of street corners as spaces that turned children into thugs and gangsters. At the assembly students fidgeted, chatted, and giggled as Jackie and Robert threatened punishments and struggled to keep the room in order. This kind of disruptive behavior was "not a symptom" of "incomplete training in public etiquette"; it was a "meaningful" refusal to follow the rules, and a way in which students conveyed something about "their relation to the adult world."[113] Students broke out laughing when Robert called them "potential thugs or gangsters" and began shouting out objections and talking loudly when they were threatened with being tried as adults. Their outbursts pointedly challenged the schizophrenic ways we treat adolescents in the United States: as children with limited rights of citizenship and yet as adults fully responsible and accountable for their actions.[114]

Youth in Oakland fought to claim what geographer Donald Mitchell calls the right to the city—access to public space and a place in the city's public sphere. Many kids were trapped outside looking in at the city's new landscapes of consumption. Their struggle for access was not always orderly. It sometimes erupted into violence. It included young people looking for a place to hang out with friends after school and young people dealing drugs as they struggled to find a place in the current economic order. Young people often resisted adult authority in ways that helped perpetuate their exclusion from public spaces. Disorderly students reinforced adult assumptions that students needed discipline and couldn't handle autonomy. One Skyline Youth Together student explained, "Teenagers are just rowdy. And we can never have anything. Some don't know how to act. That's why we don't get things when we ask for them because some of us don't know how to act." These comments hint at a complex dynamic produced by what author Jeff Chang calls "the politics of containment."[115] As the number of public spaces for youth declined, youth crowds were more likely to overwhelm the few spaces that were available to them, like Jack London Square. Then, if youth were disorderly, public policy makers used this as an argument for the need to further restrict young people's uses of public space.

Youth activists interpreted the proposed antiloitering law very differently than the older, mostly African American homeowners at the council meeting described at the start of this chapter. But it would be wrong to interpret these divergent responses simply as evidence of a generational divide between "rowdy teenagers" and "old heads" or between "respectable" and "street values."[116] Youth activists and homeowner activists were embedded in very different political mobilizations that shaped the ways they articulated the needs and problems of youth. Young people remained marginalized from many of Oakland's neighborhood political networks and centers of policy debate. But even middle school students had contact with Oakland's youth activists and were well educated about public policies like Proposition 21. Youth were organizing and developing their own kind of politics that reworked definitions of childhood and youth.

What Is "the Power of the Youth"?

Prop 21 has been okayed again
us youngstas could cast no vote, but can be sent to the Pen.
What is going on in this world we live in,
and why are we young being tried as adults?
Explain to me, America, why you have given up hope.
You've robbed our childhoods,
surrounding us with guns and dope.
You're running full ahead on punishment
but turning your back on an antidote.
Are we not a republican government, governed by the people?
Then why don't teenagers have a vote?
Are we not people?
Why in court can we be adults,
but outside the courts we are not their equal?
You need to end this awful sequel
or in the future there be a different reason
why America's called a melting pot:
It'll be because adults turned their back on their young,
who suffered moral rot
for they, the young, were suffering from gridlock.
The world had changed so fast and so much
that parents had no time for tutelage for their kids
which left their learning up to luck.
A child left with no teaching
of the real world outside the classroom
will wander aimlessly, and inevitably self-destruct.
After wandering through these urban streets,
the goodest of people are bound to be corrupt.
The parents paid attention of course,
but they failed to teach enough
they had no time because times were rough,
they had to work two times as hard as their parents
and left their child's life up to luck.

> —Dwayne The Knowledge, Alameda County
> Juvenile Hall, published in *The Beat Within*

On a sunny afternoon in April 2001, a multiracial crowd of 150 teenagers and young adults marched through downtown Oakland to demand that the Board of Supervisors abandon plans to build a "Super Jail for Kids." Months before, the county supervisors had unanimously approved plans to build a new juvenile hall, expanded from 299 to 540 beds, in a far-flung suburb of Alameda County. At first this plan attracted little attention, but that changed as youth activists began a sustained campaign. At this first protest, Latino, Southeast Asian, Tongan, black, and Jewish high school students marched alongside local college students, young teachers, and nonprofit workers towards the entrance to the Board of Supervisors offices. Many dressed in hip hop styles: young men in hooded sweatshirts and sagging pants marched alongside teenage girls in tight pants flared at the ankles. The crowd slowly filed through metal detectors, and past armed sheriff's deputies, sending backpacks and signs through the x-ray machines, as their chants echoed through the corridors—"Books not bars. Schools not jails"; "No more beds"; and the rhythmic, "Ain't no power like the power of the youth, 'cause the power of the youth don't stop. Say what?" Older men and women with suits and leather briefcases leaving the county building stopped and stared in curiosity. The crowd packed into the Board of Supervisors hearing, a sea of young people surrounding a row of county officials in suits, scattered juvenile justice experts, and a few older community representatives. I marched and chanted along with the youth activists and then retreated to watch from the back of the room, sitting uncomfortably between a youth organizer and an assistant DA, both of whom I had interviewed. The DA, James Thurman, an African American man in his early fifties, insisted that the county needed the additional beds and he worried that these protests could backfire and even lead to reinstating the death penalty if a kid on probation committed a terrible crime while out of juvenile hall.

The meeting began with a formal probation presentation to the five county supervisors explaining that the county needed a new, larger juvenile hall to plan for population growth. But this was not a standard Board of Supervisors meeting. Midway through the probation department's formal presentation, a young man with coffee-colored skin and curly brown hair interrupted, "We came here to make our case." Scott Haggerty, the president of the Board of Supervisors, repeatedly threatened to "shut down the meeting" if youth were not respectful. Shortly thereafter, youth activists were called up to testify. They performed raps and spoken word poetry, engaged in call and response with the audience, and told personal stories alongside more familiar calls for "alternatives to incarceration," "services," and jobs for youth. The first speaker, an organizer with Youth Force Coalition, asked for a moment of silence for people locked up in juvenile hall, and then launched into a freestyle rap about prisoners behind walls, as he urged the supervisors to put "freedom first, touch the skies, not concrete walls and metal doors." The supervisors listened with puzzled expressions on their faces as the young audience bounced their heads in rhythm, pumped their hands in the air, and cheered for the young rapper.

The campaign against the Super Jail won a series of victories. Youth protestors convinced the conservative Board of Corrections to turn down $2.3 million of preapproved money for the Alameda County expansion. They convinced the two African American supervisors, Nate Miley and Keith Carson, to vote against any expansion. Slowly over the next two years, the proposed juvenile hall shrank in size from 540 beds to 450 beds. Finally, in May 2003, the Board of Supervisors voted to build a 360-bed juvenile hall at the current site. To win this victory, youth activists formed close alliances with juvenile justice think tanks like the Youth Law Center, Annie E. Casey Foundation, and the National Council on Crime and Delinquency, which provided youth activists with statistics and concrete proposals for reducing the county's reliance on incarceration. They also formed a surprising alliance with homeowners in Dublin to fight against locating the new juvenile hall in this suburb far from the homes and families of most incarcerated youth. Possibly most important, youth activists challenged the punitive turn in the nation's youth policies and, in the words of one county staff person, pushed alternatives to detention to "the forefront of the county agenda."[1]

The Super Jail campaign was part of a rising tide of youth activism in California and across the nation that challenged what activists call "the criminalization of a generation."[2] Youth activist organizations throughout the 1990s developed new grass-roots strategies for engaging youth in diverse local political struggles from New York to the Bay Area, from Portland to rural Louisiana.[3] Several training centers and networks, including the Funders' Collaborative on Youth Organizing, the Haywood Burn's Institute, and the Movement Strategy Center, have begun to knit together these local grass-roots initiatives to share strategies and forge national and sometimes transnational coalitions. Popular books like Anya Kamenetz's *Generation Debt* have called for youth to organize in colleges, workplaces, and the halls of government to demand more public investment in young people. Beyond the United States, youth activism is on the rise globally, as young people from sub-Saharan Africa to Brazil have begun to organize and craft oppositional political identities in response to the potent combination of shrinking economic opportunities and expanded consumer desires driven by globalized media.[4]

This campaign built on a series of local youth activist mobilizations that challenged the punitive turn in our nation's youth policies in the 1990s, from school discipline policies to local curfews and antiloitering ordinances. In 2000, youth activists in California gained national attention in their fight against Proposition 21, a ballot initiative that increased penalties for a wide range of juvenile offenses and made it far easier to try juveniles as young as fourteen as adults. Each of these campaigns directly challenged the ways particular laws and public policies had "criminalized youth" by treating them as objects of discipline, control, or surveillance, but they also engaged in a much broader struggle to reshape the cultural and legal definition of childhood and the place of youth as citizens of the city.

Throughout this book, we have seen children and youth serve as powerful symbols in Oakland politics, central to discussions about the city's past and future and to debates about crime, education, and urban redevelopment. In most of the city's political networks, young people themselves remained marginalized or silent, more often treated as objects of reform or as symbols of neighborhood decline than as political subjects. But we have also repeatedly seen children and youth contest their exclusions from full citizenship and from public space.

Daniel HoSang, an American studies scholar, argues that this new generational political identity emerged in response to a political and economic "assault on youth citizenship" in the 1980s and '90s. Conservative attacks on the welfare state led to declining investments in young people, but also to a new round of get tough on youth policies. In the process, "youth itself became a pejorative identity, emblematic of the failure of family, values, and nation."[5] Oakland scholar-activists Shawn Ginwright and Taj James argue that young people today, like blacks before 1954, "face intense economic isolation, lack political power and are subjected to pervasive social stigma."[6] These assaults on young people certainly politicized a generation. But the complex cultural meanings we attach to youth also made it a powerful political identity. Located between childhood and adulthood, between dependence and independence, youth inevitably calls attention to the relationships among generations and to a broader terrain of social relations.[7]

Youth activists used generational identities to challenge some of the central premises of neoliberal urban governance that we have explored in this book. They used claims to youth to construct a space for protest politics and to make demands on the state in an era of partnership and community-based governance. They drew on childhood, and the notions of parental responsibility it demands, to reconstruct a vision of the state as parent, and to fight for a more comprehensive vision of the welfare state. They offered compelling critiques of the ways in which neoliberal urban policies redrew the boundaries between public and private spheres.

Youth activists rejected a model of childhood that locates children off the streets and in the private sphere. They used urban space and youth cultural practices to construct a new view of youth as active citizens with a legitimate place in the public spaces of the city and in the body politic. The youth movement's claims to public space were particularly important in the context of the local (and national) dominance of neoliberal models of urban redevelopment.[8] We have seen how youth, and particularly youth of color, have been repeatedly cleared from public space as Oakland has tried to create landscapes for middle-class consumption. Youth protests fundamentally challenged this erasure of young people from public space. By combining dance parties with street protests, they challenged the perception that youth socializing was dangerous and reclaimed public space for youth cultural practices. These political occupations of public space claimed a "right to the city" that was necessary for claiming the rights of citizenship that are often fundamentally denied to youth.[9]

Youth activists constructed a social movement that foregrounded a politics of generation instead of race. They forged new political networks that linked young people across racial lines to challenge neoliberal public policies that had abandoned and criminalized a generation. But this generational politics was not color-blind. Youth activists directly challenged the racialized images of youth crime that have been central to building support for increased state investments in police surveillance and prisons. They emphasized the ways in which state policies excluded youth of color, and black boys in particular, from childhood and from public spaces. It is important to consider why a politics of generation emerged in urban centers nationwide, and how it transformed, but did not abandon, racial political subjectivities. This politics of generation offers an intriguing alternative to the race and class political subjectivities we've seen in homeowner and parent politics.

Creating a Counterpublic

The "Super Jail" and "No on Prop 21" campaigns drew a lot of news media attention as youth movements, and the press was endlessly fascinated by what one news headline described as the "idealistic, poetic," and "jarring" form youth activism took.[10] Young people claimed moral high ground and embodied knowledge as they spoke about juvenile justice issues. High school and college students often led the protests against Proposition 21 and the Super Jail, and most, though not all participants in these overlapping campaigns were relatively young, between the ages of fourteen and thirty. Get tough on youth crime policies had politicized many young people in California. But the age of participants did not determine that activists would organize or be identified as a "youth movement."

Youth, as a political identity, provided activists with the material and symbolic space to craft a new counterpublic.[11] Youth protests included elements of political carnival, rituals that, as anthropologist Victor Turner argues, often invert existing hierarchies.[12] The initial protest at the Board of Supervisors meeting intentionally disrupted the traditional form of expert testimony. Instead of professionals speaking eloquently about youth problems while young people remained silent, young people challenged the probation department's authority and silenced the adult experts. Youth activists then symbolically put the probation department itself on trial. They often played with and inverted the form of the legal trial and the language of criminal guilt and innocence. At another protest, one speaker made this inversion explicit, saying, "This generation wasn't born to be put on trial by the system. It was born to put the system on trial" and "Youth are not criminal. Not funding education is criminal."

Youth was a powerful political identity in Oakland, partly because it symbolically connected contemporary activism to a tradition of idealism, rebellion, and radical protest with deep roots in the Bay Area. Youth are expected to challenge authority in the American cultural imagination. Vivid memories of the Black Panthers, Chicano Movement student walkouts, and Asian student movements helped consolidate this image of the revolutionary potential of youth in the Oakland imaginary. Youth activists often mobilized images of youth as revolutionary on the handheld fliers they passed out in school. In one flier for a rally against the Super Jail, a young person stands with hands on a detonator ready to blow up prison bars with dynamite. The fissures in the words "No More Cell Blocks for Youth" suggest that the walls are crumbling from the force of youth activism (See Figure 16). A flier for one of the biggest anti–Prop 21 rallies explicitly connected the activism of the hip hop generation to the youth movements of the sixties and seventies. This flier shows a brown arm thrust straight out of rolling sands, holding up a microphone in a clenched fist, a black power salute for the hip hop generation. This symbolic link between past and present social movements enhanced the power of youth as a political identity in Oakland (See Figure 17).

Figure 16. No More Cell Blocks. A flier for the campaign against the expansion of Alameda County's Juvenile Hall.

Van Jones, an African American, Yale-educated lawyer and youth advocate, described the Super Jail campaign as "traditional militant youth activism." Jones founded the Ella Baker Center, named for the organizer who most emphasized youth organizing in the civil rights movement. They used videos of civil rights protests as part of their youth organizing training, and one flier, called "The Birth of a Movement," connected contemporary activists to the young people who "led sit-ins at lunch counters that sparked a generation of protest." Jones constructed this lineage back to 1960s protests to launch a familiar critique of civil rights–era leadership. Most civil rights organizations today were "too lame and too tired. . . . I don't believe the true power of the people can be confined to a ballot box. . . . We need to be about the whup-ass. . . . You have to be creative about how you engage the enemy because if you do it on his terms, the outcome is already known."[13]

Youth activists intentionally built a political infrastructure separate from Oakland's established, adult-run civil rights networks, churches, and community organizations. Speaking as youth, they created the space for oppositional politics at a time when black and Latino political incorporation and neoliberal discourses of "community responsibility" had delegitimized protest politics.[14]

Figure 17. Hip Hop Power Salute. A flier for No on
Prop 21 protest, printed by Third Eye Movement,
designed by Local 1200, a hip hop collective.

Many of the established black churches and civic organizations developed
very close working relationships with city politicians and with the police as
the black urban regime consolidated political power in the 1980s and early
'90s. These organizations usually followed bureaucratic "problem-solving"
channels, embraced discourses of "partnership," and avoided confrontational politics. Partnerships in policing often encouraged black neighborhood activists to redefine their rights of citizenships as the right to sufficient
policing. Middle-class parent activists frequently relied on volunteer labor
to make up for public disinvestments in children's environments. Even when
adults fought for expanded investments in youth, they too often reproduced
images of youth as dangerous or deficient. Narrow visions of private, family
responsibility for youth repeatedly stood in the way of crafting a more progressive politics of childhood.

Youth activism against the Super Jail and Prop 21 was nurtured by a densely
networked infrastructure of nonprofit youth services in the Bay Area. Most
youth nonprofits in Oakland were service providers, effectively incorporated
into government and hesitant to directly challenge local politicians. Indeed,
when some nonprofit leaders expressed concerns about plans to expand juve-

nile hall during a probation service provider meeting in 2000, a county probation official explicitly warned that they represented the probation department
and so should avoid criticism of the planned expansion. But many youth organizations developed youth leadership and organizing groups during the 1990s.
These organizations trained succeeding generations of youth activists and
helped consolidate youth as a political identity.[15] One executive director drew
the distinction between these "political youth service providers" and "service
providers with no politics," which she insisted could "not create social change."

Many of the youth activist groups organized within specific high schools
or primarily along racial or ethnic lines, but repeatedly came together in
coalitions that challenged law and order responses to youth violence and
demanded expanded investments in youth. Core youth activist organizations
in Oakland in the late 1990s included Youth Together, the multiracial high
school organizing effort; AYPAL, an Asian and Pacific Islander high school
activist network; the East Bay Asian Youth Center; Leadership Excellence, an
African American youth leadership organization; Youth for Oakland United
(YOU), a youth organizing committee of People United for a Better Life in
Oakland (PUEBLO); Young Women United for Oakland, an organizing project run by and for low-income young women of color; UNYTE, the youth
organizing effort of a homeless advocacy group; Youth Alive, an antiviolence
peer education and intervention program; and Olin (later Huaxtec), a Latino
student activist group mentored by a local labor activist. Olin was one of the
few long-standing grass-roots groups that refused to become incorporated as
a nonprofit and so had no paid staff or grants.

The Kids First! Coalition (KF!C) first formally brought together a tightly
knit group of these youth service providers and high school activists in 1996
to formulate a systematic challenge to Oakland's law and order responses to
youth crime and to build support for investments in youth development. One
of the founders of KF!C explained that the directors of several youth programs were sitting around "all bellyaching about why it was so hard to raise
money for kids." They were frustrated by chronic funding problems, decimated infrastructure for youth services, and repeated repressive responses
to the problems of youth violence. Borrowing from a similar San Francisco
campaign, they decided to launch a voter initiative—Measure K—that would
mandate that the city dedicate 2.5% of its general fund for grants to nonprofit
services for children and youth.

The Measure K Kids First! Campaign used persuasive images of children
and youth to argue that the state was failing to invest in their future. Youth
researchers wrote reports documenting significant reductions in city spend-

ing for youth programs since the 1960s and charged that the city's failures to fund youth programs deprived youth of "safe havens," perpetuated "low self-esteem for youth," and demonstrated "a lack of the city's commitment to its young people."[16] Groups of children, youth, and parents canvassed neighborhoods for signatures and showed up to city council meetings wearing bright purple t-shirts with yellow line drawings of children posed in acrobatic positions to spell out Kids First. When they had collected the requisite number of signatures, a crowd of children pulled red wagons filled with boxes of signed petitions into city hall. Captured in newspaper photographs, these iconic images helped to convince 75% of voters to pass Measure K. Calling for "an Oakland children's trust fund," youth activists and children's advocates transformed the ultimate image of private privilege (a trust fund) into a demand for public investment that would help all children "succeed in life" and get "their fair share" of the city budget.[17]

Youth activist organizations helped young people develop political critiques that linked their everyday personal struggles to broader disinvestments in children's environments that had deepened racial and class inequalities. Young people in Oakland viscerally felt "their declining value in the declining physical environment" of their homes and schools.[18] As Lupe Gomez, a seventeen-year-old Latina student activist from Castlemont, explained, she lived near an active drug corner in the Elmhurst flatlands and loved her block in many ways. She knew everyone (including the drug dealers), and there were "hecka cool parties." But just a few days before we talked, a gunshot ricocheted through her living room. "Debris flew everywhere. There was a big hole in the wall." She described what it felt like the next day to come to school and "try to have a cool day."

> [You] step into an environment that's all negative. . . . Some teachers are not teaching. Other students feel like you do and don't want to put up with anybody. . . . You get so tired of the situation you in. You want to get out. You'll sit out there and deal drugs. You desperate. . . . You end up in the criminal justice system, which is what they want. Obviously they don't want you coming to school otherwise they'd fund our schools. They wonder why we have such a negative attitude about school. You got to show by example.

Politicized through youth activism, Lupe linked her daily stresses to what youth activists began to call the school-to-prison pipeline.[19] She defined the major struggles youth faced in East Oakland as "becoming a target of the criminal justice system, bad education, even the issue of poverty."

The hypercriminalization of youth had transformed Oakland schools into a confounding maze of control and punishment—into what Victor Duarte, the Youth Together member, called "a prison-state." At a youth speakout, students described the ways tardiness and suspension policies punished students even when they had done little or nothing wrong. At Oakland Tech, one young person explained that when students are late, school officials keep them out of class until fourth period. Youth activists struggled to understand the logic of punishing students for being late by keeping them out of class even longer. Another student reported that some teachers lock students out of the classroom if they are late, and if they're caught in the hall, they are suspended. At one school several kids got suspended for five days for a water balloon fight. A Tongan young man got suspended from Castlemont when his cousin got in a fight, and another African American student "got suspended for breaking up a fight." As sociologist Victor Rios has documented, in cities like Oakland, the "punitive arm of the state" has crossed into "traditionally nurturing institutions" like family, school, and community centers, leading teachers, youth workers, and even parents to label and treat young people as criminals.[20]

Youth activist networks politicized these daily experiences of exclusion on Oakland's streets and schools throughout the late 1990s.[21] Activist-oriented youth nonprofits mobilized high school students to defeat a proposed curfew in 1994; to reduce school suspensions and institute alternative discipline policies; to challenge the school district's decisions to fund its own police department, and, later, to contest efforts to bring the Oakland Police Department into the schools; and to oppose the loitering law. They fought for teen centers, ethnic studies classes, and increased funding for youth programs. In 2003 Kids First! organized a year-long campaign to win free bus passes for students because "public education is supposed to be free."[22] While many youth organizations only had a short life span, each mobilization trained a new generation of young activists, created a culture of social justice activism in the schools, and linked young people across race and geography.

The Bay Area has a dense subculture of social justice organizations that helped nurture youth activism in Oakland. Several progressive organizing training centers, like the Center for Third World Organizing and School of Organizing Unity and Liberation (SOUL), and media organizations, like Youth Media Council and We Interrupt This Message, conducted research and provided organizing training and political education for youth activists. Dahlia Smith, a 23-year-old white queer poet and activist, described the depth of formal and informal activism in the Bay Area. She said, "There's always movement. . . . There are hella young people who know what's going on and are doing shit. It takes so many different forms. Some are staging protests, making demands on big companies, policy makers or government." Others created theater or art collectives. "It's not protest, but it is part of the same thing."

The Bay Area is also home to multiple generations of progressive activists with histories in local labor movements, the Third World student movements, and groups like the Black Panthers. Jakada Imani, a youth organizer and local MC, described the impact of "alive and walking about history." As a young activist, he met a man who had been a member of the Communist Party in the thirties and regularly talked with his friend's father, who had worked security for the Panthers. Long-time Chicano Movement organizers helped nurture Latino youth activist networks in Oakland throughout the 1990s. This older generation of movement activists, who had worked with SNCC, the Black Panthers, and Chicano Movement, still often lived in the Bay Area and maintained ties to younger activists. Many students and youth organizers came together with older activists in September 1998 at the Critical Resistance conference to challenge the prison industrial complex in the United States. One conference subcommittee developed into the Youth Force Coalition, which built regional relationships among youth activists, especially when Proposition 21 was placed on the ballot.

The "youth movement" actually included activists from across a fairly wide age range, including college students and some nonprofit executive directors and hip hop producers in their thirties or forties who worked alongside teenagers in high school or even middle school. Youth activist organizations included a broad spectrum of approaches to developing youth leadership; some were more fully youth led, while others used more of an apprenticeship model that combined adult and youth leadership.[23] As one young organizer explained, "The high school students are running things now. They needed college students as mentors in the beginning, but now they can run their own meetings."[24] Through a process of generational succession, the most active high school activists sometimes moved on to become full-time staff and later directors in nonprofit youth programs, continuing to train younger students. For example, Victor Duarte began as a student activist in high school with Youth Together and Olin, and later returned to work for Youth Together after completing college. Jakada Imani, the thirty-year-old African American youth organizer and MC, first became involved in political activism in high school in East Oakland, where he got involved in campaigns against the proposed curfew in Oakland and against racist textbooks in schools. Later, with the Bay Area Universal Zulu Nation chapter, he conducted "know your rights" workshops for younger kids who complained about violent police crackdowns on hip hop parties. He was a founding member of the cultural collective Underground Railroad and of the hip hop label Freedom Fighters, both of which used hip hop music and networks to promote youth activist campaigns. In 2006, he replaced Van Jones as the executive director of the Ella Baker Center.

Adults who remained engaged activists often continued to claim the space of youth and to use youth cultural forms and institutions, particularly those associated with underground hip hop, to build an infrastructure for progressive social action. Many older leaders maintained personal ties to contemporary youth culture and performed more youthful identities. Like other older participants in youth activist rallies and planning meetings, I found myself unconsciously cultivating very different bodily practices than the bureaucratic professional styles I would adopt when meeting with city and county officials. I wore political t-shirts and jeans instead of slacks and blouses. I swore more, adopted a more informal speaking style, changed my posture, and used particular words and phrases connected to youth and hip hop cultures.

The No on Prop 21 campaign built on this local infrastructure of youth organizing. Youth activists created novel political strategies that combined hip hop concerts and voter registration drives, street protests and carefully crafted media campaigns. They also built relationships with juvenile justice think tanks that provided scientific research and statistics to support youth activist demands. After Proposition 21 passed, youth groups struggled to preserve the momentum that had been generated during the campaign. Several organizations came together to form the Youth Empowerment Center (YEC), which provided space, training, and technical support to nurture youth-led activist collaborations. The Ella Baker Center also launched a statewide campaign called Books Not Bars to focus attention on alternatives to incarceration and to demand a redistribution of state expenditures from "locking kids up" to "lifting them up." The campaign against the Alameda County Juvenile Hall expansion served as a focal point for these developing activist collaborations.

Reclaiming Childhood to Demand an Accountable State

One evening at an East Oakland neighborhood meeting in early 2000, William Johnson, a confident seventeen-year-old African American activist, took the stage to criticize police crackdowns on youth and to urge the crowd to vote against Proposition 21. As he spoke, he called his cousin, a four-foot-tall boy with the chubby, dimpled cheeks of a prepubescent child, to the stage. "Can you imagine this young man in adult prison?" "We don't need more money to fight crime. We need more money for schools so that he can go to college. That's what we need to do instead of throwing us behind bars." Already a veteran in Oakland's youth activist networks, William knew how to use children as powerful political symbols. The image of his fresh-faced cousin on the stage directly challenged racialized images of "youth criminals," "gangbangers," or adult-like "super-predators." William's stagecraft highlights the ways youth activists used the symbolic power of childhood to rework notions of family responsibility and to demand a revitalized state commitment to youth.

Since the 1970s, images of youth as dangerous have been part of an explicit political project to critique the welfare state and to promote law and order responses to urban economic and social crises. We can see the political power of this representation by examining the book *Body Count: Moral Poverty and How to Win America's War on Crime and Drugs*, written by John DiIulio and William Bennett. DiIulio first coined the term, "super-predator" in the mid-1990s to describe a new generation of youth criminals so violent that they shocked and terrified adult prisoners. DiIulio predicted massive increases in violence as this "increasingly violent" teenage population grew from 1990 to 2010. *Body Count* used this "super-predator thesis" to explicitly attack structural explanations that located the causes of youth crime in economic dislocations or racial discrimination. Instead, DiIulio and Bennett defined youth crime as caused by "moral poverty" and the failure of female-headed families to properly raise their children. High black youth crime rates were a "problem of sin not skin." With images comparing youth criminals to "savages" and "wolf-packs," the super-predator thesis encoded deep fears that a growing number of dangerous youth of color threatened the body politic. DiIulio and Bennett used these racialized fears of other people's children to create a powerful argument against state welfare programs. Their theory suggested that there was little the state could do to reform youth or to stop the impending crime wave because the future of the nation was determined solely within the family.[25] Implicitly, *Body Count* suggested that the only appropriate role for the state was that of a policeman.

The "super-predator" crime wave rather notably did not happen. Youth crime actually fell quite dramatically even as youth populations skyrocketed in the late 1990s, both in Oakland and nationwide.[26] But many of the theory's presuppositions continued to influence policy making and politics, even in the self-consciously progressive Bay Area.[27] Alameda County proponents of the expanded juvenile hall relied on remarkably similar assumptions that larger youth populations would lead automatically to more crime and that youth were becoming more violent.[28] As one letter of support for the new juvenile hall explained, the current hall was "not structured or equipped to house the increasing population of youthful offenders who commit serious and violent crimes."[29] A 2002 *Oakland Tribune* article reported that "juveniles commit about 60% of the city's homicides."[30] It turned out the reporter had completely misread a police report: that year, only two juveniles under eighteen had been arrested for murder.[31] Nevertheless the error was easy to make because of the pervasive common sense that youth were dangerous. This kind of news coverage escalated adult fears, even as youth crime fell.[32] A California poll in 1996 found that 60% of adults believed that juveniles committed most violent crime at a time when only 13% of California's violent arrests were of juveniles. As violent youth crime fell by more than 50% in the late nineties, adults still believed that teen violent crime rates were increasing.[33]

We have seen how the image of dangerous youth was a powerful force behind efforts to redefine the role and purpose of government along neoliberal lines in Oakland. Oakland increasingly "governed through crime," and a narrow logic of crime prevention, discipline, and security extended deep into the fabric of the city. Fears of crime reshaped the rhythms of daily life, the structure of local politics, where and how businesses operated, and even how parents and schools responded to the needs and problems of young people. The image of dangerous youth often served to shrink a vision of public responsibility for social welfare, since it was easy to blame faulty families for "disrespectful" young people running the streets.

Youth activists in their juvenile justice campaigns consistently portrayed youth in the juvenile justice system as children. They used the responsibility adults have for children to critique neoliberal models of choice, accountability, and individual responsibility. At anti–Prop 21 rallies, young people held paper cut-outs of prison bars in front of their faces or carried signs with arrows pointing down that said, "I could be in prison now." Often, newspapers showed images of particularly young kids behind bars, boys or girls as young as eleven, highlighting the innocence and vulnerability of the kids who would be affected by the law (See Figure 18). Another flier for a protest showed a multiracial crowd of youth holding signs that said, "CAL Prisons Taking Children," implying that the prison system was kidnapping and corrupting innocent children.

Many youth activist slogans also worked to reclaim childhood for incarcerated youth. Even the choice of the word "kid" in the slogan "Super Jail for Kids" emphasized a connection to childhood more than the word "youth."

Figure 18. Books Not Bars: The symbolic power of childhood. (Photo courtesy of Ella Baker Center for Human Rights, John Pilgrim, photographer)

The heavy circulation of the phrases "youth crime" and "youth violence" had fundamentally transformed the meaning of "youth" so that the term itself signified danger. In contrast, "kid" highlighted the incongruous juxtaposition of innocence and danger. Youth activists argued that young people needed "books not bars" and "coaches not guards." They insisted that children needed proximity to their families and communities, not exile in juvenile halls or out-of-home placements. This rhetoric that emphasized home, family, and recreation tied incarcerated youth back to idealized childhoods. With calls to "expand minds not prisons," youth activists called on the nation to invest in the unlimited potential of children.

Youth activists considered Prop 21 and the Super Jail part of a broader "War on Youth" that was "criminalizing a generation." These rallying cries rejected the fundamental premise of individual responsibility that characterized both the criminal justice system and neoliberal governance. Instead, youth activists argued that criminal justice policies and media representations of youth threatened to define all youth as dangerous. Insisting that all young people were under attack, youth activists called into question the fundamental claims that youth "chose" to become criminal and that crime was a problem of individuals who should be cut off from society. Youth activists routinely challenged the probation department's argument that the new facility was being built for the good of young people. They rejected the department's therapeutic language of reform and argued that locking kids up, even in juvenile hall, turned them into hardened criminals. While the department spoke of "numbers of beds," "youth guidance centers," and "counselors," youth activists referred to "cells," "jails," and "guards." Mariana Lopez, a Latina activist from East Oakland, criticized the new planned location for the juvenile hall next to the adult jail in Dublin. "All the young offenders could just look out the window to see their futures. What kind of message is that to send to our kids?"

Youth activists explicitly highlighted the state's role in excluding youth of color from the protections and normative spaces of childhood. Most obviously, Proposition 21 and other adult transfer policies explicitly exclude some children under eighteen from the category of childhood. Youth of color are far more likely to be tried in the adult system than white youth because courts often use race or racialized labels like "gangs" as a proxy for "dangerousness." One study in Los Angeles County found that black boys were 18.4 times, Latino boys 7.3 times, and Asian boys 4.5 times more likely to be tried as adults than white boys committing similar crimes.[34] This data provides evidence for a hierarchy of racial exclusions that positions Asians and Latinos below whites but continues to locate African Americans at the bottom of the racial hierarchy. The report *And Justice for Some* documents that "youth of color—especially African American youth—receive different and harsher treatment for similar offenses" across a juvenile justice system that is "separate and unequal."[35] More broadly, youth activists suggested that representations of youth as hardened (and adult-like) criminals created political support for get tough on youth policies. In their report *Locked Out*, Kids First! documented stark racial disparities in Oakland public school suspensions and expulsions. Youth activists pointed out the ways zero tolerance policies in schools excluded far too many youth of color from remaining in school, the ultimate normative space of childhood.[36]

Youth activists also challenged the ways media coverage created a complex equation of crime, age, and race—criminalizing youth and racializing crime.[37] One youth-led study of a TV station in Oakland showed that 63% of news stories about young people focused on youth crime. Even one-third of news stories about education concentrated on crime and violence.[38] Another report analyzed differences in representations of white youth and youth of color and showed that media representations disproportionately identified youth of color as the perpetrators of crime. Even when white youth were represented as criminal, they were framed as children, described with terms like "innocent faces," and depicted with yearbook pictures. In contrast, minority kids were shown handcuffed, in court, framed already by the justice system.[39] Youth activists critiqued the ways media images fostered public policies that excluded youth of color from childhood and from the important (if inadequate) protections of the juvenile justice system.

Youth activists worked to reclaim key elements of the modern construction of childhood, defining children as inherently reformable but also as vulnerable and in need of adult protection. These claims to childhood, and the parental obligations it entails, enabled youth activists to talk about social responsibility, not only individual responsibility, and to make explicit demands on the state. At the April 2001 protest against the Super Jail, Veronica, an eighteen-year-old Latina activist, demanded that adults, and particularly local politicians of color, stop separating themselves from youth. She carried a rosebud up to the podium and spoke in a soft voice full of emotion directly to the two African American men on the board.

> It is wonderful to see people of African American descent on the council and in such positions of power, but what about the other brothers? They can't get where you are because their schools aren't good. The expansion of juvenile hall is the destruction of young people souls. I see it everyday. We are dying. I am dying because of what you are putting us through. Our communities are crumbling. It's a bigger picture. It's about oppression. People separate themselves out from youth. "They're rowdy." You are helping the process of killing us, Keith Carson.

Here she singled out the African American board member who had previously voted for the larger hall, and people in the audience cheered loudly. "Yes we're loud and angry. Why do you want to see our destruction? We haven't even had a chance to bloom. Stop stereotyping us, waiting for us to end up in jail sometime soon."

At the same protest, another Latina young woman, who had been on probation for five years, criticized the mistreatment she encountered in the system. She said, "None of it gave me a way out. . . . In juvenile hall, there were counselors who put you down and said, 'I'm glad you're here. You're paying my bills.' . . . I sit here angry at all of you. You did not give me what you promised me." Both of these speeches called on the moral obligation adults have to nurture young people, and they argued that the state has been a negligent, even abusive, parent. This focus on the state as parent built on the juvenile justice system's formal role acting "in loco parentis" to insist that the state was failing to live up to its parental responsibilities. It explicitly challenged the privatizing discourses that blame families for youth crime and set the stage for material demands on the state.

Veronica also used images of "family" to call for racial solidarity and to challenge the ways black political incorporation had left "many brothers" behind in the city. Her comments highlighted the limits of racial solidarity in Oakland politics. At the time in Oakland, the chief of police, the city manager, and the county chief of probation were all African American, and African American professionals ran much of the city bureaucracy. These neighborhood and city leaders embodied the successes of Oakland's civil rights struggles in advancing black political and administrative power. But Veronica explicitly argued that the infrastructure that allowed for these African American men (and women) to rise to positions of power was gone. She pointed to fears of youth even within African American, Latino, and Asian communities, and she challenged the ways adults often used their own successful paths up out of poverty to condemn today's youth as undisciplined failures. Activists in the Super Jail campaign used this language of family to demand that the supervisors reclaim youth in the juvenile justice system as their own children. Youth activists focused on getting both Keith Carson and Alice Lai-Bitker to change their votes to show solidarity with the youth of color in the juvenile justice system.[40] Meanwhile, they largely ignored the white board members, Gail Steele and Scott Haggerty, apparently accepting that the white board members would fail to identify with kids in the hall.

Youth activists shifted attention from the "risky" actions of youth to the actions of politicians. At the first large protest in front of the Board of Supervisors, one young speaker redefined the meaning of "at-risk" youth: "We are at risk of police brutality, at risk of poverty, at risk of people trying to lock us up. That shit ain't right. That's not going to help us. Sorry I can't help but swear. What kind of future are you trying to build?" Similarly, at a public hearing in July, Van Jones encouraged the supervisors to do what they often asked young people to do, to stand up to the "peer pressure" of the powerful prison lobby.[41] By rhetorically stigmatizing adult behavior with language usually used to talk about problem youth, these activists shifted the focus to public policies and away from the actions of individual youth.

Youth activists proposed concrete alternatives to incarceration and challenged the county to live up to its rhetorical commitment to invest in "model programs" and follow "best practices." Michelle Darden, a leader of the Books Not Bars campaign, insisted, "There is a lot of agreement on what kinds of things need to happen." But she asked, "Where are the investments? Where's the leadership? It all ends up going back to criminal justice. . . . It's one thing to write a list of what we want to see happen. Somewhere between the idea of model programs and actual implementation, millions of dollars just sort of disappear." Youth activists challenged the tendency of public policy makers to look to the police and justice systems to secure "public safety." Instead, they consistently pointed out the links between the absence of social supports for youth and the involvement of youth in the justice system. Michelle Darden acknowledged that "a lot of our kids are messed up," but she asked, "What do they need? They don't need to be incarcerated. They don't need public funding for their schools and recreation centers and health care and social services to be spent on prisons."[42]

Youth activists' claims to childhood, and the parental obligations it entails, operated in several important ways to reconstruct social and political space in the context of early twenty-first century U.S. cities. They used generational ties to reconstruct racial community and solidarity and to critique the ways African Americans and other people of color increasingly supported tougher criminal justice policies. But they also worked to reincorporate both criminal youth and youth of color back into the family of an imagined national community. They used childhood to launch a moral critique of the ways youth of color were criminalized and youth crime was racialized in both local and national political discourses. Youth activists claimed childhood to assert membership in the family of the nation, and they drew on a broader notion of parental responsibility to demand that the state invest in their future.

Youth activism against the Super Jail created a quandary for supporters of the expanded juvenile hall. Supervisor Gail Steele, a white woman and longtime children's advocate, objected to the youth movement's "sound-bite politics" and insisted that the kids in juvenile hall are not "little fifth graders with a bad attitude." "Excuse me. That's not what we have here. These are deeply sick kids. They have been neglected forever, practically from the time they were born. . . . Their life experiences are wrong choices." But she worried that she would look like a cold-hearted bureaucrat or "ogre" when she disagreed with the youth protestors. She explained, "You take young people who really don't have a clue about how to raise children, how difficult it is, what happens to kids, and they say, 'Close the jail. Kids belong at home.' Well I'm sorry, no they don't. . . . Not these kids." Steele's frustration highlights the symbolic power of childhood to reframe the debate about youth crime and challenge the reliance on incarceration as a solution to youth problems. But her comments also point to some problems with "youth" as a political identity.

Youth activists had to work against the pervasive common sense that children and youth are not competent social and political actors with the knowledge or experience to shape public policy.[43] While children may be the future of the nation, they are generally framed as only citizens-in-the-making, not as full citizens. District Attorney Tom Orloff emphasized youth protestors' naiveté as he argued for the expanded juvenile hall: "I think their basic premise is that youth should not be detained. I wish they were right, but experience has shown me otherwise."[44] Others worked to discredit the Super Jail campaign by casting doubt on the independence or authenticity of youth protests. James Thurman, the African American assistant DA, told me that the youth protestors were being "manipulated." Supervisor Scott Haggerty insisted that the majority of activists were "adults." Protests against the Super Jail were not "a spontaneous uprising of youth" but instead the actions of "activists with an agenda they feel passionate about."[45] Opponents seemed to suggest that if young people were political activists "with an agenda," then they couldn't be seen as the "pure" voice of youth. But if they were really "youth," they were too naïve and impressionable to be good policy makers.

Youth activists offered a fundamental critique of this definition of youth as incomplete citizens. Zack, a seventeen-year-old white activist with Youth Together, explained, "The mainstream culture basically says that until you're eighteen, you don't have a brain or anything. Once you hit eighteen everything you do is righteous and legal, and fighting for your rights. But before you're eighteen, it's just kids causing trouble." Greg, an African American high school student leader in Youth Together at Skyline, challenged the exclusions of youth from basic rights of citizenship. He became involved in the Proposition 21 campaign because he was frustrated that "we couldn't vote on something that affected us. Prop 21 was for youngsters, and you have a 65-year-old voting on propositions that are not even going to affect them? Of course they are going to vote yes. Let us vote on things that affect us."

Young people's limited rights of citizenship significantly shaped their approach to political engagement. Victor Duarte explained the importance of street protests, of "making noise," given young people's limited rights of citizenship. "That's the only power that we have." Adults "have the ability to vote, ability to make noise, to contact the person that represents them. The only thing we can do is hold a rally and make noise." Both Greg and Victor worried that adults sometimes interpreted youth rallies as "childish behavior." But Victor asked adults to "put themselves in our shoes. At least try to see where we come from. If we are holding a protest, why are we doing it?" Victor's challenge raises the question of how youth activists used protests to reconfigure the rights of youth and the place of youth in the city by "making noise" in the streets.

Youth activists clearly worked to redefine our understanding of childhood and youth even as they drew on powerful symbolic associations of those cultural categories. They refused both the neoliberal definitions of youth as criminal and Gail Steele's more sympathetic definitions of youth as "deeply sick," at risk, or primarily full of negative life experiences and skills. They rejected constructions of childhood that locate responsibility for children and youth purely in a reified private sphere—in the home or "the family"—and that excluded young people from the street. They redefined youth as "agents of change" with the rights and capacity to participate in the public sphere of politics.[46]

Hip Hop Politics Reclaims the Streets

Youth activists in the Bay Area developed a distinctive form of hip hop politics that intentionally blurred the boundaries between hip hop parties and political protests. They used local DJ networks and hip hop collectives as a cultural and quasi-institutional base from which to organize. In the absence of large-scale commercial venues for hip hop in the Bay Area, a dense network of underground hip hop collectives emerged, like Black Dot Artists Collective, the Living Word Project, Underground Railroad, and Freedom Fighter, all of which trained young activists and performed at rallies for different campaigns. Organizers used hip hop promotional techniques, turning people out for protests in the way they would for a party. Young people plastered their schools and neighborhoods with posters, handed out sleek, well-produced fliers, called friends, and spread the word through classrooms and school hallways.

Protests against Proposition 21 and the Super Jail claimed public parks and open squares in the heart of both San Francisco and Oakland for outdoor parties and then moved into the streets, stopping traffic along major boulevards. Sometimes these were formal and well-advertised protests, while at other times a flatbed truck brought "guerrilla hip hop" music and No on Prop 21 messages to parks and schools.[47] Some MCs and poets also took their spoken word and raps onto public buses where they would perform, educate, and get people involved in the campaign.[48]

The mix of politics and pleasure in occupying public space was clear at a rally in front of the probation department the week before the vote on Prop-

Figure 19. Ain't No Power Like the Power of the Youth. Protestors at a No on Proposition 21 march in downtown Oakland. (Photo courtesy of Ella Baker Center for Human Rights, John Pilgrim, photographer)

osition 21. On this gray, rainy day, I joined a crowd of eighty middle school and high school students at 4:00 P.M. in the playground of a West Oakland middle school. These young protestors were primarily black and Latino, with some Asian and Pacific Islander youth, and they ranged in ages from twelve to eighteen. We marched through downtown and towards the probation department, dancing down the streets to the rhythms of the chants: "No justice no peace. We don't need police"; "21 is a prop that we gotta stop." We gathered in the street in front of the juvenile court and probation building. Speaking with microphones from the back of the flatbed truck, a couple of high school students gave brief statements against Prop 21. Young organizers asked each Oakland school to "represent," and students cheered for their schools. In a brief speech, an African American young man described the juvenile court building as "the place they take us to court before they send us to prison." But he reassured the young audience that they didn't have to worry about the police today. "We're not going to let you go."

The teenage protestors clearly enjoyed the way street protests overturned the relationship between youth and the police on Oakland's streets and challenged the emerging spatial order that excluded young people and hip hop culture from public spaces. After a few brief speeches against Prop 21, these young activists proceeded to have a dance party in the middle of the intersection. They had no permit for the event. As it got dark, a large group of black, Latino, and Pacific Islander youth danced in the middle of a downtown street, with speakers blaring hip hop dance music from a flatbed truck as dozens of police officers simply stood disinterested a block away diverting traffic. The police at these rallies protected kids' rights to the street and made no attempt to get the protestors or the dance party to disperse. As one organizer asserted, "We have the upper hand. The cops are diverting traffic. We're making them to work for us right now."

Youth activists occupied the streets as well as halls of political power in a way that enacted a fundamental right to public space.[49] Don Mitchell argues that the right to public space is not an abstract or stable right. Instead, public space is "a practice" that must be constantly recreated and defended as truly public through daily use and political protest. As youth activists danced, marched, and spoke in the streets, they reclaimed the streets for young people and youth culture. A common chant of the Prop 21 marches made these claims to public space quite clear: "Whose streets is these?" a young organizer with a bullhorn would shout out, and the crowd would respond, "These streets is ours."

These political occupations of public space were vital for youth activists' claims to citizenship. Mitchell argues that public space is vital for the "work of citizenship" because it is only in public spaces "that the desires and needs of individuals and groups can be seen, and therefore recognized."[50] As Mitchell argues, controlling public space shapes the nature of public debate, "the sorts of actions that can be considered legitimate," and the kinds of people defined as members of "the legitimate public."[51] Excluding youth from public space reinforced their exclusion from "the legitimate public" and focused attention on the needs and desires of an adult public. When youth activists protested in Oakland's streets, they made young people's needs and desires visible. They demanded more than the limited right to hang out on the corner. Instead, they used public space to claim a fundamental right to the city, which geographer David Harvey defines as a right not only to live in and use urban spaces but also "an active right to make the city different, to shape it more in accord with our heart's desire."[52]

Youth activists' hip hop politics also directly challenged dominant representations of hip hop as violent or criminal. Many adults interpreted hip hop styles as the main sign of "dangerous youth" in Oakland. As youth activists in their baggy pants and baseball hats marched through downtown streets and rapped against the new juvenile hall to the Board of Supervisors, they reframed hip hop culture and youth socializing in the street as expressive forms of citizenship. By combining politics with the pleasures of hip hop culture, youth activists demanded that youth occupations of public space be considered a legitimate part of free speech and political assembly.

Since its origins, hip hop culture has enacted young people's claims to public space. Graffiti artists splashed their names, neighborhoods, and art across buses, freeways, and buildings. Beats blaring from boom boxes or car stereos filled the air with youth music and voices. American studies scholars Robin Kelley and Tricia Rose have argued that hip hop music and cultural styles became "weapons" in an "ad hoc war of position to take back public space."[53] In late-twentieth-century Oakland, the Sideshow, cruising, spinning donuts, blasting hip hop from car stereos, and gathering in the streets were certainly youth strategies in that ongoing battle. But youth activists used hip hop much more explicitly to claim their rights to public space and to citizenship.[54]

Youth activists often described Prop 21 as an attack on hip hop and the hip hop generation. One anti–Prop 21 flier described the proposition as "a war on hip hop" and made clear that activists would fight back through the medium of hip hop as well. In simple red and white block letters on a yellow background, the flier said, "Hip-Hop Will Prevail," and in graffiti-style print, it added, "No Prop 21" and "It's not a Battle. . . . It's War." Activists singled out several provisions of Prop 21 as targeting hip hop, and particularly expressions of hip hop culture in public spaces. Proposition 21 increased penalties for graffiti, lowering the definition of felony vandalism from fifty thousand dollars of property damage to four hundred dollars. Activists also frequently criticized the proposition's gang provisions, which allowed misdemeanors to be turned into felonies if the police suspected gang membership. As one flier explained, "Any group of three or more folks who dress similar or share a common name can be labeled a 'gang.' Chillin' with your folks" or "hangin' on the street rapping" "will land you in jail."[55]

Young people worried that hip hop and other urban youth cultural styles would subject them to further surveillance and punishment on Oakland's streets. As Youth Together member Victor Duarte said, Prop 21 felt like "an attack on us," an attempt "to classify us like delinquents." When people talk about "gangs," they are "not talking about punk rockers." Victor knew he and many of his family members fit "the stereotype of a gang member." His cousins always "dressed in the same style when they went out, wearing the same colors and same shirts," and he worried that they could "get in some kind of trouble through Proposition 21." Victor himself had been stopped on the street by an older woman, who saw him wearing red and asked, "'What gang do you belong to?' It really got me mad. I didn't say anything. I just walked away. But I knew she was ignorant."

Hip hop also provided a powerful medium for turning youth anger and oppositional attitudes into fuel for political action. Activists built on the tradition of message rappers like Public Enemy, who, as Chuck D explained, "decided to take that anger [in hip hop] and direct it at something real."[56] Youth activists called the last week of the Proposition 21 campaign the "Week of Rage." They defined their rage as political, challenging interpretations of youth anger as an individual problem that should be controlled with anger management classes. Jakada Imani explained that the youth movement tried to turn the "devil-may-care," "fuck you attitude" of hip hop into militant politics. Youth activists frequently used hip hop slang, as when a youth organizer called out for "who-riders to represent" and asked "who's down to ride?" "Who-ride" means to act wild, crazy, or disruptive and also to defeat through crazy actions. Organizers used this term, which referred generally to the pleasures of acting crazy, to describe the pleasures of oppositional political action. More generally, they framed political protest as a way of participating in the pleasures of the street. Instead of suppressing anger and denying the pleasures of the street, these youth organizers, much like the Black Panthers before them, sought to channel this generation's angers and pleasures towards political action.

Activists emphasized the dangers of political protest and framed the police as an imminent danger to protestors. Common protest rituals included elaborate preparations for the possibility of being arrested. Many students at the Proposition 21 protest in front of the probation department had written the numbers of ACLU lawyers on their arms in ink for use in case of arrest. Most of the adults at this march, mostly teachers, nonprofit workers, and older college students, wore large stickers that marked us as "Legal Observers." We were to take notes in case of arrests or clashes with the police. At protests, older activists warned youth to stick together as they left to avoid being made "a target" by the police. At rallies, speakers frequently told stories of humiliation by the police and warned that the police are "looking for a reason to take you down." Even the youth organizer who reassured the crowd "We won't let them take you," reinforced the common presumption that the police and probation department wanted to jail the young protestors. This focus on the potential dangers of political protest actually made the protests more appealing to many youth who enjoyed the oppositional attitude and implicit dangers of street action.

Organizers sometimes worried that young people came to these events primarily for the pleasures of the street. At one anti–Prop 21 rally in front of the police station, when the crowd was paying scant attention to a young African American woman organizer, she complained, "I'm sick of young folks coming out to smoke blunts and cut school. You can't just go home and light a blunt and forget about it. I care about y'all. Y'all are family. I don't want to see y'all locked up in there." But younger, less politicized protestors resisted attempts to impose too much discipline on their political action. At the same rally, an organizer called for rappers to come and "bust it, represent on the microphone," but to keep the raps positive: "No disrespecting nobody." A young black man sitting near me yelled out, "We can still disrespect the Po-Po [police], right? We can still say 'Fuck the Po-Po,' right?" The organizer didn't respond, so he added, "Y'all better not get all controlling now."

Youth activists worked to turn this kind of oppositional attitude into a transformational politics. As ethnographer Paul Willis and many educational anthropologists have shown, working-class youth or youth of color often reject school and embrace oppositional identities like "hustler" or "thug."[57] But this form of agency or resistance often reifies negative stereotypes and reproduces racial and class exclusions and inequalities. African American Studies scholar and Oakland activist Shawn Ginwright has argued that youth activism provides a powerful example of how to turn this kind of oppositional resistance into "transformative resistance" that enables youth to challenge negative stereotypes as they engage in local political struggles.[58]

Youth activists have tried to realize the potential of hip hop politics by linking progressive hip hop directly to specific local campaigns for youth justice. Oakland rap artist Boots of The Coup argued for the importance of linking political hip hop to grass-roots movements:

Political rap groups [like Public Enemy in the late 1980s] offered solutions only through listening. . . . They weren't part of a movement, so they died out when people saw their lives were not changing. . . . On the other hand, gangsta groups and rappers who talk about selling drugs are a part of a movement. The drug game has been around for many years and has directly impacted lives, and for . . . many it's been positive in the sense that it earned people some money. Hence gangsta rap has a home. . . . In order for political rap to be around, there has to be a movement that will be around that will make people's lives better in a material sense.[59]

American studies scholar George Lipsitz has argued that attacks on rap music routinely imply that rap causes youth crime and inner-city decline. These attacks on youth culture, which many black adults have embraced, erase the political and economic transformations that have decimated the infrastructure for youth in cities like Oakland.[60] Youth activists—and their allies in local progressive hip hop—have tried to "embrace and transform" hip hop culture "rather than confront, isolate and marginalize" dominant youth cultural expressions.[61] By using hip hop as a resource for political mobilization, young activists posed a direct challenge to the portrayals of hip hop as criminal. Their form of hip hop politics worked to bring a structural analysis of youth crime back into public policy debates. And by reframing hip hop as the language of future leaders, they reclaimed public space for youth cultural practices.

Race and the Cultural Politics of Youth

One of the largest rallies against Prop 21 drew a crowd of almost a thousand and featured an Asian break dancing group and hip hop performances by established artists like The Coup and Dead Prez, local groups like The Company of Prophets, and up-and-coming high school acts. The crowd was incredibly diverse, almost a quarter Asian, a quarter black, a quarter Latino, and a quarter white, but that barely captures the diversity of protestors. South Asian, black, and white hip hop headz rapped at an open mike, young skateboarders, punks, and anarchists sat on the grass, queer activists passed out literature, earnest socialists sold newspapers, and older men and women sat scattered throughout the audience, watching young people run the show. During the performances, young men and women flirted and danced to the music, circulated petitions, registered voters, and chanted against Prop 21.

Jakada Imani, one of the event's MCs, emphasized the challenge that this multiracial community presented to the status quo. "The 5-o have already been here. They looked around and saw all these youth. What they gonna do? They looked around and saw lots of black ones, brown ones, yellow ones, white ones. What they gonna do?" He paused to indicate that they couldn't really do anything. "So what we're gonna do is keep it peaceful. We're gonna represent." Youth activists cultivated a generational political identity, speaking as "the hip hop generation" or simply as "youth," but this does not mean that they avoided or somehow transcended race. Youth activists worked to reconfigure, not abandon, racial political subjectivities. They constructed a collective identity as "youth of color" affected by the "war on youth."

Political alliances among youth of color certainly did not exist in any simple sense in Oakland. Oakland was home to periodic race riots in high schools between blacks and Latinos or blacks and Asians or Tongans and Latinos, depending on the school. These tensions in neighborhoods and schools often encouraged young people to draw narrow racial boundaries around their communities of interest. At Castlemont High School in the late 1990s, black and Latino riots became almost a ritual marking the beginning of each school year. One Latino counselor explained that as the Latino student population began to increase, he would "hear rumors from African American students that the school still "belongs to us, is run by us" or resentment that Latino students were "taking over." At Skyline, a fight between a couple of Asian and black students escalated over a period of days into a series of racial riots that led many Asian kids to avoid school for several days.

Even within the multiracial youth activist coalitions, tensions occasionally emerged as youth or adult observers wondered whether Asian American high school boys or Latina activists could speak for troubled youth or youth in the juvenile justice system with the same authority as African American young men.[62] At one school board hearing, many Asian American youth spoke passionately against Mayor Jerry Brown's proposal to create a military charter school, calling the proposal racist because it assumed "students of color need discipline" or were "animals to be trained into obedience." When Elmhurst NCPC leader Bill Clay heard these comments, he assumed the youth activists were talking about black kids and questioned whether Asian students could speak about racism, asking, "If they're going to talk about black kids, why can't they find more than two or four?" An Asian American director of one youth organization privately expressed similar worries that having all these Asian faces talking about racism missed significant differences in young people's experiences of racial exclusion in Oakland.

Youth activists consciously worked to produce a generational political identity as "youth of color" in the face of these ongoing racial tensions. Photos, fliers, and murals in youth activist campaigns worked to construct an imagined community of Asian, Latino, Native, and black young men and women united in struggle. Activists often emphasized unity among "youth of color" who were "overrepresented" in a "too racist" juvenile hall.[63] The imagery in the mural, We Are Our Ancestors, which graces the front cover of this book, emphasizes this unity among youth of color under attack by the prison industrial complex.

Christine Wong Yap painted the mural for the campaign against Proposition 21 protests, and it circulated to protests around the state in 2000. In

Figure 20. *We Are Our Ancestors.* Mural painted in support of the anti–Proposition 21 youth movement in California. (Christine Wong Yap, artist, 2000. Photo by Scott Braley)

the foreground, a Chinese boy and Native American girl come together in a circle, holding hands with black and Latino youth. They are surrounded and threatened by monsters representing the media, prisons, and police and by old white men and women, including Governor Pete Wilson with his "war on youth," a white history teacher "telling lies," and President Bill Clinton literally "targeting" a young Latino mother who is protecting her child from an alligator-like prison system. The figure of a black young man placed in handcuffs by Pete Wilson highlights the particularly powerful criminalization of black men, but the image represents all youth of color as under threat. The mural mounts a clear critique of the racial hierarchies that continue to reproduce white political power and privilege and that threaten freedom and opportunity for youth of color.

Mariana Lopez emphasized the importance of getting young people to understand their shared experiences of oppression across racial and gender lines. Growing up in East Oakland, she had experienced racial tensions in schools and racism from black bus drivers who assumed she didn't speak English. But since she was twelve, she had also participated in youth organizing trainings that taught her about the links among the struggles of Mexican American farm workers, the Chicano student movement, and the Black Panthers and "all the people they lost" in Oakland. She learned how to relate her experiences of getting dirty looks as a teenage mom to the suspicion her brother faced in public, where too often people saw his hip hop style and assumed he was up to no good.

> You can't be a person of color and go to Macy's and not get targeted by all the cameras. Why do you try to fight when you're both basically oppressed? The system is putting both of you down. Get together and fight the system. Everything that's happening to you isn't because they don't like you, it's because they don't like all of us. How come your schools are poor? They want to lock you up. They want to put you in a failing situation.

Youth organizing groups even used the occasional race riots in Oakland high schools as opportunities to cultivate deeper conversations about shared experiences of oppression. As a Youth Together staff person explained, "Young people were running the gauntlet. Even home was not a safe place for a lot of youth. Out the door, young people were harassed on the street, on the bus. By the time they get to school, maybe they were ten minutes late, and they were treated as criminals." There was "no drinking water, no bathrooms, no nurse to give you aspirin." When schools erupted into racial violence, Youth Together organizers helped students to "peel back the layers," to connect their everyday experiences to broader histories and "cycles of oppression, genocide, racism, and educational discrimination." Youth Together students at Castlemont created a poster that highlighted their understanding of these connections. Line drawings of a boy and girl at the center were surrounded by all the problems youth brought to school on a daily basis (their need for jobs, safe places to be after school, supportive teachers), but below in large print were the labels of "Racism," "Class Oppression," and "Violence."

Youth activists often called for Oakland schools to develop an ethnic studies curriculum that would foster both greater respect and political unity among students of color. As one African American adult organizer explained to a group of Skyline students, the kind of ethnic studies needed would have to go beyond the standard, and often apolitical, vision of multiculturalism.

> Ethnic Studies is great. But it's not just culture that you need to understand. We have a common fight against racism as people of color. We are each other's allies. I encourage you to think about ethnic studies as an anti-racism class. How have Latinos fought against racism? How have Asians fought against racism? What have African American struggles been? You could back each other up in this fight.

Youth activists didn't avoid talking about race or simply equate the experiences of all youth of color. They directly challenged racialized images of youth crime, and they frequently called attention to the ways criminal justice crackdowns specifically targeted young black men for surveillance and policing. Kids First's publication *Locked Out* emphasized the disproportionate suspension and expulsion of black boys.[64] Fliers for the campaign against the Super Jail described the proposal as generically "racist" and targeting "youth of color" but also included a pie chart that documented the massive overrepresentation of black youth in Alameda County's juvenile hall. Asian and Latino youth remained underrepresented compared to their population, although they were still incarcerated at rates higher than whites.[65]

Youth activists and adult advisors often encouraged young people to explore their own racial prejudices, as well as the structural processes that produced racial tensions and inequalities in the public schools. After a riot between black and Asian students at Skyline High school, youth organizers held a three-day mediation in which they encouraged Asian and black students to reflect on the ways academic tracking and school security practices helped to produce racial stereotypes and divisions. Asian students realized that few African Americans were in their honors or AP classes: "It's usually the same five or six in all the classes." But in the lowest division classes, "There's hella blacks. They run those classes." Black students described their resentment that Asians "didn't get as hard punishment" because administrators didn't see them "as threats." "If there are five black students by the cars, the police will come and want to jack us up. For the Asians, they just get a warning. They are approached with respect. 'Hurry on to class now.' The administration has a lot of stereotypes. When they see Asians walking down the hall, they think that they are nerds." But Asian students also described the downside of the stereotypes of Asians as model minorities. Administrators rarely responded to Asian student or parent complaints because of stereotypes that Asians were quiet and wouldn't raise a fuss. And Asian young men often felt pressured to prove they were tough enough to negotiate Oakland's streets and challenges from black students who assumed they wouldn't fight back.

Youth organizers tried to link the struggles of students across racial lines by focusing on the ways students felt disrespected by school administrators. Students at the Skyline mediation talked about feeling infantilized and criminalized by administrators who talk at us "with a bull horn, like we're animals, like we're children." One African American young woman suggested that this treatment produced violence: "We get mad, and we take it into our own hands." An Asian student organizer for Youth Together worked to turn this anger into action against the administration: "I feel you about the security. I saw it yesterday. I was walking in the hall and nobody stopped me. But security stopped a couple of black guys. I am willing to work with you on that. We can go up legally to the administration and fight. We can walk out. We can make them take a pay cut." The room erupted into cheers, as he added, "We need to come together and organize and fight for a better education."

Youth offered a flexible form of identity politics that could respond to the particularities of contemporary age and racial formations. In California, the category "youth" itself is racialized and often serves as a proxy for a stigmatized "underclass."[66] Poverty is concentrated among children and youth, and people of color constitute the majority of children and youth in California, while whites remain the majority of elderly.[67] Disinvestments in California's public schools and the growing emphasis on security have affected youth across race, class, and gender lines, even if unevenly. At a youth speakout, one student explained that security crackdowns targeted Castlemont High School because it was a "ghetto school." But another student pointed out the common struggles across Oakland public schools, none of which had sufficient books, teachers, or facilities needed for a high-quality education, saying, "All Oakland schools are ghetto schools." Youth as a political identity created the space for black, Latino, Asian, and even some white students to recognize their shared experiences in the "ghetto schools" of Oakland, while still exposing the ways that race, class, and gender intersected to produce disparate burdens.

Organizing as youth, activists could be attentive to the diversity of local racial and class formations. Crackdowns on crime and increased surveillance of youth in Oakland's schools and neighborhoods often did focus on the bodies of black boys, but they were not confined to them. In particular schools and neighborhoods, surveillance focused on Tongan, Latino, or Vietnamese youth. Activists in the Laurel district worried that a group of Tongan boys and young men, with their souped-up cars and baggy pants, might be gang members waiting to start fights on the streets near the middle school. A Chinatown mall adopted a no-loitering policy because adults were afraid of the Asian youth who hung out there after school. Black youth were massively overrepresented in juvenile hall, while on the surface both Asian and Latino youth remained underrepresented. But breaking down the pan-ethnic category Asian, some Southeast Asian and Pacific Islander youth were just as overrepresented as black boys in Oakland's juvenile hall.[68] As significant numbers of Southeast Asian, Pacific Islander, and Latino youth dropped out of school, hung out on the streets, or joined gangs, they too became hypervisible objects of fear in Oakland.

Oakland's public schools and neighborhoods brought youth together to create hybrid youth cultural styles that often destabilized simple racial categories. The white vice-principal of one public school explained that black youth culture was the dominant culture in Oakland public schools. "That's not good or bad, that's just the way it is." His daughters spoke Black English, as did the daughters of other white friends whose kids went to public school. Even young immigrant adults, like the Vietnamese guys that ran his neighborhood auto repair shop, called out to each other, "Wha's up Homes?" with a Vietnamese accent. John Turner, an African American young man, grew up in the East Oakland flatlands but went to Oakland High, where Cambodian, Laotian, Vietnamese, and Hmong kids went to school with black and Latino kids. He had never even heard of the idea of Asians as a "model minority" until he went to college. Asian kids in his high school "wore the same baggy pants, spoke the same slang, and acted up just as much as the black kids."

Two interactions at the Skyline mediation highlighted the flexible construction of racial categories in Oakland public schools. One Asian young man, dressed in baggy pants and a backwards baseball cap, complained that some blacks "try to mug at me, make me look down at the floor. They'll say things like, 'Why you tryin' to dress black, Dog?' They want me to wear the pants, tight all the way up to here [pointing to his waist] Asian Urkel style. But that's not me. I grew up in the same neighborhood as you." Another white student who attended the session for black students had grown up in the predominantly black and Latino East Oakland flatlands and previously attended an Alameda County court school. She spoke up passionately about the racism black students faced on campus at Skyline, shocked at the ways black security guards would let her roam the halls but would stop any black student.

> I never felt privileged till I came to Skyline. I was the only white girl in my school before, and everyone discriminated against me. So I know where you're coming from. The only way to get by this is to focus on the things we have in common. Maybe the Chinese didn't come over on a slave ship in chains, but we have more in common than we think.

She spoke about her own path across Oakland's racial and class boundaries. "People have all these assumptions. I got bused up here. For years I grew up on East 95th." As she spoke with the rhythms and style of the East Oakland flatlands, several black students on the sidelines commented, "She's black" and "She's hard."

Youth activists often called themselves the "hip hop generation" as a way of acknowledging and politicizing these hybrid youth cultures. While Robin Kelley and Shawn Ginwright rightly emphasize the potential for hip hop to politicize black urban youth, many Bay Area activists used hip hop as a vehicle for crafting a multiracial political identity that drew on but also reconfigured blackness as the grounds for an oppositional political identity.[69] Hip hop in the Bay Area was a multiracial youth culture, no longer (if ever) simply a black youth culture. Jakada Imani explained how the rhythms and popular appeal of hip hop worked as a unifying force. "Hip hop has become the protest music for this movement. On a march, if the chants have a hip hop flavor, young people will join. It's also been crucial for drawing together youth of all colors— because hip-hop is multiethnic from the get."[70] Even though youth activists might be "banda or techno kids" and might not "live and breathe hip hop," Jakada insisted that hip hop has become deeply incorporated into urban youth culture. Young people across racial lines performed spoken word, formed hip hop dance crews, created graffiti art, and bounced along to hip hop beats in street protests. Hip hop created a language and set of symbols that young people could use across the city and across the globe to protest the ways neoliberalism has deepened exclusions and truncated the lives of too many young people.[71]

Youth offered a more flexible political identity than race- or class-based political movements in a context where many Asian, Latino, and African American youth shared similar struggles in Oakland's neighborhoods and schools. This generational political identity worked to disrupt and transcend the often race- and class-segregated networks of local politics in Oakland. We have seen how black political networks in Oakland's flatlands often implicitly excluded Latino residents and prioritized black middle-class homeowner interests over those of young people and renters.[72] In the hills, white homeowners often linked race, class, and age to exclude public school children or children on the street from belonging in the hills. Coming together as "a youth movement" or as the "hip hop generation," activists could craft alliances across Oakland's increasingly multiracial poor and working class. They could also reach out to young people in cities and neighborhoods in California and the nation where Latino or Southeast Asian youth were seen as the most "dangerous youth."

Finally, youth activists also highlighted a politics of generation (in some ways over race) because of transformations in Oakland's urban regime that brought many black and Latino administrators, activists, and politicians into local positions of power where they often supported increased policing and incarceration to discipline youth. As African American studies scholar Angela Ards argues, "a mature hip-hop movement will have more than a race-based political analysis of the issues affecting urban youth. Increasingly, the face of injustice is the color of the rainbow, so a black-white racial analysis that pins blame on some lily-white power structure is outdated."[73] Organizing as youth, youth activists have both pointed to the limits of racial solidarity and demanded that African American elders and other adults of color reclaim youth of color as their own children.

Conclusion

Youth activists put forward two very different, and potentially contradictory, images of young people in their political practice: youth as political (even revolutionary) actors, capable of planning and executing a campaign, and youth as "children" who needed adult care and support. This tension itself makes youth activism in Oakland interesting and potentially powerful because it suggests the potential for a politics of youth that draws on family imagery but is not fundamentally grounded in paternalism. Youth activists demanded a childhood for youth in the juvenile justice system and made clear the multiple ways "youth criminals" were being excluded from the category of childhood. They used family imagery and ideas of children's dependence and vulnerability as the grounds for claims on the state. But at the same time, they reworked a commonsense understanding of "dependents."[74] They challenged the right of the juvenile justice system to determine "the best interests of the child" and articulated a clear view of youth as active citizens with rights both to social support and to political power. Youth activism in Oakland suggests at least one strategy for constructing a progressive politics of childhood that could rebuild structures and cultures of care that could challenge neoliberal ideologies of self-help and privatized family values.

Youth activists produced a very different vision of childhood and of the street than that produced by many homeowner and parent activists in Oakland. They rejected a privatized model of childhood that located children and youth only in homes, schools, or supervised after-school programs out of the public sphere. The Prop 21 protests combined hip hop dance parties and political protest in ways that explicitly reclaimed the streets for youth cultural practices. More fundamentally, they rejected the notion that childhood and "youth" could be reconstructed by clearing youth off the streets. Instead, youth activists occupied public spaces, both streets and halls of political power, in a way that enacted their claims of a fundamental "right to the city."

Youth have few formal rights as citizens, and their power to make noise in the streets was one of the few ways youth could make their daily personal struggles political. Young people's everyday struggles in dysfunctional schools and violent neighborhoods often remained invisible, known only to their parents, friends, and the youth workers who struggled with few resources to manage the constant crises of poor children's lives. Even worse, young people's problems were often blamed on the private choices of parents or young people themselves. Youth activists pointed to a significant problem with the ways parent and homeowner activists used space to save children. By clearing youth off the streets, homeowner and parent activists may have undermined their own efforts to increase state investments in children and youth. As long as youth were confined to after-school programs and other age-segregated spaces of childhood, they would be framed as incomplete citizens without the right to demand a fair share of the budget. Youth activists' claims to the street were central to their efforts to reframe the problem of youth crime as a public problem and not simply a private problem of individual choice or family failure. Claiming space in public, youth as a social group could "become public."[75]

Youth activism offers one powerful example of a grass-roots challenge to the neoliberal urban political order that has restricted the uses of public space and created "a remarkably constricted public sphere and a rather shriveled notion of rights."[76] Grass-roots struggles around the world are joining calls for "a greater right to the city, a right that includes the right to housing, the right to space, and the right to control rather than be the victims of economic policy." Reclaiming the right to the city in this expanded sense requires reclaiming "public space, not for societal order and control, but rather for the struggle for justice."[77] Youth activists made this broader claim of a right to the city. They redefined young people as members of the legitimate public and demanded that the state act to reduce the deep racial and class inequalities in children's lives.

Conclusion: Hope and Fear

Young people are growing up today in contradictory times: increasing inequality alongside expanding dreams, deep poverty beside lavish wealth, racially unequal childhoods in an era that promises equal opportunity. At a special police-youth dialogue organized by performance artist Suzanne Lacy, two young people asked questions of Oakland's black police chief that captured their experiences of this contradictory moment. An African American young woman challenged, "Y'all like to beat us down. How can we respect your authority?" In a more plaintive tone, a fifteen-year-old black young man on probation asked, "How come we can't get together? We all supposed to be rich."

The police chief had no real answer to these questions about respect, state power, and crushed structures of opportunity. But how do we answer these young people as a nation? Maybe working-class and poor kids have to lower their expectations and realize we probably can't all be rich. Maybe black parents across class lines have to teach their kids the skills they need to avoid getting "beat down" when the police stop them on the street. Maybe we should send poor kids to anger management classes so they can learn to control the raw sense of injustice they feel as they compare the nation's promises to the vast inequalities they see around them. But as a nation, can we accept these as our answers? Do we really want to be the kind of nation that abandons its commitment to create real equal opportunities for all our children?

We began this book with Jerry Brown at a community meeting embracing a central precept of neoliberal urban governance—that Oakland's communities and families were responsible on their own for trying to solve the deep problems facing young people. We have also seen the formidable efforts of parents and community activists working to construct safe and nurturing environments for the city's children. But Oakland's activists often faced unacceptable political choices. Community activists in Oakland's flatlands, overwhelmed by the social costs of our nation's drug wars, sometimes turned to the police as their only choice. As they struggled to save kids in their neighborhood, they embraced a vision of the state as disciplinary father. Parents from Oakland's lower hills with kids in the public schools often had to rely on their own volunteer labor to try to reconstruct safe and nurturing landscapes for all of Oakland's children. They tried to equalize childhood, but their volunteer labor was rarely enough to address the vast inequalities built into children's lives and landscapes. Even wealthy black parents in the hills needed to defend their children from the images of black youth crime that distorted public responses to kids in Oakland and in national public policy debates. Across the city, neighborhood activists often felt they had no choice but to clear young people off the streets as they competed for the private investment necessary for urban redevelopment. Youth activists struggled to reconstruct our ideas of youth in the face of their persistent exclusion from full citizenship and public spaces.

Over the last fifteen years, Oakland city government, pushed by its citizens, who refused to abandon a generation of poor children, has worked in fits and starts to reconstruct structures and cultures of care for kids. Youth activists and adult advocates pushed the city to create a children's trust fund that expanded after-school programs and nonprofit services for children and youth. Advocates used this growing nonprofit sector, characteristic of neoliberal governance, to create a lobby to prevent crime and invest in youth. Public-private partnerships created these new possibilities but also constrained citizens' ability to demand state action and narrowed understandings of children's needs. They succeeded in expanding after-school programs to keep kids off the street and in creating new programs to prevent youth crime and violence, but did little to address the deeper problems of child poverty and retreating state supports for poor families. Neoliberal public policies exacerbated the crises of low-income families and left poorly funded nonprofits to pick up the pieces.

Children and youth do not live in a private realm outside of politics. They serve as powerful symbols and actors in on-going struggles over how to reconstruct the state. Debates about children help redraw the boundaries of public and private responsibility and forge changing ideas about the proper role of government. The ways we frame the needs and problems of young people shape the visions of the state we promote and the kinds of state action we try to secure. The politics of youth, and our collective responses to deeply personal dilemmas of social reproduction, shape changing political and economic orders.

Oakland in the Age of Obama

Oakland cycled madly between hope and fear in 2008. When I visited Oakland in July, I saw vendors at street fairs hawking an endless variety of t-shirts, hats, and posters of Barack Obama alongside icons of the civil rights movement. On election night, happy crowds poured into Oakland's streets to cheer Barack Obama's election as a symbol of the possibilities for racial progress in a post–voting rights era. But even at that optimistic moment there were troubling reminders that all was not well on Oakland's streets. A 25-year-old biracial young man, who like Obama identifies as black, noted that as everyone celebrated in the downtown streets, there was a military line of police surrounding the crowds telling them what to do. For him at that happy moment, it was a reminder of how Oakland youth "feel quarantined all the time."

Despite the excitement about national politics, there was an escalating sense of despair and frustration with local politics. A slowing economy, plummeting housing prices, and a rash of foreclosures left gaping holes in both local and state budgets.[1] Murder and violent crime rates were on the rise again, though still lower than in the mid-1990s. Shootings in the East Oakland flatlands dominated the nightly news, and a spate of armed robberies in city restaurants made some middle-class residents afraid to go out to dinner. Oakland had a new mayor, Ron Dellums, a former congressman and nephew of civil rights leader C. L. Dellums, whose election in 2007 embodied the symbolic return of black political power and progressive politics in Oakland. But Dellums provided little leadership in the face of gathering economic and political storms. A 22-year-old African American woman in Elmhurst told me that she saw a difference in the city's mood as she rode the bus every day. Back in 2000-2002, she said, "Everybody had their paper [money]. They were driving fine cars, dressed nice. Now everybody looks hungry."

Only hours into 2009 came a more disturbing reminder that the election of the first black president had changed little in the lives of young people on Oakland's streets. A fight broke out in the Fruitvale BART station at 2:00 A.M. as revelers returned home on BART from New Year's Eve parties around the Bay Area. When BART police responded, one officer shot Oscar Grant, a 22-year-old black man, in the back as he lay already restrained on the ground. The next week, when the district attorney had still filed no charges, a peaceful protest erupted in violence as small groups of teenagers and young adults poured through downtown venting their anger at the long history of police abuse and disrespect they had experienced on Oakland's streets. The newspapers were filled with photos of young Asian, black, Latino, and white protesters carrying signs proclaiming "I am Oscar Grant," chanting, and, more rarely, dancing on police cars and smashing windows. A few months later came another harsh reminder of tension and violence on the frontline of Oakland's war on crime: on a routine police stop, a 27-year-old parolee started a shootout with Oakland police, killing four officers before he was shot down.

Two ballot measures on the November 2008 ballot crystallized opposing visions of Oakland's public policy choices as crime escalated and a new fiscal crisis loomed: the first planned a new parcel tax to fund an additional 105 police officers along with 75 police technicians. The second proposed expanding the amount of city funding set aside for youth programs through what advocates called Kids First 2. These dueling measures embodied different visions of the state and the rights of citizens that we have seen percolating through the chapters of this book. The debates that ensued highlight the important role youth play in politics and some of the core contradictions in neoliberal urban governance we have explored.

Governing through crime created a vocal and powerful constituency in Oakland that defined the core right of citizenship as a right to public safety. Community policing leaders began to organize as Safety First in 2003 and later also as the group, Oakland Residents for Peaceful Neighborhoods (ORPN). They demanded a significant expansion of Oakland's police force to twelve hundred officers, campaigned for the city to get back to the basics of governing, and defined the first priority of city government as public security. But they opposed levying new taxes to fund the expansion of the police force, insisting that the city should pay for a larger force out of the general fund. They were frustrated by city hall scandals and by the slow pace of hiring new police officers from a previous ballot initiative, Measure Y, passed in 2004 to fund police and youth violence prevention programs. These groups began to organize an incipient tax revolt in Oakland. They opposed and helped defeat the 2008 police parcel tax, which, like all taxes in the post–Prop 13 era, needed a two-thirds majority to pass.

Kids First 2 used the symbolic power of childhood to further expand the state's responsibility for children. As one advocate explained, "This initiative would go a long way" to making sure that all Oakland neighborhoods provided "a safe and nurturing environment" where families can raise their children.[2] But the initiative faced enormous opposition from the mayor and most city council members, who argued that increasing the pool of grant funding for children at a time of budget deficits would force deep cuts in other general fund spending: to parks, recreation, senior services, and policing. In the strange world of California budgets, which are often partially crafted at the ballot box, this kind of zero-sum game is increasingly common. Voters choose to expand public spending on schools, parks, or after-school programs, but voters and politicians rarely approve the new taxes that could pay for them. Kids First 2 received just over a 50% yes vote, slightly fewer votes than the police parcel tax, but since it was not a tax, it passed. In the face of a worsening budget crisis, however, youth advocates compromised for a reduced expansion of funds.[3]

Many activists in the Safety First groups opposed increasing Kids First both because of the looming fiscal crisis and because of the narrow way they defined the core responsibilities of local government. As Safety First's mission statement explained, "We believe that long-range social programs to reduce crime and violence are important; but that the funding of such programs should be subordinate to the primary goal of immediate *suppression* of street crime so that Oakland's residents can walk its streets and use its parks without fear." Oakland's expanded partnerships with nonprofits also provoked deep discomfort and new criticisms of the city's investments in youth services. Some critics framed nonprofits as "special interests," their government contracts as evidence of patronage politics, and their advocacy for more funding for youth as self-interested, not as acting in the public interest. Safety First criticized the city for "handing out grants to non-profits with no accountability."[4] ORPN accused Youth Uprising of using public funds to promote Oakland's "thug culture," which created the disorder and crime on Oakland's streets that the police then had to clean up.[5]

These debates offer several important lessons for youth advocates. Youth advocates need to beware of framing investments in youth as crime prevention programs. This strategy only reinforces the idea that the state's primary responsibility is stopping crime and that the core right of citizenship is a right to safety. It does not build support for a vision of the state as responsible for investing in children's environments. Such arguments also reproduce the idea that youth are dangerous, which encourages the disavowal of public responsibility for caring for kids and makes our investments in punishment appear absolutely necessary.[6] If we want to build and sustain investments in equal opportunity childhoods, youth advocates cannot just fight for new set-asides for children and youth programs. They must also build alliances and sufficient power to confront much broader tax and spending policies (at local, state, and national levels of government) that shift resources towards corporations and the wealthy and away from working families and their children. We have to change the zero-sum game in which gaining new after-school programs means losing health care, school funding, or parks.

Cities like Oakland face significant constraints as they try to create more just and equal environments for children. Oakland is home to a disproportionate number of poor families and children and has a lower tax base than surrounding wealthier cities. Municipalities are "poor instruments" for "social democratic projects," as urban historians have long observed, because they have limited powers to tax and "overtaxed" employers can always "flee to cities" with lower taxes.[7] But we must challenge Jerry Brown's pessimism about the power of government to improve the lives of young people. Neoliberal governance was forged out of municipal struggles, and any viable alternative may have to be forged in cities as well. The city of Oakland cannot solve these problems alone, but if Oakland does not try to create more just and equal childhoods, who will? If Oakland does not condemn the nation for abandoning its children, who will? If cities like Oakland define youth as thugs, who will see them as children?

Barack Obama's election offered at least the hope that Oakland would not have to struggle on its own to reduce the unacceptable inequalities in contemporary childhood. In Obama's now-famous speech on race in Philadelphia, he called on the nation to invest in all its children:

> This time we want to talk about the crumbling schools that are stealing the future of black children and white children and Asian children and Hispanic children and Native American children. This time we want to reject the cynicism that tells us that these kids can't learn; that those kids who don't look like us are somebody else's problem. The children of America are not those kids, they are our kids, and we will not let them fall behind in a twenty-first-century economy. Not this time.

Obama implicitly argued that racial images of childhood have too long blocked this nation's attempts to create truly equal opportunities for all its children.

We may well be entering a new era when faith in the markets has tanked and we look again to government to lay the foundation for a more prosperous, stable, and equal union, but it is far from clear that we have overcome the structuring ideologies of neoliberalism, which may quickly return as the roiling economic waters calm. It remains to be seen whether the nation is willing to face the ways racial inequities continue to structure children's lives.

We must not allow the ideal of postracial America to leave us color-blind, unable to see the inequalities staring us in the face. And the economic crisis that began in 2008 will only make inequalities in childhood deeper—as California once again severely slashed funding for schools and youth programs.

Is a Progressive "Kids First" Politics Possible?

The stories in this book offer important lessons as the nation tries to chart a new course. We have seen the power of childhood and youth to reinvigorate claims on the state, but we have also identified significant barriers to constructing a progressive politics of childhood. Some obstacles are tied to our ideas about childhood itself—the ideal that children should be nurtured by nuclear families, in safe and secure private homes, and rarely found unsupervised or on the streets. Too often we define children as "private goods" instead of as a vital social investment.[8] This conceptualization erases the ways public actions fundamentally shape family life and children's worlds, and thus determine the choices available to parents and children. Our ideal of childhood frequently presumes a distinction between public and private that simply does not exist.

This book has traced alternate ways of imagining children as a public responsibility. Black traditions of other mothers and communal fathers offer one important model for how to challenge the privatization of social reproduction in this neoliberal moment. The progressive era child savers and New Deal reformers offer others. These advocates built the initial infrastructure of America's "semi-welfare state" from the 1880s to the 1930s, in large part by organizing to expand state responsibility for children. They created Mother's Pensions (later, Aid for Families with Dependent Children), mandatory free public schools, the juvenile justice system, and publicly funded playgrounds, hoping that these children's programs would be the first steps towards constructing a more comprehensive welfare state in the United States.[9] We can draw on these traditions to reimagine nurturing children as a collective responsibility, and not just the responsibility of extended families or neighborhoods. But we also need to learn from the repeated failures of these efforts to actually deliver the support children need.

Historian Linda Gordon argues that the idea of childhood innocence itself is an impediment to creating a progressive "Kids first politics."[10] Throughout the twentieth century, child savers tried to save "innocent children" without helping their mothers, whom they often defined as morally suspect. They embraced a narrow concept of children's needs and often tried to punish poor parents who did not meet them. Child welfare agencies took kids away from "neglectful" parents instead of working with parents to improve housing, create safe neighborhoods, or reduce family poverty. But this led to the bizarre fiction that one could punish parents without punishing their children. We do the same thing today when we take away "the mother's" part of a welfare check if she doesn't comply with work requirements, while pretending that we are not depriving her children of food and shelter. Or when we reduce direct monetary payments to families (because we don't trust parents) and then pay nonprofits to help kids survive the ensuing crises. Clearly any progressive politics of childhood must neither reify "the family" nor demonize families in whatever form they take.

Race remains one of the most significant barriers to developing a broader vision of collective responsibility for and commitment to America's children. The racial distribution of poverty and punishment in America has corrupted our commitment to kids. Americans define many poor kids of color as "not our kids" and so not our responsibility. It is far too easy for white America to write off poor black children and youth as the product of faulty families or "a thug culture" and to refuse to recognize the public decisions that have produced daily crises in many of their lives. As a nation, we may pity them, at least until they become young teenagers, at which point we mostly fear them. But we repeatedly refuse to see the ways in which public policies have produced America's vast racial and class divides in childhood.

America's unequal childhoods have been built into the physical geography of its cities and suburbs in ways that create additional stumbling blocks for efforts to invest in kids. These landscapes of inequality pose two interconnected problems. First, they have created a commonsense equation of space and danger that has naturalized and justified existing racial and class inequalities as transparent expressions of culture or morality. Images of inner-city kids have undermined support for the welfare state and buttressed calls for a more law and order state. Second, these landscapes have created vast physical distances between poor and wealthy kids; they live in different neighborhoods, play in separate parks, and attend unequal schools. This physical and psychic distance impedes middle-class adults from identifying with the struggles of poor kids and undermines efforts to create a politics of inclusion. Luring more middle-class families to cities like Oakland, as we have seen, is no guarantee of a more progressive politics of youth. Instead, it can exacerbate tensions and create new efforts to control and contain poor kids. And middle-class families can always retreat to private schools and class-segregated neighborhoods.

Figure 21. *The Choice Facing America*. This mural at Youth Uprising was commissioned by Oakland's Youth Commission and designed by Ariel Shepard of Visual Elements. (Courtesy of Youth UpRising)

Constructing a more progressive politics of childhood requires that we confront these racial divides and challenge the powerful image of youth criminality that has twisted our public response to the needs and problems of youth. Our urban wars—the war on drugs, the war on gangs, and the war on street crime—have not made neighborhoods or children safer. Instead, they have consolidated an image of black and Latino boys as thugs, as threats to public safety and economic development. Unless we are willing to lock people up *forever*, and to suffer the social, moral, and financial costs that would entail, more police and suppression cannot fundamentally solve Oakland's (or the nation's) crime problems. The police must arrest people who commit violent crimes. But prisons do not make us safer.[11] Prisoners come back to Oakland's streets angrier, more violent and mentally ill, and with fewer skills than when the police "took them off the streets."[12] It is essentially unjust to abandon generations of poor, predominantly African American and Latino young men, to that fate. We have tried for the last thirty years to manage escalating economic inequality through prisons. This expensive experiment has only deepened crises in poor families and communities and escalated racial inequalities in young people's lives. We need to abandon it. We face a fundamental choice as a nation, a choice graphically illustrated by a mural at Youth UpRising (See Figure 21). We can invest in creating truly equal opportunities across our urban landscapes or we can continue to tolerate the divided landscapes of childhood that generate hopelessness and violence.

There are things we can do as a nation to create more equal and just childhoods. The United States *chooses* to have high child poverty rates and to incarcerate so many poor young people. We successfully reduced, indeed almost eliminated, poverty among the elderly through Social Security and Medicare. We can do the same with children. Many public policies would help. The United States could create a family allowance, as President Nixon once considered, or could create publicly funded savings accounts (like a trust fund) for all the country's children, as Great Britain recently did.[13] We could invest more in higher education so that access to education doesn't depend on parents' ability to pay. We could expand the earned income tax credit to raise the wages of America's lowest-paid workers and index the minimum wage to inflation to ensure that low-wage workers don't fall more behind each year. We can build high-quality low- and moderate-income housing, which would improve children's home environments and thus reduce stress and pressure within families struggling to survive on limited incomes. We can fund public day care and after-school programs to reduce the crises of care in working families. We can invest in expanding new models, like Harlem Children's Zone, that move beyond piecemeal programs to provide comprehensive supports for children and families in America's poor neighborhoods.

Finally, we must transform our juvenile justice systems so they don't resemble prisons and they provide young people with real opportunities to change their lives. States like Missouri have already demonstrated how: focus on counseling not punishment, create alternatives to incarceration, build small, home-like facilities instead of prison warehouses, so that young people can be teenagers instead of gladiators.[14] Some of these approaches may lend themselves to universal public policies that invest in all American kids. Others may focus specifically on poor kids. But they cannot be absolutely color-blind. We will only take these steps once we confront the ways racial and class exclusions from childhood pervade our national consciousness and public policies.

Revitalizing a progressive politics of youth can offer a vital challenge to neoliberal governance. Political and economic changes over the last thirty years have radically constricted both structures and cultures of care. Neoliberalism has defined dependency as the ultimate failure of citizenship and reified the long-standing emphasis on autonomous individualism in America. Children and youth may be the only legitimate dependents we have left. As such they may help us reimagine a social order that values interdependency and thus fundamentally prioritizes human relationships over profits.

Hopeful Signs

The politics of youth in Oakland embodied many of the troubling signs of this neoliberal moment: a shrinking public sphere, privatized public space, and a fearful public who sometimes supported punitive policies. But the city also developed more hopeful models that can point the nation in a new direction. Black, Latino, Asian, and white parents fought for increased investments in children's environments in and out of school. Many community activists, like Bill Clay in Elmhurst, Robert Jackson in the Laurel district, and Shirley Casey in the hills, reached out to nurture Oakland's kids. They refused to abandon kids on the street as thugs. And they worked to expand networks of care, even as they sometimes embraced policies that reinforced fears of dangerous youth.

Youth activists trained a generation of new leaders in Oakland who challenged, and sometimes changed, the ways policy makers thought about youth. They insisted that young people were not a collection of problems to be fixed, or criminals to be contained, but citizens with ideas and energy who could lead the transformation of Oakland's schools and neighborhoods. Youth activists point the way to a politics of childhood that recognizes the capacities of young people themselves as citizens with a right to the city. These young activists may become the kind of leaders in Oakland and the nation, who understand that political action, not just social services, is necessary to create more just childhoods. Oakland's youth activists have expanded alliances with parents and juvenile justice reformers throughout California in order to challenge the state's failed criminal justice policies and to demand reform. Books Not Bars and its many allies celebrated a major victory in 2007 when Governor Schwarzenegger committed to closing some of California's violent, dysfunctional, and expensive youth prisons in order to shift young people into rehabilitative placements closer to home. Progressive advocates have begun to argue that any real path out of California's repeated budget crises must include prison reform. In 2009, educators, parents, youth, and criminal justice reformers proposed "a people's budget fix" that demanded reductions in corrections spending so that education spending could be maintained.[15]

City officials, along with the Oakland Police Department, have begun to embrace other mechanisms for reducing violence in Oakland. They have created alternatives to incarceration, using street-savvy case managers to help high-risk youth turn their lives around. Many of these models were developed, campaigned for, and run out of Oakland's nonprofits (like Oakland Community Organizations, Youth UpRising, East Bay Asian Youth Center, and Youth ALIVE), which could create programs with more flexibility and street credibility than could city or county agencies. In 2008, the city funded twenty street workers to reach out to young men and women on Oakland's toughest streets on weekend nights. The police point these outreach workers to specific problem areas and potential conflicts, but the workers never share information with the police. Outreach workers hand out their cell phone numbers, call people on the street "the loved ones," and help people connect to job training and other services. Most important, they talk about their work as bringing hope and care into the streets to prevent violence.[16]

Oakland Community Organization (OCO) offers an important example of the kind of political organizing necessary to craft a more progressive politics of childhood. Organizing through Oakland's congregations since the 1970s, OCO built strong bases in black and Latino churches throughout the flatlands, creating a multiracial political network, still rare in Oakland's neighborhood politics. In the late 1990s, OCO began to recognize the power of "parental love" as a motivator for advocacy and to organize parents through churches and schools to build power "to protect the interests of their children."[17] OCO's parent organizing continuously politicized children's needs and challenged neoliberal ideology that simply blamed poor parents and communities for their children's failings. They helped win many new services for children in Oakland: homework centers at the libraries, investments in after-school programs, reduced class sizes in K–3. Most recently OCO led a powerful campaign to highlight inequalities in schools across Oakland's hills and flatlands. They seized on the openings created by core neoliberal ideologies of "choice" and "accountability" to build power among the low-income parents and to push the city to commit to create more small schools and charter schools in Oakland's flatlands. OCO remained engaged with these new schools, which trained parent leaders and improved test scores and graduation rates at some of Oakland's flatland schools.[18] OCO's campaign elevated the concept of care above control as a response to the needs and problems of Oakland's young people. The vice-principal of Elmhurst Middle School during its transition into two small schools explained the "complete culture change" she saw on campus. The halls felt completely different, attendance rates improved, suspension rates dropped drastically, and teachers and students started to get to know and care about each other.

Another principal described the change in his job, from being a "glorified cop" into being "an instructional leader."[19]

OCO linked parent leaders to a broad network of activists at the local, state, and national levels, through the PICO Network (People Improving Communities through Organizing) so they could develop and act on a more politicized understanding of their children's needs. They established a "platform for Oakland's working families" and a "vision for a city that values working families with affordable housing, after-school programs, and a model of collaboration and cooperation between the city and school district to provide more land for new schools."[20] When the state faced a budget crisis in 2001, OCO brought eight hundred leaders to Sacramento along with thirty-two hundred leaders from other PICO organizations around the state to demand a "fair share budget plan" that would "not balance the budget on the backs of California's working families and poorest citizens."[21]

Oakland's organizing efforts—especially those of OCO and youth activists—offer an important corrective to some of the problems facing kids-first politics. Middle-class sympathy for poor kids will never be enough to change the starkly unequal childhoods in contemporary cities. Too often middle-class reformers reproduce narrow understandings of children's needs and ignore the political causes of poverty and inequality. We can, and should, shame the nation into facing the unequal childhoods we have made. We should show America's wealthy and middle-class (often white) elders the ways in which their fates and futures are linked to the fates of poor children of color. But we also need organizations that will build the power among youth and working-class families across racial lines that is necessary to demand that the state invest in all our children and to challenge the punitive turn in American public policy. Oakland's activists can help us chart a path out of the politics of fear, which has led us to abandon and try to contain a generation, and towards a true politics of hope.[22]

Governing through crime endangers all our children. Prisons are robbing black, white, Latino, and Asian kids of money for education. Drug testing, locker searches, and zero tolerance policies have become the norm in urban and suburban, poor and wealthy schools alike, turning surveillance and policing into core values of American schools. These policies continue to link the struggles and fates of black middle-class kids to black poor kids, but they also consolidate an image of all America's youth as suspect. They create new links across racial lines and open the potential for new organizing efforts. These organizers may find willing foot soldiers in unlikely places: among Oakland's elderly community policing activists who desperately want a better future for children in Oakland's flatlands, within the fragile middle class where parents face their own anxieties about their children's future, and even among the wealthy in the hills. It is in all of our interests to ensure that the next generation, *all of our kids*, have the skills, capacity, and confidence they need to support us as we age.

Notes

INTRODUCTION

1. I borrow these well-known formulations from Levi-Strauss (1963: 89) and Turner (1969: 95). See Sibley 1995, James 1986, and Valentine et al. 1998 for related arguments.

2. Austin and Willard 1998: 1, Donahue et al. 1998.

3. Wyness et al. 2004.

4. Cindi Katz 2001a: 709.

5. This book builds on calls to investigate the politics of childhood and youth by Stephens 1995, Ruddick 2003, Cindi Katz 2001b, 2004.

6. Aitkin 2000.

7. Cindi Katz 2001b: 52, Mizen 2002.

8. See Lindsey 2009, Cindi Katz 2001a, Kozol 2005, and Lareau 2003.

9. Lindsey 2009.

10. See Lindsey 2009 for poverty, and Austin 1995, Crowell et al. 2001, Krisberg et al. 1987 for disparities in juvenile justice. Most national research doesn't distinguish between different Asian ethnicities, but if one compares Chinese or Japanese American kids with Tongan or Cambodian American kids, one finds radically different levels of poverty, levels of incarceration, and life trajectories (Le et al. 2001).

11. See Clarence Taylor 2009 for a powerful critique of the term "post–civil rights era." Although I use it as shorthand in this book, as will be abundantly clear I mean to suggest neither that race no longer matters nor that racial inequalities are gone.

12. Gupta and Sharma 2006, Li 2005, Mitchell 1992, Ferguson and Gupta 2002.

13. Mitchell et al. 2003: 432.

14. Abrams 1977.

15. As historians Robert Self (2003:14) and Ira Katznelson (2005) demonstrate, New Deal liberalism itself was rife with contradictions, regulating the markets and expanding paths to the middle class for white workers and families while excluding black families from equal opportunities.

16. Michael Katz 2001: 27, Hyatt 2001: 202.

17. Kingfisher and Goldsmith 2001, Morgan and Maskovsky 2003.

18. Simon 1997 and 2007: 75, Parenti 1999, Davis 1992.

19. Lancaster 2007: xiii.

20. Warren et al. 2008: 5.

21. Braman 2004.

22. Rios 2004.

23. Wacquant 2001.

24. Jeffrey and McDowell 2004: 131, Cindi Katz 2001a, 2004, Giroux 2003, Jones et al. 1992.

25. Michael Katz 2001: 104.

26. Hyatt 2001.

27. Holland et al. argue that public-private partnerships characteristic of neoliberal "market rule" pose deep challenges to democracy, but at the same time, sometimes ironically also "create an opening, albeit a small one, for democratic empowerment" and for the emergence of "counter-publics" (2007: 9).

28. Maskovsky 2006: 77-78, Rose 1996: 41.

29. Michael Katz 2001, Li 2005, and Brenner and Theodore 2002.

30. Hebdige (1988: 30), Adams 1997, Griffin 1993.

31. Buckholtz 2002 argues that youth is best defined as a "shifter" because its meaning depends on context of speaking, like deictics "this" and "there."

32. Zelizer 1994, Valentine 2004, Prout and James 1990.

33. Lesko 2001, Valentine 2004, Ackland 1995, Adams 1997, Austin and Willard 1998.

34. Pollock 2005: 47.

35. Fraser 1989: 204.

36. Goldstein 2001: 238.

37. Ritterhouse 2006: 63.

38. Lindenmeyer 2007.

39. Collins 1990.

40. This pattern reproduced the long-standing marginalization of black women from mainstream civil rights activism (Crenshaw 1996).

41. HoSang 2006: 8.

42. Jeffrey and McDowell 2004, Comaroff and Comaroff 2000, Scheper-Hughes and Sargent 1998, Jenks 1996, Ruddick 2003.

43. Finn 2001.

44. These trends cross gender and racial lines (Fussell and Furstenberg 2005: 30).

45. Robbins and Wilner 2001, Steinle 2005.

46. Arnett 2004, Feldman and Elliott 1990.

47. Juvenile justice historian Barry Feld argues that these schizophrenic policies "enable states to selectively choose between two constructs to manipulate young people's legal status, to maximize their social control, and to subordinate their freedom and autonomy" (Feld 1999: 9).

48. Males 1996: 248, Finn 2001, Schwartz et al. 1984.

49. Krisberg et al. 1987, McGarrell 1993, Zimring 1998, Feld 1999.

50. News coverage of youth crime escalated between 1990 and 1998 even as the youth crime rate dropped 20% (Dorfman and Shiraldi 2001).

51. Macallair and Males 2000.

52. Poe-Yamagata and Jones 2000: 25.

53. Deitch 2009, National Council on Crime and Delinquency 2007, Human Rights Watch and Amnesty International 2005, Males and Macallair 2000.

54. Feld 1999: 7.

55. National focus groups and polls have repeatedly documented this equation (Soler 2001: 15).

56. Katz and Stern 2005, Isaacs 2008.

57. Golden 1995: 21.

58. Center for Juvenile and Criminal Justice et al. 2002: 13-14. Criminologists have documented the influence of decisions made at many points: police patrols focusing on minority neighborhoods, racial disparities in police stops and searches, and differential rates at which youth are arrested, charged, prosecuted, and sentenced to out-of-home placements (Austin 1995).

59. Le et. al 2001: 27, Hamparian and Leiber 1997.

60. Poe-Yamagata and Jones 2000: 3.

61. Austin 1995, Males and Macallair 2000, Leonard et.al. 1995. One report found that "nearly 72% of African American youth referred for felony drug offenses were detained while 43% of white youth were detained for the same type of referrals" (Center for Juvenile and Criminal Justice et. al. 2002: 14).

62. Holloway and Valentine 2000: 15, see also Massey 1994.

63. Aitkin 2000: 20.

64. Holloway and Valentine 2000: 15. Model studies include Cindi Katz 2004, Ruddick 2003.

65. Comaroff and Comaroff 2000: 306.

66. Chang 2005.

67. Kids Count 2003, Race profile, Table 7. White families had a median income of $84,194 compared to $35,061 for black families, $37,408 for Asian families, and $37,442 for Latino families (Robert Gammon and Michele R. Marcucci. "Census: Racial Income Disparities Abound; U.S. Data Show Whites Earn Nearly Twice as Much as Members of Other Ethnic Groups." *Oakland Tribune*, Tuesday, August 27, 2002).

68. Gregory 1998, Harris-Lacewell 2004, Patillo 2007, Dawson 2001, Reed 1999, 2000, Maskovsky 2006, Self 2003.

69. Kitwana 2003, Sullivan 1996.

70. Dawson 1995, Cohen 1999.

71. Self 2003: 13.

72. Guinier and Torres 2002.

73. Scheingold 1984, Sanjek 1998.

74. Asian and Latino activists more often participated in ethnic- or language-based organizations that operated on a citywide level. Neighborhoods like Chinatown and Fruitvale that have longer histories as centers of Chinese and Mexican communities are exceptions to this trend.

75. Castells 1983, Gregory 1998, Logan and Molotoch 1987.

76. Logan and Molotoch 1987.

77. Both Sanjek 1998 and Gregory 1998 analyze the ways in which people construct racial and classed identities through local politics.

78. See Rhomberg 2004 for a wonderful historical account of the fragmentation of Oakland's public sphere.

79. Kirp 2007, Schmitt 2007.

1. Bissell 2005: 218.

2. Harris-Lacewell 2004: 30, Smith 2001.

3. Sociologist Patrick Carr (2005) found that white working-class activists in Chicago also saw community policing as a way to instill order in youth. Mike Davis 1992 and Parenti 1999 argue that the police manipulated the fears of black adults and senior citizens to secure their consent for expanded police powers.

4. Maskovsky 2006: 76. Gregory 1998, Guano 2004, Cattelino 2004.

5. Simon 2007: 114.

6. Simon 2007: 109.

7. Wacquant 1999, 2001.

8. This broad neighborhood definition is used by the city's redevelopment agency, by the Elmhurst Blight Committee, and by some neighborhood residents.

9. Molatore n.d.: 10.

10. See Self 2003, McClintock 2008.

11. The median household income in 1999 for census tract 4095 below E. 14th was $25,962, while just above E. 14th tract 4096 was $31,385 and the Toler Heights neighborhood above MacArthur (census tract 4098) was $56,063 (Census 2000 American FactFinder).

12. Census Tract 4096 (2000 American FactFinder).

13. The only racial violence in Elmhurst was caused by informal gangs of white and black youth that fought frequently at Castlemont High School in the late 1950s (May 1973).

14. See Self 2003: 150, 160ff. Between 1950 and 1960 the population in East Oakland shifted from majority white to 51.4% minority. By 1970, a smaller area from 82nd Ave. to 98th along the E. 14th flatland corridor was 70.6% black, 26.4% white, and 2.9% Indian (May 1973: 12, Regal 1967).

15. Regal 1967: 85.

16. See also Molatore n.d.: 5.

17. Self 2003: 175.

18. Self 2003: 174.

19. Rhomberg 2004: 186. See also Molatore n.d.

20. Oakland Citizens Committee for Urban Renewal 1990.

21. United Way of the Bay Area Elmhurst profile at http://www.uwba.org/helplink/data-central.php. Ed-Data [viewed July 2009], fiscal year 2000-2001, student profile, Castlemont High School, www.ed-data.k12.ca.us [viewed Aug. 2003].

22. One study in 1985 estimated that in parts of East Oakland, money from drug dealing represented an important part of the livelihood for 30-35% of residents (Molatore n.d.: 16).

23. Williams 1989.

24. Ed-Data, fiscal year 2000-2001, student profile, Castlemont High School, www.ed-data.k12.ca.us [viewed Aug. 2003].

25. Cf. Gregory 1998.

26. Molatore n.d.: 4, "Groups Get Action in Elmhurst Community," *Oakland Post*, March 17, 1974, 1.

27. "Activism Unites Elmhurst," *Oakland Tribune*, Oct. 19, 1992, A3.

28. Susser 1982: 99-100.

29. I thank Sue Hyatt for encouraging me to flesh out this piece of my argument.

30. Molatore n.d.: 10, Rhomberg 2004.

31. Valentine 1996b, Griffin 1993, and Adams 1997.

32. Drake 1945. See also Williams 2001 and Pattillo-McCoy 1999.

33. Reed 2000: 17, 19, 23-24, Prince 2002, Boyd 2008.

34. Naples 1998: 111, 36. See also Patricia Hill Collins 1990 and Gregory 1998: 135.

35. Katz 2004: 156.

36. Burton 1997.

37. Ashley et al. 1997: 170.

38. See Devine 1997.

39. Chauncey Bailey, "Jobs Program Has Tough Task," *Oakland Tribune,* May 14, 2003.

40. Duster 1987: 303. Freeman and Holzer 1986.

41. Molatore n.d.: 14.

42. Corcoran and Matsudaira 2005: 381.

43. Carole Stack's research on fast food workers in Oakland found that African American youth had a harder time getting hired, securing day shifts, and getting promoted to the management track than did Asians and Latinos (2001: 182).

44. Corcoran and Matsudaira 2005: 366.

45. Wacquant 2001.

46. Warren et al. 2008: 3.

47. Pager 2009: 3.

48. Roberts 2001, Braman 2004.

49. Pager 2009: 4.

50. Pager 2009: 3, see also NAACP Legal Defense Fund 2007.

51. Urban Health Initiative 2000: 2.

52. Go et. al. 2000.

53. Jenks 1996. See also Wyness 2000: 24.

54. See also Gregory 1998: 156.

55. Steven Gregory borrows the term "generational affinity" from Karl Mannheim to make this argument (1998: 160).

56. Maskovsky 2006: 85. See Higgenbotham 1993 for a historical account of the gendered politics of respectability.

57. Williams 2001: 88.

58. Gregory 1998: 137.

59. Sasson and Nelson 1996 also found that black elders participate in home alert groups, not only to decrease crime but also to restore the roles of "old heads" and "community mothers."

60. Gregory 1998: 230, Suttles 1972.

61. Skogan 2004. For these debates, see Greene and Mastrofsky 1988, Trajanowitz 1990, Walters 1993.

62. Bass 1998.

63. This comment hints at a shift in the way we conceptualize the relationship between the state and its citizens: instead of state authority emanating from its status above society, the neoliberal state gets its authority from the way it is embedded within community (see Ferguson and Gupta 2002).

64. Self 2003: 69-72.

65. Gilroy makes a similar argument about British policing (1982: 165).

66. Rhomberg 2004, Self 2003. See also the many Black Panther autobiographies, such as Elaine Brown's *Taste of Power* and Bobby Seale's *Seize the Time*.

67. OPD first developed the African American Advisory Committee on Crime and later added Latino and Asian advisory committees. In 2000, they began to talk about creating a youth advisory committee to address the generational fault lines in police-community relations.

68. For an analysis of community policing nationally see Trajanowitz 1990, Walters 1993, Weatheritt 1988, Skolnick and Bayley 1988, Kelling and Moore 1988.

69. In Oakland, the COPS grant brought the police department staffing above its previous high in 1972 (Stacey Wells and Harry Harris, "Program to Fund 50 More Officers," *Oakland Tribune*, May 8, 1998). In 2001, the city had to pick up the tab for the increased staffing—one factor, along with the recession, that may have led to the city budget crisis in 2003, when the city decided to temporarily freeze police hiring.

70. Oakland borrowed the COMSTAT crime mapping technique from New York, hired the former police chief of Houston as a consultant, and sent its officers for training in "problem-solving" in San Diego.

71. Klinenberg 2002: 150, see also Parenti 1999: 63ff.

72. Kelling and Moore (1988: 19) and Mastrofski (1988: 61) argue that quality-of-life policing often generates more community complaints and so requires intensified efforts to secure community consent.

73. Reed 1999: 119, Boyd 2008: xvii.

74. Bureau of Justice Statistics 2003: 55.

75. In one illustrative case, a deacon at Deputy Chief Bryant's church was stopped, frisked, and detained by the police because he supposedly matched the description of a robbery suspect. His family circulated a petition and a flurry of emails through the congregation, while the deputy chief wished they had contacted him directly so he could have tried to resolve the problem.

76. Self 2003. Skogan 1989 found that African Americans participate in civilian policing at higher rates than other racial groups.

77. Maskovsky 2006 and Cattelino 2004.

78. Gregory 1998: 156.

79. Maskovsky has argued that "neoliberal governance has had a mediocre track record in converting residents to idealized subjects in the inner-city" (2006: 79).

80. Anthropologists like Chesluk 2004, Gregory 1998, and Cattelino 2004, as well as a few criminologists like Mastrofski (1988: 37), have explored this theme.

81. See also Klinenberg 2002: 153ff.

82. See also Chesluk 2004.

83. Wilson and Kelling 1982, Gregory 1998: 154.

84. Gregory 1998: 232.

85. Anderson 1999. See Patillo-McCoy 1999 for another criticism of Anderson.

86. Through homeowner quality-of-life activism, issues of crime, drugs, or poor city services were "disarticulated from the broader structural context and framed as local and typically episodic violations of the rights of individuals to maintain a middle-class lifestyle" (Gregory 1998: 154).

87. Some national surveys suggest that support for trying juveniles as adults increases after age fifty and is higher among African American parents than among any other group (Schwartz et al. 1993).

88. Gilroy 1982: 161.

CHAPTER 2

1. Geographer Gill Valentine argues that exclusionary political projects target "other people's" kids, while projects of inclusion focus on "our kids" (1996b).

2. My argument about the volunteer state is indebted to the work and advice of Sue Hyatt 2001 and to Michael Katz 2001: 163 ff. See also Klinenberg 2002 for a critique of what he calls "the entrepreneurial state."

3. Michael Katz 2001: 137.

4. Putnam 2000.

5. 2001: 166.

6. See Sharma 2006, Li 2005, Gupta and Sharma 2006: 21ff, Ferguson and Gupta 2002, Comaroff and Comaroff 2000, Paley 2001, Cruikshank 1999.

7. The third sector, neither government nor private for-profit corporation, has developed institutions, research publications, and lobbying efforts to define, defend, and expand its interests, such as Aspen Institute and the Association for Research on Non-Profit Organizations and Voluntary Associations. The magazine *Youth Today* and the After-School Alliance work to link nonprofit youth services providers into youth-specific advocacy networks.

8. Family incomes in a single census block could range from under $10,000 to over $200,000.

9. Self 2003: 164. In 1970, the heart of the Laurel district and Redwood Heights Mac-Arthur was .1% black (Social Explorer 1970 data, available at www.socialexplorer.com).

10. Redwood Heights is mostly in census tract 4069, block group 1. For comparison, block group 3 further down the hill along MacArthur is 21% white, 41% black, and 26% Asian. One long-time white Redwood Heights resident told me that in the 1950s and '60s a local real estate agent organized residents to come together to buy any house that came on the market, so that they could be in control of who it was sold to.

11. Census block 4069, group 3 (American Fact Finder Census 2000). Unless otherwise noted all subsequent data is from Census 2000.

12. Sharon Higgens, "Lessons Learned at Public Schools in Oakland," *Oakland Tribune,* March 2, 2005.

13. Ruddick 2003: 337.

14. California Recreation Commission 1955: 29. In 1917, Oakland was one of the only cities that had a centralized system to run public youth recreation programs (Curtis 1917).

15. Oakland Community Chest 1938, Oakland Junior Chamber of Commerce 1935.

16. Kenney 1948: 4, 22.

17. Hawes 1991, Gordon 1988, 1990, Nasaw 1985. For accounts of child saving in juvenile court see Getis 2000, Schlossman 1977, Platt 1977, and Schneider 1992.

18. Kett 1977, Mintz 2004, Chudacoff 2007.

19. Skocpol 1996 makes a similar argument.

20. Boys and Girls Club history at http://www.bgcoakland.org/history/history.html [viewed May 2009].

21. Thorne reports this public program ended in the late 1960s, just as the number of mothers entering the workforce began its precipitous rise (2003: 174). On the Associated Agencies see May 1973, Self 2003.

22. Ruddick 2003: 337.

23. Self 2003, Rhomberg 2004.

24. Self 2003.

25. Hoggart 1991.

26. Rubin 1983: 24.

27. Children's Advocacy Institute 2006: I-6-7.

28. Rubin 1981 and 1983, http://www.oaklandparks.org/about_friends.htm [viewed July 2008].

29. Oakland voters passed several parcel taxes and school bonds in 1994, 2000, and 2006 that together provided $907 million to cover the estimated $1 billion of necessary repairs and seismic retrofits to aging schools (Simone Sebastian, "Schools Measure Proposed Administrator Wants to Ask Voters for $435 Million," *San Francisco Chronicle,* March 8, 2006). Voters also passed a series of bonds for acquiring and refurbishing parks and recreation facilities (Measure K in 1989, Measure I in 2000, and measure DD in 2002).

30. One study estimated that during the boom years between 1996 and 2000, total government spending per child in Oakland increased by only 1.9%, an increase that pales in comparison to growth in total government expenditures for the same period (Brecher et al. 2004: 8).

31. On California's budget deficit, see the California Budget Project 2007 and 2008.

32. Children's Advocacy Institute 2006: I-24.

33. Oakland city government had substantial budget surpluses in 2000 and 2006, but faced massive deficits in 2003, 2005, and 2007-2009. Oakland was particularly vulnerable to ups and downs in the housing market since it derived little revenue from sales tax (Heather MacDonald, "Oakland Looking at Budget Shortfall," *Oakland Tribune* March 23, 2007). The state raided local funds in 1994, 2003, and again in 2007 (Lisa Coffey Mahoney, "Supervisor Jittery over State Budget Woes," *Montclarion,* June 28, 2002).

34. Thorne 2003: 167. See also Hochschild 2004.

35. www.escore.com [viewed July 2002].

36. Cindi Katz 2001b.

37. Laurel Elementary Healthy Start Survey Results (author's files).

38. Valentine and John McKendrick (1997) argue that children's access to public play is reduced more by parental anxieties than by the availability of public play spaces.

39. Best 1990.

40. Lancaster 2007: 150-51.

41. Hawes 1991, Meucci and Redmon 1997.

42. Medrich et al. 1982 and Litt 1997 document parental hypervigilance in poor urban neighborhoods

43. Thorne 2003, Hochchild 2004, Garey 2002.

44. "After School Activities in Oakland: An Assessment of Programs and Resources." Life Enrichment Agency Report to Life Enrichment Committee, Oakland City Council, May 14, 2002.

45. For professional families, extended kin often lived scattered across the country. Extended family ties may also be more stretched and thus no longer provide as much support for black working-class parents and their children as in earlier generations (Kaplan 1997).

46. Carnegie Foundation 1992: 10.

47. Carnegie Foundation 1995: 106.

48. Carnegie Foundation 1992: 10.

49. Carnegie Foundation 1992: 1.

50. Scott et al. 2006: 696-97. Influential authors include Karen Pittman, Michelle Gambone, and Milbrey McLaughlin.

51. Urban Strategies Council 1996: 11.

52. Garey 2002.

53. Prominent California advocacy groups included The After-School Alliance, California After-School Network, and Fight Crime: Invest in Kids.

54. The federal government increased after-school funding from $40 million in 1998 to $1.08 billion in 2008 (http://www.afterschoolalliance.org/policy21stcclc.cfm [viewed July 2009]). California passed the After School Learning and Safe Neighborhoods Partnership in 1998, creating a pool of state funding for competitive grants, and in 2002, California voters passed Proposition 49, which helped to rapidly expand state funding starting in 2005.

55. Scott et al. 2006: 706.

56. Safe Passages 2007: 2.

57. After School Alliance 2001: 2.

58. This extended semidependent period of youth is not altogether new. It resembles the complex combination of dependence and independence experienced by youth in the eighteenth and early nineteenth centuries (Kett 1977).

59. Carnegie Foundation 1992: 28.

60. Mintz 2004: 380-81.

61. On middle-class fears of falling see Ehrenreich 1989, Heiman 2001, Ortner 1998.

62. California Budget Project 2007: 3.

63. California Budget Project 2008: 30. See Heiman 2001, Ortner 1998, Ehrenreich 1989 for discussions of middle-class fears of falling.

64. Hacker 2008.

65. Williams 2007.

66. Finn 2001: 176.

67. Ruddick 2003.

68. Joan Williams (2000: 36ff) argues that this is a modern twist on the ideal of domesticity. One or two generations ago, middle-class mothers were encouraged to stay home to supervise their children's development, but they spent as much time "housekeeping" as actively cultivating their children.

69. Lareau 2003.

70. Williams 2000. See Field 1995 for how education becomes endless labor in Japan.

71. This intensive parenting means both mothers and fathers spend more time with their children today than they did twenty-five years ago (Jacqueline Salmon, "Surprising Study Finds More Togetherness of Kids, Parents," *Oakland Tribune,* May 10, 2001).

72. Chudacoff 2007 describes the 1950s and '60s as a high point in children's free play, even though play was deeply commodified and somewhat colonized by adults.

73. Lareau 2000 and 2003, see also Hofferth and Sandberg 2001.

74. Carnegie Foundation 1992: 67.

75. Lareau 2000, 2003.

76. Patillo-McCoy 1999.

77. Isaacs 2008: 5.

78. Shapiro 2005, Oliver and Shapiro 1995, Conley 1999.

79. Ferguson 2000.

80. Www.ibabuzz.com/education/ [viewed Feb. 25, 2008].

81. Hays 1988.

82. On the complex role of gender and "public mothers" in the progressive era, see Smith-Rosenberg 1987: 263, Getis 2000, and Kunzel 1993.

83. Hyatt 2001.

84. Cindi Katz 2001b: 49.

85. Jones et al. trace the consolidation of this model from the 1970s to the early 1990s in New York, although they do not use the term "neoliberal" (1992: 107).

86. Lareau 2000.

87. Tucker, Jill and Robert Gammon. "Separate and Unequal: Fundraisers Give Schools an Edge." *Oakland Tribune* June 18, 2003. See also rhs.ousd.ca.campusgrid.net/home [viewed June 2008].

88. Pugh 2005: 20.

89. The value of these block grants, unlike those for the elderly, tends to fall each year since they are rarely indexed to inflation. The percent of domestic federal spending for children declined from 20.1% in 1960 to 15.4% in 2005, while spending on entitlement programs for seniors expanded from 22.1% to 45.9%. (Isaacs and Lovell 2008: 6).

90. Foundations and many state and federal agencies prefer to fund new, not existing, programs, which encourages hyperinnovation instead of stability (Landau 1988).

91. A statewide evaluation of Healthy Start–funded programs found similar struggles (http://ccsp.ucdavis.edu/sites/ccsp.ucdavis.edu/files/HSsusExeSumMay4.pdf [viewed June 2008]).

92. California State Budget Project 2001, quoted in Jill Tucker, "State's Spending Fails to Keep Pace," *Oakland Tribune*, June 16, 2003.

93. Safe Passages 2007: 5.

94. City of Oakland Mayor's Office and Park and Recreation 1994.

95. Burr et al. 2005: 4.

96. Katz and Sachsse 1996: 16-17, Wolch 1990.

97. Gilmore 2007, Rodriguez 2007.

98. Gilmore 2007: 46.

99. Rodriguez 2007: 33.

100. Miller 1993, Clarke et al. 2007.

101. Oakland Fund for Children and Youth 2003: 40.

102. Mark Friedman of the Fiscal Policy Studies Institute, quoted in Oakland Fund for Children and Youth 2003: 2.

103. Oakland Fund for Children and Youth 2003: Appendix D.

104. Social services have focused on individual reform (or salvation) since the early twentieth century (Finn 2001: 170, Sarri and Finn 1992).

105. Oakland Fund for Children and Youth 2003: Appendix D9-10.

106. Goode and Maskovsky 2001: 20.

107. See also Halpern 2003: 96.

108. Garey 2002.

109. California Budget Project 2008: 54.

110. Katz 2001b: 51-52.

111. Tilde Herrera, "Eastlake YMCA Needs Volunteers, Now Is the Time for Support," *Oakland Tribune*, March 5, 2003.

112. KTVU, "Budget Cuts Force Oakland Schools to Cut 700 Jobs," May 17, 2003, http://www.ktvu.com/news/2211021/detail.html [viewed June 2003].

CHAPTER 3

1. Heyman 1963: 34.

2. Bonilla-Silva 2006, Gilroy 1987, Balibar and Wallerstein 1992. Ann Stoler argues that the emphasis on cultural distinctions is not new but was always part of colonial racial hierarchies (1995).

3. Bonilla-Silva outlines the central frames of color-blind liberalism (2006: 25ff).

4. Skyline High School's history is documented in Kirp 1982: 217-50, Heyman 1963, and Crain et al. 1969, who refer to Oakland as Lawndale. My account also relies on news coverage in *The Montclarion* and *Oakland Tribune*.

5. Pollock 2005: 46.

6. Self 2003: 166.

7. Roland 1965: 27, Kirp 1982: 217.

8. Heyman 1963: 42, Kirp 1982: 224.

9. "The School Board," *Montclarion*, Jan. 13, 1965, 10.

10. Heyman refers to parent letters expressing worries that academic standards might be diluted and fears of "violence," "different moral standards (especially sexual) and fears that their children would be bused to predominately Negro schools" (1963: 32).

11. "School Board Open Plan," *Montclarion*, Feb. 3, 1965, 1. "School Board," *Montclarion*, Feb. 10, 1965, 9.

12. "School Board Hears Charge: Myth of Privilege Provoked Violence at Skyline High," *Montclarion*, Oct. 22, 1969.

13. "Serious Racial Strife Could Develop Only at One High School in Oakland—Skyline," *Montclarion*, March 3, 1976, 1.

14. Ladson-Billings 2004: 4.

15. Kirp 1982: 235.

16. Rhomberg 2004 and Self 2003.

17. The census tract near the high school (4081) is 48% white, 32% black, and 18% Asian, with negligible numbers of Latinos. But there is significant divergence between different areas of this tract. Hillcrest Estates is 71% white, while another block group is 45% black and 50% white (U.S. Census 2000, American FactFinder).

18. Conley 1999: 1 and Oliver and Shapiro 1995.

19. Votes were frequently split between the hills and flatlands (Laura Counts and Paul Rosynsky, "Pattern in Voting for Mayor Splits Hills, Flatlands," *Oakland Tribune*, March 18, 2002).

20. Pugh 2005: 8.

21. Between 1990 and 2000, Skyline's white student population declined from 23% to 12%, continuing a trend from the 1980s (www.ed-data.k12.ca.us/StudentTrends [viewed July 2003]). All statistics for OUSD can be found at Ed-Data.

22. Nakao 1998.

23. Oakland History Clipping File, Oakland Hills, Skyline. Most hills neighborhoods are organized into homeowners' associations for each separate development although a Hills Homeowner Coalition unites these different groups in fights against further development in the hills.

24. Elmhurst has several parks, but most are grassy areas between two and five acres with a few trees and sometimes a recreation building. A couple of larger 14-16-acre parks exist outside of the hills, but are dwarfed by the open space in the hills (www.oaklandnet.com/Parks/ [viewed Aug. 2008]).

25. Buses poorly serve the area, though the East Bay Regional Park District does try to provide some subsidized transportation for low-income schools and organized groups serving low-income families.

26. Rieder explores the ways "talk collectivized the experience of danger" (1995: 67).

27. Davis 1992, Caldeira 2001, and Low 2003.

28. Cobern and Riley 2000.

29. Survey in author's files.

30. Gregory 1998 Sugrue 1998, and Hirsch 1983 all examine the ways race was built into the post–World War II urban spaces through urban redevelopment and national housing policies.

31. See Hartigan on racial etiquette (1999: 157).

32. Gregory 1999: 110.

33. Hartigan 1999: 167.

34. Bonilla-Silva 2006: 25ff.

35. Frankenberg 1993: 147.

36. Pollock 2005: 44 and Pollock 2004.

37. Rieder 1995 and Hirsch 1983 document this kind of prevalent belief in ancestral bootstrapping.

38. Hartigan 1999: 241.

39. Self 2003, Oliver and Shapiro 1995 Conley 1999, Katznelson 2005.

40. Ed-Data http://www.ed-data.k12.ca.us/StudentTrends.

41. Bonilla-Silva 2006: 68, see also Hartigan 1999: 155.

42. Rhomberg 2004: 167.

43. Ginwright 2004: 72.

44. Wilson 1987, 1996, Murray 1984. For critiques see Vincent 1993 Zinn 1989, Katz 1992.

45. Collins 1989: 876-82.

46. Lawrence 1983: 50.

47. Gilroy 1987: 43.

48. Gilroy 1987: 43.

49. Schrag 1999. Sugrue 1998 traces the history of how U.S. policy transfers wealth from the cities to suburbs, while Howard 2006 details how the "invisible welfare state" benefits middle-class homeowners and not the poor.

50. Gilmore quoted in HoSang 2006: 9-10.

51. Pugh 2005: 14.

52. HoSang 2006: 8.

53. Ed Source 2003, California Budget Project 2007: 1. These rankings also do not take into account the high cost of living in California, which, because of higher teacher salaries, means that the same funding goes less far in California than in other states.

54. Reported by school board member in a Beat 25X NCPC meeting, May 2000.

55. "Census: Oakland among Brainiest Cities," *Oakland Tribune*, Dec. 20, 2000.

56. Cobern and Riley 2000: 10.

57. Cobern and Riley 2000: 10-11.

58. Cindi Katz 2001a: 51.

59. Ferguson argues that the mirror images of black men as an endangered species and as criminals both "frame black men as individually responsible for their own fate" (2000: 80-82).

60. These tracking patterns are common in public schools throughout the country (Street 2005: 82ff., Darling-Hammond 2004, Fischer et al. 1996).

61. Here I draw on interviews and Nakao 1998.

62. Nakao 1998.

63. Ferguson 2000: 61.

64. Shah et al. 2009: 8-9.

65. Jill Tucker and Robert Gammon, "Teachers Key to Top Schools: Senior Instructors in Oakland Hills Earn an Average of $10,000 More Than Those in Flatlands," *Oakland Tribune*, June 17, 2003. See also Education Trust West 2005.

66. Ladson-Billings 2004: 9.

67. Www.decent.schools.org [viewed July 2009].

68. Pollock 2005: 45. See Darling-Hammond 2004, Street 2005, and Kozol 2005.

69. Fine 2004: 255.

70. California Budget Project 2001: 3-4.

71. Shah et al. 2009: 8-9.

72. Ferguson 2001: 80.

73. Ferguson 2001: 84, 90.

74. Ferguson 2001: 125.

75. NAACP Legal Defense Fund 2007, Advancement Project and Harvard Civil Rights Project 2000, Skiba et al. 2000.

76. Kids First 2000. Youth and parent activism helped reduce suspensions (especially for defiance of authority) so that by 2007 Oakland had a suspension rate only slightly higher than the state average (Nanett Asimov, "Suspensions Point to Trouble in Schools," *San Francisco Chronicle*, May 19, 2008).

77. Darling-Hammond 2004: 226.

78. Annie Nakao, "Peer Power: Blacks Can't Just Drop Their Kids Off at School and Assume They'll Get the Same Education as Whites," *San Francisco Examiner*, June 9, 1998.

79. Collins 1990.

80. See www.naacpldf.org and http://www.childrensdefense.org for information on these campaigns.

81. See Darling-Hammond 2004.

82. Pollock 2005: 45, 47.

83. Sanjek 1998: 300ff.

84. Sanjek 1998: 390.

85. See for example, Davis 1992, Smith 1996, Parenti 1999, Mitchell 2004.

CHAPTER 4

1. This portrait draws on the work of Rhomberg 2004: 120 and Self 2003.

2. Oral History Interview, conducted by Oakland Living History Program, at http://www.deepoakland.org/project?id=20 [viewed Aug. 2008].

3. I draw on my observations of Eastmont Mall, as well as Mall 2000 and Cielo 2005.

4. Mall 2000.

5. This description draws on some of my own observations, videos, and news reports (Sahagun 2005, Gammon 2005, Cielo 2005, and J. Douglass Allen-Taylor's articles at http://www.safero.org/sideshows.html [viewed June 2007]).

6. Cielo 2005: 21.

7. The Richie Rich and the 415 song "Sideshow" released in 1989 was the first of many to celebrate the Sideshow. More recently, E-40 boosted the popularity of the event with his video featuring lyrics and images of ghost riding in "Tell Me When to Go" in 2006.

8. Cielo 2005: 21. The city mandated that the owners of parking lots erect fences and lock them at night to keep out cruisers (Gammon 2005).

9. Krisberg et al. found similar phenomena in Washington, DC, where all crime was also characterized as a "youth issue" (2009: vi).

10. Matless 1995: 96. See also Valentine 2004, 1996b, Aitkin 2001.

11. Youth activists defeated a proposed curfew in 1996, but African American city council members brought the idea back in 1998, 2000-2001, and, most recently, February 2009. Each time they were defeated because of youth activism and broader concerns that they criminalized youth.

12. Mary Douglas 1966: 50. See also Lees 2003: 625 and Gregory 1998, who make related arguments drawing on Douglas.

13. Lees (2003: 613, 614), Smith 1996, Mitchell 2004, Brenner and Theodore 2002, and Zukin 1995, who provided one of the earliest explorations of the new importance of image and culture in urban redevelopment.

14. Smith 2002: 439.

15. Peck and Tickell 2002, Merry 2001, Chelsuk 2004, Sorkin 1992, Maskovsky 2001.

16. Merry 2001: 16, 20.

17. Merry 2001: 3.

18. Lees 2003 and Breitbart 1998 are significant exceptions. See also Gilroy et al. 1982, Gilroy 1987, Katz 2005, and Gough 2002.

19. Miller 1998, Lasch 1977, Nasaw 1985.

20. Kett 1977, Fass 1977. Early urban redevelopment efforts in Oakland sometimes used juvenile delinquency, as well as race, as markers of urban decline (Marr 1938). But these early-twentieth-century efforts did not suggest that youth on the street created urban decline and that clearing youth off the street was necessary for urban renewal.

21. Valentine 2004, Cahill 1990.

22. Mitchell 2004: 4. I borrow the phrase "geographic fix" from Mitchell 2004.

23. Parenti 1999, Sorkin 1992.

24. Kirkpatrick called this an "aggressively entrepreneurial regime" (2007: 347). Rhomberg 2004: 190.

25. Michael Duffy, "Jerry Brown Still Wants Your Vote," *Time Magazine*, May 21, 2006. Jerry Brown, Inaugural Address 2003.

26. Kirkpatrick 2007: 347. Ryan Tate, "Dealmaker: Jerry Brown," *San Francisco Business Times,* March 24, 2006.

27. Logan and Molotoch argue that pro-growth urban coalitions routinely make this argument, but that growth is often a "mixed blessing" for low-income populations (1987: 85).

28. Michael Katz 2001.

29. Smith 2002.

30. Kirkpatrick 2007: 349.

31. Kirkpatrick 2007: 347-48.

32. Chauncey Bailey, "Brown, Riles Clash in Debate," *Oakland Tribune,* Feb. 18, 2002.

33. Jobs and Housing Coalition, http://jobsandhousing.com/ [viewed Feb. 2009].

34. MacDonald 1999.

35. Chris Thompson 2000.

36. Rhomberg 2004: 190.

37. Alex Katz, "Empty Seats May Shut Down Schools," *Oakland Tribune,* Oct. 23, 2003.

38. Rhomberg 2004, Salazar 2006.

39. MacDonald 1999.

40. Wilson and Kelling 1982, Mitchell 2004: 200.

41. On gated communities in Brazil and the United States, see Caldeira 2000, Low 2003.

42. For Jack London and Oak to 9th plans see http://www.jacklondonsquare.com/ [viewed June 2009] and http://www.oakto9th.com [viewed June 2009].

43. Smith 2002: 443.

44. Oakland Community Economic Development Agency 2005: 8-9.

45. Rhomberg (2004: 187) reports that in 1977 the central business district downtown still had seven department stores, while ten years later the whole city had only four. Two of these closed with the decline of the Eastmont Mall, and by 2005 there was only one Sears store downtown (Oakland Community Economic Development Agency 2005: 2).

46. Lees 2002: 620.

47. Lees 2002: 614.

48. CEDA website (http://www.business2oakland.com/main/demographics.htm).

49. Bill Picture, "In Oaktown, Unpolished Is the New Glam," *San Francisco Magazine,* October 2007, http://www.sanfranmag.com/node/2592 [viewed July 2008].

50. Ruddick 2003: 334.

51. Ruddick 2003: 353, 351.

52. Ruddick 2003: 344.

53. Picture 2007.

54. Burt 2007.

55. Shuman 2000. See Rose (1991: 276) for an analysis of the "institutional policing" of rap.

56. Burt 2007.

57. Davey D, "How & Why Hip Hop Is Darkening Oakland's Nightlife—or Is It?" Nov 12, 2007. www.daveyd.com [viewed June 2008].

58. Bass 1998. Police harassment of black youth at the Lake goes back into the 1940s and '50s, according to some of my informants and to Bass (1998: 219).

59. Bass 1998: 232.

60. Bass 1998: 214ff, Austin 1988. Bass argues that the festival turned into "a festival of the haves and have nots" since young people often did not have the escalating price of admission to the popular festival (1998: 223). She estimated that 95% of cruisers were black and 75-80% were between the ages of fifteen and twenty-five (1998: 216).

61. The city spent between $400,000 and $1 million a year to disperse the Sideshow (Mike Martinez, "New Sources Eyed to Fund Cruise Patrol," *Oakland Tribune*, Jan. 2, 2003; Zusha Elinson, "City Steps In: Sideshows Could End," *Oakland Post*, July 6, 2005).

62. Zusha Elinson, "City Steps In: Sideshows Could End," *Oakland Post*, July 6, 2005. In 1999, an Elmhurst community policing officer told me that a study he conducted in 1997 found closer to 50% of cars from out of the city.

63. City council person Desley Brooks, an African American woman who represented one of East Oakland's flatland districts, accused Brown of putting his career ahead of the safety and security of black children: "It's unfortunate you sacrifice *our* children for your career" (Bobby Caina Calvan, "A Car Culture Inflames a Culture War," *Boston Globe*, June 10, 2005).

64. In 2007, the city settled a lawsuit and agreed to no longer seize and sell cars participating in the Sideshow (Henry K. Lee, "Seizure Lawsuit Settled," *San Francisco Chronicle*, July 19, 2007).

65. Gammon 2005. The Sideshow slowed in 2005-2006, but by 2009 was active again.

66. J. Douglas Allen-Taylor. "Applying Critical Thinking to Another Oakland Shooting Death," *Berkeley Daily Planet* February 11, 2005.

67. Jim Herron Zamora, "Profiling a Dilemma for Oakland: Residents Don't Want to Sacrifice Civil Liberties for Police, Protection," *San Francisco Chronicle*, May 12, 2002. Lakiesha McGhee, "NAACP Probe Reveals Problems with Police," *Oakland Tribune*, April 18, 2002.

68. Peggy Stinnett, "Videos Heat Up Sideshow Debate," *Oakland Tribune*, June 27, 2005.

69. An African American police captain who worked in East Oakland told me that he had recently concluded that he'd need an officer "on every corner" to sweep the Sideshow out of the city. By 2001, he supported exploring legalized venues.

70. Davey D., "Oakland's Oppressive Sideshow Ordinance Passes," July 20, 2005, www. daveyd.com [viewed June 2008].

71. LCAP website www.support.net/lcap/info.cfm [viewed October 2002].

72. Goode and Maskovsky 2001: 9.

73. Youth scholars have often pointed to the ways groups of youth within suburban malls are constructed as threatening presences, potential shoplifters to be actively monitored and moved along by security guards (Ruddick 1996, Matthews et. al. 1996, and Shields 1989).

74. Steve Chawkins, "No Appetite for Classical Music," *Los Angeles Times*, June 28, 1998. The Mosquito teen deterrent device is now marketed in the United States, but in a wonderful inversion, teenagers are now using this sound as a cell ring tone that can't be heard by adults (www.mosquitogroup.com [viewed Aug. 2009]).

75. Matthews et al. 1996: 257, Shields 1989, Valentine 1996a: 214.

76. Lees 2002: 624, see also Wyn and White 2000: 307.

77. Klein 2000: 311.

78. Dominguez 1994, also Stoler 1995.

79. Hall 1904: xv.

80. Bennet et al. 1996: 18. Anthropologist Johannes Fabian's analysis of metaphors of time suggests that these temporal metaphors may serve to distance adults from children, as they did anthropologists from racialized "Others" (1983).

81. Fleetwood 2004: 36.

82. Kelley 1996: 136.

83. Thorne 2003: 167. See also Aitkin 2000.

84. Zukin 1994: 5.

85. Valentine 1996a: 211-12, Cahill 1990. Valentine and John McKendrick 1997 argue that children's access to public play is reduced more by parental anxieties than by the availability of public play spaces.

86. Valentine 1996b: 590.

87. Lower-class and minority youth have long been represented as "dangerous" kids who required social control (Finn 2001: 171, Kett 1977).

88. Valentine 1999.

89. Valentine 2004: 1.

90. Douglas 1966: 50.

91. Leslie Miller argues that the creation of the concept of dangerous street and safe home occurred at exactly the same time as the creation of the idea of innocent, fragile children (1998).

92. Laws like Proposition 21 that transferred kids to the adult criminal justice system were passed all over the country in the 1990s (Feld 1999), see Barry Krisberg et. al. 1987 Steinhart 1991 for detrimental effects on recidivism.

93. See Jenks 1996, Wyness 2000: 24.

94. Mitchell 2004: 211.

95. Sally Merry argued that different strategies of governance often coexist, "interlocking and layered" one with another (2001: 25).

96. Devine 1997, Ayers et al. 2001.

97. See also Meucci and Redmon 1997, Ashley et al. 1997.

98. High schools were not eligible for Prop 49 funding, and only 3% of California high schools received federal funding for after-school activities (After-School Programs Fact Sheet 2004 at http://www.preventviolence.org/press/articles/AfterSchool_factsheet.pdf [viewed Jan. 2010].

99. Mitchell 2004: 33.

100. Safe Passages 2007: 29-30.

101. Hall et al. 1999: 506. See also Matthews et al. 2000, O'Neil 2002: 64-65.

102. Austin 1988: 678.

103. Hall et al. 1999: 512.

104. I borrow this phrase from Valentine et al. 1997. See Katz 2004, Stephens 1995, Meucci and Redmon 1997 for the importance of paying attention to children's own understandings of their environments.

105. Ashley et al. 1997: 175.

106. Meucci and Redmon 1997: 5.

107. Youth activists published the result of a survey of three hundred youth in 1997 that documented these findings. But over ten years later, the Oakland Youth Commission survey and my own focus groups documented very similar comments, despite the passage of Kids First, which increased funding for youth programs (Ashley et al. 1997: 172, interviews with Youth Commission members and staff).

108. Tilton 2009.

109. Sibley 1995.

110. Mitchell 2004: 211.

111. Bernard Harcourt, "The Broken-Windows Myth." *New York Times*, September 11, 2001. See also Harcourt 2001, Gregory 1998, Mitchell 2004.

112. Davey D, "Boots Heats Up on Oakland Mayor Jerry Brown," Jan. 25, 2000, www.daveyd.com [viewed July 2003].

113. Cahill 1990: 398.

114. Feld 1999: 9.

115. Chang 2005.

116. Cf. Anderson 1990, 1999.

CHAPTER 5

1. Ashley 2001.

2. Youth Rights Media in New Haven, CT, Justice for DC Youth, Friends and Families of Louisiana's Incarcerated Youth, and Justice 4 Youth Coalition in New York all have engaged in similar kinds of campaigns.

3. Ginwright 2006, Ginwright and James 2002, HoSang 2003 and 2006.

4. Comaroff and Comaroff 2000, Durham 2000, 2004, Sherrod et. al 2006.

5. HoSang 2006: 6.

6. Ginwright and James (2002: 27) have offered an important critique of mainstream youth development models, arguing for Social Justice Youth Development initiatives that emphasize a "political understanding of race, economic inequality and political power."

7. Durham 2004.

8. On neoliberal spatial transformations generally, see Brenner and Theodore 2002, Smith 2002, Peck and Tickell 2002, Calderia 2001, Davis 1992, Sorkin 1992, Maskovsky 2001.

9. Mitchell 2004.

10. Ashley 2001.

11. I use "counterpublic" in the tradition of feminist and black scholars, who have critiqued and reframed Habermas's work on the public sphere (Fraser 1989, Harris-Lacewell 2004, Gregory 1998).

12. Turner 1969: 178ff.

13. Van Jones, quoted in Ards 2004.

14. See Gregory 1998, Reed 1999.

15. HoSang 2003: 6.

16. The Kids First! Initiative youth researchers found that the city spent only 1% of the city budget on youth programs and recreation in 1995 compared to 15% in 1960 (1998: 2). HoSang 1997 argued that the city of Oakland spent far less on nonprofit services than surrounding cities, only $200,000 in 1995.

17. Kids First! Coalition 1998: 17-18.

18. Cindi Katz 2004: 159.

19. NAACP Legal Defense Fund 2007. The Children's Defense Fund renamed this the "cradle to prison pipeline."

20. Rios 2004: 50. See videos produced by Oakland students for similar evocative stories of young people's experiences at http://urbandreams.ousd.k12.ca.us/video/index.html [viewed July 2008].

21. For descriptions of youth activist political education efforts in Oakland, see Rios 2004, Ginwright 2006, HoSang 2003.

22. HoSang 2003.

23. See Ben Kirschner 2006 for an analysis of apprenticeship models and the importance of not reifying the notion of "youth leadership."

24. Quoted in Martinez 2000.

25. Bennet, DiIulio, and Walters 1996: 39-56. See also John DiIulio, "Moral Poverty: The Coming of the Super-Predators Should Scare Us into Wanting to Get the Root Causes of Crime a Lot Faster," *Chicago Tribune*, Dec. 15, 1995, 31.

26. In fact crime rates plummeted as youth populations peaked in the early 2000s (Macallair and Males 2000). Between 1991 and 1998, as youth populations skyrocketed in Alameda County, felony arrests dropped 41% (Rosser International 1998: 1-3).

27. Males 1996: 104ff, Zimring 1998, Macallair and Males 2000.

28. Rosser International originally developed the proposal for a 540-bed juvenile hall. Bart Lubow from the Annie E. Casey Foundation said their estimate didn't "seem to be based on any sort of science." Since Rosser was in the juvenile detention construction business, Lubow commented, "That's like asking Lockheed Martin how many bombers the U.S. needs to protect itself" (Books Not Bars press release, "Youth-Led Movement against Prisons Is Gathering Steam San Diego," Thursday, May 17, 2001).

29. Alameda County Chiefs of Police and Sheriff's Association, October 18, 2001 (author's files).

30. Cecily Burt, "Oakland Moves to Trace Sales of Guns to Minors," *Oakland Tribune*, July 24, 2002, Local section. In fact, the report had found that 60% of guns recovered from arrested juveniles had been purchased in the Bay Area (personal communication).

31. Mike Males, "Oakland Murders Not Youth Violence," *San Francisco Chronicle*, Nov. 27, 2002.

32. Dorfman and Schiraldi 2001.

33. Youth Media Council 2002, Soler 2001.

34. Macallair and Males 2000: 5. Stereotypes of gang members as black, Asian, and Latino contribute to these disparities (Villaruel and Walker 2002).

35. National Council on Crime and Delinquency 2007: 37.

36. See Ayers et al. 2001.

37. Comaroff and Comaroff 2004: 804.

38. Youth Media Council 2002.

39. We Interrupt This Message & Youth Force 2001. These youth media organizations also drew on the work of Males 1996, Dorfman and Schiraldi 2001.

40. Keith Carson quickly did, while Alice Lai-Bitker wavered between votes for a smaller facility and the larger juvenile hall (Donna Horowitz, "420-Bed Juvenile Hall OK'd," *Oakland Tribune*, Oct. 10, 2001).

41. Quoted on Davey D's Hip Hop Corner July 25, 2001 at www.daveyd.com [viewed July 2007].

42. Overall, the expanded juvenile hall would cost the county $176 million to build, only $33 million of which would be provided by a grant from the state. The rest of the money would come from the county's Emerald Fund, which activists insisted should be used instead to rebuild mental health facilities or to create youth centers in communities (Donna Horowitz, "Surprise Vote for Smaller Juvenile Hall: Youth Activists Cheer as 2 Sites, Options to Detention, Weighed," *Oakland Tribune*, Sept. 26, 2001).

43. O'Neil 2002 and Jenks 1996 document the links between innocence (seen both as ignorance and goodness) and dependence in modern concepts of childhood. See also Noguera et al. 2006 for a set of academic and activist challenges to this idea that youth are incomplete citizens.

44. Ashley 2001.

45. Quoted in Ashley 2001.

46. Sean Ginwright and Taj James (2002), two theorists of youth activism with roots in Oakland, have written extensively about this new social justice approach.

47. Ginwright 2006.

48. Shuman 2000.

49. Mitchell 2004: 4.

50. Mitchell 2004: 23.

51. Mitchell 2004: 182.

52. Harvey 2003: 939.

53. Kelley 1996: 206, Rose 1991, 1994.

54. Low 2003 and Holston 1999 also explore the links between the rights to public space and citizenship.

55. Youth Force flier "Fight Pete Wilson's War against Youth," February 2000 (author's files).

56. Perkins 1996: 21.

57. Willis 1981, Fine 1991, Ferguson 2000.

58. Ginwright 2006. See also Rios 2004, who talks about Olin's use of hip hop to transform youth "from knucklehead to revolutionary."

59. Boots quoted in Ards 2004. Many hip hop scholars have looked eagerly for signs of hip hop's political awakening (Chang 2005, Kitwana 2003, Perry 2004).

60. Lipsitz 1998.

61. Representative Maxine Waters urged that adults engage hip hop in this way during the gangsta rap hearings (Chang 2005: 454).

62. Kwon 2006.

63. Books Not Bars and Youth Force Coalition flier, 2001, "Inside: Everything You Need to Know to Stop the Super Jail for Kids" (author's files)

64. Kids First! Coalition 2000.

65. Books Not Bars and Youth Force Coalition flier, 2001, "Inside: Everything You Need to Know to Stop the Super Jail for Kids" (author's files).

66. Comaroff and Comaroff (2000: 303) note that in much of the English-speaking world "teenager" is racially marked as white and "youth" invariably as black and male.

67. Males 1996.

68. Le et al. 2001.

69. Kelley 1996, Ginwright 2006.

70. Quoted in Martinez 2000.

71. Comaroff and Comaroff 2000, Spady et al. 2006.

72. As in Gregory 1998, black political subjectivities cultivated in these homeowner-dominated meetings often defined "respectability" in ways that often excluded younger residents and renters of the "core black community."

73. Ards 2004: 320.

74. As Durham has written, if "invoking youth is a pragmatic act," then "in the prag-matic and political processes in which such namings take place, the category itself is reconstructed" (2004: 592-93).

75. Mitchell 2004: 129.

76. Mitchell 2004: 9.

77. Mitchell 2004: 222.

CONCLUSION

1. Between 2005 and 2008, one-quarter of Oakland's single-family homes went into fore-closure ("Oakland Faces a Daunting Foreclosure Problem," *Oakland Tribune*, Nov. 12, 2008).

2. Kelly Rayburn, "Kids First! Group Says It Has Signatures Needed for November Ballot Measure," *Oakland Tribune*, June 9, 2008.

3. On a state level, the crises facing investments in children looked even more dire as California cut funding for education, children's health, and child care.

4. Safety First statement of principles and purpose, http://safetyfirstoakland.blogspot.com/ [viewed July 2009].

5. Oakland Residents for Peaceful Neighbors, www.orpn.org [viewed Jan. 12, 2010].

6. HoSang 2006: 8.

7. Self 2003: 326, Peterson 1981.

8. Interview with Timothy Smeeting in Susan Phillips, "Choosing Child Poverty," http://www.connectforkids.org/node/577 [viewed Aug. 2009], See also Thorne 2003.

9. Gordon 2009, Michael Katz 2001.

10. Gordon 2009.

11. Males et al. 2006.

12 Scott Duke Harris, "Listening to Oakland: The City Is a Stark Example of How Tough Laws Are Putting More Seasoned Criminals on the Streets of California," *Los Angeles Times*, July 6, 2003.

13. Lindsay 2009.

14. Youth Transitions Funders Group 2006.

15. Books Not Bars (http://www.ellabakercenter.org/index.php?p=bnb_peoples_budget [viewed Jan. 2010]).

16. Sean Maher. "Hometown Heroes: Commissioned to Improve the Mean Streets of Oakland," *Oakland Tribune*, July 26, 2009.

17. Snyder 2008: 106.

18. An Evaluation of the Oakland New Small Schools Initiative, Sept. 2007. New Small Autonomous Schools Evaluation 2007 at http://www.bayces.org/article.php/nsaseval [viewed Nov. 2009].

19. Katy Murphy, "Oakland Small Schools Ten Years Later," *Oakland Tribune*, May 5, 2009.

20. Http://www.piconetwork.org/ [viewed Jan. 2010].

21. OCO 2002 Annual Report [viewed July 2004] www.oaklandcommunity.org.

22. Chang 2005.

Bibliography

Abrams, Philip. 1977. Notes on the Difficulty of Studying the State. *Journal of Historical Society* 1 (1): 58-91.

Ackland, Charles. 1995. *Youth, Murder, Spectacle: The Cultural Politics of "Youth in Crisis."* Boulder, CO: Westview.

Adams, Mary Louise. 1997. *The Trouble with Normal: Postwar Youth and the Making of Heterosexuality*. Toronto: University of Toronto Press.

Advancement Project and Harvard Civil Rights Project. 2000 [viewed Aug. 2008]. *Opportunities Suspended: The Devastating Consequences of Zero Tolerance and School Discipline*. Harvard University. Www.civilrightsproject.harvard.edu.

After School Alliance. 2001 [viewed Aug. 2008]. After-School Alert Poll Report, July/August 2001. Http://www.afterschoolalliance.org/documents/polling/school_poll_01085_final.pdf.

Aitkin, Stuart. 2000. Play, Rights, and Borders: Gender-bound Parents and the Social Construction of Childhood. In *Children's Geographies: Playing, Living, Learning*, ed. Sarah L. Holloway and Gill Valentine. New York: Routledge.

———. 2001. *Geographies of Young People: Morally Contested Spaces of Identity*. New York: Routledge.

Anderson, Elijah. 1990. *Streetwise: Race, Class, and Change in an Urban Community*. Chicago: University of Chicago Press.

———. 1999. *Code of the Streets: Decency, Violence, and the Moral Life of the Inner City*. New York: Norton.

Ards, Angela. 2004. Rhyme and Resist: Organizing the Hip-Hop Generation. In *That's the Joint: The Hip-Hop Studies Reader*, ed. Murray Forman and Mark Anthony Neal. New York: Routledge.

Arnett, Jeffery. 2004. *Emerging Adulthood: The Winding Road from Late Teens through the Twenties*. New York: Oxford University Press.

Ashley, Guy. 2001. Poetic, Idealist Politics of Youth Activists Jarring. *Contra Costa Times*, Oct. 21, 2001.

Ashley, Jermaine, et al. 1997. How Oakland Turns Its Back on Teens: A Youth Perspective. *Social Justice* 24 (3): 170-76.

Austin, James. 1995. The Overrepresentation of Minority Youth in the California Juvenile Justice System: Perceptions versus Realities. In *Minorities in Juvenile Justice*, ed. Kimberly Kempf Leonard, et al. Thousand Oaks, CA: Sage.

Austin, Joe, and Michael Nevin Willard. 1998. Angels of History: Demons of Culture. In *Generations of Youth: Youth Cultures in Twentieth-Century America*, ed. Joe Austin and Michael Willard. New York: New York University Press.

Austin, Regina. 1988. Not Just for the Fun of It: Government Restraints on Black Leisure, Social Inequality, and the Privatization of Public Space. *Southern California Law Review* 71: 667-714.

Ayers, William, et al. 2001. *Zero Tolerance: Resisting the Drive for Punishment in Our Schools*. New York: New Press.

Balibar, Etienne, and Immanuel Wallerstein. 1991. *Race, Nation, Class: Ambiguous Identities*. New York: Verso Press.

Bass, Sandra Jean. 1998. *Politics, Policymaking, and the Police: Institutionalized Value Systems, Political Practicalities, and the Politics of Police Policy Making*. Ph.D. diss., University of California, Berkeley.

Bennet, William J., John DiIulio, and John Walters. 1996. *Body Count: Moral Poverty and How to Win America's War on Crime and Drugs*. New York: Simon & Schuster.

Best, Joel. 1990. *Threatened Children: Rhetoric and Concern about Child-Victims*. Chicago: University of Chicago Press.

Bissell, William Cunningham. 2005. Engaging Colonial Nostalgia. *Cultural Anthropology* 20 (2): 215-48.

Bonilla-Silva, Eduardo. 2006. *Racism without Racists: Color-Blind Racism and the Persistence of Racial Inequality in the United States*. New York: Rowman and Littlefield.

Boyd, Michelle. 2008. *Jim Crow Nostalgia: Reconstructing Race in Bronzeville*. Minneapolis: University of Minnesota Press.

Boyd-Franklin, Nancy. 2000. *Boys into Men: Raising our African American Teenage Sons*. New York: Dutton.

Braman, Donald. 2004. *Doing Time on the Outside: Incarceration and Family Life in Urban America*. Ann Arbor: University of Michigan Press.

Brecher, Charles, et al. 2004. *What Does Government Spend on Children? Evidence from Five Cities*. Center for Urban and Metropolitan Policy, Brookings Institute, March 2004.

Breitbart, Myrna. 1998. "Dana's Mystical Tunnel": Young People's Designs for Survival and Change in the City. In *Cool Places: Geographies of Youth Cultures*, ed. Tracey Skelton and Gill Valentine. New York: Routledge.

Brenner, Neil, and Nik Theodore. 2002. Preface: From the "New Localism" to the Spaces of Neoliberalism. *Antipode* 34(3): 342-47.

Buckholtz, Mary. 2002. Youth and Cultural Practice. *Annual Review of Anthropology* 31: 525–52.

Bureau of Justice Statistics. 2003 [viewed July 2009]. *Sourcebook of Criminal Justice Statistics*. Http://www.albany.edu/sourcebook/.

Burr, Elizabeth, et al. 2005 [viewed June 2008]. Services for Youth in West Oakland: Understanding Local Comunity-based Organizations. Stanford: Gardner Center. Http://gardnercenter.stanford.edu/docs/FINAL_FINAL_CBO%20Survey.pdf.

Burt, Cecily. 2007. Violence Darkening Oakland's Nightlife: Downtown Hip-Hop–Oriented Clubs Closing in Face of Security Problems. *Oakland Tribune*, Nov. 12, 2007.

Burton, Linda. 1997. Ethnography and the Meaning of Adolescence in High-Risk Neighborhoods. *Ethnos* 25 (2): 208-17.

Cahill, S. 1990. Childhood and Public Life: Reaffirming Biographical Divisions. *Social Problems* 37: 390-402.

Caldeira, Theresa. 2001. *City of Walls: Crime, Segregation, and Citizenship in São Paulo*. Berkeley: University of California Press.

California Budget Project. 2001 [viewed July 2008]. *What Do the 2000 API Results Tell Us about California's Schools?* Budget Brief, March. Http://www.cbp.org/pdfs/2001/bb010301.pdf .

———. 2007 [viewed July 2008]. *A Generation of Inequality: The State of Working California, 1977-2006.* San Francisco. August. Www.cbp.org .

———. 2008 [viewed July 2008]. *Two Steps Back: Should California Cut Its Way to a Balanced Budget?* San Francisco. Www.cbp.org.

California Recreation Commission. 1955. *Recreation in California: Annual Report.* Oakland.

Carnegie Foundation. 1992. *A Matter of Time: Risk and Opportunity in the Non-School Hours.* New York: Carnegie Foundation.

———. 1995. *Great Transitions: Preparing Adolescents for a New Century.* New York: Carnegie Foundation.

Carr, Patrick. 2005. *Clean Streets: Controlling Crime, Maintaining Order, and Building Community Action.* New York: New York University Press.

Castells, Manuel. 1983. *The City and the Grassroots: A Cross-Cultural Theory of Urban Social Movements.* London: E. Arnold.

Cattelino, Jessica. 2004. The Difference That Citizenship Makes: Civilian Crime Prevention on the Lower East Side. *PoLAR* 27 (1): 114-37.

Center for Juvenile and Criminal Justice. 2006 [viewed July 2008]. *California Youth Crime Declines: The Untold Story.* Http://www.cjcj.org/files/CAYouthCrimeSept06.pdf .

Center for Juvenile and Criminal Justice et al. 2002 [viewed Jan. 2003]. *Alameda County at the Crossroads: A National Disgrace or a National Model?* Www.cjcj.org.

Chang, Jeff. 2005. *Can't Stop Won't Stop: A History of the Hip-Hop Generation.* New York: St. Martin's.

Chesluk, Benjamin. 2004. Visible Signs of a City out of Control: Community Policing in New York City. *Cultural Anthropology* 19 (2): 250-75.

Children's Advocacy Institute. 2006 [viewed June 2008]. *California's Children's Budget, 2004-2005.* Http://www.caichildlaw.org/childrens-budget.htm.

Children's Defense Fund. 2007 [viewed July 2009]. *Cradle to Prison Pipeline.* Http://cdf.childrensdefense.org/site/PageServer?pagename=c2pp_report2007.

Chudacoff, Howard. 2007. *Children at Play: An American History.* New York: New York University Press.

Cielo, Cristina. 2005. *Civic Sideshows: Communities and Publics in East Oakland.* UC Berkeley Institute for the Study of Social Change, Working Paper Series.

City of Oakland Mayor's Office and Park and Recreation. 1994. *Shining Stars Directory.* Oakland, CA.

Clarke, John, et al. 2007. *Creating Citizen Consumers: Changing Publics and Changing Public Services.* New York: Sage.

Cobern, K. Gwynn, and Patricia Riley. 2000 [viewed Feb. 2001]. *Failing Grade: Crisis and Reform in the Oakland Unified School District.* San Francisco: Pacific Research. Http://www.pacificresearch.org/pub/sab/educat/oakland.pdf.

Cohen, Kathy. 1999. *Boundaries of Blackness: AIDS and the Breakdown of Black Politics.* Chicago: University of Chicago Press.

Collins, Patricia Hill. 1989. A Comparison of Two Works on Black Family Life. *Signs* 14 (4): 875-84.

———. 1990. *Black Feminist Thought: Knowledge, Consciousness, and the Politics of Empowerment*. New York: Routledge.

Comaroff, Jean, and John Comaroff. 2000. Millennial Capitalism: First Thoughts on a Second Coming. *Public Culture* 12 (2): 292-334.

———. 2004. Criminal Obsessions, after Foucault: Postcoloniality, Policing, and the Metaphysics of Disorder. *Critical Inquiry* 30: 800-824.

Comer, James P., and Alvin Poussaint. 1992. *Raising Black Children: Two Leading Psychiatrists Confront the Educational, Social, and Emotional Problems Facing Black Children*. New York: Plume Press.

Conley, Dalton. 1999. *Being Black, Living in the Red: Race, Wealth, and Social Policy in America*. Berkeley: University of California Press.

Corcoran, Mary, and Jordan Matsudaira. 2005. Is It Getting Harder to Get Ahead? Economic Attainment in Early Adulthood for Two Cohorts. In *On the Frontier of Adulthood: Theory, Research, and Public Policy*, ed. Richard Settersten, Frank Furstenberg, and Ruben Rumbaut. Chicago: University of Chicago Press.

Crain, Robert, et al. 1969. *The Politics of School Desegregation*. Garden City, NY: Doubleday.

Crenshaw, Kimberle. 1996. Mapping the Margins: Intersectionality, Identity, Politics, and Violence against Women of Color. *Critical Race Theory: The Key Writings That Formed the Movement*, ed. Kimberle Crenshaw et al. New York: New Press.

Crowell, Nancy, Joan McCord, and Cathy Widom. 2001. *Juvenile Crime, Juvenile Justice*. Washington, DC: National Academy Press.

Cruikshank, Barbara. 1999. *The Will to Empower: Democratic Citizens and Other Subjects*. Ithaca, NY: Cornell University.

Curtis, Henry Stoddard. 1917. *The Play Movement and Its Significance*. New York: Macmillan.

Darling-Hammond, Linda. 2004. The Color Line in American Education: Race, Resources, and Student Achievement. *Du Bois Review* 1 (2): 213-46.

Davis, Mike. 1992. *City of Quartz*. New York: Vintage.

Dawson, Michael. 1995. *Behind the Mule: Race and Class in African-American Politics*. Princeton, NJ: Princeton University Press.

———. 2001. *Black Visions: The Roots of Contemporary African-American Political Ideologies*. Chicago: University of Chicago Press.

Deitch, Michelle. 2009. *From Time Out to Hard Time: Young Children in the Adult Justice System*. Austin, TX: LBJ School of Public Affairs.

Delpit, Lisa. 1995. *Other People's Children: Culture Conflict in the Classroom*. New York: New Press.

Devine, John. 1997. *Maximum Security: The Culture of Violence in Inner-City Schools*. Chicago: University of Chicago Press.

Dominquez, Virginia. 1994. *White by Definition: Social Classification in Creole Louisiana*. New Brunswick, NJ: Rutgers University Press.

Donohue, Elizabeth, et al. 1998. *School House Hype: School Shootings and the Real Risks Kids Face in America*. San Francisco: Justice Policy Institute. Http://www.justicepolicy.org.

Dorfman, Lori, and Vincent Schiraldi. 2001. *Off Balance: Youth, Race, and Crime in the News*. Washington, DC: Building Blocks for Youth.

Douglas, Mary. 2002 (1966). *Purity and Danger: An Analysis of Pollution and Taboo*. London: Routledge Classics.

Drake, St. Clair. 1945. *Black Metropolis: A Study of Negro Life in a Northern City*. New York: Harcourt, Brace.

Duffy, Michael. 2006. Jerry Brown Still Wants Your Vote. *Time Magazine*, May 21, 2006.

Durham, Deborah. 2000. Youth and the Social Imagination in Africa. *Anthropological Quarterly* 73(3): 113-120.

———. 2004. Disappearing Youth: Youth as a Social Shifter in Botswana. *American Ethnologist* 31 (4): 589-605.

Duster, Troy. 1987. Crime, Youth Unemployment, and the Black Urban Underclass. *Crime and Delinquency* 33: 300-316.

Ed Source. 2003 [viewed May 2003]. *How California Ranks: The State's Expenditures for K-12 Education*. Www.edsource.org.

Education Trust-West. 2005. *Hidden Teacher Spending Gaps in Oakland School District: A Tale of Two Schools*. Oakland CA: Education Trust. Www.edtrust.org.

Ehrenreich, Barbara. 1989. *Fear of Falling: The Inner Life of the Middle Class*. New York: Pantheon.

Fabian, Johannes. 1983. *Time and the Other: How Anthropology Makes Its Object*. New York: Columbia University Press.

Fass, Paula.1977. *The Damned and the Beautiful: American Youth in the 1920s*. New York: Oxford University Press.

Feld, Barry. 1999. *Bad Kids: Race and the Transformation of the Juvenile Court*. New York: Oxford University Press.

Feldman, Shirley, and Glen Elliott. 1990. *At the Threshold: The Developing Adolescent*. Cambridge, MA: Harvard University Press.

Ferguson, Ann Arnett. 2000. *Bad Boys: Public School in the Making of Black Masculinity*. Ann Arbor: University of Michigan Press.

Ferguson, James, and Akhil Gupta. 2002. Spatializing States: Towards an Ethnography of Neoliberal Governmentality. *American Ethnologist* 29 (4): 981-1002.

Field, Norma. 1995. The Child as Laborer and Consumer: The Disappearance of Childhood in Contemporary Japan. In *Children and the Politics of Culture*, ed. Sharon Stephens. Princeton, NJ: Princeton University Press.

Fine, Michelle. 1991. *Framing Dropouts: Notes on the Politics of an Urban High School*. New York: State University of New York Press.

———. 2004. Witnessing Whiteness/Gathering Intelligence. In *Off White: Readings on Power, Privilege, and Resistance*, ed. Michelle Fine et al. New York: Routledge.

Finn, Janet. 2001. Text and Turbulence: Representing Adolescence as Pathology in the Human Services. *Childhood* 8 (2): 167–91.

Fischer, Claude, et al. 1996. *Inequality by Design: Cracking the Bell Curve Myth*. Princeton, NJ: Princeton University Press.

Fleetwood, Nicole. 2004. "Busing It" in the City: Black Youth, Performance, and Public Transit. *TDR* 48 (2): 33-48.

Folbre, Nancy. 2001. *The Invisible Heart: Economics and Family Values*. New York: New Press.

Frankenberg, Ruth. 1993. *White Women, Race Matters: The Social Construction of Whiteness*. Minneapolis: University of Minnesota Press, 1993.

Fraser, Nancy. 1989. *Unruly Practices: Power, Discourse, and Gender in Contemporary Social Theory*. Minneapolis: University of Minnesota Press.

Fraser, Nancy, and Linda Gordon. 1994. A Genealogy of Dependency: Tracing a Keyword of the U.S. Welfare State. *Signs: Journal of Women in Culture & Society* 19 (2): 309-37.

Freeman, Richard B., and Harry Holzer. 1986. *The Black Youth Unemployment Crisis*. Chicago: University of Chicago Press.

Fussell, Elizabeth, and Frank Furstenberg. 2005. Transition to Adulthood in the 20th Century: Race, Nativity, and Gender Differences In *On the Frontier of Adulthood: Theory, Research, and Public Policy*, ed. Richard Settersten et al. Chicago: University of Chicago Press.

Gammon, Robert. 2005. Sideshows RIP? Oakland's Illegal Street Parties Have Vanished. *East Bay Express,* August 10, 2005.

Gammon, Robert, and Michele R. Marcucci. 2002. Census: Racial Income Disparities Abound; U.S. Data Show Whites Earn Nearly Twice as Much as Members of Other Ethnic Groups. *Oakland Tribune,* Aug. 27.

Garey, Anita Ilta. 2002. Social Domains and Concepts of Care: Protection, Instruction, and Containment in After-School Programs. *Journal of Family Issues* 23: 768.

Getis, Victoria. 2000. *Juvenile Court and the Progressives*. Chicago: University of Illinois Press.

Gilmore, Ruth Wilson. 2007. In the Shadow of the Shadow State. In *The Revolution Will Not Be Funded: Beyond the Non-profit Industrial Complex*, ed. INCITE! Women of Color against Violence. Cambridge, MA: South End Press.

Gilroy, Paul. 1987. *"There Ain't No Black in the Union Jack": The Cultural Politics of Race and Nation*. London: Hutchinson.

Gilroy, Paul, et al. 1982. *The Empire Strikes Back: Race and Racism in 70s Britain*. London: Hutchinson.

Ginwright, Shawn. 2004. *Black in School: Afrocentric Reform, Urban Youth, and the Promise of Hip-Hop Culture*. New York: Teachers College Press.

———. 2006 [viewed July 2008]. Toward a Politics of Relevance: Race, Resistance, and African American Youth Activism. Social Science Research Council Youth Activism Web Forum. Http://ya.ssrc.org/african/Ginwright/.

Ginwright, Shawn, and Julio Cammarota. 2002. New Terrain in Youth Development: The Promise of a Social Justice Approach. *Social Justice* 29 (4): 82-95.

Ginwright, Shawn, and Taj James. 2002. From Assets to Agents of Change: Social Justice, Organizing, and Youth Development. *New Direction for Youth Development* 96 (2): 27-46.

Giroux, Henry A. 2003 [viewed May 2005]. Public Time and Educated Hope: Educational Leadership and the War against Youth. *The Initiative Anthology.* Www.units.muohio.edu/eduleadership/anthology/OA/OA03001.html.

Go, Charles, et al. 2000 [viewed Aug. 2003]. *Oakland Baseline Indicators Report*. Alameda County Interagency Children's Policy Council. Www.co.alameda.ca.us/icpc.

Golden, Marita. 1995. *Saving Our Sons: Raising Black Children in a Turbulent World*. New York: Doubleday.

Goldstein, Donna. 2001. Microenterprise Training Programs: Neoliberal Common Sense and Discourses of Self-Esteem. In *The New Poverty Studies: The Ethnography of Power, Politics, and Impoverished People in the United States*, ed. Judith Goode and Jeff Maskovsky. New York: New York University Press.

Goode, Judith, and Jeff Maskovsky. 2001. *The New Poverty Studies: The Ethnography of Power, Politics, and Impoverished People in the United States*. New York: New York University Press.

Gordon, Linda. 1988. *Heroes of Their Own Lives: The Politics and History of Family Violence, Boston, 1880-1960*. New York: Viking.

———. 1990. *Women, the State, and Welfare*. Madison: University of Wisconsin Press.

———. 2009. The Perils of Innocence; or, What's Wrong with Putting Children First? *Journal of the History of Childhood and Youth* 1 (3): 331-50.

Gough, James. 2002. Neoliberalism and Socialisation in the Contemporary City: Opposites, Complements, and Instabilities. *Antipode* 34 (3): 405-26.

Greene, Jack, and Stephen Mastrofski. 1988. *Community Policing: Rhetoric or Reality*. New York: Praeger.

Gregory, Steven. 1998. *Black Corona: Race and the Politics of Place in an Urban Community*. Princeton, NJ: Princeton University Press.

Griffin, Christine. 1993. *Representations of Youth: The Study of Youth and Adolescence in Britain and America*. Cambridge: Polity Press.

Guano, Emanuela. 2004. The Denial of Citizenship: "Barbaric" Buenos Aires and the Middle-Class Imaginary. *City and Society* 16 (1): 69-97.

Guinier, Lanier, and Gerald Torres. 2002. *The Miner's Canary: Enlisting Race, Resisting Power, Transforming Democracy*. Cambridge, MA: Harvard University Press.

Gupta, Akhil, and Aradhana Sharma. 2006. Introduction: Rethinking Theories of the State in an Age of Globalization. In *The Anthropology of the State: A Reader*, ed. Aradhana Sharma and Akhil Gupta. New York: Blackwell.

Hacker, Jacob. 2008. *The Great Risk Shift: The New Economic Insecurity and the Decline of the American Dream*. New York: Oxford University Press.

Hall, G. Stanley. 1904. *Adolescence: Its Psychology and Its Relation to Physiology, Anthropology, Sociology, Sex, Crime, Religion, and Education*. New York: Appleton.

Hall, Stuart, et al. 1978. *Policing the Crisis: Mugging, the State, and Law and Order*. New York: Holmes and Meier.

Hall, Tom, et al. 1999. Self, Space and Place: Youth Identities and Citizenship. *British Journal of Sociology of Education* 20(4): 501-513.

Halpern, Richard. 2003. *Making Play Work: The Promise of After-School Programs for Low-Income Children*. New York: Teachers College Press.

Hamparian, Donna, and Michael Leiber. 1997. *Disproportionate Confinement of Minority Juveniles in Secure Facilities: 1996 National Report*. Champaign, IL: Community Research Associates.

Hansen, Julia. 1996. Residential Segregation of Blacks by Income Group: Evidence from Oakland. *Population Research and Policy Review* 15: 369-89.

Harcourt, Bernard E. 2001. *Illusion of Order: The False Promise of Broken Windows Policing*. Cambridge, MA: Harvard University Press.

Harris-Lacewell, Melissa. 2004. *Barbershops, Bibles, and BET: Everyday Talk and Black Political Thought*. Princeton, NJ: Princeton University Press.

Hartigan, John Jr. 1999. *Racial Situations: Class Predicaments of Whiteness in Detroit*. Princeton, NJ: Princeton University Press.

Harvey, David. 2003. The Right to the City. *International Journal of Urban and Regional Research* 27 (4): 939-41.

Hawes, Joseph. 1991. *The Children's Rights Movement: A History of Advocacy and Protection*. Boston: Twayne.

Hays, Sharon. 1988. *The Cultural Contradictions of Motherhood*. New Haven, CT: Yale University Press.

Hebdige, Dick. 1988. *Hiding in the Light: On Images and Things*. London: Routledge.

Heiman, Rachel. 2001. Ironic Contradictions in the Discourse on Generation X; or, How "Slackers" Are Saving Capitalism. *Childhood* 8 (2): 274-92.

Heyman, Ira M. 1963. *Oakland: Civil Rights U.S.A.: Public Schools in the North and West*. Washington, DC: U.S. Civil Rights Commission.

Higginbotham, Evelyn Brooks. 1993. *Righteous Discontent: The Women's Movement in the Black Baptist Church, 1880-1920*. Cambridge, MA: Harvard University Press.

Hirsch, Arnold. 1983. *Making the Second Ghetto: Race and Housing in Chicago, 1940-1960*. New York: Cambridge University Press.

Hochschild, Arlie. 2004. Love and Gold. In *Global Woman: Nannies, Maids, and Sex Workers in the New Economy*, ed. Barbara Ehrenreich and Arlie Hochschild. New York: Holt.

Hofferth, Sandra, and John F. Sandberg. 2001. Changes in American Children's Use of Time, 1981-1997. In *Children at the Millennium: Where Have We Come from, Where Are We Going?*, ed. T. Owens and S. Hofferth. New York: Elsevier Science.

Hoggart, Keith. 1991. Adjusting to Fiscal Stress: City Expenditure in the San Francisco-Oakland Metropolitan Area. *Local Government Studies* 17 (2): 57-75.

Holland, Dorothy, et al. 2007. *Local Democracy under Seige: Activism, Public Interests, Private Politics*. New York: New York University Press.

Holloway, Sarah, and Gill Valentine. 2000. Children's Geographies and the New Social Studies of Childhood. *Children's Geographies: Playing, Living, Learning*. New York: Routledge.

Holston, James. 1999. *Cities and Citizenship*. Durham, NC: Duke University Press.

HoSang, Daniel. 1997 [viewed 2003]. Organize! Oakland Campaign Puts Kids First. Shelterforce Online. Http://www.nhi.org/online/issues/96/organize.html.

———. 2003 [viewed 2004]. *Youth and Community Organizing Today*. Funders' Collaborative on Youth Organizing. Http://www.fcyo.org/attachments/Papers_no2_v4.qxd.pdf.

———. 2006. Beyond Policy: Ideology, Race, and the Reimagining of Youth. In *Beyond Resistance! Youth Activism and Community Change*, ed. Pedro Noguera, Julio Cammarota, and Shawn Ginwright. New York: Routledge.

Howard, Christopher. 2006. *The Welfare State Nobody Knows: Debunking Myths about U.S. Social Policy*. Princeton, NJ: Princeton University Press.

Human Rights Watch (HRW) and Amnesty International. 2005 [viewed June 2009]. *The Rest of Their Lives: Life without Parole for Child Offenders in the United States*. Www.hwr.org/reports/2005/us1005/TheRestofTheirLives.pdf.

Hyatt, Susan. 2001. From Citizen to Volunteer: Neoliberal Governance and the Erasure of Poverty. In *The New Poverty Studies: The Ethnography of Power, Politics, and Impoverished People in the United States*, ed. Judith Goode and Jeff Maskovsky. New York: New York University Press.

Isaacs, Julia. 2008 [viewed August 2008]. Economic Mobility of Black and White Families. In *Getting Ahead or Losing Ground: Economic Mobility in America*, ed. Isabell Sawhill et al. The Brookings Institute. Www.brookings.edu/reports.

Isaacs, Julia, and Phillip Lovell. 2008 [viewed July 2008]. *Priority or Afterthought: Children and the Federal Budget*. First Focus. Http://www.buildinitiative.org/files/03childrenfamilies.pdf .

James, Allison. 1986. Learning to Belong: The Boundaries of Adolescence. In *Symbolizing Boundaries: Identity and Diversity in British Cultures*, ed. Anthony Cohen. Manchester, England: Manchester University Press.

Jarrett, Robin. 1999 [viewed June 2009]. Successful Parenting in High-Risk Neighborhoods. *When School Is Out* 9 (2): 45-49. Www.futureofchildren.org.

Jeffrey, Craig and Linda McDowell. 2004. Youth in Comparative Perspective. *Youth and Society* 36(2): 131-142.

Jenks, Chris. 1996. *Childhood*. London: Routledge.

Jones, Delmos, et al. 1992. Declining Social Services and the Threat to Social Reproduction: An Urban Dilemma. *City and Society* 6 (2): 99-114.

Kamenetz, Amy. 2006. *Generation Debt: How Our Future Was Sold Out for Student Loans, Bad Jobs, No Benefits, and Tax Cuts for Rich Geezers—and How to Fight Back*. New York: Riverhead Press.

Kaplan, Elaine Bell. 1997. *Not Our Kind of Girl: Unravelling the Myths of Black Teenage Motherhood*. Berkeley: University of California Press.

Katz, Cindi. 2001a. The State Goes Home: Local Hypervigilance of Children and the Global Retreat from Social Reproduction. *Social Justice* 28 (3): 47-56.

———. 2001b. Vagabond Capitalism and the Necessity of Social Reproduction. *Antipode* 33 (4): 709-28.

———. 2004. *Growing Up Global: Economic Restructuring and Children's Everyday Lives*. Minneapolis: University of Minnesota Press.

———. 2005. Partners in Crime? Neoliberalism and the Production of New Political Subjectivities. *Antipode* 37 (3): 623-31.

Katz, Michael. 1992. *The Underclass Debate: Views from History*. Princeton, NJ: Princeton University Press.

———. 2001. *The Price of Citizenship: Redefining the American Welfare State*. New York: Henry Holt.

Katz, Michael, and Christoph Sachsse. 1996. Introduction. *Mixed Economy of Social Welfare in England, Germany, and the United States from the 1870s to the 1930s*. Baden-Baden, Germany: Nomos Verlagsgesellschaft.

Katz, Michael, and Mark Stern. 2005. The New African American Inequality. *Journal of American History* 92: 3.

Katznelson, Ira. 2005. *When Affirmative Action Was White: An Untold History of Racial Inequality in Twentieth-Century America*. New York: Norton.

Kelley, Robin. 1996. *Race Rebels: Culture, Politics, and the Black Working Class*. New York: Free Press.

Kelling, George, and Mark Moore. 1988. From Political Reform to Community: The Evolving Strategy of Police. In *Community Policing: Rhetoric or Reality*, ed. George Kelling and Mark Moore. New York: Praeger.

Kenney, John. 1948. *A Study in Juvenile Control by the Police Department, Oakland, California*. Oakland, CA: California Youth Authority.

Kett, Joseph. 1977. *Rites of Passage: Adolescence in America, 1790 to Present*. New York: Basic Books.

Kids Count. 2003 [viewed November 2003]. *Kids Count Census Data Online.* Http://www.
aecf.org/kidscount/census/.

Kids First! Coalition. 1998. *The Kids First! Initiative: A Guide to How One Community Successfully Campaigned for Funding for Children and Youth Services.* Oakland, CA: Kids
First! Coalition.

———. 2000. *Locked Out: Exposing the Suspension Epidemic in Oakland Public Schools.*
Oakland, CA: Kids First! Coalition.

Kingfisher, Catherine, and Marlene Goldsmith. 2001. Reforming Women in the United
States and Aotearoa/New Zealand: A Comparative Ethnography of Welfare Reform in a
Global Context. *American Anthropologist* 103 (3): 714–32.

Kirkpatrick, Lucas Owen. 2007. The Two "Logics" of Community Development: Neighborhoods, Markets, and Community Development Corporations. *Politics & Society* 35
(2): 329-59.

Kirp, David. 1982. *Just Schools: The Idea of Racial Equality in American Education.* Berkeley:
University of California Press.

———. 2007. *The Sandbox Investment: The Preschool Movement and Kids First Politics.* Cambridge, MA: Harvard University Press.

Kirschner, Ben. 2006. Apprenticeship Learning in Youth Activism. *Beyond Resistance:
Youth Activism and Community Change; New Democratic Possibilities for Policy and Practice for America's Youth,* ed. Pedro Noguera et al. Oxford, England: Routledge Press.

Kitwana, Bakari. 2003. *The Hip Hop Generation: Young Blacks and the Crisis in African
American Culture.* New York: Basic Civitas Books.

Klein, Naomi. 2000. *No Logo: No Space, No Choice, No Jobs.* New York: Picador Press.

Klinenberg, Eric. 2002. *Heat Wave: a Social Autopsy of Disaster in Chicago.* Chicago: University of Chicago Press.

Kozol, Jonathan. 2005. *Shame of the Nation: The Restoration of Apartheid Schooling in
America.* New York: Crown.

Krisberg, Barry, et al. 1987. The Incarceration of Minority Youth. *Crime and Delinquency*
33: 173-205.

———. 2009. *Youth Violence Myths and Realities: A Tale of Three Cities.* Washington, DC:
Annie E. Casey Foundation and National Council on Crime and Delinquency.

Kunzel, Regina. 1993. *Fallen Women, Problem Girls: Unmarried Mothers and the Profession-
alization of Social Work, 1890-1945.* New Haven. CT: Yale University Press.

Kwon, Soo Ah. 2006. Youth Organizing for Juvenile Justice. *Beyond Resistance: Youth
Activism and Community Change: New Democratic Possibilities for Policy and Practice for
America's Youth,* ed. Pedro Noguera et al. Oxford, England: Routledge.

Ladson-Billings, Gloria. 2004. Landing on the Wrong Note: The Price We Paid for Brown.
Educational Researcher 33 (7): 3-17.

Lancaster, Roger. 2007. Preface. *New Landscapes of Inequality: Neoliberalism and the Erosion of Democracy in America.* Santa Fe, NM: School for Advanced Research Press.

Landau, Madeleine. 1988. *Race, Poverty, and the Cities: Hyperinnovation in Complex Policy
Systems.* Institute for Governmental Studies. University of California, Berkeley.

Lareau, Annette. 2000. *Home Advantage: Social Class and Parental Intervention in Elementary Education.* New York: Rowman & Littlefield.

———. 2003. *Unequal Childhoods: Class, Race, and Family Life.* Berkeley: University of
California Press.

Lasch, Christopher. 1977. *Haven from the Heartless World: The Family Besieged*. New York: Basic Books.

Lawrence, Errol. 1983. Just Plain Common Sense: The Roots of Racism. In *The Empire Strikes Back: Race and Racism in 70s Britain*, ed. Center for Contemporary Cultural Studies. London: Hutchinson.

Le, Thao, et al. 2001. *Not Invisible: Asian Pacific Islander Juvenile Arrests in Alameda County*. Oakland, CA: National Center on Crime and Delinquency.

Lees, Loretta. 2003. The Ambivalence of Diversity and the Politics of Urban Renaissance: The Case of Youth in Downtown Portland Maine. *International Journal of Urban and Regional Research* 27 (3): 613-35.

Leonard, Kimberly Kempf, Carl E. Pope, and William H. Feyerherm, eds. 1995. *Minorities in Juvenile Justice*. Thousand Oaks, CA: Sage.

Lesko, Nancy. 2001. *Act Your Age: The Cultural Construction of Adolescence*. New York: Routledge.

Levi-Strauss, Claude. 1963. *Totemism*. Boston: Beacon Press.

Lewis, Earl. 1991. *In Their Interest: Race, Class, and Power in Richmond, Virginia*. Berkeley: University of California Press.

Li, Tanya. 2005. Beyond "The State" and Failed Schemes. *American Anthropologist* 107 (3): 383-94.

Lindenmeyer, Kriste. 2007 [viewed July 2009]. Moving into the Mainstream: Childhood, Dependency, and Independence in U.S. History. *Society for the History of Children and Youth Newsletter*. Http://www.history.vt.edu/Jones/SHCY/Newsletter10/Lindenmeyer.html.

Lindsey, Duncan. 2009. *Child Poverty and Inequality: Securing a Better Future for Our Children*. Oxford: Oxford University press.

Lipsitz, George. 1998. The Hip Hop Hearings: Censorship, Social Memory, and Intergenerational Tensions among African Americans. In *Generations of Youth*, ed. Joe Austin and Michael Willard. New York: New York University Press.

Litt, Jacquelyn. 1999. Managing the Street, Isolating the Household: African American Mothers Respond to Neighborhood Deterioration. *Race, Gender, and Class* 6 (3): 90.

Logan, John, and Harvey Molotch. 1987. *Urban Fortunes: The Political Economy of Place*. Berkeley: University of California Press.

Low, Setha. 2003. *Behind the Gates: Life, Security, and the Pursuit of Happiness in Fortress America*. New York: Routledge.

Macallair, Daniel, and Michael Males. 2000 [viewed Oct. 2003]. *Dispelling the Myth: An Analysis of Youth and Adult Crime Patterns in California over the Past Twenty years*. Center for Juvenile and Criminal Justice. Www.cjci.org/pubs/myth.

MacDonald, Heather. 1999. Jerry Brown's No-Nonsense New Age for Oakland. *City Journal*, Autumn 1999.

Males, Mike. 1996. *Scapegoat Generation: America's War on Adolescents*. Monroe, ME: Common Courage Press.

Males, Mike, and Dan Macallair. 2000. *The Color of Justice: An Analysis of Juvenile Adult Court Transfers in California*. Washington, DC: Building Blocks for Youth.

Males, Mike, et al. 2006 [viewed July 2008]. *Testing Incapacitation Theory: Youth Crime and Incarceration in California*. Center on Juvenile and Criminal Justice. Www.cjcj.org.

Mall, Joan Obra. 2000. Adjusted: Will the Former Eastmont Mall Succeed in Transforming Itself from a Failed '60s-Era Shopping Plaza to a Model Inner-City Community Center? *East Bay Express*, June 14, 2000.

Marinoff, Joani. 1997. There Is Enough Time: Rethinking the Process of Policy Development. *Social Justice* 24 (4): 234-46.

Marr, John G. 1938. *Statistical and Geographical Analysis of a Specific Housing Area: Project Area Number 1 8th-12th Cypress-Adeline*. Oakland City Planning Department, map collection.

Martinez, Elizabeth. 2000 [viewed January 2002]. The New Youth Movement in California. *Z Magazine online*. Http://www.zmag.org/ZMagSite/zmoarch.html.

Maskovsky, Jeff. 2001. The Other War at Home: The Geopolitics of U.S. Poverty. *Urban Anthropology* (Summer-Fall): 215-30.

———. 2006. Governing the "New Hometowns": Race, Power, and Neighborhood Participation in the New Inner City. *Identities:Global Studies in Culture and Power* 13 (1): 73-99.

Massey, Doreen. 1994. *Space, Place, and Gender*. Minneapolis: University of Minnesota Press.

Massey, Douglas, and Nancy Denton. 1993. *American Apartheid: Segregation and the Making of the Underclass*. Cambridge, MA: Harvard University Press.

Mastrofski, Stephen. 1988. Community Policing as Reform: A Cautionary Tale. In *Community Policing: Rhetoric or Reality*, ed. George Kelling and Mark Moore. New York: Praeger.

Matless, David. 1995. The Art of Right Living: Landscape and Citizenship, 1918-39. In *Mapping the Subject: Geographies of Cultural Transformation*, ed. Steve Pile and Nigel Thrift. New York: Routledge.

Matthews, Hugh, et al. 1996. The Unacceptable Flaneur: The Shopping Mall as a Teenage Hangout. In *Childhood: Critical Concepts in Childhood*, vol. 1, ed. Chris Jenks. London: Routledge.

———. 2000. The Street as Third Space. *Children's Geographies: Playing, Living, Learning*. New York: Routledge.

May, Judith. 1973. *Struggle for Authority: A Comparison of Four Social Change Programs in Oakland, California*. Ph.D. diss., University of California, Berkeley.

McClintock, Nathan. 2008. *From Industrial Garden to Food Desert: Unearthing the Root Structure of Urban Agriculture in Oakland, California*. Berkeley: Institute for the Study of Social Change Working Paper No. 32.

McDonald, Katrina Bell. 1997. Black Activist Mothering: A Historical Intersection of Race, Gender, and Class. *Gender and Society* 11 (6): 773-95.

McGarrell, Edmund. 1993. Trends in Racial Disproportionality in Juvenile Court Processing: 1985-1989. *Crime and Delinquency* 39 (1): 29-48.

McNeil, Donald. 2005. Narrating Neoliberalism. *Geographical Research* 43 (1): 113-55.

Medrich, Elliot, et al. 1982. *The Serious Business of Growing Up: A Study of Children's Lives outside School*. Berkeley: University of California Press.

Merry, Sally. 2001. Spatial Governmentality and the New Urban Social Order: Controlling Gender Violence through Law. *American Anthropologist* 103 (1): 16-29.

Meucci, Sandra, and Jim Redmon. 1997. Safe Spaces: California Children Enter a Policy Debate. *Social Justice* 23 (3): 139-51.

Miller, Leslie. 1998. Safe Home, Dangerous Street. In *Cool Places: Geographies of Youth Cultures*, ed. Tracey Skelton and Gill Valentine. New York: Routledge.

Miller, Toby. 1993. *The Well-Tempered Self: Citizenship, Culture, and the Postmodern Subject*. Baltimore, MD: Johns Hopkins University Press.

Mintz, Steven. 2004. *Huck's Raft: A History of American Childhood*. Cambridge, MA: Harvard University Press.

Mitchell, Don. 2004. *The Right to the City: Social Justice and the Fight for Public Space*. New York: Guilford Press.

Mitchell, Katharyne, Sallie Marston, and Cindi Katz. 2003. Life's Work: An Introduction, Review, and Critique. *Antipode* 35 (3): 415-42.

Mitchell, Timothy. 1992. *The Return of the State*. Ann Arbor: University of Michigan.

Mizen, Phillip. 2002. Putting the Politics Back into Youth Studies: Keynesianism, Monetarism, and the Changing State of Youth. *Journal of Youth Studies* 5 (1): 5-20.

Molatore, Toni. N.d. *East Oakland Pathways to Community Revitalization: A Special Report to the Koshland Fund*. Oakland History Room, Vertical File Folder, Elmhurst.

Morgan, Sandra, and Jeff Maskovsky. 2003. The Anthropology of Welfare "Reform": New Perspectives on U.S. Urban Poverty in the Post-Welfare Era. *Annual Review of Anthropology* 32: 315-38.

Murray, Charles. 1984. *Losing Ground: American Social Policy, 1950-1980*. New York: Basic Books.

NAACP Legal Defense Fund. 2007 [viewed July 2009]. *Dismantling the School to Prison Pipeline*. Http://www.naacpldf.org/content/pdf/pipeline/Dismantling_the_School_to_Prison_Pipeline.pdf.

Nakao, Annie. 1998. Stacked Odds: The Ways Students Are Classified Often Derail African Americans from the Educational Fast Track. *San Francisco Examiner*, June 8, 1998.

Naples, Nancy. 1998. *Grassroots Warriors: Activist Mothering, Community Work, and the War on Poverty*. New York: Routledge.

Nasaw, David. 1985. *Children of the City: At Work and at Play*. Garden City, NY: Anchor Press/Doubleday.

National Council on Crime and Delinquency. 2007 [viewed July 2009]. *And Justice for Some*. Http://www.nccd-crc.org/nccd/pubs/2007jan_justice_for_some.pdf .

National Council on Crime and Delinquency and Resource Development Associates. 1997. *Juvenile Justice Local Action Plan Update*. Alameda County Probation Department, March 13, 1997.

Newman, Katherine. 2001. Hard Times on 125th Street: Harlem's Poor Confront Welfare Reform. *American Anthropologist* 103 (3): 762-78.

Noguera, Pedro. 2008. *The Trouble with Black Boys: And Other Reflections on Race, Equity, and the Future of Public Education*. San Francisco: Jossey-Bass.

Noguera, Pedro, et al. 2006. *Beyond Resistance: Youth Activism and Community Change: New Democratic Possibilities for Policy and Practice for America's Youth*. Oxford, England: Routledge.

Nybell, Lynn. 2001. Meltdowns and Containments: Constructions of Children at Risk as Complex Systems. *Childhood* 8 (2): 167-91.

Oakland Citizens Committee for Urban Renewal. 1990. *Neighborhood Profile, Elmhurst*. Oakland: OCCUR (author's files).

Oakland Community Chest. 1938. *They Would Rob You of Health, Happiness, Security*. Pamphlet, Oakland History Room Public Library (Oakland Community Chest Vertical Files).

Oakland Community Economic Development Agency (CEDA). 2005. Retail Development Strategy Report, December 13, 2005.

Oakland Fund for Children and Youth. 2001. *An Assessment of Opportunities to Support Oakland's Youth*. May 31, 2001.

——. 2003. *Interim Evaluation Report, FY2002-2003*.

Oakland Junior Chamber of Commerce. 1935. *Report on the Activities of the Committee on Juvenile Supervision and Recreation*. Oakland History Room.

Oliver, Melvin, and Thomas Shapiro. 1995. *Black Wealth/White Wealth: A New Perspective on Racial Inequality*. New York: Routledge.

O'Neil, Mary Lou. 2002. Youth Curfews in the United States: The Creation of Public Spheres for Young People. *Journal of Youth Studies* 5 (1): 49-67.

Ortner, Sherry. 1998. Generation X: Anthropology in a Media-Saturated World. *Cultural Anthropology* 13 (3): 414-40.

Osborne, David, and Ted Gaebler. 1992. *Reinventing Government: How the Entrepreneurial Spirit Is Transforming the Public Sector*. Reading, MA: Addison-Wesley.

Pager, Devah. 2009. *Marked: Race, Class, and Finding Work in an Age of Mass Incarceration*. Chicago: University of Chicago Press.

Paley, Julia. 2001. *Marketing Democracy: Power and Social Movements in Post-Dictatorship Chile*. Berkeley: University of California Press.

Parenti, Christian. 1999. *Lockdown America: Police and Prisons in the Age of Crisis*. New York: Verso.

Pattillo, Mary. 2007. *Black on the Block: The Politics of Race and Class in the City*. Chicago: University of Chicago Press.

Pattillo-McCoy, Mary. 1999. *Black Picket Fences: Privilege and Peril among the Black Middle Class*. Chicago: University of Chicago Press.

Peck, Jamie, and Adam Tickell. 2002. Neoliberalizing Space. *Antipode* 34 (3): 380-404.

Perkins, William Eric. 1996. The Rap Attack: An Introduction. In *Droppin' Science: Critical Essays on Rap Music and Hip Hop Culture*, ed. William Erik Perkins. Philadelphia: Temple University Press.

Perry, Imani. 2004. *Prophets of the Hood: Politics and Poetics in Hip Hop*. Durham, NC: Duke University Press.

Peterson, Paul. 1981. *City Limits*. Chicago: University of Chicago Press.

Picture, Bill. 2007 [viewed July 2008]. In Oaktown, Unpolished Is the New Glam. *San Francisco Magazine*, October. Http://www.sanfranmag.com/node/2592.

Platt, Anthony M. 1977. *The Child Savers: The Invention of Delinquency*. Chicago: University of Chicago Press.

Poe-Yamagata, Eileen, and Michael A. Jones. 2000. *And Justice for Some: Differential Treatment of Minority Youth in the Justice System*. Washington, DC: Building Blocks for Youth.

Pollock, Mica. 2004. Race Bending: "Mixed" Youth Practicing Strategic Racialization in California. In *Youthscapes: The Popular, the National, and the Global*, ed. Sunaina Maira and Elisabeth Soep. Philadelphia: University of Pennsylvania Press.

———. 2005. *Colormute: Race Talk Dilemmas in an American School*. Princeton, NJ: Princeton University Press.

Prince, Sabiyha. 2002. Changing Places: Race, Class, and Belonging in the "New" Harlem. *Urban Anthropology and Studies of Cultural Systems and World Economic Development* 31 (1): 5-25.

Prout, Alan, and Allison James. 1990. A New Paradigm for the Sociology of Childhood? Provenance, Promise, and Problems. In *Constructing and Reconstructing Childhood: Contemporary Issues in the Sociological Study of Childhood*, ed. Allison James and Alan Prout. London: Falmer Press.

Pugh, Alison. 2005 [viewed July 2007]. The Social Context of Childrearing: Public Spending in Oakland, 1970-2000. Institute for the Study of Social Change. *ISSC Fellows Working Papers*. ISSC_WP_04. Http://repositories.cdlib.org/issc/fwp/ISSC_WP_04.

Putnam, Robert. 2000. *Bowling Alone: The Collapse and Renewal of American Community*. New York: Simon & Schuster.

Reed, Adolph. 1999. *Stirrings in the Jug: Black Politics in the Post-Segregation Era*. Minneapolis: University of Minnesota Press.

———. 2000. *Class Notes: Posing as Politics and Other Thoughts on the American Scene*. New York: New Press.

Regal, J. M. 1967. *Oakland's Partnership for Change*. City of Oakland, Department of Human Resources. Oakland, California.

Rhomberg, Christopher. 2004. *No There There: Race, Class, and Political Community in Oakland, California*. Berkeley: University of California Press.

Rieder, Jonathan. 1995. *Canarsie: The Jews and Italians of Brooklyn against Liberalism*. Cambridge, MA: Harvard University Press.

Rios, Victor. 2004. From Knucklehead to Revolutionary: Urban Youth Culture and Social Transformation. *Journal of Urban Youth Culture* 3 (1).

———. 2006. The Hyper-Criminalization of Black and Latino Male Youth in the Era of Mass Incarceration. *Souls* 8: 40-54.

Ritterhouse, Jennifer Lynn. 2006. *Growing Up Jim Crow: How Black and White Southern Children Learned Race*. Chapel Hill: University of North Carolina Press.

Robbins, Alexandra, and Abby Wilner. 2001. *Quarterlife Crisis: The Unique Challenges of Life in Your Twenties*. New York: Tarcher/Putnam Books.

Roberts, Dorothy. 2001. Criminal Justice and Black Families: The Collateral Damage of Over-Enforcement. *UC Davis Law Review* 34: 1005-18.

Rodriguez, Dylan. 2007. The Political Logic of the Non-Profit Industrial Complex. In *The Revolution Will Not Be Funded: Beyond the Nonprofit Industrial Complex*, ed. INCITE! Women of Color against Violence. Cambridge, MA: South End Press.

Rogers, Adam. A New Brand of Tech Cities. *Newsweek*, April 30, 2001.

Roland, Tom. 1965. Analysis: Oakland Crisis Next Door. *The CORE-lator* 1 (2): 26-32. Online Archive of California. Http://content.cdlib.org.

Rose, Nikolas 1996. The Death of the Social? Refiguring the Territory of the Government. *Economy & Society* 25: 327-56.

Rose, Tricia. 1991. Fear of a Black Planet: Rap Music and Black Cultural Politics in the 1990s. *Journal of Negro Education* 60 (3): 276-90.

———. 1994. *Black Noise: Rap Music and Black Culture in Contemporary America*. Hanover, NH: Wesleyan University Press.

Rosser International. 1998. *Alameda County Juvenile Justice Complex Needs Assessment and Master Plan, Executive Summary*. Alameda County Probation Department.

Rubin, Victor. 1983 [viewed June 2008]. Responses to Local Fiscal Stress: Privatization and Coproduction of Children's Services in California. In *Services to Children and the Urban Fiscal Crisis: A Comparison of Experiences among States and Localities*, ed. Victor Rubin and Elliot Medrich. Chapter 4. U.S. National Institute of Education, Education Resource Information Center # ED311098 online at http://www.eric.ed.gov/.

Rubin, Victor, and Elliot Medrich. 1980. Children's out of School Services and the Urban Fiscal Crisis: A Report to the U.S. National Institute of Education, Education Resource Information Center #222588 online at http://www.eric.ed.gov/.

Ruddick, Susan. 1996. *Young and Homeless in Hollywood*. New York: Routledge.

———. 2003. The Politics of Aging: Globalization and the Restructuring of Youth and Childhood. *Antipode* 35 (2): 334-62.

Russel, Katheryn. 1999. *The Color of Crime: Racial Hoaxes, White Fear, Black Protectionism, Police Harassment, and Other Macro-Aggressions*. New York: New York University Press.

Safe Passages. 2007 [viewed July 2009]. *After-School Landscape, Analysis, and Recommendations for Sustainability in Oakland, California*. Oakland: Safe Passages. Http://www.safepassages.org/PDF/afterSchoolSustainability_Oakland.pdf.

Sahagan, Louis. 2005 [viewed Jan. 2006]. Deadly Swerves and Spins. *Los Angeles Times*, March 7. Www.latimes.com.

Salazar, Alex. 2006. Designing a Socially Just Downtown: Mayor Brown's Plan for a New Downtown in Oakland Was Stymied by a Resurgence of Grassroots Housing Advocacy. *Development News* #145.

Sanjek, Roger. 1998. *The Future of Us All: Race and Neighborhood Politics in New York City*. Ithaca, NY: Cornell University Press.

Sarri, Rosemary, and Janet Finn. 1992. Child Welfare Policy and Practice: Rethinking the History of Our Certainties. *Children and Youth Services Review* 14 (3/4): 219-36.

Sasson, Theodore, and Margaret Nelson. 1996. Danger, Community, and the Meaning of Crime Watch: An Analysis of the Discourses of African-American and White Participants. *Journal of Contemporary Ethnography* 25: 171-200.

Scheingold, Stuart. 1984. *The Politics of Law and Order: Street Crime and Public Policy*. New York: Longman.

Scheper-Hughes, Nancy, and Carolyn Sargent. 1998. *Small Wars: The Cultural Politics of Childhood*. Berkeley: University of California Press.

Schlossman, Steven L. 1977. *Love and the American Delinquent: The Theory and Practice of "Progressive" Juvenile Justice, 1825-1920*. Chicago: University of Chicago Press.

Schmitt, Mark. 2007. "Kids First" Politics, Round Two. *American Prospect*, November 19, 2007.

Schneider, Eric. 1992. *In the Web of Class: Delinquents and Reformers in Boston, 1810s-1930s*. New York: New York University Press.

Schrag, Peter. 1999. *Paradise Lost: California's Experience, America's Future*. Berkeley: University of California Press.

Schwartz, Ira, Richard J. Gelles, and Wanda Mohr.1984. The Hidden System of Juvenile Control. *Crime and Delinquency* 30: 371-85.

Schwartz, Ira, et al. 1993. The Impact of Demographic Variables on Public Opinion Regarding Juvenile Justice: Implications for Public Policy. *Crime and Delinquency* 39 (1): 5-28.

Scott, Richard, et al. 2006. Advocacy Organizations and the Field of Youth Services: Ongoing Efforts to Restructure a Field. *Nonprofit and Voluntary Sector Quarterly* 35 (4): 691-714.

Self, Robert. 2003. *American Babylon: Race and the Struggle for Postwar Oakland*. Princeton, NJ: Princeton University Press.

Settersten, Richard, et al. 2005. *On the Frontier of Adulthood: Theory, Research, and Public Policy*. Chicago: University of Chicago Press.

Shah, Seema, et al. 2009. *Building a District-Wide Small Schools Movement: Oakland Community Organizations*. Providence, RI: Annenberg Institute for School Reform, Brown University.

Shapiro, Thomas. 2005. *The Hidden Cost of Being African American: How Wealth Perpetuates Inequality*. New York: Oxford University Press.

Sharma, Aradhana. 2006. Crossbreeding Institutions, Breeding Struggle: Women's Empowerment, Neoliberal Governmentality, and State (Re)Formation in India. *Cultural Anthropology* 21 (1): 60-95.

Shields, R. 1989. Social Spatialization and the Built Environment: The W. Edmonton Mall. *Environment and Planning D: Society and Space* 7: 147-64.

Shuman, Aaron. 2000 [viewed February 2002]. This Is How We Do It. *Bad Subjects: Political Education for Everyday Life*. Http://eserver.org/bs/editors/prop21d.html.

Sibley, David. 1995. *Geographies of Exclusion: Society and Difference in the West*. New York: Routledge.

Simon, Jonathan. 1997. *Poor Discipline: Parole and the Social Control of the Underclass*. Chicago: University of Chicago Press.

———. 2007. *Governing through Crime: How the War on Crime Transformed American Democracy and Created a Culture of Fear*. New York: Oxford University Press.

Skiba, Russell, et al. 2000. The Color of Discipline: Sources of Racial and Gender Disproportionality in Schools. *Urban Review* 34 (4): 317-42.

Skocpol, Theda. 1996 [viewed July 2008]. Unravelling from Above. *American Prospect* 25: 20-25. Http://epn.org/prospect/25/25-cnt2.html.

Skogan, Wesley G. 1989. Communities, Crime, and Neighborhood Organization. *Crime and Delinquency* 35: 437-57.

———. 2004. *Community Policing: Can It Work?* Evanston, IL: Northwestern University.

Skolnick, Jerome, and David Bayley. 1988. *Community Policing: Issues and Practices around the World*. Washington, DC: U.S. Department of Justice.

Smith, Neil. 1996. *The New Urban Frontier: Gentrification and the Revanchist City*. New York: Routledge.

———. 2002. New Globalism, New Urbanism: Gentrification as a Global Urban Strategy. *Antipode* 34 (3): 427-50.

Smith, Preston H. 2001. Self-help, Black Conservatives, and the Re-Emergence of Black Privatism. In *Without Justice for All: The New Liberalism and the Retreat from Racial Equality*, ed. Adoph Reed. Boulder, CO: Westview Press.

Smith-Rosenberg, Carroll. 1987. *Disorderly Conduct: Visions of Gender in Victorian America*. New York: Oxford University Press.

Snyder, Ron. 2008. Faith-Based Organizing for Youth: One Organization's District Campaign for Small Schools Policy. *New Directions for Youth Development* 117: 93-107.

Soler, Mark. 2001. *Public Opinion on Youth, Crime, and Race: A Guide for Advocates*. Washington, DC: Building Blocks for Youth.

Sorkin, Michael. 1992. *Variations on a Theme Park: The New American City and the End of Public Space*. New York: Noonday Press.

Spady, James G., Samir Meghelli, and H. Samy Alim. 2006. *Tha Global Cipha: Hip Hop Culture and Consciousness*. Philadelphia: Black History Museum Press.

Stack, Carol. 2001. Coming of Age in Oakland. In *The New Poverty Studies*, ed. Judith Goode and Jeff Maskovsky. New York: New York University Press.

Steinhart, David. 1991. *Juvenile Justice Policy Statement*. San Francisco: National Council on Crime and Delinquency.

Steinle, Jason. 2005. *Upload Experience: Quarterlife Solutions for Teens and Twentysomethings*. Evergreen CO: Nasoj Publications.

Stephens, Sharon. 1995. *Children and the Politics of Culture*. Princeton, NJ: Princeton University Press.

Stoler, Ann. 1995. *Race and the Education of Desire: Foucault's History of Sexuality and the Colonial Order of Things*. Durham, NC: Duke University Press.

Street, Paul. 2005. *Segregated Schools*. New York: Taylor and Francis.

Sugrue, Thomas. 1998. *Origins of the Urban Crisis: Race and Inequality in Postwar Detroit*. Princeton, NJ: Princeton University Press.

Sullivan, Lisa. 1996. The Demise of Black Civil Society: Once upon a Time When We Were Colored Meets the Hip-hop Generation. *Social Policy* 27 (2): 6-10.

Sum, Andrew, and Robert Taggart. 2002. *The National Economic Recession and Its Impacts on Employment among the Nation's Young Adults (16-24 Years Old): The Untold Story of Rising Youth Joblessness*. Center for Labor Market Studies, Northeastern University, Boston, Massachusetts.

Susser, Ida. 1982. *Norman Street: Poverty and Politics in an Urban Neighborhood*. Oxford: Oxford University Press.

Suttles, Gerald D. 1972. *The Social Construction of Communities*. Chicago: University of Chicago Press.

Taylor, Clarence. 2009. Hurricane Katrina and the Myth of the Post–Civil Rights Era. *Journal of Urban History* 35: 640-55.

Thompson, Chris. 2000. The Soul of a New Machine, the City Council. *East Bay Express*, March 3-9, 2000.

Thorne, Barrie. 2003. The Crisis of Care. In *Work-Family Challenges for Low-Income Parents and Their Children*, ed. Nan Crouter and Alan Booth. Hillsdale, NJ: Lawrence Erlbaum.

Tilton, Jennifer. 2009. Youth Uprising: Gritty Youth Development and Community Tranformation. *Childhood, Youth, and Social Work in Transformation: Implications for Policy and Practice*, ed. Lynn Nybell et al. New York: Columbia University Press.

Tough, Paul. 2008. *Whatever It Takes: Geoffrey Canada's Quest to Change Harlem and America*. New York: Houghton Mifflin.

Trajanowitz, Robert. 1990. Community Policing Is Not Police-Community Relations. *FBI Law Enforcement Bulletin* 59: 6-11.

Turner, Victor. 1969. *The Ritual Process: Structure and Anti-Structure*. Chicago: Aldine.

Urban Health Initiative. Fall 2000 [viewed Sept. 2003]. *Urban Seminar Series Probes Youth Violence Trends and Factors*. Www.urbanhealth.org/urban_seminar_violence.

Urban Strategies Council & Youth Development Initiative Working Group. 1996. *Call to Action: An Oakland Blueprint for Youth*. Oakland, CA: Urban Strategies Council.

Valentine, Gill. 1996a. Children Should Be Seen and Not Heard: The Production and Transgression of Adults' Public Space. *Urban Geography* 17 (2): 205-20.

———. 1996b. Angels and Devils: Moral Landscapes of Childhood. *Environment and Planning D: Society and Space* 14: 581-99.

———. 1999. Oh Please Mum. Oh Please Dad. In *Gender, Power, and the Household*, ed. Linda McKie et al. New York: St. Martin's Press.

———. 2004. *Public Space and the Culture of Childhood*. Burlington, VT: Ashgate.

Valentine, Gill, and John McKendrick. 1997. Children's Outdoor Play: Exploring Parental Concerns about Children's Safety and the Changing Nature of Childhood. *Geoforum* 28 (2): 219-55.

Valentine, Gill, Tracey Skelton, and Deborah Chambers. 1998. Cool Places: An Introduction to Youth and Youth Cultures. In *Cool Places: Geographies of Youth Cultures*, ed. Tracey Skelton and Gill Valentine. New York: Routledge.

Vanderbeck, Robert, and James Johnson. 2000. That's the Only Place Where You Can Hang Out: Urban Young People and the Space of the Mall. *Urban Geography* 21: 5-25.

Villaruel, F., and N. E. Walker. 2002. *¿Donde esta la Justicia?* Washington, DC: Building Blocks for Youth.

Vincent, Joan. 1993. Framing the Underclass. *Critical Anthropology* 13 (3): 215-30.

Wacquant, Loic. 1999. How Penal Common Sense Comes to Europeans: Notes on the Transatlantic Diffusion of Neoliberal Doxa. *European Societies* 1 (3): 319-52.

———. 2001. Deadly Symbiosis. *Punishment & Society* 3 (1): 95-133.

Walters, Paul. 1993. Community-Oriented Policing: A Blend of Strategies. *FBI Law Enforcement Bulletin* 62: 20-23.

Warren, Jenifer, et al. 2008 [viewed Aug. 2008]. *One in 100: Behind Bars in America, 2008*. Pew Center on the States and the Public Safety Performance Project Report. Http:// www.pewcenteronthestates.org/uploadedFiles/8015PCTS_Prison08_FINAL_2-1-1_ FORWEB.pdf.

We Interrupt This Message. 2001 [viewed July 2003]. *Soundbites and Cellblocks: Analysis of the Juvenile Justice Media Debate* and *A Case Study of California's Proposition 21*. Http:// www.interrupt.org.

We Interrupt This Message & Youth Force. 2001 [viewed July 2003]. *In Between the Lines: How the* New York Times *Frames Youth*. Http://www.interrupt.org/inbetw.html.

Weatheritt, Molly. 1988. Community Policing: Rhetoric or Reality. In *Community Policing: Rhetoric or Reality*, ed. George Kelling and Mark Moore. New York: Praeger Press.

Williams, Brett. 2001. The Great Family Fraud of Postwar America. In *Without Justice for All: The New Liberalism and the Retreat from Racial Equality*, ed. Adoph Reed. Boulder, CO: Westview Press.

———. 2007. The Precipice of Debt. In *New Landscapes of Inequality: Neoliberalism and the Erosion of Democracy in America*. Santa Fe, NM: School for Advanced Research Press.

Williams, Joan. 2000. *Unbending Gender: Why Family and Work Conflict and What to Do about It?* New York: Oxford University Press.

Williams, Terry M. 1989. *The Cocaine Kids: The Inside Story of a Teenage Drug Ring*. Reading, MA: Addison-Wesley.

Willis, Paul. 1981. *Learning to Labor: How Working-Class Kids Get Working-Class Jobs*. New York: St. Martin's Press.

Wilson, James Q., and George Kelling. 1982. Broken Windows: The Police and Neighborhood Safety. *Atlantic Monthly*, March.

Wilson, William J. 1987. *The Truly Disadvantaged: The Inner City, the Underclass, and Public Policy*. Chicago: University of Chicago Press.

———. 1996. *When Work Disappears: The World of the New Urban Poor*. New York: Knopf.

Wolch, Jennifer. 1990. *The Shadow State: Government and Voluntary Sector in Transition*. New York: Foundation Center.

Wyn, Johanne, and Rob White. 2000. Negotiating Social Change: The Paradox of Youth. *Youth and Society,* December.

Wyness, Michael G. 2000. *Contesting Childhood.* New York: Falmer Press.

Wyness, Michael, et al. 2004. Childhood, Politics, and Ambiguity: Towards an Agenda for Children's Political Inclusion. *Sociology* 38 (1): 81-99.

Youth Media Council. 2002. *Speaking For Ourselves: A Youth Assessment of Local News Coverage.* San Francisco: We Interrupt This Message.

Youth Transitions Funders Group. 2006 [viewed June 2008]. A Blueprint for Juvenile Justice Reform. Http://www.ytfg.org/knowledge_pubs.html.

Zelizer, Viviana. 1994. *Pricing the Priceless Child: The Changing Social Value of Children.* Princeton, NJ: Princeton University Press.

Zimring, Franklin. 1998. *American Youth Violence.* New York: Oxford University Press.

Zinn, Maxine Baca. 1989. Family, Race, and Poverty in the 80s. *Signs* 14 (4): 856-75.

Zukin, Sharon. 1995. *The Culture of Cities.* New York: Blackwell.

Index

Chang, Jeff, 189

Chicano Movement, 196, 202, 220

childhood: and equal opportunity, 2, 4, 5, 8, 134, 142, 149, 229; gated, 177; ideals of, 83–84, 182; as "natural category," 11; normative definition of, 51; as period of dependence, 11–12; "privatized," 88, 89 fig. 7, 183; progressive politics of, 10, 119, 235–36; symbolic power of, 2, 4, 8–10, 179, 194, 204, 210–12, 230, 232–33. *See also* adolescence; youth

children: and crisis of care, 77, 92, 95, 263n3; dangers of free time, 77, 84; innocence of, 8, 235–36, 259n91; public responsibility for, 4, 76, 83, 200, 235, 250n30; as reformable, 208; shaping of urban space by, 161, 176–78

Children's Defense Fund: on "cradle to prison pipeline," 4–5, 148; and politics of childhood, 9–10

Chuck D, 216

citizenship: definitions of, 34, 60; exclusion of youth from, 194, 211, 227, 230, 239; neoliberal ideas of, 10, 13, 15, 60, 101; and police protection, right to, 7, 35, 58, 63, 65, 198, 232, 233; and public space, 227, 262n54

civil rights networks, 197–98

Clinton, Bill, 220

Clinton, Hillary, 10

Collins, Patricia Hill, 10, 140

color blind ideology, 17, 132–34, 235; resistance to, 143, 238; in Skyline Task Force, 133, 143

color blind liberalism, 120, 132

Comaroff, Jean and John, 14

community activists, 2, 7–8, 11, 58; in Laurel district, 91, 99, 102, 109–10, 170, 172, 223; and partnerships with the police, 51–52, 59, 66, 67, 198, 247n59; and Sideshows, 168–69

community, notions of, 140

Community Oriented Policing Services (COPS), 56, 247n69

community policing: and Black middle class power, 34, 60, 63; and broken win-

dows thesis, 61; and calls for self-help, 55; and COPS program, 56, 247n69; as deterrent to political action, 60–61; and disciplining Black boys, 34, 52, 246n3; emphasis on problem-solving, 60–61, 247n70, 247n72; and neoliberalism, 34, 35, 58; Oakland initiative, 55–56, 59–61; relationship with police, 55, 247n59; Skogan on, 55. *See also* Elmhurst Middle School; Elmhurst neighborhood; Laurel district; Neighborhood Crime Prevention Councils

Concerned African American Parents at Skyline, 147

conservatism: "nanny state," 6; and self-help, 33

Coontz, Stephanie, 40

Coordinating Council of the Community Chest, 84, 85 fig. 6

Coup, The, 188, 217, 218

crime: as disciplinary problem; juvenile, 1, 205, 207, 261n26; prevention of, 1; rates of, 231. *See also* Black youth; community policing; Neighborhood Crime Prevention Councils; youth; youth of color

criminal justice; models of accountability, 65, 206–7; and neoliberalism, 206–7, 210; punitive logic of, 7, 179–80, 200, 222; reform, calls for, 239; and surveillance; 179. *See also* Proposition 21

crisis of care: and neoliberalism, 7; and working families, 88, 92, 95

Critical Resistance, 21, 202

cruising, 41–42, 167, 215. *See also* Sideshows

culture: biological notions of, 140; as dynamic process, 149; linked to space, 140; as source of race and class inequalities, 120, 139–41

curfew laws, 160–61, 194, 201, 256n11

Davey D, 167

De La Fuente, Ignacio, 38

Dellums, C. L., 231

Dellums, Ron, 231

Devine, John, 46

MacArthur freeway, 155

Marked: Race, Crime, and Finding Work in the Era of Mass Incarceration (Pager), 47–48

Maskovsky, Jeff, 33, 170, 247n79

Matter of Time, A, 92–93

McClymonds High School (Oakland), 138

McCullum, Donald, 122

Men of Tomorrow (service club), 39

Merry, Sally, 161

Miley, Nate, 117–18, 124–25, 185, 193

Miller, Leslie, 3

Mitchell, Don, 183, 188, 214

Molotoch, Harvey, 20

NAACP, 122, 168; Legal Defense Fund, 148

Naples, Nancy, 43

neighborhood activism: public/private partnerships, 8, 51–52, 59, 66

Neighborhood Crime Prevention Councils (NCPCs), 1, 19, 26, 31; and black self-help, 55; creation of, 55; demographics of, 31, 35; effect on activism, 61–62; Elmhurst, 31–33, 46, 52–53, 219; Hillcrest Estates, 129; Laurel, 70, 75–76, 80, 82, 90, 111, 153, 171, 178–79; membership of, 38–39, 63; as outside activist infrastructure, 60; as source of community power, 57–58; support of public schools by, 53–54; and racial profiling, 64. *See also* community policing; Elmhurst Middle School; Elmhurst neighborhood; Laurel district

neoliberal governance, 5–8: and community governance, 17, 34, 58, 102; contradictions of, 232; decline of public services under, 27, 78, 195, 200; inequality, reproduction of, 141; pro-growth policies of, 163, 257n27; urban redevelopment under, 160, 162–64, 166, 170, 187. *See also* Brown, Jerry; children; Neighborhood Crime Prevention Councils; nonprofit organizations; public/private divide

neoliberalism: and citizenship, 6, 10, 13, 15, 60, 101; and community partnerships, 7–8, 17, 66, 67, 194–95, 244n27; and

community policing, 34, 35, 55–56, 58; and crisis of care, 7, 238–39; dependence upon volunteerism, 7, 99–101; and non-profits, 7, 105–8, 230; as overturning of Great Society, 164; political action under, 67, 197; privatized family values in, 9, 133, 226; and punitive governance, 6–7, 10; as reigning ideology, 78; and self-help ideology, 9–11, 106–7; as shaped by youth, 8, 14–15; structuring ideologies of, 234, 247n63; welfare policies of, 108; youth critiques of, 205–206. *See also* Brown, Jerry; Neighborhood Crime Prevention Councils; public/private divide

New Deal, 6, 235, 243n15

news media, 193, 207–8, 244n50

Nixon, Richard, 238

No Child Left Behind, 93

nongovernmental organizations (NGOs), 77

non-profit organizations: and after-school programs, 7, 78; political limitations of, 105–6, 233; public-private partnerships in, 7, 105, 230, 233; as youth service providers, 7, 40, 184, 198–99, 201, 240

nostalgia, 6; for disciplined youth, 33, 35, 40–42, 43–44, 65; for family discipline, 50, 52–53; for Jim Crow South, 41; for parental authority, 49; in post–Civil Rights Era, 40; Reed on, 41; Williams on, 50–51

Notorious B.I.G., 31

Oakland, CA: ballot measures, 232; black unemployment in, 37; black urban regime of, 16, 39, 40, 57, 124, 135, 209, 231; bond measures in, 87, 250n29; class geography of, 18, 23, 36, 79, 103, 136–37, 246nn11, 14; college graduation rates in, 142; community organizing in, 17, 39, 240–41; community policing initiative of, 7, 34, 55–57, 59–60; crime rates in 1, 38, 61, 231; decline of public infrastructure, 86–87; demographics of, 13–16, 14 fig. 1, 15 fig. 2, 245n67; effects of globalization on, 49; geography of, 13; politics of, 5, 124–25; public schools of, 1; racial geography of, 13, 18, 23, 126, 135, 139, 144; racial politics in, 15; unequal distribution of resources in, 88, 119; urban redevelopment in, 23, 157–58, 162–65, 257n45; white flight from, 25, 37, 86, 119, 121, 123, 155–56; youth activists in, 9; youth violence in, 20. *See also* Oakland, CA, neighborhoods of

Oakland, CA, neighborhoods of: Elmhurst (*see* Elmhurst neighborhood); flatlands, 1, 31, 60, 69, 82, 86, 88, 120, 121, 160, 231; Fruitvale, 38, 231; Hillcrest Estates, 124, 126–28, 130; hills, the 113–14, 114 fig. 9, 123. Laurel district, (*see* Laurel district); Piedmont, 170; Redwood Heights, 75, 79, 80, 138, 173, 249n10; Rockridge, 170; Uptown, 166–67. *See also* Oakland hills

Oakland Club (women's club), 84

Oakland Community Organization (OCO), 36, 39, 49, 60, 67; and activist mothering, 53; challenges to neoliberal policies, 240–41; as corrective to kids-first politics, 241; on educational inequality, 144–45

Oakland Department of Parks and Recreation, 75, 77, 83, 85, 249nn14, 21; Friends of, 87; post-Prop 13, 8

Oakland Federation of Teachers, 122–23

Oakland Fund for Children and Youth (OFCY), 105–6, 107 fig. 8

Oakland Gone Wild, 168

Oakland hills, 113–14; black parent activism in, 147–48; demographics of, 123; erasure of race in, 134–35, 139, 149; map of, 114 fig. 9; "neighbors" v. "parents" in, 118, 119, 125, 128–30; as "private" space, 130–31; public investment in, 127; white denials of racism in, 133–36, 138–39; as "white" space, 131, 139

Oakland Housing Authority, 39

Oakland Police Department (OPD): on community policing, 60, 198; community relations, 29, 56, 58–59; and COPS program, 56; as disciplinary force, 53 fig. 4; harassment by, 48, 169, 257n58; in schools, 134; juvenile bureau, 84; on developing alternatives to jail, 239; Sideshows, responses to, 156, 167–68; sweeps by, 8, 29, 31, 57, 156, 160, 167; youth activism, responses to, 213–14. *See also* community policing; Neighborhood Crime Prevention Councils; police

Oakland Residents for Peaceful Neighborhoods (ORPN), 232, 233

Oakland Tribune, 110, 155, 205

Oakland's Youth Commission, 237, 259n107

Obama, Barack, 231, 234

Office of Civil Rights, U.S. Department of Education, 148

Omega Boys Club, 93

Orloff, Tom, 211

Pager, Devah, 47–48

Parent Teachers Associations (PTAs), 19; Castlemont, 43; Laurel, 70, 72, 80, 82, 100–101; Redwood Heights, 103; Skyline, 113, 114

parenting: Black middle class practices, 23, 99; of Black youth, 71; and child development, 4; and discipline, 27–28; structured time, importance of, 94, 96–97, 181–82, 251n72; middle class practices, 8, 77, 94, 97, 99, 100–101, 103, 251nn68, 71. *See also* Black youth; childhood; youth; youth of color

Pattillo, Mary, 17. *See also* Pattillo-McCoy, Mary

Pattillo-McCoy, Mary, 98. *See also* Pattillo, Mary

People Improving Communities through Organizing (PICO), 241

police: disciplinary role of, 42, 53 fig. 4, 66, 246n3; as male authority figures, 53; partnerships with neighborhood activists, 51–52, 198. *See also* community policing; Neighborhood Crime Prevention Councils; Oakland Police Department

police brutality, 22, 56, 229, 231; Black Panther response to, 56

Rios, Victor, 201
riots: at Castlemont High School, 219; in Los Angeles, 56; racial, 219, 221, 246n13; at Skyline High School, 132, 219; youth as signifier of, 172
Ritterhouse, Jennifer, 10
Roosevelt, Franklin, 10
Rose, Tricia, 215
Ruddick, Susan, 11, 86, 166

Safety First, 232, 233
San Francisco Magazine, 166
Sanjek, Roger, 149–50
Saving Our Sons (Golden), 12
school shootings, 134
Schrag, Peter, 141
Schwarzenegger, Arnold, 239
segregation: de facto, 119, 121; racial, 16
self-help ideology, 50; and community policing, 55; as conservative ideology, 33–34; as neoliberal ideology, 5, 9
Self, Robert, 18, 37, 121–22
Sideshows, 156–58, 168–69, 256n7; public space, as claim to, 157, 215; shut down, attempts to, 156, 167–68
Simon, Jonathan, 34–35, 65
Skogan, Wesley, 55
Skyline High School (Oakland), 23, 101, 113, 115; catchment area of, 121–22, 122 fig. 10, 137; demographics of, 123, 137, 253n17; dropout rates, 142–43; flatlands kids at, 135; history of, 119, 121, 253n4; honors classes at, 144; integration of, 119, 123, 253n10; lack of resources at, 150–51; open enrollment at, 122, 137–39; students as outsiders, 120, 126–28, 131, 140, 148; tracking at, 147; youth activism at, 211, 221; Youth Center at, 117–19, 128, 136, 150, 185. *See also* Skyline Task Force
Skyline Task Force, 116–19, 123, 129, 150–51; and color blind ideology, 133, 143, 149; racial animosity in, 132
social reproduction, 3, 48, 230; public responsibility for, 120; privatization of, 235; state investments in, 10

space: children, as shaped by, 161, 176–77; government regulation of, 161; neoliberal governance of, 61, 162, 165–66, 260n8; politics of, 148; urban planning, 161; youth use of, 160, 179, 194. *See also* geography; public space
Spees, Dick, 183–84
state, the, 5–6, 58; as disciplinarian, 17–18, 34, 52–53, 61, 65, 66, 230; as idea, 6; as negligent parent, 4, 9, 209; as policeman, 204; as set of relationships, 6; as volunteer state, 75, 77–78, 249n2. *See also* neoliberal governance; neoliberalism
Steele, Gail, 209, 210, 212
Street Corner Society (Whyte), 161
Sydewayz, 168

teenager, as term, 8, 262n66
Thorne, Barrie, 88
Till, Emmett, 10
Torres, Gerald, 18
Turner, Victor, 196, 243n1

United States: child poverty rates in, 4; Department of Justice, 56; housing policy, 4; urban redevelopment policies, 4
urban redevelopment, 4, 162–65; and displacement, 28, 254n30; and diversity, 166; role of youth in, 161, 165–69, 230. *See also* neoliberal governance; neoliberalism
urban renewal, displacement in, 39, 164

Valentine, Gill, 13–14, 178, 249n1, 250n38
volunteerism: Bush on, George H. W., 77; and class privilege, 91–92; Clinton on, Bill, 77; and inequality, 103–5; Katz on, 77; limits of, 102–5; in public schools, 7, 39, 54, 100–101, 109, 230. *See also* children; neoliberal governance; public schools, CA; public schools, Oakland; volunteer state, the
volunteer state, the, 75, 77–78, 99–100, 249n2

Wacquant, Loic, 7, 47
War on Drugs, 48
Waters, Maxine, 262n61
Way We Were, The (Coontz), 40
welfare state: California spending on, 108; critiques of, 204; and Democratic Party, 33; effect on families, 49, 236; "invisible" middle class benefits of, 254n49; and neoliberal governance, 108, 183; punitive nature of, 4; restructuring of, 6; youth vision of, 194–95. *See also* neoliberal governance; neoliberalism; New Deal
white boys, as "good kids," 146
white flight, 25, 37, 86, 119, 121, 139, 155–56, 253n21. *See also* Oakland, neighborhoods of
Williams, Brett, 50–51, 95
Williams v. State of California (2000), 144
Willis, Paul, 217
Wilson, Pete, 220
women: volunteer labor of, 100; political marginalization of, 244n40
Word, Richard (OAK Chief of Police), 55, 57, 58, 61, 156
Works Progress Administration (WPA), 85, 127

youth: as "broken windows," 178, 188; clearing streets of, 153, 182–83, 195, 226, 230, 256n20; concerns for safety of, 96, 106–7; as consumers, 171; criminalization of, 50, 113, 119, 120, 132, 136, 159–60, 188, 194, 201, 215–16; as dangerous, 141, 177, 198, 204–5, 233; dangers of free time for, 84; disciplining of, 1–2, 9, 27–29, 32–34, 40–43; drug use among, 27; as endangered, 2–3; exclusions from full citizenship, 194; fear of, 23, 42–43, 134, 136–37, 172, 179; geography of, 175 fig. 14; job-training programs for, 62; lack of economic opportunities for, 2; as liminal category, 45; loitering ordinances, 154; moral panics about, 3; as "our kids," 3, 150, 209, 242; police

harassment of, 131, 169; as political identity, 196, 199, 211, 225; politics of, 2, 3, 10, 13, 226, 238–39; as racialized category, 18, 174, 178, 223, 262n66; reform of, 118; as "slippery concept," 8–9; state investment in, 106; as "super-predators," 204; as threat to economic development, 153–54, 171; 20th-century ideals of, 83–84; unemployment rates of, 46–47; wealthy, 2. *See also* adolescence; Black boys; Black girls; Black youth; childhood; children; youth activism; youth, Asian American; youth of color; youth, Latino; youth, white
youth activism, 192–94, 202, 213; childhood, claims to, 208, 210, 226; as corrective to kids first politics, 241; critiques of media representations, 207–8; critiques of neoliberalism, 205; law and order politics, challenges to 199; public space, claims to, 195, 212–14, 227; racial diversity of, 218, 219, 223; and "right to the city," 195, 214, 226–27, 239; on school-to-prison pipeline, 200, 209–10; and "War on Youth," 206. *See also* youth; youth of color
youth activist organizations, 21, 193, 199, 201–3
youth, Asian American, 5, 173–74, 219; activists, 159–60, model minority myth, 222, 243n10; rates of incarceration, 223; at Skyline, 119, 125, 133–34, 221. *See also* youth of color
youth development organizations, 93
Youth Empowerment Center, 203
Youth Force Coalition, 193, 202
youth, Latino, 5, 6, 10, 12, 173–74, 219, 221; activists, 159–60; rates of incarceration, 223; and Sideshows, 156. *See also* youth of color
youth of color: and child labor, 10; childhood, exclusions from, 12, 207; criminalization of, 10, 50, 204, 210, 222, 237; fear of, for 8, 17; as gang members, 6; as generational identity, 218, 219; incarceration rates of, 5; public space,

About the Author

JENNIFER TILTON is an anthropologist and assistant professor of Race and Ethnic Studies at the University of Redlands.